In the Service of
the Emperor

In the Service of the Emperor

The Rise and Fall of the Japanese Empire 1931–1945

N.S. 'Tank' Nash

Pen & Sword
MILITARY

First published in Great Britain in 2022 by
PEN & SWORD MILITARY
an imprint of Pen & Sword Books Ltd
Yorkshire – Philadelphia

Copyright © N.S. Nash, 2022

ISBN 978-1-39909-007-0

Typeset by Concept, Huddersfield, West Yorkshire, HD4 5JL.
Printed and bound in England by CPI Group (UK) Ltd, Croydon CR0 4YY.

Pen & Sword Books Ltd incorporates the imprints of Aviation, Atlas, Family
History, Fiction, Maritime, Military, Discovery, Politics, History, Archaeology,
Select, Wharncliffe Local History, Wharncliffe True Crime, Military Classics,
Wharncliffe Transport, Leo Cooper, The Praetorian Press, Remember When,
White Owl, Seaforth Publishing and Frontline Books.

For a complete list of Pen & Sword titles please contact
PEN & SWORD BOOKS LTD
47 Church Street, Barnsley, South Yorkshire, S70 2AS, England
E-mail: enquiries@pen-and-sword.co.uk
Website: www.pen-and-sword.co.uk
or
PEN & SWORD BOOKS
1950 Lawrence Rd, Havertown, PA 19083, USA
E-mail: uspen-and-sword@casematepublishers.com
Website: www.penandswordbooks.com

Contents

List of Maps vii

Acknowledgements ix

Glossary xi

1. Preamble 1

2. 1926–39: The Emperor 3

3. 1904–37: Aspirations for Empire 7

4. 1937–45: The Second Sino-Japanese War 22

5. 1938–45: The Russian Threat, the Chinese War and the Burma
   Road 39

6. 1938–41: The Path to World War 50

7. August–December 1941: Manipulation and Misunderstanding . . . 60

8. December 1941–February 1942: Pearl Harbor, Thailand, Guam,
   Malaya and Singapore 67

9. December 1941: The Philippines, Wake Island, Hong Kong and
   Bataan 92

10. 1931–45: Comfort Woman 114

11. December 1941–May 1942: Burma, Battles of Ceylon and the
    Coral Sea 120

12. June–July 1942: The Ebb of the Tide – The Battle of Midway . . . 136

13. 1415–1945: Inconvenient Guests and their Treatment 143

14. August 1942–February 1943: The Kokoda Trail, Guadalcanal,
    the Battle of Savo Island and the Battle of the Bismarck Sea 155

15. November 1942–3: Food, the Bengal Famine and the First Chindit
    Operation 178

16. January–December 1943: Yamamoto, Attu, Casablanca, Cairo,
    Quebec and Teheran 184

17. April–December 1943: Operation CARTWHEEL, Bougainville
    and Rabaul 190

18. November 1942–August 1943: Co-prosperity, Tarawa, Makin and
    Mountbatten 194

19. January 1944: Kwajalein, Roi-Namur, Truk, Food and Eniwetok . . 203

20. February 1944–August 1945: Kohima, Imphal, the Second Chindit
    Operation, Marauders and the Recapture of Burma 209

21. April–July 1944: Hollandia, Aitape, Biak Island, Mopping up,
    Saipan and the Marianas 'Turkey Shoot' 230

22. July–September 1944: Trophies, Logistics, Guam, Tinian,
    Morotai and Peleliu 244

23. October–December 1944: Leyte 259

24. October 1944–August 1945: Kamikaze 275

25. December 1944–March 1945: Mindoro, Luzon and Massacre 280

26. February–June 1945: Iwo Jima 286

27. April–June 1945: Okinawa 293

28. 1945 303

Epilogue 308

Bibliography 317

Index 324

List of Maps

Theatre of the Sino-Japanese War   8

The Japanese Empire, 1914 11

The Manchukuo Rail Network 34

Japan's operations in China 1911–45 36

The disputed border between Nomonhan and Khalkhin Gol 40

South of the Burma Road 46

Japanese Fleet's approach to Pearl Harbor 68

The Japanese invasion of Thailand 76

Malaya in 1941 82

Japanese air attack on the Philippines 93

Japanese invasion of the Philippines 96

Situation on Bataan 100

The Dutch East Indies in 1942 104

Wake Island 107

Japanese conquest of Burma 123

The Leeward and Windward Islands 134

Battle of Midway 141

The battlefield at Agincourt 145

The peninsula of Iges 151

The Death Railway 153

The Kokoda Trail 156

Battle of the Bismarck Sea 161

Guadalcanal 167

The route of Admiral Mikawa Gunichi 168

Disposition of ships prior to the Battle of Savo Island 171

The Battle of Truk Lagoon 205

The campaign in northern Burma and Assam, March–July 1944 214

Second Chindit expedition, the fly-in 216

Saipan Island 239

Battle of Guam 251

Invasion of Leyte 261

Battle of Leyte Gulf 269

Battle of Iwo Jima 287

Invasion of Okinawa 296

Battle of Okinawa 298

Acknowledgements

This book is not intended to be either a blow-by-blow account of the battles fought by the Japanese in the service of their emperor nor a blood-soaked and depressing chronicle of the conduct of the Japanese as they swept across Asia. Because Japanese behaviour was so egregious and so consistent, its behaviour is an integral element in its expansionist, militarily led policy. This policy led to the second Sino-Japanese War (1937–45), which was a major conflict and an integral part of the wider war that convulsed the world. However, China was never conquered, was not incorporated into the Japanese Empire and thus is not a centre of focus.

The aim is to produce a melange that puts diplomatic, political, strategic and military operations into context and by so doing provide a relatively short, overall view of world affairs and the part played by Japan in the period 1931–45. Many of the events described were taking place concurrently and so thwart my aim of presenting a chronological text. Of necessity, some of the fine detail of political and military has had to be excluded in the pursuit of brevity.

In considering the behaviour of the Japanese during the period of empire, I have placed its conduct into historical context and compared it, albeit very briefly, to that of its contemporary ally – Germany. The taking and care of prisoners is an element of warfare which, over centuries, has been inconvenient and problematic and is an issue addressed here. 'Victor's justice' is considered and the measure of retribution that was delivered leads on to a summary of the Japanese Empire and all its works.

In this text I had followed the Japanese practice of putting the family name first. I have drawn on a wide circle of sources and considered the views of historians who have gone before me. John Toland makes for compelling reading, but his history is not neutral in its judgements as he writes from a discernible American standpoint. S.C.M. Paine was a valuable source and the reproduction of her masterly map on page 36 is gratefully acknowledged. John Costello provided carefully balanced and neutral views. Sir Max Hasting is the historian's historian. His painstaking research and balanced judgements have influenced my view. FM Lord Slim, Lord Russell and many others have been consulted, as the bibliography shows.

This text, as in all my previous books, has been reviewed by Lieutenant Colonel Tom Gowans and I am grateful to him for his usual meticulous observations. My editor at Pen & Sword was, again, the punctilious and efficient Linne Matthews, whose forensic eye for detail added value to my work. She polished the text and excised my errors, and I am, once again, very grateful to her. The design team at Pen and Sword, led by Matt Jones, have produced a most handsome book, as is their wont.

I have acknowledged, where possible, the sources of maps and photographs where the copyright is available. In many cases the copyright has expired and I can only offer grateful thanks to the originators of sources that are unknown.

Finally, any errors or omissions are mine alone.

Tank Nash
Malmesbury, Wiltshire
nsnash39@gmail.com
March 2022

Glossary

AASC – Australian Army Service Corps
ABDA – American-British-Dutch-Australian forces
ABDACOM – American-British-Dutch-Australian Command
ADC – Aide-de-Camp
ANZUK – Australia, New Zealand and the United Kingdom
BEF – British Expeditionary Force
BPF – British Pacific Fleet
BURCORPS – Burma Corps
CAP – Combat Air Patrol
CASEVAC – casualty evacuation
CEF – Chinese Expeditionary Force
COMAIRSOLS – Commander Air, Solomon Islands
COSMOPA – Command of the South Pacific Area
CW – policy chemical weapons policy
DUKW – 6-wheeled amphibious truck
EAC – Eastern Assault Convoy
GEACS – Greater East Asia Co-prosperity Sphere
GOC – General Officer Commanding
GOC-in-C – General Officer Commanding-in-Chief
FEAF – Far East Air Force
HMAS – His Majesty's Australian Ship
HMG – His Majesty's Government
HNLMS – Her Netherlands Majesty's Ship
IJA – Imperial Japanese Army
IJN – Imperial Japanese Navy
INA – Indian National Army
JAG – Judge Advocate General
LRP – Long Range Penetration
LST – Landing Ships, Tank
MTB – motor torpedo boat
NSDAP – Nazi Party
NVA – North Vietnam Army
OP – observation post
PT – boat patrol torpedo boat

RAAF – Royal Australian Air Force
RAN – Royal Australian Navy
SEAC – Supreme Allied Commander Southeast Asia Command
SIGINT – signals intelligence
SIS – Signal Intelligence Service (US Army)
SRB – Special Reserve Battalion
TG – Task Group
ULTRA – wartime signals intelligence
USAAF – United States Army Air Force
USAFFE – US Army Forces in the Far East
USMC – United States Marine Corps
USN – United States Navy
WAC – Western Assault Convoy
WPO – War Plan Orange

Chapter One

Preamble

The Second World War had been over for twenty-six years when I was posted to Singapore in 1971 to join 28 ANZUK Brigade. I was a captain, with aspirations of a majority – one day. On arrival I reported to my new commanding officer. He made me feel welcome but then spoiled my day by asking me to take on the role of Officers' Mess Secretary as an extramural appointment.

Sembawang Officers' Mess was a building redolent of colonial times, atop a hill and overlooking the airstrip and, in the distance, the Straits of Johore. The brigade headquarters shared the mess with 6th Battalion, Royal Australian Regiment (6 RAR), recently arrived from Vietnam.

Several weeks into my tour I decided to inspect the rooms of the 'living-in' officers and to this end I asked Mr Tan, the senior of the locally employed people who made the mess function, to accompany me. He was 'No. 1 Boy', an appellation left over from the colonial era that had ended only the year before. Mr Tan relished the title.

Mr Tan was a gem; he had been employed by the Crown in Sembawang Officers' Mess since about 1935 and I was grateful for his practical common sense, experience and unremitting hard work. Together we made a start on our tour of the bedrooms, which were arranged in a series of quadrangles around patches of grass, each about 20 yards square (24km²).

I went into the room of one Australian subaltern and found that the occupant had clearly dismantled his motorbike. The bedroom was covered in oil, cogs, chains, spanners and unidentified pieces of metal. It looked like a regimental workshop, and it was a complete shambles.

I was not going to expect the mess staff to clean this room and I went to the door and called out to Mr Tan to tell him. He was on the opposite side of the quadrangle. Mr Tan walked very deliberately around the quadrangle, and by this circuitous route, he met me at the door.

I said to him, 'Why on earth did you walk all the way round; why didn't you cut the corner and cross the grass?'

He replied, 'I can't walk there; it's sacred ground.'

'Sacred'?

'In 1942, I stood here and watched the Japanese behead Colonel Henderson, Major Black, Major Allan and …' Tan then recited six or eight names.

He continued: 'The Japs threw their heads down there,' pointing to a boundary wire fence. 'I retrieved the heads and put them with the right body. These were all my officers; it all happened just there, just there.'

Tan showed no outward emotion, but he stood silently reliving the horror of that day. I looked over his shoulder at the innocuous, unremarkable patch of grass. Somehow, the unholy mess in the subaltern's bedroom did not seem quite so important ...

Chapter Two

1926–39
The Emperor

The creation of empires across the world has always left a trail of bloodshed. The Romans, Ottomans, French, Germans, Belgians and British are examples of empire builders, but all eventually surrendered their territorial gains as their subject peoples demanded and gained self-determination. Only the British, with the oldest and largest, managed a dignified withdrawal from empire. The creation of a democratic Commonwealth is, arguably, Britain's greatest legacy.

However, one of the bloodiest empires was also one of the shortest, but not the sweetest. It lasted only from 1931 until 1945, at a cost of millions of lives. This was the merciless Japanese version of empire, which embraced swathes of Southeast Asia. It was wide-reaching, and it had reached its zenith by 1942 – but, within three years, it had collapsed, not from pressure from within but by the external force of arms.

This book will trace that brief, fourteen-year period and the meteoric success of the Japanese armed forces as they took possession of the homes and lives of millions of other Asiatic people. It will recognise the courage of its armed forces but will record the grotesque barbarity of its soldiers and the insouciance of its political leaders. It will seek an explanation for Japan's aspirations for empire and the context and impact on the rest of the world. The text will explore the Japanese culture in which Japanese willingly and happily forfeited their lives in the service of their emperor. It would be a massive understatement to say that there was a clash of cultures in the Far East from 1931. Indeed, it is this clash and the irreconcilable difference in values and priorities that provide the bones of this book. The text fleshes out those bones.

Emperor Hirohito was a constitutional monarch, who reigned but did not rule. He did not participate in the taking of strategic political or military decisions and had a diffident, self-effacing personality. He had come to the throne on 26 December 1926 when he was 25 years of age and, to the Japanese, with a status bordering on that of a deity. All Japanese activity flowed from his all-embracing authority and his unseen presence.

Hirohito (1901–89), Emperor of Japan 1926–89.
(*Atomic Heritage Foundation*)

His empire dated back 2,600 years and its two guiding principles were '*Hakkō ichiu*' and '*Kodo*'. The first of these aimed at making the world one big family and the second made clear that laudable aim could be obtained solely through loyalty to the Emperor.

Politicians who embraced military aggression frequently turned it into a moral issue by invoking the names of *Hakkō ichiu* and *Kodo*. It was argued frequently and publicly by Dr Ōkawa Shūmei (known as the Japanese Goebbels) from 1924, that Japan was the first state in existence, and it was her 'divine mission to rule the world'. It was a dangerous creed, but one that found ready adherents.

Fortunately, Hirohito had wise men about him and he was well prepared for his role; his principal tutor had been Prince Saionji, who had impressed on his charge that he had to play the part of a father figure to his nation. He had to accept responsibility for 'all affairs of State but never issue any positive order of his own volition'.[1]

Hirohito was influenced by a tour of Europe that he made during the summer of 1921. He was feted wherever he went and, while in the UK, collected honorary doctorates from Cambridge and Edinburgh universities. His meeting at Windsor with King George V and the future King Edward VIII gave him a close view of constitutional monarchy and their influence remained with him for the rest of his life. In London, he attended the theatre, visited the Bank of England and HM Tower of London. In short, he was accorded all the deference and hospitality due to the future monarch of a valued ally. He went on to Italy and then visited some of the First World War battlefields. Apart from the academic and chivalric honours, he also brought back from the UK a taste for single malt whisky and golf.

When he ascended to the throne, he was, at least in theory, master of all he surveyed. However, it was not quite like that in practice. Although he was assumed to have plenary power and all matters of state required his acquiescence, the reality was that once his ministers or generals had agreed on a course of action, he was obliged to give that action his tacit support. Like British monarchs, he was able to exercise his influence as he was entitled to advise and warn his subordinates, but without ever getting into the mucky and detailed business of politics. He trod a fine line, with caution as his watchword. He was not a political person, and from choice, he would spend all his time on marine biology, which was his abiding interest. Hirohito was an unprepossessing man with no presence. He was:

> an unlikely-looking emperor, slouching around the Palace in frayed, baggy trousers and crooked tie, dreamily peering through glasses as thick as portholes, so oblivious of his appearance that occasionally his jacket

would be fastened with the wrong button. He disliked buying new clothes, on the ground that he couldn't 'afford' them. He was so frugal that he even refrained from buying books … and … wore down every pencil to a stub.[2]

Notwithstanding his appearance and demeanour, his people regarded him as akin to a deity. From birth, all Japanese were indoctrinated to believe that he was all-powerful and that merely to look upon his face would bring blindness. In public gatherings the mere mention of the 'Emperor' was sufficient to stiffen the backs of attendees. Japanese people not only revered their emperor but viewed him with the fondness, even affection, accorded a family member. They felt a sense of commitment to him as he was seen to be the very embodiment of fatherhood. The members of his armed forces believed that it was an honour to lay down their lives in pursuit of the Emperor's wishes.

Those who fought the Japanese often used the word 'fanatical' to describe their selfless courage. In the Japanese military culture, surrender was a disgrace, and death was much to be preferred. This total devotion to the cause was also exhibited by the Chinese and North Koreans during the Korean War (1950–3) and the Vietnamese (1945–75). However, these were communist states and not monarchies, so this degree of devotion was to an ideal, a political aim, and not to an individual. It is of interest that all these latter examples are Asians. Russian troops in the assault on Berlin also used human wave tactics; perhaps indoctrination played a part there, but so too did the commissars who shot the unwilling.

When Hirohito took the throne in 1926, Japan was rated as a great power. It had the third-largest navy, after Great Britain and the USA. It was at the top table as the ninth-largest economy. Japan had been allied to Great Britain, France, USA and Italy during the First World War and, as one of the victors, had a permanent seat on the Council of the League of Nations, which, incidentally, the USA did not join. All of this made Hirohito a major player in world affairs, whether he wanted to be or not.

Notes

1. Toland, J., *The Rising Sun: The Decline and Fall of the Japanese Empire, 1936–45* [1970] (Modern Library, New York, 2003), p. 23.
2. Ibid., p. 24.

Chapter Three

1904–37
Aspirations for Empire

Japanese expansionist imperial ambitions can probably be traced back to 1904–5 when it went to war with Russia over their shared designs on Manchuria and Korea. The battlefields in Manchuria, a Chinese province, were in the southern part of the Liaodong Peninsula and Mukden (now Shenyang). Naval engagements were fought in the Yellow Sea as Russia sought to secure the warm-water Port Arthur. The need for a warm-water port was a pressing issue for the Russians because Vladivostok, their main naval base, was ice-bound for at least two months of the year. However, much to the surprise of the great powers, Japan not only won the war, but by doing so enhanced its grip on Korea, where it had had a foothold since 1894. It thwarted Russian territorial aspirations and enhanced its international standing. As a result, Japan was perceived to be the major military power in the East. It now held a very small slice of Chinese territory, the Liaodong Peninsula (see Dairien, sometimes spelt Dalian) as well as Port Arthur.

By 1910, the Japanese Empire was a modest affair as the map (page 11) demonstrates. It held Formosa (Taiwan), Korea, and some small offshore islands. In 1910, the importance of the Liaodong Peninsula was not its size but its location on the Chinese mainland. The sketch map clarifies its shape. Here, the Japanese inherited the railway system from the previous Russian occupation. To circumvent any international criticism and to cement a place in the imperialist community of Great Britain, France, Belgium et al, Japan invested heavily in the territory. It administered a form of law and order necessary to police the thousands of economic immigrants flooding into Manchuria. Japan was represented in the region by the Kwantung Army; the Japanese force was stationed in Liaodong, under a curious lease arrangement, 'to protect Japanese interests'.

From 1910, Manchuria was the focus of Japan's attention. It was a province of Northeast China and a vast tract of land about the size of Spain, France and Germany combined. Then, in 1911, China, as a nation, dissolved in a curious but spontaneous revolution and as a result there was no central Chinese government. Power was seized by several opportunist officials and soldiers. In these circumstances, the greater part collapsed. Manchuria fell into the hands

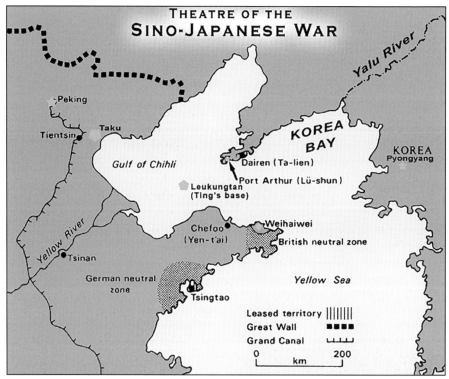

(*David White*)

of a bandit, soldier and warlord, Zhang Zuolin/Chang Tso-lin. Despite his violent career he was an effective leader, and under his aegis, Manchuria was further developed and became an economic powerhouse.

The Japanese considered themselves to be ill-used by the other great powers and the Japanese press voiced dissatisfaction on the inequalities that permitted the USA to annex the Philippines, but Japanese seizure of Formosa as its first colony in 1895 was disapproved. 'Why', it asked, 'was there no opposition to Great Britain's control of India but Japan's control of Korea (1894–1945) was subject to criticism?' A feeling of victimhood was generated and fuelled by the press.

Clearly, political forces were gathering and Japan's relations with other powers were at risk. Japan noted and envied the USA, which had a record of interfering in the affairs of other sovereign states, evidenced by its occupation of Haiti (1915–34), Nicaragua (1912–33), Cuba (1892–1902 and 1906–9), the Dominican Republic (1916–24) and Columbia (1902). Troops from the USA made incursions into Panama in 1908, 1912 and 1918.[1] Not unreasonably, and understandably, the Japanese view was, 'If they can do it why can't we?'

The USA, although nominally allied to Japan, sought to keep it on a short economic and political leash. The Japanese enquired, 'If the USA could seize a piece of Panama for a canal why could the Japanese not take enough of Manchuria to build a railway?' It was an ingenuous question because the proposed railway could only serve Japanese interests; on the other hand, the canal was an international asset.

The expansion of the Japanese Empire beyond Formosa and Korea was to start in Liaodong, and the Kwantung Army was central to a conspiracy to move out from its base in the peninsula, move north and annex the whole of Manchuria. The first step was to initiate 'regime change' – a device later polished by the USA and employed as a tool of foreign policy.

In Manchuria, regime change was put into effect on 2 June 1928 when Zhang Zuolin was assassinated by the Japanese in what became known as the 'Huanggutun Incident'. Zhang's train was blown up by a bomb at Huang-gutun railway station, in a clumsy, ill-conceived act. The front men and prime movers for the killing were two middle-ranking Japanese officers, Colonel Itagaki Seishirō and Lieutenant Colonel Ishiwara Kanji.

Their shared motive was their belief that Manchuria was vital to the well-being of Japan. They believed that it was not only a barrier to future Russian

Lieutenant General Itagaki Seishirō (1885–1948), executed for war crimes.

Lieutenant Colonel Ishiwara Kanji (1889–1949), as a major general in 1945.

expansion, but it was an area that could be widely cultivated and thus changed into a civilised, semi-autonomous, democratic and prosperous Japanese state. To the Kwantung Army, Manchuria represented a treasure house of gold, coal, livestock, soya beans, cotton and rice. The abundant raw materials when sent to Japanese manufacturers could then be marketed back in Manchuria, which they saw as the economic and strategic panacea to Japan's ills.

The colonels' motivation was not personal gain. There can be no doubt as to their devotion to their homeland and to the Emperor but, quite specifically, not to the Japanese Government. They did not preclude violence in their pursuit of economic well-being. However, after the killing of Marshal Zhang Zuolin/Chang Tso-lin, the perpetrators and their support by the Kwantung Army provoked strong condemnation not only in Tokyo, but around the world. The furore was such that the conspirators laid low until the heat had died right down.

Although the miscreants were readily identified, they were never punished. Tokyo realised that its army in Liaodong was out of control and Itagaki and Ishiwara were using the organisation to their own ends. Viewed from the distance of almost a century, this is a state of affairs that beggars belief. The disproportionate influence of these two officers could only be the result of the active support of their superiors in the command chain.

Given that in Liaodong there was clearly a corrupt command structure, it was decided, in Tokyo, that an independent, on-the-spot review of the situation was needed. However, there was no sense of urgency, and it was not until three years later that a General Tatekawa Yoshitsugu was sent, on 18 September 1931, to investigate at first hand.

He was not a good choice because he too was a member of the conspiracy! On arrival he dined with Colonel Itagaki at the Shinyokan Inn and, afterwards, the general was not inclined to 'talk shop'. Itagaki left his visitor to his own devices as he had other military fish to fry. Tatekawa commented that, during that evening, 'I was entertained by geisha girls while listening to the sound of firing in the distance. I retired later and slept soundly until called in the morning.'[2]

Tatekawa's absence gave the two colonels plenty of time and space to manoeuvre. They had positioned troops strategically and in sufficient numbers to overrun Manchuria, and now waited only for a reason to act. That same evening of 18 September 1931, a Lieutenant Kawamoto Suemori led a small party that placed a charge of dynamite on a line of the South Manchurian Railway near Mukden. The subsequent explosion was too weak to inflict any serious damage, but the object of the exercise was to create the desired *casus belli*. Immediately, the Kwantung Army accused Chinese 'dissidents' of this act of sabotage and opened hostilities. By the next morning, Mukden was in

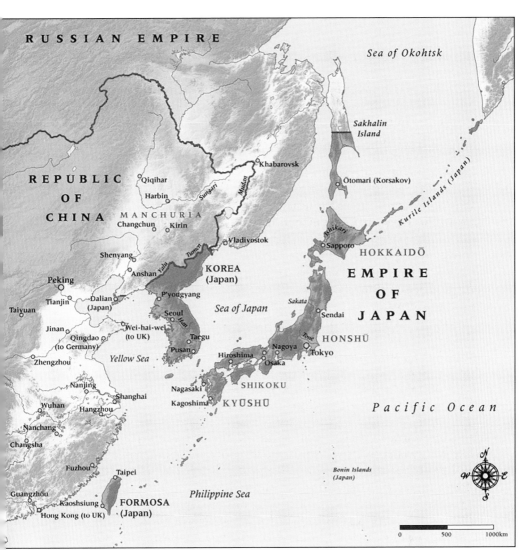

The Japanese Empire in 1914. (*New Zealand History*)

Japanese hands. Allegedly, it had cost the Japanese only two fatalities, but Chinese dead numbered 500.[3]

The Kwantung was intent on taking the whole of Manchuria and, despite being vastly outnumbered, the trained professional Japanese soldiers rode roughshod over their opponents and in the process killed thousands of non-combatant Chinese, most of whom were ethnic Han. By 1933, Manchuria had been pacified. However, 'The occupation of Manchuria did not sate the Japanese, who continued to expand their zone of occupation in North China between 1933 and 1936.'[4]

Tokyo was appalled, as was the rest of the civilised world. The advance of the Kwantung Army caused a mixture of anger and distress in Tokyo.

Immediately, the Army General Staff issued an order for the Kwantung Army to cease hostilities but, in an act of extraordinary disobedience, that order was completely ignored.

By any yardstick, this was mutiny on a heroic scale. This rejection of lawful orders was to be made manifest in the homeland. To further muddy the waters there were any number of conspirators in Tokyo, many of them members of the 'Cherry Blossom Society' (Sakurakai), all committed to a war in Manchuria and a coup d'état at home. In March 1931, a coup had been planned but it was completely ineffective and came to nothing.

Having failed to replace the Government with a desired totalitarian military dictatorship in March, the instigators tried again in October. Allegedly, 120 members of the Sakurakai, ten companies of troops from the Imperial Guard and some air-

The Sleeping Giant Begins to Feel It

London Evening Standard, **1931.**

craft from the Imperial Japanese Navy (IJN) were recruited. But, notwithstanding the boots on the ground, this uprising also failed miserably. The plans for the coup leaked and all the players were arrested on 17 October 1931.[5]

The Sakurakai was disbanded, and the leader of the conspiracy was brought to trial and sentenced to: twenty days' confinement. His right-hand man had to endure ten days. Others were merely reprimanded. This pathetic, supine response to an insurrection only served to feed the forces of dissent and further weaken the standing of the Government.

The governance of Japan was very turbulent from 1931, from which time the large army in Manchuria was, in effect, a separate state. A variety of governments attempted to produce manageable domestic policies that would bring the armed forces under political control whilst at the same time develop a coherent foreign policy in particularly complex times.

Japanese society was riven by competing political factions, and attempted coups and assassinations were commonplace. It was not until General Tōjō Hideki was appointed on 18 October 1941 that the country had a measure of stable government. The table opposite lists successive governments from the Mukden Incident in September 1931.

Prime Minister	Tenure	Duration
Baron Wakatsuki Reijirō	April 31–Dec 31	244 days
Inukai Tsuyoshi	Dec 31–May 32	156 days
*Viscount Saitō Makoto	May 32–July 34	2 yrs, 44 days
*Admiral Okada Keisuke	July 34–March 36	1 yr, 246 days
Hirota Kōki	March 36–Feb 37	331 days
*General Senjūrō Hayashi	Feb 37–June 37	123 days
Prince Konoye Fumimaro	June 37–Jan 39	1 yr, 216 days
Baron Kiichirō Hiranuma	Jan 39–Aug 39	238 days
*General Abe Nobuyuki	Aug 39–Jan 40	140 days
*Admiral Yonai Mitsumasa	Jan 40–Jul 40	189 days
Prince Konoye Fumimaro	July 40–Oct 41	1 yr, 89 days
*General Tōjō Hideki	Oct 41–Jul 44	2 yrs, 279 days
*General Koiso Kuniaki	July 44–April 45	260 days
*Admiral Baron Suzuki Kantarō	April 45–Aug 45	133 days

* Denotes a military background, eight of the fourteen named.

During the 1930s, Japan ravaged China, courted Germany, feared Russia, envied Great Britain, Holland and France, and needlessly provoked the USA. By 1939, and while smarting from a disastrous local war with Russia, Japan prepared plans to seize all European colonies in the Far East and invade and hold the Philippines, and Wake and Guam islands.

That latter aspiration was of long-standing, and it was fuelled by Japan's benefits from its participation in the First World War. Not least of these benefits was its being charged with the government, by mandate, of German possessions in the Pacific region to include the Micronesian islands north of the equator. In 1914, these small islands were judged to have 'low cultural, economic and political development'.[6] Initially, they were a financial burden. However, they were well suited for the growing of sugar cane.

The provisions of the mandate required that the islands should not be fortified in any way, and they were subject to League of Nations inspection. By 1930, Japan's constant rejection of inspection visits allowed it to militarise the islands and to turn their economy, based on sugar, to such good effect that it was a net contributor to the national income.

It was not all about sugar: the Japanese Navy established a military organisation and split the scattered islands into five separate naval districts, headquartered at Truk under two-star command. The other four districts were Palau, Saipan, Jaluit Atoll and Ponape.[7] Japan had some 6,852 islands, but only about 430 were inhabited. During the 1930s, wherever it was practical, airstrips were built, and harbours and ports constructed. The islands were seen as the outer perimeter of the defensive system of the five home islands;

Honshu is the largest, and Okinawa the southernmost, of which we will hear more later.

The War Minister issued a spineless message to the mutinous army now rampaging over Manchuria. Presumably with the concurrence of the elderly Prime Minister Inukai Tsuyoshi, he signalled:

> The Kwantung Army is to refrain from any new projects such as becoming independent from the Imperial Army and seizing control of Manchuria and Mongolia.
>
> The general situation is developing according to the intentions of the army, so you may be completely reassured.[8]

The government in Tokyo was powerless to exercise any measure of authority over its renegade army. The Vice Minister of War, taking his lead from the above, burst into print and penned the following, which set a new benchmark in appeasement. He advised the mutineers that:

> We have been united in making desperate efforts to solve the existing difficulty ... trust our zeal, act with great prudence ... Guard against impetuous acts such as declaring the independence of the Kwantung Army and wait for a favourable turn of events on our side.[9]

The Japanese referred to the invasion of Manchuria as the 'Mukden Incident' but this attempt to downplay a massive military operation deceived no one. Any subterfuge had to be abandoned when the invading army declared the formation of the new state of Manchukuo, a Japanese entity independent of the homeland and its law but dependent upon it for logistic support and manpower.

The economic imperative was plain to see, as Japan depended upon Chinese imported raw materials such as 90 per cent of its iron, 75 per cent of its lead, zinc oil, dyes and chemicals, 64 per cent of its coal and 46 per cent of cast iron. Manchuria provided China with about 33 per cent of its total trade.[10] For Japan, Manchuria was a major acquisition, notwithstanding the curious administrative and command arrangements.

The Japanese were brutal conquerors; they did not discriminate between military and civilian prisoners, or between men, women or children. Between 1931 and 1945, they killed hundreds of thousands who fell into their hands, and they earned the deepest hatred of the Chinese. The League of Nations had watched the Japanese invasion with dismay. The very essence of the League's being was to prevent war. The Council of the League issued an instruction to Japan to withdraw its forces. Japan, or at least its army, treated the order with studied contempt. The League of Nations then formed a commission to be headed by the Earl of Lytton.[11]

The Lytton Commissioners examine the site of the Mukden Incident in 1932.

The Commission visited the site of the Mukden Incident – but there really was nothing to see. Lytton reported in the spring of 1932 and outlined the events of the previous year. He concluded that Japan governed the leased territory with practically full rights of sovereignty. Through the South Manchuria Railway, it administered the railway areas including several towns such as Mukden and Changchun. In these areas it controlled the police, taxation, education, and public utilities. It maintained armed forces in many parts of the country. Lytton continued:

> there is probably nowhere in the world an exact parallel to the situation, no example of a country enjoying in the territory of a neighbouring state such extensive administrative privileges. A situation of this kind could conceivably be maintained ... if it were freely desired or accepted by both sides but in the absence of such conditions, it could lead to friction and conflict.[12]

The Lytton Report was an ineffective, political tool and demonstrated publicly the inability of the League of Nations to enforce any form of international discipline. The whole reporting process had taken far too long, and in the meantime, Japan had reinforced its position. The following year, 1933, Japan withdrew from the League of Nations, further weakening the League's standing.

The Mukden Incident, minor in its immediate physical effect, was, arguably, the trigger of the Second World War. This is a view espoused by several historians who think that the successful creation of the state of Manchukuo fed the imperialistic ambitions of a generation of Japanese politicians and military leaders. Demonstrably, at this stage there was no single nation with either the desire or the capability to prevent further Japanese expansion.

During the 1930s, the Government of Japan was a mess. Political assassinations were commonplace, and the army and navy were out of control. For practical purposes the country was in the firm grip of an unelected junta. In China, there was a power struggle in process between the Nationalist faction led by Generalissimo Chiang Kai-shek and the burgeoning Communist Party of China led by Mao Zedong/Mao Tse-tung. There was deep enmity between the two but, in the national interest, they agreed to combine their forces to resist the Japanese. Together, they played a role in the defeat of the Japanese Empire, a contribution largely disregarded in the West. It would be a mistake to view the now imminent Sino-Japanese War (1937–45) and Second World War as two unrelated and distinct events. The reality is that the Sino-Japanese War was a factor in Japan's attack on Pearl Harbor in 1941.[13]

In Tokyo, insurrection was in the air and, on 11 February 1932, Finance Minister Inoue Junnosuke was assassinated. It was a pointless gesture but significantly, the two killers, although convicted, were sentenced to life imprisonment with the strong likelihood that they would only serve a short term of confinement. Only three months later, on 15 May, Prime Minister Inukai Tsuyoshi was assassinated by an eleven-strong group of young naval officers. This murder was triggered by his refusal to recognise the new state of Manchukuo. Forty conspirators were tried for this murder, all of whom were found guilty and received terms of imprisonment. The death of Inukai ended civilian-led government of Japan. Thereafter, the affairs of state were largely in military hands.

Despite the ascendancy of the military, there was continued rumbling dissent within the army. This came to a head in August 1935, when General Nagata Tetsuzan was murdered by Lieutenant Colonel Aizawa Saburō. The assassin believed that the Government of Japan was in the hands of corrupt officials, that Japan's diplomats had failed by agreeing to a limitation on the size of the fleet, and that powerful bureaucrats and financiers were influencing national affairs for their personal gain. He killed the General and, in his view, it was his duty to do so.[14]

At his court martial, on 25 February 1936, the five military judges trod very lightly in their dealing with the self-confessed murderer. He was given licence to make political attacks and his counsel warned: 'If the court fails to

Lieutenant Colonel Aizawa Saburo (1889–1936).

understand the spirit which guided Colonel Aizawa, a second Aizawa and even a third may appear.'[15] Found guilty, Aizawa was shot on 3 July.

Neither the lawyer nor those present in court at the time realised how prophetic were the lawyer's words. A major coup was planned for the following day, and it became yet another 'incident' in Japanese history – known as the '26 February Incident' or the '26-2 Incident'.

The basis for the uprising was to resolve the philosophical differences between two factions in the army. The aim of a group of young officers of the Imperial Japanese Army (IJA) was 'to purge the government and military leadership of their factional rivals and ideological opponents'. The IJA had a long history of factionalism among its senior officers, which originated in rivalries from the Meiji period of 1886–1912. Decades later, and by the early 1930s, the officers of the IJA were divided into two main schools of thought.

Those of a traditionalist bent favoured the Kōdō-Ha or 'Imperial Way'. The leader of this body of opinion was General Araki Sadao, who enjoyed the support of General Masaki Jinzaburō. The aim of the Kōdō-Ha was the preservation of army and national culture. It laid emphasis upon individual spiritual purity over material quality. It was by no means passive and advocated an attack on Russia which lurked north of Manchuria, or Manchukuo, as it now was. Aizawa had been allied to this Kōdō-Ha group.

The other group was the Tōsei-Ha. The adherents were opponents of the status quo. They were modernisers in thrall to German general staff systems and supported central economic and military planning (total war theory), technological modernisation, mechanisation and expansion within China. There was a philosophical chasm between the two factions. Tōsei-Ha wanted change and it wanted it at once. Its leader was General Nagata Tetsuzan – and he had just been assassinated.

On 26 February, the Kōdō-Ha dissidents, who were about 1,500 strong, had the initial success that always accompanies a surprise attack. They succeeded in assassinating several leading officials (including two former prime ministers) but they failed to eliminate their principal target, the serving Prime Minister Okada Keisuke. They took possession of several public buildings but not the Imperial Palace, which had been their aim. The coup petered out as it was unable to counter the massive force of 20,000 men and twenty-two tanks mustered against it, and the uprising was all over by 29 February.[16] Immediately after the surrender, several of the coup leaders committed suicide, well knowing the fate that awaited them.

Previously, political violence had been dealt with very leniently, but this time the established government took an uncompromising line and brought the full power of the law to bear. All the participants faced trial and seventeen of the ringleaders were executed.[17] Forty of the lesser lights went to prison. The Kōdō-Ha grouping in the army was severely damaged. It was forced to take a much lower profile and the Government had enhanced, in some small measure, its control over the army – at least domestically. However, its writ did not run as far as Manchukuo, where, very soon, violence on an unprecedented scale was about to be unleashed.

The commander of the Kwantung Army in 1937 was General Doihara Kenji, who was making ruthless sorties into North China. This was a general who was not subservient to his political masters but one who had his own agenda. He had contrived to convince the Chinese war lords that there was merit in occupying five northern provinces to form an autonomous government under the protection of the IJA. This was far beyond his authority, and little wonder the Western press was calling him the 'Lawrence of Manchuria'. Attempts to curb Doihara failed and his nation-forming attempts flourished as Japanese entrepreneurs arrived in droves to exploit the opportunities now on offer. The General claimed that what he had created was a buffer state between Manchuria and China, and to strengthen his hand, he imported 5,000 troops to provide 'protection from bandits'. These soldiers can

General Doihara Kenji (1883–1948). Executed for war crimes.

only have come from Japan and only with the direct cooperation of the Japanese Government or the autocratic ruling of the Ministry of War.

Lieutenant Colonel Ishiwara Kanji, who had been such an enthusiastic proponent of a Japanese Manchuria had, ten years on, changed his mind. His ability was widely recognised and, as a lieutenant colonel, he had a level of influence disproportionate to his rank. He now took the view that these 5,000 troops were to be employed in a major foray into China. He dismissed Doihara's buffer state as a 'poisonous flower' that should be abandoned before it inflamed the ongoing war with Chiang Kai-shek and his Nationalist forces. Ishiwara urged the removal of troops from likely trouble spots, of which the Marco Polo bridge was one.[18]

In late 1936, against all the odds but very pragmatically, Mao Tse-tung sent his right-hand man, Chou En-lai, to hold discussions with Chiang Kai-shek's

Mao Tse-tung (1893–1976) and Chou En-lai (1898–1976), the two leaders of the Communist Party of China in 1936.

envoy, Chang Hsueh-liang. The Communists conceded that Chiang Kai-shek was best placed to lead the Chinese opposition against the Japanese and, furthermore, agreed that Red (Communist) generals would serve under Chiang. The quid pro quo was the release of Communists held in Nationalist jails and acceptance that, after Japan's defeat, the Communist Party could operate legally.

Initially, there was domestic upheaval in the Nationalist camp, which need not detain us, because eventually and after months of wrangling, on 5 July 1937, the agreement between these two factions was signed. It was a game changer. It brought a unified command to China and the first period of relative domestic tranquillity for ten turbulent years.

Generalissimo Chiang Kai-shek (1887–1975), leader of the Chinese Nationalists and commander of all Chinese forces 1936–45.

Meanwhile, in 1936, Britain was in the throes of a severe financial crisis. There was not the money to maintain the large, modern fleet needed to support its colonial territory worldwide. The USA was no better off, with rampant unemployment and a population that had readily embraced 'isolationism'. The Anglo-American presence in the Far East was weak although both countries recognised fully the threat that an aggressive Japan posed to the Philippines, Burma, Malaya, Singapore and Hong Kong.

Back in 1932, the Committee of National Defence had considered the situation in the Crown Colony of Singapore, the centre of British commercial activity. It warned, 'it would be the height of folly to perpetuate Britain's defenceless state there.'[19] Unfortunately, the naval assets to defend Singapore did not exist. Britain's military weakness and America's isolationism and anti-colonial posture were a lethal combination that gave the servants of Hirohito every encouragement to pursue an aggressive expansionist foreign policy.

Notes

1. Paine, S.C.M., *The Wars for Asia 1911–1949* (New York, Cambridge University Press, 2012), p. 24.
2. Russell, Lord of Liverpool, *The Knights of Bushido* (London, Cassell, 1958), p. 8.
3. Behr, E., *The Last Emperor* (New York, Bantam Books, 1987), p. 182.
4. Paine, p. 123.
5. Russell, p. 9.

6. Perez, L.G., *League of Nations, Mandates. Japan at War* (ABC-CLIO, ed., 2013), p. 204.
7. Balley, D.E., *WWII Wrecks of the Truk Lagoon* (North Valley Diver Publications, 2001).
8. Toland, J., *The Rising Sun: The Decline and Fall of the Japanese Empire, 1936–45* [1970] (Modern Library, New York, 2003), pp. 8–9.
9. Ibid.
10. Paine, p. 28.
11. Victor Bulwer-Lytton, 2nd Earl of Lytton, KG, GCSI, GCIE, PC, DL (1876–1947).
12. Russell, pp. 2–3.
13. Paine, p. 3.
14. In 1922, a treaty was signed in Washington that limited the number of capital ships of the Royal Navy, US Navy and Japanese Navy on scale of 5:5:3. This was amended in 1930 and 1936 to 10:10:7. The Japanese bitterly resented this restriction.
15. Toland, p. 12.
16. Jansen, M., *The Making of Modern Japan* (Harvard University Press, 2002), p. 598.
17. Kita Hiroaki, *Ni Niroku Jiken Zenkenshō* (Asahi Shimbun, 2003), pp. 147, 150.
18. Toland, p. 37.
19. Louis, W.R., *British Strategy in the Far East 1919–39* (Oxford, Clarendon Press, 1971), p. 211.

Chapter Four

1937–45
The Second Sino-Japanese War

Costly wars are often initiated by relatively small *casus belli* and these are often contrived. The Mukden Incident is one example; and on 7 July 1937, there occurred another. Domestically, Japanese public affairs were in constant turmoil. The military was out of control in Manchuria, where the Kwantung Army held sway. It had positioned a small force, numbering a few hundred, overlooking the Marco Polo Bridge and the Fortress of Wanping on the far side of the Yongding River, about 15 miles (24km) south-west of Peking (now Beijing).[1] At this point there was no evident threat to either side.

A Japanese soldier, Private Shimura Kikujiro, left his post to relieve himself and did not return to his post at once. His commanding officer, for no obvious reason, concluded that the man was in Chinese hands and demanded that the Chinese permit his troops to cross the bridge and search for Shimura in the fortress.

Predictably, the Chinese rejected the demand. The Japanese commander apparently overreacted and, despite the return of Shimura from his wanderings, advanced on the Chinese-held fortress and mounted an assault upon it. The likelihood that a local commander, perhaps a lieutenant colonel, could initiate such an attack is very remote. It is suggested that this attack was premeditated and planned at a senior but anonymous level.

This made no sense in 1937, nor does it today.

The Japanese were repulsed, but nevertheless, and again for no cogent reason, issued an ultimatum. General Feng Zhian, the GOC of 37th Chinese Division, was given a warning order to put his division in a state of readiness. What had started as a soldier briefly leaving his post had, by now, all the makings of a very serious confrontation. In fact, it was the start of the Second Sino-Japanese War, and it would last for eight years and cost millions of lives.[2]

The two sides fought an 'asymmetric war'. The Japanese had anticipated a short, conventional war which would limit the logistic burden and the cost. The Chinese, particularly Chiang Kai-shek, favoured what would later be termed 'revolutionary or guerrilla' war. The Generalissimo, who had been

The Marco Polo Bridge. The likelihood of Private Shimura wandering across this bridge in the middle of the night seems to be remote.

fighting the Japanese since 1931, knew that the longer he could prolong the war the more likely he was to exhaust the Japanese.

The Japanese were somewhat complacent, and on 11 July 1937, the War Minister, Field Marshal Sugiyama Hajime, advised Hirohito that the 'incident probably can be resolved in a month'.[3] He added that only five divisions would be needed to quell any Chinese opposition. Six days after the first clash, the Japanese embassy in China informed Chiang Kai-shek: 'This time when Japan sends troops the central Government (i.e., you) will be the target.'[4]

Japan was very serious about targeting Chiang Kai-shek and immediately sent three reinforcement divisions to Manchukuo, with a further two in August. On 28 July, the Japanese initiated its general advance in China. The front was 'over an area roughly equivalent to the United States east of the Mississippi River' – a vast and vulnerable front, but even so, Beijing and Tianjin were taken at once.[5] The railways were key to the Japanese advance and the First Army followed the Beijing–Wuhan line and Second Army took the route from Tianjin to Pukou.

By the end of 1937 there were twenty-one divisions, numbering 600,000 Japanese in China. In addition, it had two divisions in Korea. Japanese estimates of time, space, logistic support and the cost of this war were hopelessly inaccurate. By year's end it had suffered 100,000 casualties. A year later, the Japanese had 1.1 million men under arms in China and had achieved nothing except well-advertised international contempt.

In August 1937, the Japanese assaulted and took Shanghai deep in Nationalist country. Chinese resistance was obdurate, and it inflicted heavy casualties on the invader. However, 2,900 of its 5,255 factories were destroyed and the inhabitants had to endure thirteen poison gas attacks – this despite Japan being a signatory to the 1899 and 1907 Hague conventions, which banned its use. According to historians Yoshimi Yoshiaki and Matsuno Seiya, it was Emperor Hirohito himself who authorised the use of chemical weapons in China, a decision that he came to regret – and which could have cost him his life.[6]

It took until November for the city to fall, by which time the Chinese had lost 187,200 killed and 85,000 wounded. The Japanese admitted to 9,115 dead and 31,257 wounded.[7] However, the Chinese claimed 98,417 Japanese dead and wounded. The high casualty rate was a disincentive to the Japanese, but nevertheless, on 1 December it was decided to take Nanking (Nanjing), at that time the capital of China and thus a prestigious target.

On the way to Nanking the Japanese did not neglect provincial capitals, because they were economically important and were also transport hubs. Baoding (Zhili) was taken on 24 September, Shijiazhuang (Hebei) on 10 October, Taiyuan (Shanxi) on 9 November, and Hangzhou (Zhejiang), south of Shanghai, would follow on 26 December. The Yangtze River provided a convenient route to Nanjing and the campaign to take the city was launched on 1 December.[8]

The behaviour of the Kwantung Army had drawn attention since the Mukden Incident. The wholesale killing of prisoners had been noted and deplored but, in November 1937, during the early months of the Sino-Japanese War, the Japanese set a new, very low benchmark. The mindset of its officer corps is exemplified by Second Lieutenants Toshiaki Mukai and Tsuyoshi Noda.

These two apologies for soldiers had a competition to see who could be first to decapitate 100 Chinese. The time frame was mid-November to 13 December 1937, at about the time of the assault on Nanking.[9]

Their exploits were reported in a series of four articles in the *Japan Advertiser* implying that their kills were during battle. However, by the time each man had beheaded his 100 victims, the competition was so close that it was difficult to identify the winner. On that basis they decided to extend the competition to 150 heads.

The competition attracted public attention and publicity was given in *Tokyo Nichi-Nichi Shimbun*. Journalists Asami Kazuo and Jiro Suzuki's jointly written article had the headline:

Incredible Record [in the Contest to behead 100 People] – Mukai 106 – 105 Noda – Both 2nd Lieutenants go into Extra Innings

These two men did nothing remotely heroic. They were murdering passive Chinese captives for sport and, worryingly, being applauded by the Japanese public for doing so. The myth was that they had killed the 211 people in hand-to-hand fighting. Tsuyoshi himself destroyed that myth by saying:

> I didn't kill more than four or five people in hand-to-hand combat … We'd face an enemy trench that we'd captured, and when we called out '*Ni, Lai-Lai!*' (You come here!), the Chinese soldiers were so stupid, they'd rush toward us all at once. Then we'd line them up and cut them down, from one end of the line to the other. I was praised for having killed a hundred people; but almost all of them were killed in this way. The two of us did have a contest, but afterwards, I was often asked whether it was a big deal, and I said it was no big deal.[10]

After the war the deeds of Toshiaki and Tsuyoshi had faded from public memory until a brave Japanese historian, Hora Tomio, wrote a paper about

The two 'sportsmen', Toshiaki and Tsuyoshi, in 1937. Both were executed for war crimes.

the events in Nanjing and the horror of what had been done in the service of the Emperor. The paper was stoutly ignored until 1971, when journalist Katsuichi Honda dragged its detail into a series of articles he wrote for *Asahi Shimbun*. The two competitors faced retribution after the war. They were tried by the Chinese Government and, on 28 January 1948, were executed for their crimes.

In December 1937, although it had made large territorial gains in China, Japan felt threatened by communist foes. In the north, Stalin had 'bombers in Vladivostok less than 700 miles [1,127km] away from Tokyo and, in the west, the bourgeoning legions of the Chinese communists under command of the determined peasant Mao Tse-tung'.[11]

The Japanese forces assaulting Nanking were commanded by Prince Asaka Yasuhiko, Hirohito's paternal great-uncle; that familial connection would save his life. The Japanese were able to swarm into the city of Nanking because Chiang Kai-shek had decided to withdraw into the Chinese hinterland and save his troops for a later day. The result was that the defence, although spirited, was unable to withstand the overwhelming power of Asaka's army and on 13 December, the city fell. What followed is one of the bleakest times in human history. The Japanese put the inhabitants of Nanking to the sword – literally. The death toll is difficult to establish and estimates of Chinese dead vary between 40,000 and 300,000.[12] The international consensus is 'about 200,000'. On the other hand, Japanese sources say it never happened. The number of rapes committed by Japanese soldiers has not been calculated but any Chinese woman left un-raped was in a minority.[13]

The heads of about ninety murdered Chinese arranged, presumably, for the benefit of the officer in the background, perhaps Toshiaki.

Lieutenant General Prince Asaka Yasuhiko (1887–1981).

The killings in Nanking were not the work of a handful of undisciplined men, rather it was a major war crime in which there were tens of thousands of active and enthusiastic participants. The commanders of these soldiers abrogated their responsibilities and were, thus, complicit in the crime. A feature of the mayhem was the humiliation, torture and mutilation inflicted on the victims. Clearly there was serious hate at the root of the massacre. It is germane to pause to consider the reasons why the Japanese acted with such unvarnished brutality.

* * *

The mutilation of enemy bodies before or after death is proscribed, although the Japanese did not acknowledge any such constraints. The behaviour of the Japanese in Nanking has no evident explanation. There was no sound military reason, no tactical or strategic benefit. Similarly, there were no medals to win, no accolades to receive.

Most humans would shrink at the prospect of killing another human being, but there are exceptions. Grossman argued that proximity to the victim is a key element. Dropping a bomb from 30,000 feet is an impersonal act, usually with no effect on the airman because he cannot see the people he is killing.[14] However, the closer the killer gets to his victim, the greater his stress – usually.

The reason that, elsewhere in the Second World War, SS killer squads shot people in the back of the head was to avoid looking the victim in the eye. Even so, mass killing by shooting was so stressful that another methodology had to be found and the gas chambers were the result. The desire to avoid bayonet fighting is normal among Western soldiers. In the First World War, the British casualties caused by bayonets number only 0.32 per cent of the total.[15] It is reasonable to assume a similar miniscule percentage for the other armies involved. During the American Civil War (1861–5), an examination of all those wounded and hospitalised revealed that only 922 had bayonet wounds. This does ignore those who were treated in the field and all of those killed by bayonet. A Union doctor reported that he only treated thirty-seven men with bayonet wounds.[16]

The corpses of victims line the bank of the Qinhuai River in Nanking. *(Moriyasu Murase)*

Empirical research shows that close-quarter fighting is highly unpleasant and that killing an enemy with a bayonet is distressing. A German soldier, Stephen Westman, observed that:

> We got an order to storm a French position and during the ensuing melee a French Corporal stood before me, both our bayonets at the ready, he to kill me I to kill him … Pushing his weapon aside I stabbed him through the chest. He dropped his rifle and fell, the blood shot out of his mouth, I stood over him for a few seconds and then gave him the *coup de grace*. After we had taken the position, I felt giddy, my knees shook, and I was sick.

Westman had had a different upbringing and in a different Western culture. There was, and presumably still is, a culture gap of wide proportions between Western and Asian soldiers, specifically Japanese – because the Japanese favoured the sword and bayonet. These two weapons are for 'up close and personal' killing. Any reluctance to use the bayonet was markedly absent in the Japanese Army and there is every indication, not least in Nanjing, that its use was relished. These weapons enabled an atrocity, a subject that Grossman gave thought to, and he observed that:

> Atrocity can be a powerful tool. But it is also a wretched and hateful servant that must be kept on a short leash, lest it turn on its would-be

master and deny them even short-term benefits. Yet there is undeniably, a simple, horrifying and obvious value resident in atrocity. The Mongols were able to make entire nations submit without a fight just on the basis of their reputation.[17]

The Japanese were going to face obdurate adversaries in their quest for empire and knowledge of their barbarous behaviour shaped the attitudes of their latter-day enemies in the field. It is not unreasonable to suggest that the Nanking massacre caused the deaths of tens of thousands of Japanese soldiers who were denied the ability to surrender but were shot out of hand. This text will cite examples in support of that assertion.

In Nanking, the despatch of captives allowed for a degree of inventiveness in making death as awful as possible. Burying captives alive achieved nothing, other than providing something different for the audience. The victims suffered unbearable mental anguish before death released them from the horror of it all.

This book is not intended to be a chronicle of war crimes, but the Japanese Empire was founded on war crimes of loathsome brutality. Because these crimes had a deleterious effect on the moral compass of the Allied soldiers they faced, reference to them is inevitable as we trace the campaigns of the Second World War.

'Indoctrination is the process of inculcating a person with ideas, attitudes, and cognitive strategies. Humans are a social animal species, inescapably shaped by cultural context, and it follows that some degree of indoctrination is implicit in the parent–child relationship.'[18] In a group context, this leads to the formation of stable communities with shared corporate values – at least, it did and still does in the West, but that pattern seemed not to apply in Japan.

John Toland, on his way to a Pulitzer Prize, tried to explain Japanese mentality and to rationalise the behaviour of its representatives in uniform:

> to the Western observer the Japanese were an incomprehensible con- tradiction: polite and barbarous, honest, and treacherous, brave and cowardly, industrious and lazy – all at the same time. To the Japanese these were not anomalies at all, but one united whole. To the Japanese a man without contradictions could not be respected; he was just a simple person ... The strong recognition of death gave Japanese not only the strength to face disaster stoically but an intense appreciation of each moment which could be their last. This was not pessimistic but a calm determination to accept the inevitable.[19]

Toland concluded that although the Japanese were religious, they had and still have no single god, no divine being, to worship. *They were sincere but had*

Execution by the sword, c.1938, for the entertainment of a Japanese audience.
The perpetrator of this war crime was never identified and probably died in his
bed in the 1970s.

no concept of sin. They felt sympathy but lacked humanity. They formed clans but
had no society in Western terms. The family provided security but that
sapped individuality. In Toland's opinion, they were a great and energetic
people driven by opposing forces and seeking to move in diametrically
opposed directions at the same time.[20]

In every army, initial training is designed to mould new recruits from those stable communities, mentioned above, into new, acceptable military norms. The training aspires to develop a strong team spirit by shared physical, mental and social experiences. For the individual the transition from civilian to soldier does not, or should not, expunge core values learned in childhood.

Having completed basic training, it is expected that an individual will willingly abandon his individuality and obey instantly an order given by a superior. This may well involve the exposure to extreme danger and the killing of perceived enemies. The fail-safe in the system is always that the soldier is acting as a member of a trained and disciplined team, led by an experienced officer, and that all activity is in accordance with an acceptable code of behaviour.

In the IJA at Nanking, there was, by any military standard, a complete and catastrophic breakdown in discipline. However, although the Japanese could not be expected to conform to the values of a Western culture, nevertheless,

December 1937, an interested, but dispassionate, group of Japanese watch the entombment and murder of Chinese captives. (*Keystone*)

murder was proscribed in Japanese society and punishable by death, and Japanese soldiers knew that. Perhaps the most reprehensible aspect of this business was that, in Tokyo, the government of Prince Konoye Fumimaro was aware of the excesses and took no action to punish the culprits or to prevent a recurrence elsewhere.

This text will show how the behaviour of the Japanese, epitomised by the Nanking Massacre, adversely affected all with whom they later came into contact. War is an uncivilised and brutal business, but until December 1937 there had remained room for a modicum of humanity.

'For the avoidance of doubt,' as lawyers are wont to say, all those who opposed, physically, the Japanese Empire, ostensibly committed retaliatory war crimes, in that they did not take Japanese prisoners and killed perhaps 95 per cent of defeated Japanese. The defence argument might be, 'They started it', just as the leaders of British Bomber Command would take as a justification for the destruction of German cities the precedent of London, Bristol, Coventry et al. However, the specific question posed is, 'What does a soldier do if a defeated enemy refuses to surrender and any negotiations with him are seriously life-threatening for the captor?' There is but one pragmatic solution and that is, 'Kill him'.

*   *   *

Great Britain and the USA were powerless to prevent the massacres in Nanking, but they had a responsibility for expatriates living in the city. Both countries maintained a flotilla of river gunboats on the Yangtze and, on 12 December 1937, USS *Panay* was attacked by Japanese aircraft, from the aircraft carrier *Kaga*, and hit with two 132lb (60kg) bombs. Four people were killed and forty-eight wounded in this inexplicable incident, which caused *Panay* to sink in mid-river.[21] That same day, HMS *Ladybird* was also fired upon; two men were killed but the gunboat, along with HMS *Bee*, was able to rescue survivors from the *Panay*. There followed the inevitable post-mortem. The Japanese claimed that the ships could not be identified as neutrals but did accept responsibility and, on 22 April 1938, it paid the USA $2,214,007.36 in recompense.[22] USS *Panay* was the first American ship to be lost to Japanese air power – it was by no means the last.

It was noted that, after the fall of Nanking and the USS *Panay* incident, casualty lists from the China theatre mounted; 100,000 Japanese troops were killed or wounded by December 1937. Japanese War Ministry and General Staff officers tried to bring hostilities to a rapid conclusion.

In general terms, these officers may be divided into expansionists and anti-expansionists. The expansionists believed that any show of weakness

USS *Panay*, sunk by Japanese aircraft in the Yangtze River on 12 December 1937.

by the Japanese would only encourage Chinese resistance. The anti-expansionists viewed the China war as a debilitating effort that was bleeding the IJA white while the main enemy, the USSR, continued a military build-up in the Soviet Far East and menaced Japan and Manchuria from the north. However, both groups accepted the premise that the Soviets were indeed Japan's number one foe. The expansionists preferred to eliminate any potential Chinese threat to the Japanese flank in operations against the USSR. The anti-expansionists opted to end the drain on IJA resources to use such resources to prepare for war with the USSR. Nevertheless, Japan's military and civilian leaders could not find a means to stop the fighting and, by 1939, the IJA had about 1 million men committed on the endless China front.[23]

Not the least of the consequences of the Second Sino-Japanese War was the extreme impact on the Chinese population, of whom 95 million, or about 26 per cent, of the population became refugees between 1937 and 1945. This social disruption led to epidemics of cholera, malaria and the plague.[24] The conduct of the Japanese and its deleterious effects across Chinese society generated a deep-seated hatred of the invaders and strengthened the resolve of the Chinese to continue the fight.

After the suppression of Nanking, the Japanese Army was engaged in the Xuzhou Campaign between March and May 1938 (see '5' on the map on page 36) involving the participation of 600,000 men. The Japanese aim was to take the city of Xuzhou, a transport hub served by three strategically important railway lines. The east–west line connected Zhengzhou with Shanghai (and the sea), the north–south, Tianjin–Pukou, line was the connection for

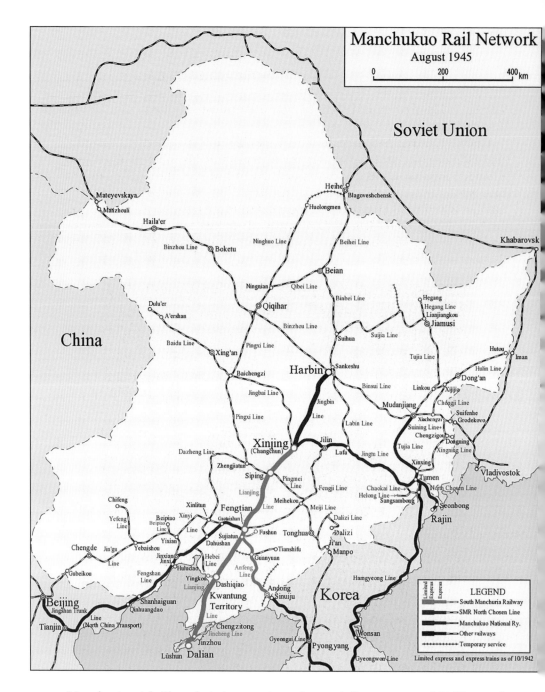

Manchuria with Shanghai. A second north–south line connected Beijing and Wuhan.

The fighting around Xuzhou was savage and Chinese losses were in the tens of thousands, and included nine generals. The surviving Chinese generals, not least Li Zongren, Bai Chongxi and Tang Enbo, became national heroes.[25] The first named went on to be President of China, vice Chiang Kai-shek, in January 1949.

Chiang Kai-shek had suffered great losses in the fighting around Shanghai and Nanking and had withdrawn the remnants of his force. The residual Chinese opposition was poorly trained, but it had Russian logistic support and was provided with armour and artillery. The heroism of the Chinese soldiers contributed greatly to the major defeat of the Japanese at Taierzhuang in April 1938, when General Li Zongren destroyed two Japanese divisions and, at a stroke, 'dispelled the myth of Japanese invincibility, greatly boosting Nationalist morale'.[26]

General Li Zongren (1890–1969).

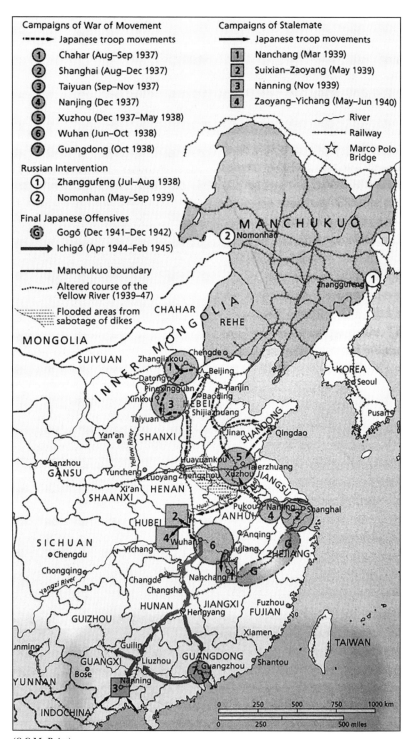

Campaigns of War of Movement

······► Japanese troop movements

- ① Chahar (Aug–Sep 1937)
- ② Shanghai (Aug–Dec 1937)
- ③ Taiyuan (Sep–Nov 1937)
- ④ Nanjing (Dec 1937)
- ⑤ Xuzhou (Dec 1937–May 1938)
- ⑥ Wuhan (Jun–Oct 1938)
- ⑦ Guangdong (Oct 1938)

Russian Intervention

- ① Zhanggufeng (Jul–Aug 1938)
- ② Nomonhan (May–Sep 1939)

Final Japanese Offensives

- ⓖ Gogō (Dec 1941–Dec 1942)
- ──► Ichigō (Apr 1944–Feb 1945)

─── Manchukuo boundary

·········· Altered course of the Yellow River (1939–47)

Flooded areas from sabotage of dikes

Campaigns of Stalemate

──► Japanese troop movements

- 1 Nanchang (Mar 1939)
- 2 Suixian–Zaoyang (May 1939)
- 3 Nanning (Nov 1939)
- 4 Zaoyang–Yichang (May–Jun 1940)

~~~ River

········ Railway

☆ Marco Polo Bridge

(*S.C.M. Paine*)

Once Xuzhou had been taken, the Japanese moved on Wuhan. (See map opposite, '6'). At this point, Chiang was responsible for an atrocity that killed more Chinese than the Japanese. Chiang ordered that the dikes alongside the Yellow River should be breached where the river joined the Grand Canal. The resultant floods covered an area of 23,316 square miles (60,388km^2) of high-quality farmland. Estimates of the number of those who were drowned or died of starvation vary but 'about 900,000' is generally quoted.[27] The human cost of this one act was astronomic: 3.9 million refugees were created, and their life expectancy was much reduced. The Yellow River flowed outside its previous dikes for ten years. The floods did deny the Japanese access to Wuhan by road; however, they went up the Yangtze River instead. After spirited resistance, Wuhan, 714 miles (1,150km) south of Beijing, finally fell on 25 October 1938, having caused attrition in Japanese ranks and extended its logistic and commensurate financial burden.

War is an expensive business, especially so when one fights with the source of strategic material upon which one depends for economic health. Japan had assumed that its military strategy and war with China would produce financial benefits. The reality was the opposite. The value of Shanghai's trade sank from $US 31 million per month to 6.7 million. At this point it was evident that Japan's military strategy was incompatible with its economic aspirations. In addition, it undermined its relations with the Western powers, who resented the closure of the Yangtze River and the exclusion of Western traders from the Chinese market. Japan was locked into a war with an intractable opponent. It had now to support logistically its island chain and their garrisons as well as an army in China a million strong. In the face of reason and in an act of crass stupidity, it decided to tweak the tail of its most formidable neighbour – it went to war with Russia.

Notes

1. The bridge is an eleven-arch granite bridge of architectural value. It was erected under the Jin dynasty (1115–1234) and later restored by the Kangxi Emperor in 1698. The explorer Marco Polo made mention of the bridge in his book, written in the thirteenth century.
2. The First Sino-Japanese War was fought in 1894–5 and was settled in Japan's favour.
3. Takafusa Nakamura, *History of Shōwa Japan* (University of Tokyo Press, 1998), p. 142.
4. Taylor, G.E., *Struggle for North China 1940* (Institute of Pacific Relations, 1940), p. 20.
5. Paine, S.C.M., *The Wars for Asia 1911–1949* (New York, Cambridge University Press, 2012), p. 131.
6. Yoshimi, Y. & Matsuno, S., *Dokugasusen kankei shiryō II, Kaisetsu* (1997).
7. Yang Tianshi, *Chiang Kai-shek and the Battles of Shanghai and Nanjing* (Baihua Literature and Art Publishing House, 2000), pp. 153–4. Lai, B. (2017), *Shanghai and Nanjing 1937: Massacre on the Yangtze* (Oxford, Osprey Publishing, 2017), p. 87.
8. Paine. p. 133.
9. Bob Tadashi Wakabayashi, 'The Nanking 100-man killing contest debate. War guilt amid fabricated illusions 1971–75' (*The Journal of Japanese Studies*, Vol. 26, No. 2, Summer 2000).

10. Katsuichi, Honda, *The Road to Nanjing* (M.E. Sharp, Pacific Basin Institute, 1987), p. 82.
11. Toland, J., *The Rising Sun: The Decline and Fall of the Japanese Empire, 1936–45* [1970] (Modern Library, New York, 2003), p. 38.
12. Levene, M. & Roberts, P., *The Massacre in History* (Oxford, Berghahn Books, 1999), pp. 223–4. Totten, S. & Bartrop, P., *Dictionary of Genocide* (Greenwood, 2007), pp. 298–9.
13. Chang, I., *The Rape of Nanking* (New York, Basic Books, 1997).
14. Grossman, D., *On Killing* [1995] (New York, Back Bay Books, 2009), pp. 97–8.
15. T.J. Mitchell & G.M. Smith, *Official History of the War, Casualties and Medical Statistics, Imperial War Museum* (HMSO, reprinted London, 1997).
16. Norris, J., *Fix Bayonets* (Barnsley, Pen & Sword, 2015), p. viii.
17. Grossman, p. 21.
18. Funk, A. & Wagnalls, B., 'To instruct in doctrines; esp., to teach partisan or sectarian dogmata', I.A. Snook, ed. (*Concepts of Indoctrination*, London, Routledge & Kegan, 1972).
19. Toland, p. 38.
20. Ibid.
21. Toland asserts (p.49), incorrectly, that HMS *Ladybird* was 'destroyed' in this incident. She was not and went on to fight elsewhere in the Second World War.
22. *Miami Daily News Record* (Associated Press, 22 April 1938), p. 1.
23. Drea, E.J., *Nomonhan: Japanese-Soviet Tactical Combat 1939* (US Army Command and General Staff College, Fort Leavenworth, 1981).
24. Larry, D., *The Chinese People at War: Human suffering and Social Transformation 1937–45* (Cambridge University Press, 2010), p. 120.
25. MacKinnon, S.R., *Wuhan 1938* (Berkeley University Press, 2008), p. 32.
26. Garver, J.W., *Chinese-Soviet Relations 1937–45* (New York, Oxford University Press, 1988), p. 39.
27. Lary, D. (1 April 2001), 'Drowned Earth: The Strategic Breaching of the Yellow River Dikes, 1938' (*War in History*, 2001 **8** (2)), pp. 191–207.

Chapter Five

1938–45
The Russian Threat, the Chinese War and the Burma Road

Japan had viewed Russia as its prime threat since the turn of the century. It had cause to worry because Russia did not conceal its negative attitude towards Japan. This became manifest in open warfare in the summer of 1938 at the Battle of Lake Khasan (29 July–11 August 1938). In the Japanese manner this was known as the 'Changkufeng Incident'. It was all about the possession of an obscure hilltop on the Manchurian–Russia border. This was contested and there was a brief two-week engagement in which the Russian Air Force and Army inflicted sufficiently serious casualties that the Japanese sought an armistice followed by a settlement.

On 11 May 1939, fighting broke out again and this time it included the first tank battle in history, fought at Khalkhin Gol, so named for the river that flowed through the battlefield. The Japanese term it the 'Nomonhan Incident', and:

> it clearly illustrates what happens when an independent military organi-sation, such as the Kwantung Army, is given unilateral control to make strategic decisions without regard to the impact of national policy. In Nomonhan, the Kwantung Army unilaterally invaded a foreign country (Outer Mongolia) by ground and air, without Imperial sanction and without a declaration of war. It manipulated the High Command in Tokyo, withheld information, and even duped higher headquarters on occasion. It evaded national policy and ignored the home government. The Kwantung Army was a prima donna which proved insensitive to the central controls of the High Command and the civilian government. By its actions, the Kwantung Army was making foreign policy at gunpoint and risking all-out war. So, how did this field army come to exert such a flippant disregard for higher authority and a despised 'weak-kneed' civilian diplomacy?[1]

It is argued that the answer lay in Japan's overly aggressive leadership doctrine, which placed great emphasis upon *dokudansenko*, a word that meant

BATTLE OF KHALKIN-GOL

The disputed border between Nomonhan and Khalkhin Gol. (*Vantage Art*)

'initiative and originality in emergencies', and fostered tactical flexibility when perhaps communications were poor. However, the principle was at risk from 'headstrong staff officers in the field who were determined to interpret guidance as they deemed fit'.[2]

It was two months after hostilities were opened before any notice was taken by disinterested Western nations. The *New York Times* commented on 'A Strange War' in an editorial about the fighting between the Soviet Red Army and the Imperial Japanese Army on the Mongolian steppes. *The Times* derided both combatants' claims as exaggerated but, inadvertently, touched on the distinctive feature of the fighting when it described the battle as 'raging in a thoroughly out-of-the-way corner of the world where it cannot attract a great deal of attention'.[3]

A combination of the geography, the two combatants' unfailing secrecy, and the outbreak of the Second World War in Europe on 3 September 1939 served to conceal the very significant first use of massed armour by the Russians, led by General Georgi K. Zhukov. The IJA, essentially an infantry force, fared poorly and fell victim to a Soviet double envelopment. This was a serious war; the Russians committed about 500 tanks and 27,000 men, of whom 9,703 were killed or missing. The Japanese matched the Russians numerically and admitted having 8,440 killed and 8,766 wounded. The tank battle was one-sided as Russian losses were 253, and the Japanese only 29. The arithmetic is a reflection on Zhukov, who had demonstrated that, at this stage, he was no expert in armoured warfare.

There was considerable aerial combat and Russia lost 163 fighters and 44 bombers. Japanese combat losses were 97 fighters, 25 bombers and 41 others (mostly reconnaissance), while 128 fighters, 54 bombers and 38 others required repairs due to combat damage. The Japanese air-force suffered 152 dead and 66 severely wounded. This was the first time in military history that air power was used to obtain an objective.

This savage little war, little known in the West, established the pattern of warfare that applied throughout the Second World War. The great tank battle of Kursk (July–August 1943) had its genesis on the banks of this obscure Chinese river.

The battle was won by the Russians and, despite the disparity in material losses, it took possession of the battlefield and had won a pyrrhic victory. The Kwantung Army, already in great disfavour in Tokyo, went even deeper into disfavour and not least for initiating and escalating a war without reference to

Mongolian troops oppose a Japanese counter-attack on the western beach of the river Khalkhin Gol, 1939.

the government of the day. Its defeat not only damaged national pride but, more importantly, the continued resistance of the Chinese under Chiang Kai-shek in combination with the German-Soviet Non-aggression Pact called for a reconsideration of Tokyo's war plans.[4]

The knock-on effects of this war were considerable. There was a hint of paranoia in the Russian response. Although its position in the Far East was secure, it feared another incursion by the Japanese. On this basis, it maintained enormous forces to counter the perceived threat. On 1 July 1942, there were 1,446,012 troops, 11,759 artillery pieces and 2,589 tanks and self-propelled guns. In addition, it had 3,178 combat aircraft.[5] This massive force was not considered strong enough to resist an invasion, in the opinion of the commander, General A.K. Kazakovtsev. He pronounced that 'if the Japanese enter the war on Hitler's side … our cause is hopeless.'[6] Not a shot had been fired and, with this judgement, Kazakovtsev must surely have secured a place in the Pessimists' Hall of Fame.

*   *   *

In March 1938, the 717-mile (1,154km) long 'Burma Road' was completed. It was vital for the continuing logistic support of China by the British during the Second Sino-Japanese War. The criticality of this line of supply was caused by the loss of all ports in China by the Nationalist forces of Chiang Kai-shek.

The architect of this massive piece of civil engineering was Chin-Ping Chen, who employed 220,000 Burmese and Chinese labourers, working with hand tools in extreme conditions. Chin-Ping Chen went on to a highly successful diplomatic career.

In September 1939, Great Britain was facing an aggressive European enemy intent on its invasion and subjugation. The overriding priority was the retention of the independence of the British Isles. The very survival of the nation was at stake. To add to Britain's political burden, the Japanese Government, recognising the impact the Burma Road was having on operations in China, exerted strong pressure on Britain and eventually, in July, briefly, the British acquiesced and closed the road.

For the British the war in Europe took priority over events in the Far East. Malaya (now Malaysia), Burma (now Myanmar), Singapore and Hong Kong could not be given the level of military support they needed to deter the acquisitive Japanese. The United States was disinclined to give aid to a colonial regime as Roosevelt held well-known anti-colonial and Anglophobic views. Russell Mead, the American historian, considers:

> Franklin Roosevelt to be the most Anglophobic American president of the 20th century: while loudly and enthusiastically proclaiming solidarity

Casualties of a mass panic during a Japanese air raid in Chongqing. (*Carl Mydans*)

with Churchill and the Brits during the war, FDR also ensured, as John Maynard Keynes put it, that the US would 'pick the eyes out of the British Empire'. FDR aimed to help Britain win the world war while ensuring Britain lost its supreme place in the world.[7]

Roosevelt's personal opinions would always be a factor in Anglo-American relations but equally, not all British servicemen and politicians were enamoured by the United States. In the war to come there was antipathy between senior commanders of both nations, not least domestically, and the personal ambition of some was a constant factor that impacted upon operations.

Anglophobia will raise its head later in this book and it is as well to get it into perspective. This author served two very happy years in the US Army, as an exchange officer in the mid-1970s, and was offered only warmth, kindness and unlimited, generous hospitality. Most Americans know little of the UK, have never met a British person, and give no thought to the UK and the people who live there. The converse is much the same. Anglophobia is not rife in the USA today and nor was it in 1941.

The views of governments are quite different; they are corporate, entirely political and owe little to personal relationships. It could be argued that although Roosevelt was a devious hypocrite, his only interest was the well-being of his country – and that is, after all, the function of a president. It was unfortunate that at a critical time a number of senior Anglophobes congregated at the head of American public life.

On a wider scale, there are absolutely no friends in international relations. There are allies, but any relationship between them is invariably dependent upon treaty obligations and a shared enemy. Lord Palmerston judged that 'we have no eternal allies, and we have no perpetual enemies. Our interests are eternal and perpetual, and those interests it is our duty to follow.'[8]

Henry Kissinger expressed the same sentiment from an American standpoint when he said, accurately, 'America has no permanent friends or enemies, only interests.'[9]

For the British, the exception is perhaps the Commonwealth. This is an association of countries that share a history and the same democratic values. The mythical 'Special Relationship' between the USA and Great Britain has been *usually* based on shared aims. However, when the aims are not in accord, then each looks to its own best interests. The refusal by the USA to aid the British in Tientsin (see page 8) is just one example. Similarly, Britain declined the invitation to join in the Vietnam War in 1964. In the twenty-first century it is emotional nonsense to advertise a completely unbalanced relationship as being the least 'special' in any way.

Perceived altruism in diplomatic issues always has a political aim, perhaps in the very long term. A wise man once said, 'There is no free lunch,' and that truism applied in international relations in 1939 just as it still does in 2022.

From February 1938, the Japanese embarked on a bombing campaign and focussed their attention on Chongqing, which it assailed with incendiary bombs, little realising how vulnerable Japanese cities were to a similar assault. The Japanese bombing would destroy civilian morale. However, just as London, Coventry, Bristol, Hamburg and Dresden would show, bombing had the effect of strengthening the resolve of the bombed and fed their anger. The killing of 11,889 civilians in Chongqing achieved nothing and was militarily counterproductive.

Ground operations against the Chinese continued with the attendant barbarism that was now de rigueur for Japanese troops. However, no one could doubt the courage of individual Japanese soldiers. They fought with total commitment to their nation's cause and a comment on their performance at Nomonhan is:

> Outnumbered, outgunned, and outmanoeuvred, the Japanese officers and men of the 2nd Battalion, 28th Infantry Regiment, 7th Infantry Division, held their positions until they received orders to withdraw. Tradition, unit esprit, training, and doctrine all contributed to this exceptional display of courage in the face of awesome enemy superiority.[10]

The behaviour of Japanese, before and after an action, was strongly disapproved of by Germany, which, since 1933, had supported Nationalist China. Colonel General Hans von Seeckt, former Commander-in-Chief of the German Army, became a consultant to Chiang Kai-shek and it was von Seeckt who polished Chiang's tactics and was indirectly responsible for forcing Mao Tse-tung into his 'Long March'.

German officers were incorporated into Chiang's army. German assistance took many forms: it provided engineering expertise in the development of the railway system and German banks granted loans and fostered commercial links. However, German interest in China waned in 1937, although Adolf Hitler tacitly endorsed German support of China until September 1940, when the Tripartite Treaty with Italy and Japan was signed.

Until the signing of that treaty, Nazi Germany had provided 80 per cent of the Nationalist weapons, but based on 'no free lunch', it imported tungsten in return.

> Tungsten was a critical war material as it was a component in heavy metal alloys, machine tools, light bulbs, vacuum tube filaments. Germany had

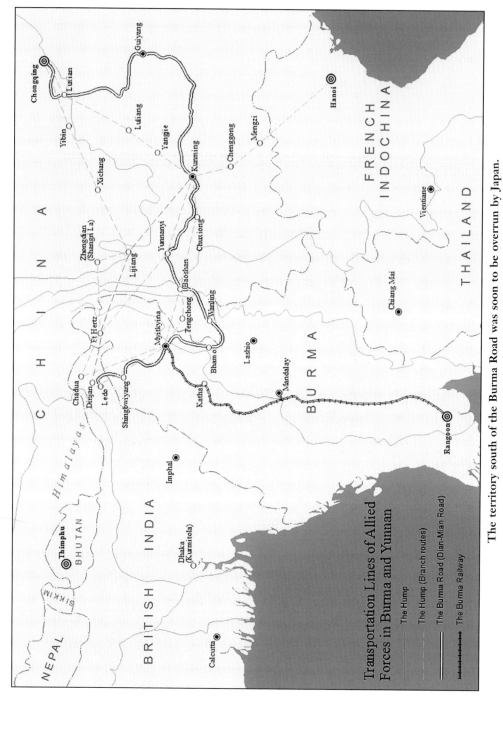

Transportation Lines of Allied Forces in Burma and Yunnan

_____ The Hump

_____ The Hump (Branch routes)

━━━━━━━ The Burma Road (Dian-Mian Road)

┼┼┼┼┼┼┼ The Burma Railway

The territory south of the Burma Road was soon to be overrun by Japan.

bought half of the world supply of tungsten and the weapons it produced were used against Allied soldiers.[11]

After the Tripartite Treaty there was an:

alliance between culture and power, art and politics in Germany and Japan as both countries moved toward nationalism and imperialism in the 1930s. German and Japanese fascism hijacked symbols, myths, rituals and ceremonies and resettled them in the new communication of militarist ideology ... to wage a total war.[12]

In the convoluted political atmosphere of the late 1930s, German-Japanese-Chinese-Russian relations was a melting pot of intrigue and mistrust. Russia had become China's new best friend in January 1938 and from that date had

Sign in Beijing, May 1940.

provided loans of $173 million. In addition, and in between 1937 and 1941, Russia sent 1,235 aeroplanes, 16,000 artillery pieces, 14,000 machine guns, 50,000 rifles, 300 advisors, 2,000 pilots and 3,000 engineers.[13] By the spring of 1940, Japan had occupied Beijing and was adopting an increasingly belligerent tone in its dealing with the British, and that is evidenced by the photo. Britain, meanwhile, provided training facilities in India for Chinese soldiers and airfields for the USA, which was flying in logistic support, and it was maintaining the strategically important Burma Road.[14]

Given the active support being provided by the UK and USA to China – its enemy – it is little wonder that the Japanese were hostile and had for some time been formulating plans to make war on both the Western nations. It might be reasonable to ask at this juncture why would a nation deeply embroiled in a war with the most populous country on earth decide, concurrently and in addition, to fight the greatest empire in the world and also the wealthiest and most militarily powerful?

The answer is multi-faceted.

First and foremost, the Japanese really believed that they were a superior race and that it was their destiny to rule the world. Second, the grip on public affairs by the armed forces gave control of the Government. Third, the central location of Japan was strategically important and allowed it to make effective use of its army and navy. Fourth, the Japanese state was economically depressed, living standards were low and the only way to redress the situation was to obtain cheap (or free) raw materials and wider markets without the competition of the UK and USA. Finally, Japan had to respond to the high tariffs being imposed on Japanese goods by the USA and other key markets.

This amalgam of reasons, the first of which does not bear objective scrutiny, are scant justification for initiating a conflict that would cause a death toll in the millions. The Government of Japan was unstable and in the eighteen months from January 1939, there were three prime ministers and the fourth, Prince Konoye Fumimaro, was only in office from July 1940 until October 1941.

It was not until General Tōjō Hideki took control in October 1941 that Japan was given the strong, resolute leadership that it required. It was Tōjō who initiated armed hostilities against the Dutch, French, Siamese, British and Americans. Ultimately, he was to be hanged for his trouble, in 1948.

Notes

1. Otterstedt, Lieut. Col. C., *The Kwantung Army and the Nomonhan Incident: Its Impact on National Security* (Pennsylvania, US Army War College, 2000).
2. Ibid.
3. *NYT*, 20 July 1939, p. 18.
4. Beevor, A., *The Second World War.* (London, Weidenfeld & Nicolson 2012), p. 18.

5. Glantz, D., *The Soviet Strategic Offensive in Manchuria, 1945: 'August Storm'* (Abingdon, Routledge, 2004), p. 8.

6. Coox, A.D., *Nomonhan: Japan against Russia 1939*, 2 Vols. (Stanford University Press, 1985).

7. Mead, R., *Go, and Gold: Britain, America, and the Making of the Modern World* (University of Michigan, A.A. Knopf, 2007).

8. Lord Palmerston, British statesman; Prime Minister 1855–8, 1859–65. Speaking in the House of Commons on 1 March 1848.

9. Kissinger, H., *The White House Years* (Simon & Schuster, 2011).

10. Richardson, Lieut. Gen. W.R. USA. In a foreword to Drea's paper (1981), 'Nomonhan: Japanese – Soviet Tactical Combat 1939'.

11. Paine, S.C.M., *The Wars for Asia 1911–1949* (New York, Cambridge University Press, 2012), p. 143.

12. Jorgenson, N.-J., *Culture and Power in Germany and Japan* (Global Oriental, 2006).

13. Paine, p. 44.

14. Perry, J.K., 'Powerless and Frustrated: Britain's relationship with China during the Opening years of the Second Sino-Japanese War, 1937–39 (*Diplomacy and Statecraft*, 2011), pp. 408–30.

Chapter Six

1938–41
The Path to World War

The military defeat by the Russians in 1939 did nothing to quell the Japanese ambition for further expansion, but that ambition was shrouded in naïvety because it ignored the economic, political and logistic facts of life. The Foreign Minister, Matsuoka Yōsuke, presumed to announce that:

> In the battle between democracy and totalitarianism the latter adversary will, without question, win and control the world. The era of democracy is finished and the democratic system bankrupt. There is not room in the world for two different systems or two different economies.[1]

This splendid and absurd self-assurance took no account of Japan's trade imbalance in strategic material. From 1931, Japan's most important trading partner was the USA, which took 40 per cent of its exports and accounted for 34.4 per cent of its imports. The USA provisioned 49.1 per cent of Japan's iron, 53.6 per cent of its machine tools and a highly critical 75.2 per cent of its oil.[2] The availability from US sources of manganese and molybdenum was no less important. Japan was obliged to import aluminium and nickel from elsewhere. By any economic yardstick, Japan, already deeply engaged in a war with China, was in no position to contemplate further military adventures. However, Japan noted the aggressive posture being adopted by Germany in Europe, which gave every indication that Germany shared Japan's intentions to expand.

The hope was that, if Germany could be enlisted as an ally, it would deter any future Russian assaults. Accordingly, there was deep dismay in Tokyo when, to the surprise of all and deep concern of most, Germany and Russia agreed a non-aggression pact on 23 August 1939. Japan had clearly been bypassed and was excluded from any top-level negotiations. On the plus side, Japanese/Russian relations still remained hostile but were non-violent. From a Russian standpoint it was advantageous for the Japanese to be engaged with the forces of Chiang Kai-shek because the two enemies of Russia would weaken each other, and the winner would be easy meat at some time in the future.[3]

Surgeon General Ishii Shirō (1892–1959).

Japan continued to pursue its operations against the Chinese with unrelenting barbarity and then hit a new low when it started to use germ warfare and poison gas weapons during 1938. One of the attractions of these weapons was that they were less expensive than bullets and bombs.[4] The infamous Unit 731 was established in Manchukuo and commanded by Surgeon General Ishii Shirō. His organisation employed a group of people about 300 strong, of whom some were medical doctors. They were responsible for many of the most egregious crimes in history. Ishii's grotesque experiments made those of Dr Josef Mengele at Auschwitz almost pale into insignificance. One product of Ishii's work was the wholesale production of biological and chemical weapons used extensively against the Chinese but *not* against the Western powers:

> Based upon interrogations and an examination of recorded incidents of chemical weapons use, it may be concluded that Japanese CW policy permitted the use of chemical weapons in China where the enemy did not possess the capacity to retaliate in kind, but largely prohibited their use in the Pacific against the Allies, whom they feared could respond with overwhelming force. Thus, the threat of retaliation in kind served as a successful deterrent to CW employment in the Pacific Theatre.[5]

Japan's use of poison gas was discontinued when the inefficiency of the weapon became clear – it was as lethal to the initiator as it was to the target. Nevertheless, the damage had been done and further alienated Western public opinion. Japan was, by 1939, an international pariah.

Japan's relations with the USA were strained and the machinations of diplomats on both sides for the two years 1939–41 were complex and fraught with misunderstandings. The sinking of USS *Panay* still rankled, despite the apology, and Roosevelt sent an emissary to London to explore the possibility of a joint US/UK naval blockade of Japan. Initially, HMG was positive but, on 13 January 1938, British Prime Minister Neville Chamberlain unexpectedly rejected a suggestion that he attend a conference to discuss the principles of international law in order to thwart what Roosevelt called 'bandit nations'. 'This sent a signal that his government would take no part in a quarantine of an aggressor in the Orient or in Europe.'[6]

Chamberlain and his policy of appeasement was soon to be totally discredited and particularly so when the Tripartite Pact between Germany, Italy and Japan was signed on 27 September 1940. Chamberlain had left office in May 1940 and been replaced by Churchill. This three-sided alliance was ominous, and the threat to Britain's colonial possessions in the Far East was now evident.

A key player in the diplomatic manoeuvring was the US Ambassador to Japan, Joseph Grew, who had been in post since 1932, and in one despatch to the State Department he opined that:

> We should not lose sight of the fact, deplorable but true, that no practical and effective code of international morality upon which the world can rely has yet been discovered ... To shape our foreign policy on the unsound theory that other nations are guided and bound by our present standards of international ethics would be to court sure disaster.

Grew was quite correct; events would show that the conduct of the Japanese baffled and angered all those who encountered them.

Wars are always the result of a *casus belli*. This may be real (Pearl Harbor), manufactured (Mukden), or merely the result of a fertile imagination (Marco Polo Bridge). On 9 April 1939, in an obscure and now long-forgotten British-administered Tientsin (now Tianjin) Foreign Concession Area, there was a murder that very nearly became a *casus belli*.

The Federal Reserve Bank of North China in Tientsin was Japanese owned and managed by one Cheng Hsi-Keng. When attending a local theatre, he was killed by a bomb laid and detonated by a group of Chinese Nationalists allied to Chiang Kai-shek. Bombs are imprecise weapons and the explosion of this one, in a crowded place, killed several entirely unconnected people.

The Japanese authorities accused six Chinese men, residents in Tientsin, of the mass murder, probably correctly.[7] The British police moved swiftly and arrested four of the six men named. Based on a promise that the men would not be tortured, they were handed over to the Japanese. With the benefit of hindsight, that was a tactical error. The judicial responsibility was confused in that the British were operating a commercial entity on Chinese territory occupied by the Japanese. Realistically, it was the Japanese who had the military clout.

Under torture, two of the four men 'confessed' and all four were returned to British custody, and from here the situation rapidly escalated. Madame

Soong Mei-ling, the wife of Chiang Kai-shek, met the British Consul in Chongqing and told him that the assassins were indeed part of Chiang's organisation, and she requested his support in keeping the four men out of Japanese hands. The Consul, Sir Archibald Clark Kerr, did not cover himself in glory when, notwithstanding the pleas of Madame Soong, he agreed to return the four men … but neglected to tell London. There, the Foreign

Barrier erected by Japanese troops around the British and French concessions of Tientsin in the summer of 1939.

Secretary, Lord Halifax, advised that the confessions had been extracted by torture and ordered that the killers be retained in British hands, and Clark Kerr had to backtrack.

General Yamashita Tomoyuki, Chief of Staff of the Japanese North China Army, was hostile to Britain and was only too happy to be given a cause to end not only the British concession in Tientsin, but those enjoyed by other Western nations elsewhere. Using the refusal of the British to hand over the men, he initiated a blockade that it was hoped would end Britain's economic support of China.[8]

Judicial authority lay at the heart of this matter and that was complicated by Britain's refusal to acknowledge the Wang regime in Nanking. The situation worsened and there was serious concern that war would be the result – something the British were only too anxious to avoid, despite the insults and humiliation inflicted on their 1,500 citizens, half of whom were soldiers.

The Japanese press mounted an anti-British campaign and the all-so-brief government of Baron Kiichirō Hiranuma gave willing support. The American diplomatic code had been broken and so the Japanese were fully aware of contacts between the USA and Great Britain. They knew that Britain had asked for American support and that support, in any form, had been refused.[9] The refusal was based on the advice of the American Ambassador to China, who believed that any sanctions imposed by the USA on Japan might well cause a war. This intercepted message served to reinforce the Japanese Government's aggressive stance against the British in Tientsin and, in addition, it also gave an impression of American weakness and confirmed that the Americans feared a war with Japan and would pay almost any price to avoid it.[10]

Intense diplomatic negotiations were held in Tokyo between Sir Robert Craigie, the British Ambassador, and the Japanese Foreign Minister, Arita Hachirō. The two men agreed, based on a settlement in which Britain recognised that Japan was at war with China and that the situation called for a robust Japanese response. Britain agreed not to oppose Japanese activity. On 20 August 1939, while Britain was fully focused on the worsening situation in Europe, the four Chinese murderers were handed over to the Japanese – a diplomatic victory for the Japanese. Predictably, the four men were promptly and publicly beheaded. This was in violation of the diplomatic agreement and in Britain this dishonourable action caused outrage, quickly overshadowed by the outbreak of the Second World War.

The inexorable move to war accelerated when the USA started to develop a Two-Ocean Navy by enacting legislation on 19 July 1940. This made provision for 70 per cent expansion of the United States Navy (USN) budget. The result would be naval assets with four times the tonnage and four times the air power of Japan. The strategic implication was that, although Japanese naval power would peak in late 1941 with approximate parity with the USA, thereafter it would decline.[11]

In June of that year, the Japanese Army General Staff held a meeting at which it agreed that an attack should be made on Singapore without delay. This resolution was not acted upon, but it was indicative of the prevailing atmosphere in military circles.

Soon after that meeting, the Prime Minister, Admiral Yonai Mitsumasa, resigned after only 189 days in office. Prince Konoye Fumimaro was persuaded to re-enter politics as Prime Minster in July 1940. On so doing he made two important appointments, and of these the first was Matsuoka Yōsuke, who took up the role of Foreign Minister. He was a mercurial man, highly intelligent, educated in the USA, fluent in English, loquacious to a fault, and very capable. The second was a soldier, General Tōjō Hideki. He was an appointed War Minister. He was an incorruptible, hard-working, stern disciplinarian.[12] They made a strong team, but it was a team without a coherent, coordinated foreign and defence policy.

General Tōjō Hideki (1884–1948), Minister of War (1940–4) and Prime Minister (1941–4). Executed for war crimes.

Matsuoka was the driving force; his quick mind jumped from topic to topic, and he floated bold ideas to provoke a response. He gave assurances that, with his education, he was pro-American but then contradicted himself by criticising the USA in the most robust terms. The new cabinet, of which Matsuoka was now a leading member, met just four days after its formation to establish a policy to deal with what was described as 'a great ordeal without precedence'.

The object of the exercise was 'to bring about World Peace and to establish a new order in Greater East Asia'. That sounds simple, but of course, it was anything but. The aim was to be achieved by uniting Manchukuo, Japan and China into a single nation but, predictably, governed from Tokyo. The entire Japanese nation was to be mobilised in support of the policy and a planned economy developed to pay for it. The Diet (Japanese Government) established in 1889 was to be reformed.[13] This way forward, although it made no mention of military operations, was nothing if not ambitious – grandiosely so. With the wisdom that comes with 20/20 hindsight it can be seen to have been political pie in the sky.

There were some propositions arising that were achievable in the short term and the Tripartite Treaty with Germany and Italy was one, quickly concluded on 27 September 1940. On that same day, bristling with aggression, Japan invaded French Indochina, and specifically, Vietnam. The French were a defeated nation and although there was token resistance, the Japanese were able to blockade the Chinese/Vietnamese border and stop any logistic supplies reaching China by way of the Vietnamese port of Haiphong. The Japanese permitted the French colonial system to remain nominally in control. However, this armed incursion into French territory was an act of war and it sent strong warning signals to both the USA and the UK – they had a tiger at the gate.

Matsuoka visited Germany in March and April 1941 and received strong hints that German operations against Russia were imminent. Nevertheless, and despite the hints, he made it clear that he was working towards a non-aggression pact with Russia. He achieved that aim soon after leaving Germany on 13 April. The Germans were, understandably, vastly discommoded. The Pact had the effect of freeing up Russian troops to fight the Germans, Japan's allies, only two months later when Hitler initiated Operation BARABAROSSA and invaded Russia. The law of unintended consequences had shown its face – it would emerge again. This also showed that the Germans and Japanese did not, at this stage, coordinate their strategies.

From a German standpoint, the treaty with their Japanese ally looked to be very shaky as it had failed its first test. It is suggested that 'perhaps Matsuoka believed that he was paying Germany back for its neutrality pact with Russia concluded during the battle of Nomonhan, when Japan would have greatly appreciated Germany's opening a second front on Russia.'[14]

On 15 June 1941, German forces swept across Russia in Operation BARBAROSSA and the world changed for ever. Perhaps international politics should be above petty point-scoring, although history shows that it is not. If this was such a case, then Matsuoka thought that he had killed two birds with one stone: retribution on the one hand and the cutting of Russian aid to Chiang on the other. He believed that the latter was a sound strategy in a regional war – he had no reason to suppose that the world was now engaged in global warfare.

German/Japanese relations, already fraught, were strained further when Japan's other treaty partner, Russia, allied itself with the USA and Great

Britain. The contradictions of the Tripartite Treaty and the Non-aggression Pact were manifest. In July 1942, in an act of quite unacceptable duplicity, Matsuoka proposed breaking the pact with Russia. The Government, of which he was part, fell in October 1941 and Matsuoka joined the unemployed.

A characteristic of the Second World War was the rise in signals intelligence (SIGINT), something in which the British excelled and which led to the ULTRA intercepts. The official historian of British Intelligence in the Second World War, Sir Harry Hinsley, argued that ULTRA shortened the war, 'by not less than two years and probably by four years', and that, in the absence of ULTRA, it is uncertain how the war would have ended.[15]

> Even before First World War I, the United States had been regularly deciphering coded messages sent by foreign diplomats. On the basis of decoded diplomatic messages, for example, the United States and Great Britain knew what arms limitations the Japanese would accept in the peace talks following that war, and negotiators bargained accordingly. The effort to break Japanese diplomatic codes continued into the 1920s and 1930s under the direction of William Friedman, a Russian immigrant who was appointed chief cryptanalyst of the (US) Army Signal Intelligence Service (SIS) in 1922. In the late 1930s, SIS cryptanalysts succeeded in breaking the purple code, also designated AN-1, which was the principal cipher Japan used to send diplomatic messages.[16]

In September 1940, the complete Japanese diplomatic code was deciphered in an operation designated MAGIC. The naval codes were more difficult to access but there was sufficient progress to allow the USN, later in the war, to achieve two significant successes.

The Japanese resisted German urging to join them in operations against Russia, although it did increase the size of its forces in Manchukuo without breaching its agreement with Russia. One of the great 'what ifs' of history is, 'What if Japan had attacked Russia during BARBAROSSA – would the Germans have won at Stalingrad and taken Moscow?' Had the Japanese attacked Russia it would certainly have had a seriously deleterious effect on Russia's capacity to defend itself on two fronts.

Earlier, on 11 March 1941, Roosevelt had initiated his Lend-Lease Act and smoothed the passage of war material to Britain, and later to China and Russia. In 1941, Chiang's Nationalist forces received $26 million worth of aid, and that rose to $100 million in 1942. The aid budgeted to China had reached $1.1 billion by 1945. It follows that the Japanese made every effort to restrict the flow of logistic aid to its enemy, hence the pressure on Great Britain to close the Burma Road again.

The MAGIC intercepts were of the greatest value as Japanese diplomats debated the merits of various courses of action open to them and the USA had no doubts as to the likely outcome. Having already invaded French Indochina in July in order to seal the Chinese border with that country, the Japanese were spoiled for choice for their next target. Thailand was a possibility, Wake and Guam – both US islands in the Pacific, the Philippines, even Hawaii, Burma and Malaya could provide rich pickings.

While the Japanese considered their options, Roosevelt took strong measures. The first, to freeze all Japanese assets, and then, on 1 August 1941, very significantly he imposed an oil embargo on a country that had the capacity to produce about 2.7 million barrels domestically from wells at Akita, Niigata and Natsu. To put this into context, it amounted to only

Franklin D. Roosevelt (1882–1945). President of the United States of America, 1933–45. (*Leon Perskie, 1944. FDR Presidential Library and Museum*)

about 0.1 per cent of world production in 1941. The seizing of wells in Manchuria and Korea produced a further 1 million barrels whilst a similar amount could be obtained from Formosa. Total indigenous assets were then about 4.7 million barrels. The annual requirement was of the order of 36 million barrels. The very significant logistic gap was to prove critical.

In late 1941, Japan had about two years' worth of oil stockpiled for peacetime activity. Nevertheless, to maintain that stockpile, Japan was obliged to import 87 per cent of its oil to satisfy its domestic economy and to fuel its vast armed forces. Most of that 87 per cent came from the USA. The Japanese now had two options; one was to pursue peace, the other was to make up the oil deficiency by taking more oil by conquest.

The decision made by Roosevelt was promptly endorsed and supported by the British, Dutch, New Zealand and the Philippines governments. The response was immediate and, as predicted by the British, Japan prepared for war. The Imperial Japanese Army believed that the 'Greater East Asia Co-Prosperity Sphere' had to be expanded to include the oil fields of the Dutch East Indies. It was considered that the war in Europe had opened a window of opportunity and an advance to the south offered attractive chances. The Imperial Japanese Navy suggested that Hawaii should be added to the list of targets. The desire for war was far from unanimous within government circles and Prime Minister Prince Konoye Fumimaro was emphatically in favour of a diplomatic resolution.

There had to be concessions by both sides and unless found and implemented, war now seemed to be inevitable. The unknowns were, when and where?

Notes

1. Bix, H.P., *Hirohito and the Making of Modern Japan* (New York, Harper Collins, 2000), p. 374.
2. Burkman, T.W., *Japan and the League of Nations* (University of Hawaii, 2008), p. 107.
3. Paine, S.C.M., *The Wars for Asia 1911–1949* (New York, Cambridge University Press, 2012), p. 117.
4. Ishijima Noriyuki, *A History of China's Anti-Japanese War* (Tokyo, Aoki Shoten, 1984), p. 171.
5. Grunden, W.E., 'No Retaliation in Kind: Japanese Chemical Warfare Policy in World War II' (Conference paper, *One Hundred Years of Chemical Warfare: Deployment Consequences*, 2017), p. 259.
6. Toland, J., *The Rising Sun: The Decline and Fall of the Japanese Empire, 1936–45* [1970] (Modern Library, New York, 2003), p. 49.
7. Watt, D.C., *How War Came* (New York, Pantheon Books, 1989), p. 352.
8. Satō, Kyozo, 'Japan's position before the outbreak of the European War in September 1939' (*Modern Asian Studies*, Vol. 14), p. 139.
9. Drea, E., 'Reading Each Other's Mail: Japanese Communication Intelligence, 1920–41' (*The Journal of Military History*, Vol. 55, Vol. 2, April 1991), p. 200.
10. Ibid.
11. Baer, G.W., *One Hundred Years of Sea Power: The US Navy 1890–1990* (Stanford University Press, 1993), pp. 134–7.
12. Toland, p. 60.
13. Ibid, p. 62.
14. Harries, M. & Harries, S., *Soldiers of the Sun* (New York, Random House, 1991) p. 310.
15. Hinsley, F.H. & Stripp, A., eds, *Codebreakers: The Inside Story of Bletchley Park* (Oxford University Press, 1992).
16. O'Neal, M., 'Breaking of Japanese Naval Codes' (*Encyclopedia.com*).

Chapter Seven

August–December 1941
Manipulation and Misunderstanding

Churchill and Roosevelt met on HMS *Prince of Wales* at Placentia Bay, Newfoundland, on 10 August 1941. At the end of the meeting, Churchill is reported as saying to the US Acting Secretary of State, Sumner Welles, that he did not think 'there was much hope left, unless the United States makes such a clear-cut declaration of preventing Japan from expanding further to the south in which event the prevention of war between Great Britain and Japan seems to be hopeless'.[1]

In their further discussions Churchill made it clear that he favoured a strong line with Japan, and he believed that he had persuaded Roosevelt; perhaps that was unnecessary as both the USA and Great Britain were actively allied to China, with whom Japan had been locked in a brutal war for four years. Certainly, on his return to the USA, Roosevelt sent for the Japanese Ambassador and made his position clear. There were four principles upon which the USA would insist, and these were eventually contained in what became known as 'The Hull Note' as they were drafted by Cordell Hull.[2]

(1) The principle of inviolability of territorial integrity and sovereignty of each and all nations.

(2) The principle of non-interference in the internal affairs of other countries.

(3) The principle of equality, including equality of commercial opportunity and treatment.

(4) The principle of reliance upon international cooperation and conciliation for the prevention and pacific settlement of controversies and for improvement of international conditions by peaceful methods and processes.

These four points were at odds with Japan's core objective of expanding its empire further, and therein lay the very bones of the problem. To comply with Hull's four principles, Japan would have to withdraw from Indochina, the invasion of which, on 28 July, had triggered the trade embargo and cut off Japan's supply of oil. However, withdrawal would involve a massive loss of face by Japan and was entirely impractical in a very short time frame.

Joseph Grew (1880–1965),
US Ambassador to Japan, 1932–41.

Only high-level talks, and positive attitudes on both sides, could resolve the tension. Soon after, Ambassador Grew met Japanese Foreign Minister, Toyoda Teijirō, and the suggestion was made that Roosevelt could meet, face-to-face, Prime Minister Prince Konoye Fumimaro. The path to peace seemed to lie ahead. It was an illusion; the meeting did not take place.

In Tokyo, in some political circles there were those still striving to head off any movement to war. However, the government propaganda of recent years was now firmly rooted, and the general atmosphere was resolutely anti-British and anti-American. The Japanese Government decided that if a satisfactory agreement could not be reached by 10 October 1941, then plans to wage war concurrently against Great Britain, the USA and the Netherlands would be implemented.

As Japan contemplated war with the USA, it had developed the *Kantai Kessen* (Decisive Battle Doctrine). This determined the scale of the offensives required to seize from the Dutch East Indies and Malay the oil, rubber and tin that Japan lacked. An anticipated American naval response, in support of its allies, would then face crippling attacks from the Imperial Japanese Navy's submarine force. It was a simplistic plan that flew in the face of the facts. An American armed response, aiding colonial powers, was unlikely in the political atmosphere of the late 1930s.

Admiral Isoroku Yamamoto was the voice of caution, who had lived and studied in the USA. A war game, in 1939, had shown that the Japanese submarine force was not big enough to fill the role delegated to it. The exercise was mounted a second time and failed again. Nevertheless, and in the face of reason, the plan was not altered until Yamamoto assumed the appointment of Commander-in-Chief of the IJN in August 1939. In the event of war, Yamamoto favoured a massive pre-emptive strike on the American fleet but, in the short-term, geography was against him.

In the summer of 1940, Roosevelt ordered the redeployment of the US Pacific Fleet, 2,455 miles (3,950km) from San Diego to Hawaii. The move was designed to deter Japanese aggression. The decision was taken despite American war games, from as early as 1925, when General 'Billy' Mitchell drew attention to the vulnerability of a fleet at anchor in Pearl Harbor. In 1932, a larger war game firmly endorsed the earlier conclusion by Mitchell that Pearl was a good place for the US fleet not to be!

The IJN Naval Academy had been studying the possibility of an attack on Pearl Harbor for several years and in 1936 students were posed the exam question, 'How would you carry out a surprise attack on Pearl Harbor?' Despite the evidence, Roosevelt insisted on the redeployment and by doing so placed the fleet within range for Yamamoto's pre-emptive strike.

The diplomatic manoeuvring took up valuable time and on 6 September, there was a conference at which Hirohito was present and he heard the head of the Japanese Navy, Admiral Nagano, assert that if Japan's minimal demands were not met then the only solution was 'aggressive military operations despite America's unassailable position, her vaster industrial power, and her abundant resources'.[3]

To the amazement of all present, the Emperor spoke! For most, this was the first time they had heard his voice as he interjected a question and, from that, the meeting inferred that the Emperor favoured more efforts to avoid war. There is no doubt that Prime Minister Konoye was sincere in his efforts to avoid war, and he and Grew met and talked through the issues. Konoye was confident that he could broker a peace deal and he was clearly an honest and honourable man. He accepted personal responsibility for the 'China incident' and the Tripartite Treaty but, not surprisingly, said of Hull's principles, 'When it comes to applying them various problems will arise and to solve them, I must have a meeting with the President [Roosevelt].' This was a significant understatement, and he did not mention that he was working with a deadline less than five weeks hence. He claimed to have the support of Generals Tōjō and Sugiyama; Grew was impressed by Konoye's frank approach and signalled Washington accordingly.

A measure of the heat the diplomatic situation was causing is illustrated by an attempt to assassinate Konoye on 18 September, but fortunately his protective screen foiled the attempt. He lived to press for a peaceful resolution of the issues.

Over the next few weeks, the Japanese moved their position and made a series of concessions. They offered to leave Indochina and to vacate China *once a peace had been agreed*. They agreed in future not to make any military advances south of Japan.

The diplomatic machinery worked slowly and valuable time slipped by; the delays at the American end caused the Japanese to think (correctly, as it happens) that the USA was merely playing for time. Roosevelt had not responded to Konoye's request for a meeting and, as the deadline drew nearer, so Japan's offers became more urgent. It now proposed peace terms with China, a blending of the Nationalists with the puppet Chinese government of Wang Ching-wei, no annexations, no indemnities, economic co-operation, and the withdrawal of all Japanese troops from China except those needed to fight the Communists.[4]

Roosevelt did not respond to these placatory offers despite increasingly strong signals from Grew, whose views were shared by his British counterpart, Ambassador Sir Robert Leslie Craigie, GCMG, CB, PC. Hull finally responded on 2 October. Although he 'welcomed' the idea of a summit meeting and was 'gratified' by Konoye's acceptance of his four principles, the machinations of the Japanese Government from here led swiftly to the resignation of Konoye, who had done his best to promote peace. On 16 October, he recommended Prince Naruhiko Higashikuni to the Emperor as his successor, but Hirohito ignored the advice, explaining, in 1946, that:

> I thought Prince Higashikuni suitable as chief of staff of the Army; but I think the appointment of a member of the imperial house to a political office must be considered very carefully.[5]

General Tōjō, the second choice, became Prime Minister on 18 October 1941. On 2 November, Tōjō, accompanied by Field Marshal Sugiyama Hajime and Marshal Admiral Nagano Osami, reported to the Emperor. Tōjō explained that despite a complete review of the situation there was no other option open to Japan but war. Hirohito accepted the advice and gave his consent and thereafter the Emperor was a participant in Japan's war effort. This participation made him complicit in what was to be done in his service.

Three days later, Tōjō opined, 'America may be enraged for a while, but later she will come to understand [why we did what we did].'[6,7] Later he argued that risking a war with the USA was 'better than being ground down without doing anything'.

On 26 November, Hull threw fuel on the fire when he issued his final note to say that concessions offered by Japan were not in themselves sufficient and that *all Japanese troops in China had to be withdrawn without delay*. Only then could a meeting take place.

This American demand for Japanese troops to leave China at once was patently impossible. In that theatre of war more than 2 million combatants were locked in one of the most ferocious conflicts in human history: 600,000 Japanese had already died, and expecting Japan to disengage immediately was nothing short of arrogant absurdity.

However, Hull must be given the credit for knowing just how impractical his demand was. The reality was that he did not seek agreement, but quite the reverse. What Hull and Roosevelt sought was a *casus belli*. The aim of the latest demand was to provoke Japan into some form of aggression that would then justify a full-blown American assault … perhaps the arrest of a US flagged ship or a minor thrust at somewhere unimportant, like Wake Island. The Philippines was another likely target because it was conveniently close to Japan.

On 27 November, Henry Stimson, the American Secretary for War, became aware of a Japanese expeditionary force moving out of Shanghai and he contacted Roosevelt to suggest that perhaps some sort of warning order should be issued to Lieutenant General Douglas MacArthur, Commander of US Army Forces in the Far East (USAFFE). The signal was sent, and it is very revealing:

> Japanese future action unpredictable but hostile action possible at any moment. If hostilities cannot, repeat cannot, be avoided the *United States desires that Japan commit the first overt act* [author's emphasis]. This policy should not, repeat not, be construed as restricting you to a course of action that might jeopardize your defence.[8]

The nature and magnitude of any possible Japanese aggression was an unknown. The USA was reading Japan's diplomatic traffic; communications were inaccurate and misleading. They painted a dangerously slanted picture and by so doing accentuated American mistrust. An example of this is a signal by Tōjō that, in the original, read:

> now that we make the utmost concession in the spirit of complete friendliness for the sake of a peaceful solution. We hope earnestly that the United States will, on entering the final stage of negotiations reconsider the matter and approach the crisis in a proper spirit with a view to preserving Japanese-American relations.[9]

When this perfectly reasonable signal was translated, it reached Hull reading: 'This time we are showing the limit of our friendship: This time we are making our last possible bargain and I hope that we can settle all our troubles with the United States peaceably.'[10]

Diplomatic exchanges are carefully nuanced by the originators to ensure that they accurately reflect the situation. Their translation merits the most meticulous scholarship, but that was sadly lacking in the State Department in late 1941 (unknown to Hull). There were any number of mistranslations and the cumulative effect was to cost thousands of lives across Southeast Asia.

Later, and in clarification, it was suggested that when Hull responded and referred to 'China', he did not include Manchuria; unfortunately, he did not specifically say so … perhaps, but it was still impractical and unacceptable.

Cordell Hull (1871–1955), the instigator of the war between the USA and Japan and, later, the recipient of the Nobel Peace Prize in 1945. (*Nobel Prize archives*)

The USA was actively preparing for a war and Hull was indeed playing for time, but he overplayed his hand. In effect, America had been 'hoist' with 'their own petard' of legend and Hull's intransigence had short-circuited the path to war.[11]

War is nasty, brutal business; there are few discernible rules. It is not at all like cricket; a coin is not spun to see who is to bat first. A pre-emptive war is one launched in anticipation of immediate aggression by another party, and in this case, the attack on Pearl Harbor has entered the history books as 'The Day of Infamy'.[12] The reality is that it was a very powerful but not unreasonable response by Japan to the impossible, non-negotiable demands made upon it by the USA. Since then, the USA has, on occasions, employed pre-emptive strikes itself, not least in 2003 in the war with Iraq.

The attack on Pearl Harbor had several wide-reaching effects. Domestically it destroyed the 'isolationist' faction that still supported the views, expressed by Abraham Lincoln, who had asked rhetorically:

> Shall we expect some transatlantic military giant to step the ocean and crush us at a blow? Never! All the armies of Europe, Asia and Africa combined with all the treasure of the earth, with a Bonaparte for a commander, could not by force take a drink from the Ohio or make a track on the Blue Ridge in a trial of a thousand years.[13]

The answer to that was that the world had moved on and the USA could not now, or ever again, expect to isolate itself against hostile forces. This position was underscored on 11 December when Germany and Italy declared war on the USA – an act triggered by their Tripartite Treaty with Japan. This declaration removed from the US Government the need to make any decision about a two-front war – one had just been imposed.

Internationally, the USA was perceived to be the victim of a brutal, unprovoked and cowardly attack. The myth spun around The Day of Infamy is an example of effective propaganda such that it is still given credence eighty years later. The USA loaded the gun, and Japan squeezed the trigger, just as the USA hoped it would. The diplomatic machinations of Roosevelt and Hull cost 2,403 American lives only ten days later – a prime example of the 'Law of unintended consequences'.

Notes

1. Toland, J., *The Rising Sun: The Decline and Fall of the Japanese Empire, 1936–45* [1970] (Modern Library, New York, 2003), p. 91.
2. Cordell Hull (1871–1955), the longest-serving US Secretary of State, 1933–44.
3. Toland, p. 98.
4. Ibid., p. 104.
5. Wetzler, P., *Hirohito and War* (University of Hawaii Press, 1998), p. 41.
6. Coox, A.D., Pacific War (*The Cambridge History of Japan*, Vol. 6, 1988), p. 329.
7. Ike, N., trans & ed., *Japan's Decision for War* (Stanford University Press, 1967) p. 239.
8. Toland, p. 174.
9. US Government archive. Quoted by Toland, p. 134.
10. Ibid.
11. 'Hoist with his own petard' is a phrase from a speech in Shakespeare's *Hamlet*. The phrase's meaning is literally that a bomb-maker is blown up: 'hoist' off the ground by his own bomb. (A 'petard' is a small explosive device.)
12. Beres, I.R., 'On Assassination as Anticipatory Self-Defense: The case of Israel' (*Hofstra Law Review*, 1991), p. 321.
13. Lincoln, A., in a speech to the 'Young Men's Lyceum of Springfield Illinois' on 27 January 1838.

Chapter Eight

December 1941–February 1942 Pearl Harbor, Thailand, Guam, Malaya and Singapore

In December 1941, the United States Government, suffering from a degree of paranoia, had a fear of the 'Yellow Peril' but nevertheless viewed Japan's military with contempt. Was it this sense of superiority that tempted some Americans, including Hull and Roosevelt, to drive the Japanese to the limit of their patience and by so doing give cause for war?

A war that need not have been fought was about to be fought because of mutual misunderstanding, language difficulties and mistranslation as well as Japanese opportunism, *gekokujō* (the low overcomes the high), irrationality, honour, pride and fear, American racial prejudice, distrust, ignorance of the Orient, rigidity, self-righteousness, national pride and fear.[1]

The Americans were planning to attack Japan and might well have launched a pre-emptive operation, but their timing was poor and their defence against an attack negligible. Admiral Harold Stark, the Chief of Naval Operations in Washington, was later judged to be culpable for failing to interpret the intelligence he had to hand. A coded Japanese message was read on 6 December, and it made clear that an attack was imminent. Stark's warning to his fleet in Hawaii was sufficiently ambiguous that it drew no response from Admiral Husband Kimmel, the recipient. This officer decided against launching air reconnaissance. Later, both officers were summarily retired. For the operation at Pearl Harbor, Yamamoto allocated six carriers, two battleships, three cruisers and eleven destroyers to Vice Admiral Nagumo Chūichi.

During the Second World War, the Japanese committed countless corporate and individual war crimes and all of these are very well, albeit harrowingly, documented. The attack on Pearl Harbor (in the opinion of this author) was not one of these crimes although others may disagree.[2] The attack was unannounced and in an unexpected quarter – the very essence of a pre-emptive strike.

The Japanese plan was to hit, almost simultaneously, at multiple targets to achieve surprise and the benefits that provided. The attack on Pearl Harbor is

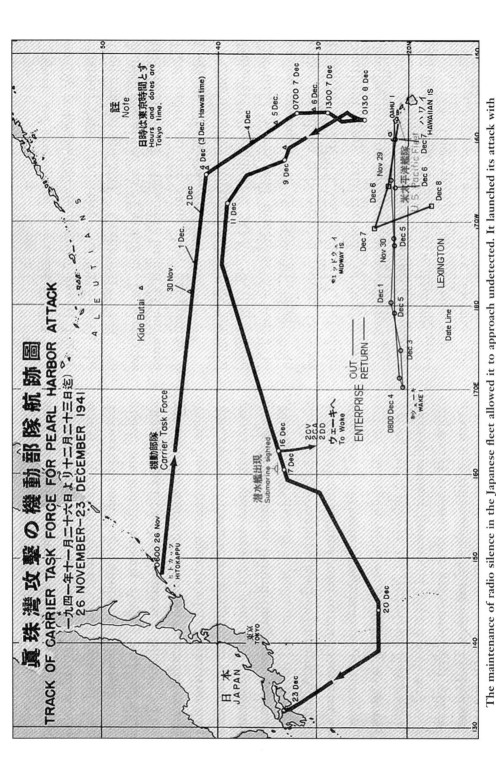

The maintenance of radio silence in the Japanese fleet allowed it to approach undetected. It launched its attack with 353 aircraft from the carriers *Akagi*, *Kaga*, *Sōryū*, *Hiryū*, *Shōkaku* and *Zuikaku*. Sixty-seven aircraft were in reserve. (*NHHC*)

the element of the plan most publicised but it was in fact just one of many significant targets.

West of the International Date Line the Japanese population slept blissfully during the night of 7/8 December, unaware that 169 of their ships, 2,000 aircraft, and hundreds of thousands of their compatriots were about to set the Pacific ablaze at the approaching dawn. The sequence of their attacks was carefully timed to explode across 6,000 miles (9,700km) of ocean like a firecracker and as the sun rose westward from Hawaii to Wake, Guam, Hong Kong, the Philippines, Thailand, Malaya and Singapore. The plan was masterly and the execution superb. The shattering attacks that began at midnight on 7 December, in Hawaiian waters, presaged six months of defeat and humiliation for the Anglo-Saxon powers as Japan came within an ace of establishing her dominance over the Pacific.[3]

Air Chief Marshal Sir Robert Brooke-Popham, the Commander-in-Chief, broadcast to the people of Malaya and Singapore. It was a message long on rhetoric but short on reality. There could be no doubting Japanese intentions or its capability, notwithstanding the 3,303 miles (5,316km) distance between Singapore and Tokyo.

It will aid the reader to see, in tabular form, the sequence of events of 7 December across Southeast Asia.

6 December

2359 hrs (Hawaiian time): Five Japanese midget submarines launched off Waikiki.

7 December

0200 hrs (0730 hrs Washington time): US Naval intelligence decipher a Japanese signal saying, 'The Japanese Government regrets it is impossible to reach an agreement through further negotiations.' *This message to be delivered to US Government at 1300 hrs Washington time.* (Author's emphasis)

0300 hrs: Japanese Strike Force 230 miles (370km) north of Oahu.

0350 hrs: Periscope sighted by USS *Condor* patrolling beyond the harbour booms.

0430 hrs: Midget submarine enters Pearl Harbor, circles Ford Island, reports position of US ships.

0530 hrs: Washington sends warning signals to Panama, San Francisco, the Philippines and Hawaii.

0530 hrs: Strike Force Less than 200 miles (322km) from Oahu. Aircraft launched for reconnaissance.

0545 hrs Kota Bharu, Malaya (1145 hrs Singapore time): Bombardment of shore defences, 5,000 Japanese invade.

0600 hrs Singapore (1200 hrs Singapore time): General Percival alerted to invasion at Kota Bharu.

0630 hrs: USS *Ward* attacks submarine off Pearl Harbor.

0702 hrs: Incoming aircraft seen on Kahuku Point radar; warning passed; no action taken.

0730 hrs Kra Peninsula, Thailand: Fourteen transports anchor off Singora beach. Thai units overrun.

(1300 hrs Washington time) Japanese telephone to delay meeting with Cordell Hull, *originally arranged for 1300 hrs, until 1330 hrs.* (Author's emphasis)

0756 hrs Hawaii: First wave of eighteen dive-bombers strikes Hickam Field, Pearl Harbor.

0810 hrs (1340 hrs Washington time): Signal from Admiral Kimmel received, telling of attack.

It was at this point that the Japanese diplomats arrived to meet Cordell Hull and to *deliver the message intercepted earlier*. The diplomats were at a loss to understand Hull's icy anger. Hull made a pretence of examining the document and then erupted, saying, 'In all my fifty years of public service I have never seen such a document that was more crowded with infamous falsehoods and distortions.'[4] The Japanese diplomats did not know, at this stage, that hostilities had commenced. Had they kept to the original timing for the meeting, the 'note' would have been presented on time and the diplomatic niceties observed.

0840 hrs: Second-wave attack made by eighty-six dive-bombers, fifty-four 'level' bombers and thirty-six Japanese fighters. Eleven attackers shot down.

0930 hrs (1500 hrs Washington time): Roosevelt and Churchill speak on the telephone.

1000 hrs Shanghai, China (1600 hrs China time): Japanese seize USS *Wake*, a gunboat. HMS *Petrel* resisted but silenced by land-based artillery.

1000 hrs Manila, Philippines (0400 hrs Philippine time): General Gerow, Chief of US Army War Plans Division, signalled MacArthur to confirm the news of the Pearl Harbor attack and said that he 'wouldn't be surprised if you get an attack there in the near future'.[5]

1000 hrs Formosa, Taiwan (0400 hrs Formosa time): Fog grounds 300 aircraft from IJN 11th Air Fleet and IJA 5th Air Group. Together they were tasked to destroy all Luzon airfields and wipe out MacArthur's air power. Admiral Takahashi, the commander, anticipated an American air strike as he felt sure that news of hostilities would have reached the Philippines. The attack was never made.

1130 hrs Tokyo (0700 hrs Tokyo time): Japanese citizens told of their country's declaration of war.

1000 hrs Singapore (0400 hrs Singapore time): Japanese bombers from Saipan, about 100 miles (160km) away, attack the city. The city was fully illuminated because the street lights could not be turned off. Sixty-three people were killed, a further 133 were injured.

1300 hrs Wake Island (1200 hrs Wake time): Thirty-six bombers attack and destroy seven aircraft on the ground. Eighteen killed. This was the prelude to an invasion.

1500 hrs Manila, Philippines (0900 hrs Philippine time): Japanese bomb both cities of Baguio and Tuguegarao. MacArthur does not retaliate.

1730 hrs Luzon, Philippines (1200 hrs Philippine time): Devastating aerial attack on Clark Field. US Air Force in the Far East eliminated.

2200 hrs Kota Bharu, Malaya (1600 hrs Malaya time): Japanese well established, all RAF and RAAF aircraft evacuated south to Kuantan.

2335 hrs Singapore (1735 hrs Singapore time): HMS *Repulse* and *Prince of Wales* leave Singapore. In the words of Captain Tennant of the *Repulse*, 'We are off to look for trouble.' Little did he know how much trouble he and his men would soon be in.

8 December

0031 hrs Midway Island, 1,073 miles (1,727km) from Pearl Harbor (1031 hrs Midway time): Japanese destroyers *Ushio* and *Sazanami* make a token raid, shelling the island and killing one Marine officer.

The Americans were at first complacent and then outraged when Japan beat them to the punch. Their premier naval base outside the continental United States was completely unprepared when the carrier-based planes under the command of Vice Admiral Nagumo Chūichi delivered a devastating, and moderately successful, attack on the US fleet at anchor in Pearl Harbor.

Nagumo was not the most inventive or charismatic of Japan's naval leaders and his appointment to command of this operation was by dint of his seniority – a criterion in the Imperial Japanese Navy that could not be breached. He was warned six hours before the attack that the prime targets, the three aircraft carriers USS *Enterprise*, *Lexington* and *Saratoga*, had all, fortuitously, recently left Pearl Harbor. Nagumo had the option of calling off the operation, but he decided to go ahead.

The attack was a short-term tactical success but a strategic failure that would unify the American public in a quest for retribution and ultimately lead to the destruction of all Japanese aspirations.

The initial aerial assault achieved the destruction of six ships and damage to another fifteen, 188 US aircraft were destroyed and a further 159 damaged. However, vital facilities such as the power station, dry docks and submarine piers were damaged but not destroyed. The Japanese failed to hit the fuel installations and the 650 million litres of stored fuel. The destruction of the fuel dump would have been far more significant than the loss of four battleships. Nagumo had the option of making a second strike. He had the means, and the men busting to go again, but he erred on the side of caution and withdrew his fleet. Nagumo left in his wake 2,403 dead Americans and 1,178 wounded.[6] On 7 December 1941, the Japanese ushered in a new era of warfare. From this point on, the capital ships in every navy were their aircraft carriers. The days of the big gun battleships were almost over.

The operation had been meticulously planned and executed at a cost of twenty-nine of the 353 aircraft employed and five midget submarines. Sixty-four Japanese were killed, and one made captive.

USS *West Virginia* sinking after being struck by six torpedoes and two bombs; 106 members of her crew were killed.

American pride and self-assurance were also both very badly damaged. It now faced a Japanese Navy commanded by Admiral Yamamoto, who had under his command 10 battleships, 6 aircraft carriers, 4 auxiliary carriers, 18 heavy cruisers, 20 light cruisers, 112 destroyers, 65 submarines and 2,274 aircraft. This was a serious navy and only the British and Americans could begin to match it.

This photograph [below], by a Japanese pilot, was taken shortly after the beginning of the Pearl Harbor attack. The view is to the east, with the supply depot, submarine base and fuel tank farm in the right centre distance.

A torpedo has just hit USS *West Virginia* on the far side of Ford Island (centre). Other battleships moored nearby are (from left): *Nevada*, *Arizona*, *Tennessee* (inboard of *West Virginia*), *Oklahoma* (torpedoed and listing) alongside *Maryland* and *California*. On the near side of Ford Island, to the left, are light cruisers *Detroit* and *Raleigh*, target and training ship *Utah* and seaplane tender *Tangier*. *Raleigh* and *Utah* have been torpedoed, and *Utah* is listing sharply to port. US Navy planes on the seaplane ramp are on fire. Japanese writing in the lower right states that the photograph was reproduced by authorisation of the Navy Ministry.[7]

In England, Churchill was entertaining the US Ambassador John Winant and the Lend-Lease co-ordinator Averell Harriman, as house guests, at Chequers. It was about an hour and a half after the first bombs fell that the BBC announced news of the attack. Very soon thereafter, Churchill and Roosevelt spoke on the telephone. Churchill, in response to Roosevelt's remark 'We are all in the same boat', expressed the view that, 'This actually simplifies things. God be with you.'

It is alleged that, after the attack, Yamamoto remarked, 'I fear all we have done is to awaken a sleeping giant and fill him with a terrible resolve.' How prescient that was.

* * *

Inevitably, after the attack on Pearl Harbor there was a backlash in the USA against those of Japanese ethnicity. Unfortunately, much of the anger was directed at perfectly loyal Americans who were perceived as tainted by their Japanese heritage. Roosevelt's response was delayed until 19 February 1942, but then it was all-encompassing. Of the approximately 127,000 people of Japanese ancestry in the USA, the majority, 112,000, were resident on the West Coast.[8] About 80,000 of these were second- and third-generation American citizens. In total, 120,000 were interned.

Concentration camps were established and to qualify for internment an individual had only to have 1/16th of Japanese lineage.[9] Colonel Karl Bendetsen, responsible for the execution of the policy, went so far as to affirm that 'one drop of blood' was reason to doubt the loyalty of a Japanese American.[10] The policy was a blunt instrument; divisive, unfair and cruel.

On the day that Roosevelt's edict was promulgated, fear of the Japanese was fuelled by the shelling of Ellwood, California, by the Japanese submarine *I-17*. The boat fired seventeen shells at the Richfield oil storage facility. The shooting was poor and did no material damage, but it initiated a panicked response from the local population. Thousands fled inland and fear of a Japanese invasion was widespread. *I-17* withdrew and, for the expenditure of only seventeen rounds, it had won a propaganda victory and given rise to significant social unrest amongst its enemy.

This fear was further evidenced the following night when the anti-aircraft guns defending Los Angeles were fallaciously warned of the presence of enemy aircraft. There were none within thousands of miles. Notwithstanding, during 'a thirty-minute fusillade, 1,440 rounds of 3″ ammunition was loosed into the night sky in what was later termed the Battle of Los Angeles. About 10 tons of shrapnel and unexploded ammunition fell back on the city.'[11]

* * *

The die was firmly cast and, on 8 December, Japan formally declared war on 'America and England', but not the Netherlands – a curious omission. In its comprehensive plan for domination of Southeast Asia, Japan saw Thailand as a stepping stone to Malaya, Burma and India. The Japanese High Command believed that India, the jewel in the British crown, could be 'liberated' to the unalloyed joy and gratitude of its vast population.

Thailand had a small but effective army, about 50,000 strong, which it had used when it invaded French Indochina, in late 1940, to regain territory lost in the Franco-Siamese War of 1893. Japan had designs on Indochina, and it had ulterior motives when it acted as the mediator and brokered a settlement between the two warring countries in January 1941.

Japan needed the airfields, railways and ports of Thailand to further its wider aims but, from choice, did not want to fight for them. Germany supported the overall Japanese aim of expansion as it would divert British forces to the Far East and weaken resistance in the Western theatre.[12]

There were discussions between the Japanese and the Thai Prime Minister, Phibun Songkhram, the object being the granting of passage for Japanese forces through Thailand. A fly in this diplomatic ointment was the British-Thai Non-aggression Pact, signed in June 1940.

The Thais and Japanese could not reach an agreement, and so Japan invaded and brushed the Thai defences aside. Phibun Songkhram promptly signed up to an armistice. On 14 December 1941, he went further and agreed to provide troops for land operations in Malaya. Very soon after, freedom to use Thai airfields and air space was granted and, only one week later, Thailand formally became a Japanese ally and declared war on Britain and the USA in December 1941.

*   *   *

It is germane to consider the position of each of the main participants in world affairs in December 1941. Japan, allied with Germany, Italy and Thailand, was at war with the USA, Great Britain and its empire, the Netherlands and China. It had a powerful navy, a very large and seasoned army, but did not have the industrial capacity to replace, in a timely manner, any ships lost in action.

The Japanese presumption was that, following its pre-emptive strike, the invasion of Thailand, Malaya, the Philippines and Guam all on 8 December, followed by an invasion of the Dutch East Indies, Borneo, Burma and Hong Kong (18 December) and Wake Island (25 December), it would be offered a negotiated peace. It assumed that, for the peace discussions, it would have a strong negotiating position. In fact, it had hopelessly misread the situation. In the USA and Britain, Japan had two adversaries who would wage total

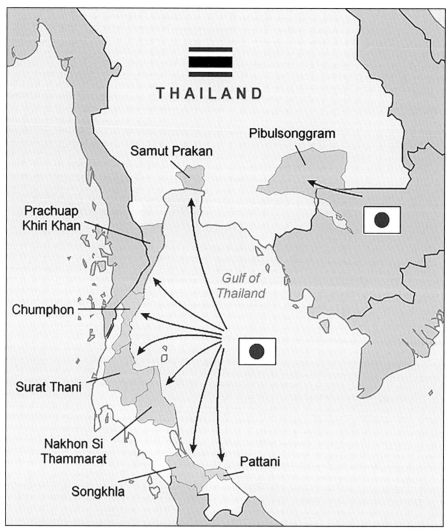

The Japanese invasion of Thailand. The cost to the Japanese was between 115 and
217 dead and 300+ wounded. The Thais lost 37 dead and 27 wounded.

war, seek unconditional surrender, and would cease hostilities only when
Tokyo fell.

The more successful the expansion of the Japanese Empire, the greater
would be the logistic burden of supplying these distant acquisitions. It would
be obliged to depend on surface transport to resupply many of its conquests.
The ability of the IJN and its merchant fleet to control all sea routes would
soon be put to the test.

Germany held most of Europe in its grip. It, too, was now at war with Great Britain and its empire, the USA, Russia and China.[13] It had enjoyed unparalleled military success in Europe over the eighteen months from September 1939. Then, in a moment of outright lunacy, Germany had declared war on the USA, 'a diplomatic blunder of suicidal proportions'.[14] Hitler's decision was akin to that of Napoleon III, who, in 1870, had capriciously declared war on the vastly superior Prussia. In both cases, hubris led to total defeat.

At a stroke, Germany had added the logistic might of the USA and its vast manpower to the balance. There was no evident 'upside' to this decision and Germany did not enjoy a productive and well-co-ordinated relationship with Japan. Unknowingly, the Tripartite Treaty triggered an action that would prove to be instrumental in the future demise of all three signatories.

A wise man once said of the Allies that the 'USA provided the materiel, Russia the manpower and Britain the minds'. The USA, with its unmatched wealth and industrial clout, was the 'quartermaster' of the Allied cause. In every battle and in every war, the side with the strongest logistic support chain wins. Field Marshal Erwin Rommel remarked later in the war, 'Before the fighting proper, the battle is fought and decided by the quartermasters.' He was correct and was to be defeated in North Africa by Montgomery's superior supply system.

There can be no doubting that American industrial strength and its capacity to supply both Britain and Russia were the keys to Allied success in the Second World War. What was certainly true, as history would reveal, both Germany and Japan had bitten off rather more than they could chew. Churchill and Roosevelt had agreed that the priority was Europe first. This would provide support for Russia as soon as a second front could be opened. However, in the meantime, Japanese expansion across Southeast Asia continued apace.

On 7 December, Japanese forces landed in Thailand, and barely thirty minutes later, on a beach in Malaya. An hour after that, Pearl Harbor was bombed. Concurrently, Guam was invaded, and the bombing of Wake Island commenced. It did not end there because, later that day, the US Clark Air Base in the Philippines was bombed, as was Hong Kong. The International Settlements in Shanghai were overrun. All these actions epitomised the value of surprise and the application of balanced force. In scope, depth, and with total success, arguably the Japanese military activity on 6–8 December was unique in the history of warfare.

Lieutenant Commander Eiichiro Jo, a naval ADC to Hirohito, recorded in his diary: 'Throughout the day the emperor wore his naval uniform and seemed to be in a splendid mood.'[15] Little wonder, because the process that had just started would stun the world at its success.

In the first five months of 1942, Japan took more territory over a greater area than any country in history and did not lose a single major ship. The statistics are overwhelming. Japan took 250,000 Allied prisoners, sank 105 Allied ships and seriously damaged a further 91, while it lost only 7,000 dead, 14,000 wounded, 562 planes and 27 ships, but no cruisers, battleships or carriers.[16]

The coordination of these widely dispersed operations was an excellent demonstration of high-grade and skilful staff work. The logistic plan to support the differing and widely dispersed operations invites admiration.

The tailor-made forces and the allocation of assets to deal with each objective nonplussed Japan's opponents who, in every case, were caught flat-footed. Resistance was in most cases determined, stoic and courageous, but unavailing. This text will consider the assaults across Southeast Asia in their approximate chronological sequence.

*   *   *

Despite the anti-colonial posture of Roosevelt in 1941, the USA was in fact a minor colonial power. It had, by various means, established its sovereignty by the turn of the century on several territories (see table opposite). However, the Japanese aspired to occupy territories that were within striking distance of Japan.

Guam is the southernmost island of the Mariana group. The US Government decided in early 1941 that it was impractical to defend Guam and accordingly graded it 'F'. This designation meant that on the outbreak of war the garrison was expected to destroy all facilities and then withdraw. The island was a civilian, logistic asset as a refuelling and cable station but, from a military standpoint, indefensible.

The invasion of Guam on 8 December 1941 was a brief affair, and the residual occupants who were unable to withdraw were quickly overwhelmed as the Japanese, under Major General Horii Tomitarō, committed four heavy cruisers, four destroyers and a host of minor vessels carrying 5,900 troops to the invasion. The US forces amounted to only 547 lightly armed marines and sailors. Their resistance cost seventeen American and Guamanian soldiers killed. The Japanese lost just one soldier killed. The Japanese were to occupy Guam for the next two and a half years, with the attendant torture and murder.

*   *   *

Malaya was one of the most important of Japan's early invasion targets and the British had no illusions as to Japanese intentions. To defend the colony

US overseas territories listed by the 1940 census. Territories with no indigenous populations, such as Wake Island, are listed as unpopulated, although the US often stationed military outposts on them. The many islands claimed by the US but not listed in the census (all uninhabited) are not included.

Territory	Years held	1940 population
Philippines*	1899–1946	16,356,000
Puerto Rico	1899–present	1,869,255
Hawaii	1898–1959 (state after)	423,330
Alaska	1867–1959 (state after)	72,524
Panama Canal Zone	1903–1977	51,827
US Virgin Islands	1917–present	24,889
Guam*	1899–present	22,290
American Samoa	1899–present	12,908
Midway and Brooks	1859–present	–
Howland and Baker	1857–present	–
Wake Island*	1899–present	–
Corn Islands	1914–1971	–
Johnston Atoll	1858–present	–
Jarvis Island	1858–present	–
Total		18,883,023

* Territories within striking distance of Japan.
Source: Immerwahr, D., 'The Greater United States: Territory and Empire in US History' (*Diplomatic History*, Vol. 40, Issue 3, 2016), pp. 373–91.

the prime formation was III Indian Corps, composed of two infantry divisions – the 9th and 11th – supplemented by elements of the 8th Australian Division. In all, Lieutenant General Arthur Percival, CB, DSO*, OBE, MC, the General Officer Commanding, Malaya, had under his command 88,600 troops. Percival's forces were deployed to defend against beach landings on the east coast of the long peninsula of Malaya, which was furnished with copious accessible sandy beaches. The population was a mixture of Malay, ethnic Chinese and Indian. Singapore's population mix was much the same.

The Japanese forces were components of the 70,000-strong 25th Army, led by Lieutenant General Yamashita Tomoyuki, a capable and ruthless soldier soon to be christened 'The Tiger of Malaya'. Yamashita was spoilt for choice but, predictably, he chose to land his 18 Division at Kota Bharu, an assault supported by 5 Division invading from the Thailand border. The landings were made from three troopships, the *Awazisan Maru*, *Ayatosan Maru* and *Sakura Maru*; these were protected by a small fleet of warships commanded by Rear Admiral Hashimoto Shintarō. They were the light cruiser *Sendai* and the four destroyers *Uranami*, *Isonami*, *Ayanami* and *Shikinami*. Other smaller support vessels completed his force.

The British had contingency plans in place to forestall any invasion but, when the invasion force was spotted at sea, Air Marshal Sir Robert Brooke-Popham, the General Officer Commanding-in-Chief (GOC-in-C) of the British Forces in the Far East, vacillated and, not wanting to provide Japan with a *casus belli*, he did not commit his air force. Thus, in the early stages the landings were unopposed and made in strong winds and rough sea conditions.

The first wave of Japanese came under effective fire as they reached the beach and ran into the defences of 3/17th Battalion, the Dogra Regiment, who were manning trenches and pillboxes along a 10-mile (16km) stretch of the beach. The Dogras' defence was aided by the guns of 73 Field Battery RA; in combination, they drew from a Colonel Tsuji Masanobu the comment, 'The enemy pillboxes were well prepared, reacted violently with such heavy force that our men lying on the beach, half in and half out of the water, could not raise their heads.'[17] This officer was one of the most culpable war criminals of the Second World War and, had he succumbed on the beach at Kota Bharu, thousands of lives

Colonel Tsuji Masanobu.

would have been saved. He survived and fled to Thailand at the end of the war and, by so doing, avoided the rope he so richly deserved.

While the Indian Army was engaged with the Japanese, thousands of miles away, in London, the Prime Minister was addressing the House of Commons. He said:

When we think of the insane ambition and insatiable appetite which have caused this vast and melancholy extension of the war, we can only feel that Hitler's madness has infected the Japanese mind, and that the root of the evil and its branch must be extirpated together.

It is of the highest importance that there should be no under-rating of the gravity of the new dangers we have to meet, either here or in the United States. The enemy has attacked with an audacity which may spring from recklessness, but which may also spring from a conviction of strength.[18]

There was more stirring stuff to follow that but, in Kota Bharu, the situation was fraught. The RAAF had ten Lockheed Hudson aircraft based at RAAF Kota Bharu and with these they attacked the troopships. All three vessels were hit and *Awazisan Maru* was sunk. However, two Hudsons were shot down and three damaged. One of the Hudsons, piloted by Flight Lieutenant John Leighton-Jones, presumably deliberately, crashed into a fully laden landing craft and killed all sixty of the occupants.[19] Nevertheless, the Japanese were able to reinforce their beachhead; soon they had numerical superiority. They took not only the town, but the airfield, held tenaciously by 2/12 Frontier Force under the command of Lieutenant Colonel Arthur Cummings.[20] It became evident that there was a need to regroup and so the British force withdrew to the south having killed about 300 and wounded 500 of the enemy.

In 1941, most of Malaya was covered in rainforest, much of it allegedly impenetrable. North/south movement was by means of the two coast roads and they provided the route to Johore Bharu and Singapore. Lateral movement was restricted to only a very few single-track roads. The Indian Army attempted to block the coastal roads and blew bridges as they retreated south.

The Japanese were undaunted by roadblocks and persistently and successfully took to the jungle to outflank the block. Then they attacked it from the rear. This was a tactic difficult to counter and which required the jungle skills that the Indian Army did not have at the time.

This was skilful soldiering and went some way to building the myth that the Japanese were a special form of 'jungle soldier'. The Japanese were mildly innovative in their use of the bicycle. They were not the first: from before the First World War, the British, Americans, Germans and Italians had all seen the benefit of bikes. During the Vietnam Wars of 1945–75, the North Vietnam Army (NVA), and its guerrilla arms the Vietminh and Viet Cong, all used bicycles to great effect, particularly so in the logistic chain operating along the Ho Chi Minh Trail.

The map on page 82 charts the inexorable progress of the invaders down Malaya, and in London and Singapore there was the very greatest concern about the land war. It was acknowledged that the Royal Navy presence in the Far East and centred on Singapore was insufficient to counter the powerful Japanese Navy. In December 1941, the Royal Navy's Far East Fleet had no integrated air cover.

Admiral Tom Phillips arrived in Singapore on 4 December, having come from a conference with General Douglas MacArthur and Admiral Thomas Hart USN in the Philippines. In his new role of Commander-in-Chief Far East Fleet he commanded Force Z, composed of the battle cruiser *Repulse* and the battleship *Prince of Wales*. These powerful units had an inadequate screen in

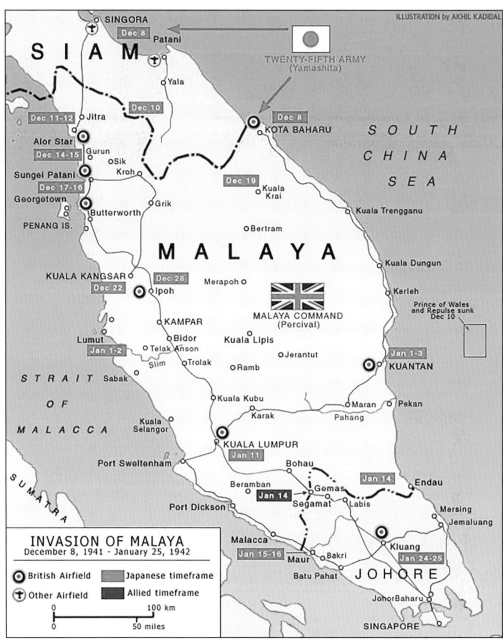

ILLUSTRATION by AKHIL KADIDAL

SINGORA
Dec 8 Patani

S I A M

Yala

TWENTY-FIFTH ARMY
(Yamashita)

Dec 10

Dec 11-12 Jitra

Alor Star
Dec 14-15 Gurun
oSik
Kroh
Sungei Patani
Dec 17-16
Georgetown
Butterworth
Grik

Dec 8
KOTA BAHARU

Dec 19 Kuala
Krai

S O U T H

C H I N A

S E A

Kuala Trengganu

PENANG IS.

Bertram

M A L A Y A

Kuala Dungun

KUALA KANGSAR
Dec 22 Dec 28 Ipoh
Merapoh

Kerleh

MALAYA COMMAND
(Percival)

Prince of Wales
and Repulse sunk
Dec 10

KAMPAR
Bidor
Lumut Telak Anson
Jan 1-2
Slim Trolak

Kuala Lipis

Jerantut

Ramb

Jan 1-3
KUANTAN

S T R A I T   Sabak

O F

M A L A C C A   Kuala
Selangor

Kuala Kubu
Karak

Maran Pekan
Pahang

KUALA LUMPUR
Jan 11

S U M A T R A

Port Sweltenham

Bohau

Beramban
Jan 14
Port Dickson

Jan 14
Gemas
Segamat Labis

Jan 14 Endau

Mersing
Jemaluang

INVASION OF MALAYA
December 8, 1941 - January 25, 1942

⊙ British Airfield   ▮ Japanese timeframe
✝ Other Airfield   ▮ Allied timeframe

0 ———————————— 100 km
0 ———————————— 50 miles

Malacca
Jan 15-16
Maur Bakri
Batu Pahat

Kluang
Jan 24-25

J O H O R E

Johor Baharu

SINGAPORE

Malaya in 1941 was heavily forested and north to south routes followed the coast.
Note the location of the sinking of HMS *Repulse* and *Prince of Wales* (centre right).
On the east coast the only towns of any size were Kota Bharu and Kuantan.
There was a crude road from Pekan to Mersing on the east but not shown on
the map. Johore Bharu was a small town until the 1960s. (*Vijaya Kumar Ganapathy*)

Japanese Bicycle Infantry. The bicycle allowed the rider to carry a heavier burden than on foot and it was a quick, inexpensive means of travel. (*cilos.my*)

the shape of the three ageing destroyers HMS *Tenedos*, *Express* and HMAS *Vampire*. Phillips recognised the vulnerability of his flotilla, which would operate without air cover. HMS *Indomitable*, the carrier designated to join Phillips, had run aground in the Caribbean and was not now available. Nevertheless, he determined to sail north and confront the Japanese fleet supporting the invasion of Malaya.

Admiral Sir Tom Phillips, KCB (1888–1941).

Phillips, like many of his generation, underestimated the capability of the Japanese. On the basis that no capital ship in action had ever been defeated from the air, he ignored the very germane attack on Pearl Harbor, took no heed of the intelligence flooding in from that attack and sailed from Singapore on 9 December without an awareness of the lethality of the specially trained torpedo bomber crews he was to confront.

The following day, 70 miles (113km) off Kuantan on the east coast of Malaya, Force Z was assailed by ninety-six naval torpedo bombers. *Repulse* was the first target and, well handled by her captain, William Tennant, she dodged a salvo of

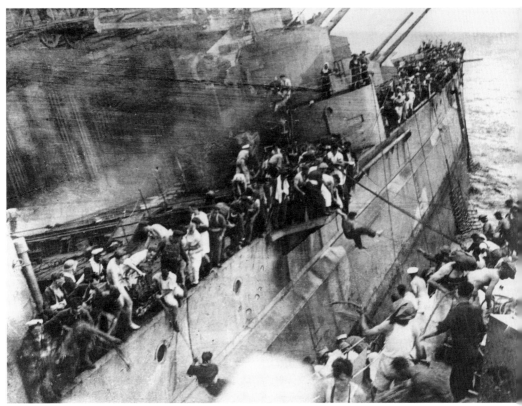

The Battleship *Prince of Wales* listing to port and being abandoned by her crew. HMS *Express* is alongside. At the top of the photograph can be seen guns which could not be sufficiently depressed to engage the sea-skimming torpedo bombers.
(Cartwright, IWM)

nine torpedoes. However, *Prince of Wales* was not so fortunate, and she was hit, immediately listing 13° to port. The ship was clearly 'not under control' and she signalled to that effect. Both her port shafts had been damaged and she would not answer to the helm. *Repulse* moved towards her consort to give assistance just as another wave of nine hostile aircraft was spotted. They all focused on the battlecruiser; she was hit by two torpedoes and her fate was sealed. Captain Tennant ordered 'abandon ship' and prepared himself to go down with her but he was manhandled by his staff to a place of safety.

The aerial attacks had been highly effective, and the effect was catastrophic. Both ships sank, and 840 men were lost. Four bombers were shot down and twenty-eight were damaged. Eighteen Japanese airmen were killed. For Great Britain, the loss of these two ships was a disaster and caused General Sir Alan Brooke, Churchill's right-hand man, to observe:

> We were hanging by our eyelids! Australia and India were threatened by the Japanese, we had temporarily lost control of the Indian Ocean, the Germans were threatening Iran and our oil, Auchinleck was in

precarious straits in the desert [North Africa], and the submarine sinkings [of convoys from the USA] were heavy.[21]

Brooke was soon to face even greater disappointment as the Japanese progressed steadily and had taken Alor Star, the largest city in Northwest Malaya.

Lieutenant General Arthur Percival,
CB, DSO*, OBE, MC **(1887–1966).**

General Percival was headquartered in Singapore, hundreds of miles to the south, and considering his reducing options. The general did not lack personal courage, as his decorations testify. In addition, he had some priceless experience and was reasonably to be considered the best man for the job. From March 1936 until 1938, as a colonel he had been filling a senior staff appointment in Singapore. The GOC, Lieutenant General Sir William Dobbie, GCMG, KCB, DSO, had tasked Percival to carry out a study on a likely attack on Singapore from the north and determine how it should be confronted. Percival concluded, with great prescience, that a Japanese invasion of Malaya would be launched through Thailand. He was then a supportive party to Dobbie's plan to build fixed defences in Southern Johore. The aim was to deny access to the causeway across the Johore Strait, Singapore city and the vital naval base. Unfortunately, Dobbie's plan was not put into place.

No defensive arrangements were made to deter the Japanese, who were hellbent on reaching Southern Johore.

In six weeks, and despite spirited resistance, Yamashita's force advanced about 500 miles (800km) down the length of Malaya. There was particularly savage fighting around Maur, which cost about 3,000 Allied casualties. A mixed force of Australians and Indians commanded by Lieutenant Colonel Charles Anderson resisted for several days but, when further resistance was impossible, Anderson told his surviving men to disperse into the jungle.

* * *

General Wavell, recently appointed as the supreme commander of unified American-British-Dutch-Australian forces (ABDA) in the Far East, visited Singapore. This was part of his command and at the behest of Churchill, who wanted to know the detailed plan for the defence of the Fortress. Wavell then reported to Churchill on his findings. He wrote:

> I discussed the defence of the island when recently at Singapore, and have asked for detailed plans. Until quite recently all plans were based on repulsing seaborne attacks on [the] island and holding land attack in Johore or farther north, and little or nothing was done to construct defences on north side of [the] island to prevent crossing the Johore Straits, though arrangements have been made to blow up the causeway. The fortress cannon of heaviest nature have all-round traverse, but their flat trajectory makes them unsuitable for counter-battery work. Could certainly not guarantee to dominate enemy siege batteries with them.[22]

All of this came as an unwelcome shock to Churchill, who confided in his dairy his amazement that there were no permanent fortifications covering the landward side of the naval base and of the city and that no measures worth speaking of had been taken by any of the commanders since the war began. He was aghast that since the Japanese had established themselves in Indochina no one had though to construct any form of field defences. The ABDA organisation was no panacea and ABDACOM had a very complicated command, involving four army, four navy and six air organisations. Admiral Hart, the commander of the US Asiatic Fleet, commented:

> there was, too, the difference in language, always a handicap, even in such small ways as the inability of our officers to read Dutch charts and sailing instructions, which were superior to ours for Netherlands East Indies waters. Finally, beyond the major common interest, there were differences in national attitudes which made it difficult to frame our ultimate strategy. For instance, when the time came it was the natural and courageous determination of the Dutch to make a desperate, last-ditch stand in Java. The British view was that it was more important to preserve our forces intact for a moment when they might be used to greater advantage. How could such views be reconciled?[23]

*　*　*

In Malaya, Colonel Anderson with his fit and walking wounded hastened into the cover of the jungle. The wounded were left, and 133 of the 135 were tortured and murdered in an event called the Parit Sulong Massacre. On 27 January, Percival withdrew all his forces from Malaya and concentrated them on the small island of Singapore. Given his previous experience, it is amazing that Percival did not select southern Johore as the site for his defence of the ill-named 'Fortress' of Singapore.

He had the men and the time available and had formulated the plan three years earlier. In late 1941, when his Chief Engineer, Brigadier Ivan Simpson, OBE, pressed him on the issue, he refused permission for the construction of fixed defences in Johore or on the north coast of Singapore on the basis that 'defences are bad for morale'.[24] If there was a compendium of asinine military pronouncements this would be included. If defences are bad for morale, it could be argued that, so too, is abject surrender. Percival was the victim of his own poor judgement. Thousands of his soldiers were victims of that too.

Percival's intelligence told him that he was facing 60,000 Japanese and although 15,000 of his own were either untrained or poorly armed, he still had a numerical superiority with a force of 85,000. The intelligence was seriously wrong because the Japanese fighting in Johore were only 30,000 strong.

Instead of fighting the enemy in Johore, and now with the acquiescence of General Wavell, his superior, Percival withdrew across the causeway and decided to defend the 70-mile (110km) coastline of the island. This was a difficult task consequent to an absurd decision, as was the destruction of the causeway, an act of strategic suicide. The decision when to blow a hole in the causeway can only have been made by Percival but, in principle, it had been authorised by Wavell. Given that at low tide the straits could be waded across, this was, on the face of it, not a particularly critical military decision. However, the island's water supply came from Malaya (and much of it still does today) and it entered Singapore by way of a pipeline that ran across the causeway. Singapore's days of freedom were now running short.

Yamashita arrived in Johore Bharu and set up his headquarters in the palace built for the Sultan of Johore, overlooking the straits. From here he marshalled his logistic train. Over the next few days, materiel, including hundreds of folding boats, flowed into the area. These boats were carried to their prospective launch sites and concealed from view. On 7 February, a diversionary invasion of the island was preceded by an artillery stonk and 400 men took possession of a small island overlooking Seletar in the north-east of the island. The next day, the British reinforced the Seletar area as Yamashita intended. That evening, at 2230 hrs, 4,000 men carried 300 folding boats to the water-line and assaulted the north-west corner of the island in the Kranji area. They were faced by 2,500 Australians. The sound of the boats' engines was drowned by artillery fire directed at the naval base and its oil tanks.

Only 48 hours before the invasion of Singapore Island by the Japanese, a composite battalion of Australian soldiers, was formed to strengthen the defence of the northwest corner of the island. Known as the Special Reserve Battalion (SRB), it comprised men from the Australian Army Service Corps (AASC), Ordnance units and a company from the 2/4th Machine Gun Battalion. The AASC (cooks, mechanics, drivers, clerks etc.) were relatively untrained. Such was the desperation of the time. The Japanese invasion on the night of the 8 February 1942, saw fierce fighting. With a combat strength of 15,000 men, the Japanese easily overwhelmed the Australian 22nd Brigade (only 3,000 men) and forced it and the SRB to retreat.[25]

The Australians of 8 Division bore the brunt of a two-division assault. The Australians gave a good account of themselves but were overcome. Thereafter the Japanese advanced quickly across the island against faltering opposition. In 1942, the middle of Singapore was rainforest. This did not deter Yamashita but, by the time he held about half of the island, he started to experience logistic difficulties. His long line of communication could not keep up with his demand for artillery ammunition. The significant differences in the two opposing forces had been evident from the first days of the invasion. Many of the Japanese soldiers were battle hardened from service in China; in comparison, the British Empire soldiers were inexperienced and poorly trained. Secondly, the Japanese came to the party with 200 tanks; the British had not one. Thirdly, the Japanese Navy held sway in the South China and Pacific seas. The Royal Navy presence was too small to have any impact on the Japanese invasion fleets and the logistic chain.

General Yamashita Tomoyuki, 'The Tiger of Malaya' (1885–1946). Executed for war crimes.

The man who held the future of the British Empire in his hands was not a man who inspired confidence. Percival was unprepossessing, lanky, with buck teeth and spoke with a lisp. His advance from colonel in 1938 to acting/

lieutenant general in 1941 was swift, but not unusual in wartime. However, his defence of Singapore was completely inept, and many held him culpable for the debacle that followed.

He was at odds with Lieutenant General Sir Lewis Macclesfield Heath, KBE, CB, CIE, DSO, MC, his commander of 111 Corps. There was a degree of angst between them because previously Macclesfield Heath had been the senior. Percival was dissatisfied with the performance of 111 Corps and considered sacking the commander but, weakly, allowed him to continue, unproductively, in post. Similarly, Percival did not get on with the Australian commander of 8 Australian Division, Major General Gordon Bennett, a particularly self-opinionated officer. 'Bennett's dealings with British senior officers, especially with the general officer commanding, Malaya, Lieutenant General A.E. Percival, were devoid of harmony.'[26] Commanders do not have to be friends, but it makes for greater efficiency if they are *d'accord*. There was little of that to be found in Singapore in February 1942.

Percival attributed his surrender to the 'imminent collapse of the water supply'. The Senior Water Engineer, David Murnane, had warned Percival of the problem and asked for the resources to alleviate it. He needed 100 Royal Engineers and ten trucks. They were not provided.[27]

Percival surrendered on 15 February 1942 in the greatest defeat ever suffered by Britain. It was a catastrophe of the most enormous magnitude, with huge political implications. With hindsight, the capitulation of Singapore signalled the beginning of the end of the British Empire. The humbling of Britain encouraged independence movements in Malaya, Burma and India. It was a watershed moment and unfortunate that a man of Percival's mediocrity had been in such an important post at such a critical time.

The capitulation of Singapore vastly overshadowed the retreat from Kabul in 1842 in which about 16,500 soldiers and camp followers were killed and the more recent surrender of Kut, in 1916, and the loss of 13,000 men. Some historians ascribe the fall of Singapore to inept political management over several years and not least to Churchill and his government, which had diverted 466 Matilda and Valentine tanks, intended for Malaya, to Russia.[28] The parlous state of the RN in eastern waters gave Japanese invasion fleets freedom of the seas. This writer would readily concede that poor political judgement was a major factor. Nevertheless, he would argue that Percival's failure to capitalise on his numerical superiority and to defend Singapore from hard defensive positions in Johore was the immediate cause of failure.

Yamashita heaped humiliation on Percival and his senior officers and would only grudgingly concede that 1,000 British soldiers should retain their arms to preserve law and order. Empire losses were 13,234 killed, 10,000 wounded, and 138,708 taken prisoner by a Japanese force of about 30,000.[29] Japanese losses were 3,507 killed and 6,150 wounded. The arithmetic says it all.

Percival endured four years of captivity but was not held to account in 1945. The only visible sign of disfavour was the lack of a knighthood, the usual sign of approbation for a British officer of his rank. Gordon Bennett was not among the captured; he had fled Singapore and made his way back to Australia.

Nearly ten years after the event, Churchill accepted responsibility for the humiliating defeat, and he said:

> I do not write this in any way to excuse myself. I ought to have known. My advisers ought to have known and I ought to have been told, and I ought to have asked. The reason I had not asked about this matter, amid the thousands of questions I put, was that the possibility of Singapore having no landward defences no more entered my mind than that of a battleship being launched without a bottom. I am aware of the various reasons that have been given for this failure: the preoccupation of the troops in training and in building defence works in Northern Malaya; the shortage of civilian labour; pre-war financial limitations and centralised War Office control; the fact that the Army's role was to protect the naval base, situated on the north shore of the island, and that it was therefore their duty to fight in front of that shore and not along it. I do not consider these reasons valid. Defences should have been built.[30]

Singapore may have fallen on 15 February 1941, but the horror was yet to come.

Notes

1. Toland, J., *The Rising Sun: The Decline and Fall of the Japanese Empire, 1936–45* [1970] (Modern Library, New York, 2003), p. 147.
2. Yuma, T., *The Tokyo War Crimes Trial* (Harvard University Asia Centre, 2009), p. 57. *See also* McCaffrey, S.C., *Understanding International Law* (Author House, 2004), pp. 210–29.
3. Costello, J., *The Pacific War 1941–45* [1981] (New York, Harper Collins, 2009), p. 128.
4. Ibid, p. 138.
5. Ibid, p. 141.
6. Parillo, M., 'The United States in the Pacific' (University Press of Kentucky, eds Higham, R. & Harris, S., *Why Air Forces Fail: The Anatomy of Defeat*, 2006), p. 288.
7. This image and text are from an internet source in the public domain.
8. Okihiro, G.Y., *The Columbia Guide to Asian American History* (Columbia University Press, 2005), p. 104.
9. Collins, C., *Representing Wars from 1860 to the Present* (Brill-Rodopi, collection 'Textxet: Studies in Comparative Literature', 2018), p. 105.
10. Weglyn, M.N., *Years of Infamy* (Seattle, University of Washington, 1996), pp. 76–7.
11. Young, D.J., 'Phantom Japanese raid on Los Angeles' (Wayback Machine, *World War II Magazine*, 2003).

12. Churchill, Sir W.S., 'The Japanese Envy' (*The Second World War: The Grand Alliance*, Vol. II, London, Cassell & Co, 1950), pp. 156–7.
13. Chiang Kai-shek declared war on Germany on 9 December 1941.
14. Paine, S.C.M., *The Wars for Asia 1911–1949* (New York, Cambridge University Press, 2012), p. 187.
15. Bix, H., *Hirohito and the Making of Modern Japan* (New York, Harper Collins, 2000), p. 247.
16. Paine, p. 188.
17. Tsuji, M. (ed., 1997), *Japan's Greatest Victory, Britain's Worst Defeat* (1997, ed. Howe, H.V., tr. Lake, M.E.), p. 75.
18. Churchill, W.S., *Hansard*, 8 December 1941.
19. Burton, J., [2006] *Fortnight of Infamy: The Collapse of Allied Airpower West of Pearl Harbor* (Annapolis, Maryland: Naval Institute Press, 2006), p. 96.
20. Cummings was awarded the Victoria Cross later in the campaign.
21. Olsen, L., *Citizens of London* (London, Random House, 2010).
22. Churchill, W.S., *The Hinge of Fate* (London, Cassell & Co. Ltd., 1951), p. 42.
23. *Java Sea Campaign* (Naval History and Heritage Command, Office of Naval Intelligence 1943).
24. Murfett, M.H., Miksic, J., Farrell, B. & Chiang Ming Shun, *Between 2 Oceans* (2nd ed.): *A Military History of Singapore from 1275 to 1971* (Marshall Cavendish International Asia Pte Ltd., 2011), pp. 190, 224, 340–4.
25. Saggers, Maj A.E., *To Hellfire, Purgatory and Back* (Perth WA, Optima Press, 2000).
26. Lodge, 'A.B., Bennett, Henry Gordon (1887–1962)', *Australian Dictionary of Biography*, Vol. 13 (Melbourne University Press, 1993), pp. 165–7.
27. Allen, L., *Singapore 1941–1942* (1977) (Frank Cass, Abingdon 2005), p. 11.
28. www.historynet.com
29. Corfield, J. & Corfield, R., *The Fall of Singapore* (Singapore, Talisman Books, 2012), p. 743.
30. Churchill, p. 92.

Chapter Nine

December 1941
The Philippines, Wake Island,
Hong Kong and Bataan

The Associated Press had a representative in Manila. He had been writing a series of articles deriding the quality of the Japanese Army, its equipment, and its training. It is unclear on what he based his misleading judgements. This man, Clark Lee, got it all wrong when he advised his readers that the Japanese Army (unknown to him, on its way to the Philippines) was composed of an 'ill-uniformed, untrained mass of young boys between fifteen and eighteen equipped with small calibre guns'.[1] It was perhaps what those readers wanted to hear. However, Lieutenant General Douglas MacArthur knew this to be rubbish. MacArthur was a very well-known and, ostensibly, popular army character. He had retired from the army in 1937 but was recalled by Roosevelt to take command in the American colony of the Philippines.

MacArthur had made a study of the Russo-Japanese War of 1904–5 and, as a young man, had noted the observations of officers like General John Pershing who expressed admiration for Japanese soldiers' 'intelligence, patriotism, abstemiousness, obedience to and respect for legally constituted authority to go forward achieving victory'. There was more in a similar vein, and in December 1941, MacArthur knew what he was up against – an army already four years into a major war with China that had produced a host of battle-hardened and ruthless veterans.

The Americans had always perceived the Philippines to be at risk from Japanese aggression, probably

**General Douglas MacArthur
(1880–1964).**

to be launched from Formosa (Taiwan), about 750 miles (1,200km) away. What is more, they had made detailed plans to counter any invasion. Throughout the 1930s, the plan had been studied at West Point by the army's prospective second lieutenants, and by the Japanese exchange officers who studied there as well. MacArthur had protested the West Point's policy since 1935.[2]

Douglas MacArthur, in his role of Commander United States Army Forces in the Far East had been alerted, on 27 November, of a likely Japanese attack, and warned not to strike the first blow: this, of course, handed the initiative to the aggressor, who could and would attack at will.

The impact and importance of the Pearl Harbor attack was made clear to the American commander when he was briefed on the events at around 0330 hrs on 8 December. (The Philippines are eighteen hours ahead of Hawaii.) However, and not in accordance with his orders, at 0500 hrs MacArthur, through his chief of staff, forbade his air commander, Major General Lewis Brereton, to fly any missions against Formosa. This was about

The effect of the Japanese attack on the Philippines, 8 December 1941. (*Correll*)

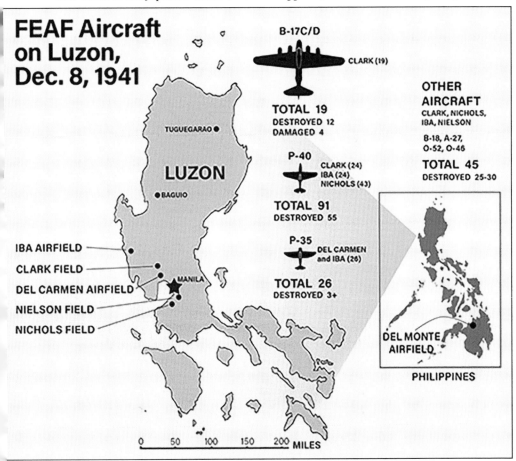

five and a half hours since the attack on Pearl Harbor. A little later, there was a half-hearted Japanese air raid north of Manila when bombs were dropped but to no great effect. MacArthur's thought process is difficult to fathom. He now had ample reason to take an offensive posture – but he did not.

Brereton could see the danger on hand and, at 0715 hrs, approached the Chief of Staff, Brigadier General R.K. Sutherland, and asked again for permission to retaliate. He got the same dusty answer. Less than an hour after that, MacArthur changed his mind and Brereton managed to get some of his assets airborne.

Communications failed and messages were not passed on. When 196 Japanese aircraft appeared, they were clearly headed for Clark Field, the main Far East Air Force (FEAF) base in the Philippines, about 45 miles (72km) north of Manila. Others were heading for the fighter base at Iba. Attempts to warn Clark Field failed, and twenty-seven Mitsubishis, followed by another wing of thirty-five, dived down on the neatly parked Flying Fortresses and a group of eighteen P-40B fighters waiting patiently to refuel.

It was easy pickings for the Japanese. They destroyed twelve B-17 bombers, fifty-five P-40 fighters and about forty other assorted aircraft. Eighty men were killed and 150 wounded. The Japanese force of 108 bombers and eighty-four fighters lost only seven.[3] Not for nothing was this called the second Pearl Harbor. The results were devastating; the strength of FEAF was reduced by half and eliminated as an effective fighting force.[4]

The raid had also savaged the docks about 8 miles (13km) south-west of Manila and columns of smoke rose from the ruins. The loss of 500 men was grievous as was the destruction of the entire stock of the Asiatic Fleet's torpedoes. Two submarines had been damaged and, with them out of commission, there were no assets capable of preventing Japanese invasion convoys reaching the Philippines.

Inevitably there was a post-mortem, given that ten hours had passed since the Pearl Harbor attack at 0755 hrs on 7 December. In the Philippines, that was 0225 hrs on 8 December. MacArthur and his subordinates should have been much better prepared and far more proactive as reports of enemy activity were sent and received very soon after. MacArthur did not initiate any action, other than his reluctant acquiescence to Brereton's request.

After the event, Major General H.H. Arnold, Chief of the Army Air Forces, spoke to the commander of FEAF, Air Commander, Major General L.H. Brereton, and apparently asked, 'How in hell could an experienced airman like you get caught with your planes on the ground? That's what we sent you out there for, to avoid just what happened. What in the hell is going on there?' The question has never been answered satisfactorily.[5]

At this distance it seems apparent that the person ultimately responsible must be the man in command: that was MacArthur, who perhaps shared the blame with his chief of staff, Brigadier General R.K. Sutherland. After the event both men attempted to shift all blame on to General Brereton – the only person who was proactive.

One of the burdens of the Allies in the Second World War was accommodating the towering ego of General MacArthur, who made it a practice never to concede that he had made a mistake and had raised self-aggrandisement to an art form. He had been recalled from retirement as a general, reinstated as a major general and swiftly promoted to lieutenant general. After the debacle of Pearl Harbor, there were no less than ten official enquiries. They resulted in the premature retirement of Admiral H.E. Kimmel and General W.C. Short. Curiously, and in comparison, there were no official investigations of the air attack on the Philippines, and no one was ever held to be responsible. Notwithstanding his inaction, MacArthur was re-promoted to general.

By 8 December, the Japanese had aerial superiority over the Philippines and that set the scene for the land invasion that immediately followed. The invasion had three interconnected aims. These were to deny the Americans the use of the islands as a base for future operations; to secure, for Japan, a firm base from which to dominate the Dutch East Indies; and finally to provide a stable line of communication between recently occupied areas in the south and Tokyo.

The Grand Alliance of four disparate nations each with its own armed forces did not begin to have military interoperability. The Dutch, defeated in Europe and occupied by the Germans, nevertheless fought on in its colonies. A Dutch submarine sank two Japanese transports and damaged a destroyer, but it was not enough to prevent a landing in the south-east of Luzon on 8 December. The Imperial Japanese Navy had put together a convoy of eighty-five ships and it was to bear General Homma Masaharu and his army of 43,110 men to the shores of Luzon and Mindanao, the two principal islands of the Philippines archipelago. Awaiting this invasion force was a large but untrained and very poorly equipped American/Filipino army.

MacArthur, to his credit, had realised the military deficiencies of his new command on his arrival and he had sought to correct them. He made a start on the manpower by initiating the raising of ten infantry divisions, but he was hampered first by the language difficulties – his American trainers could not converse with Filipinos, who spoke any of one of seventy dialects, and secondly by the shortage of facilities and small arms. His troops were equipped with M1917 pattern Enfield rifles, and not unreasonably he asked for 84,500 M1 Garand rifles to replace them. He was told that Garands were unavailable due

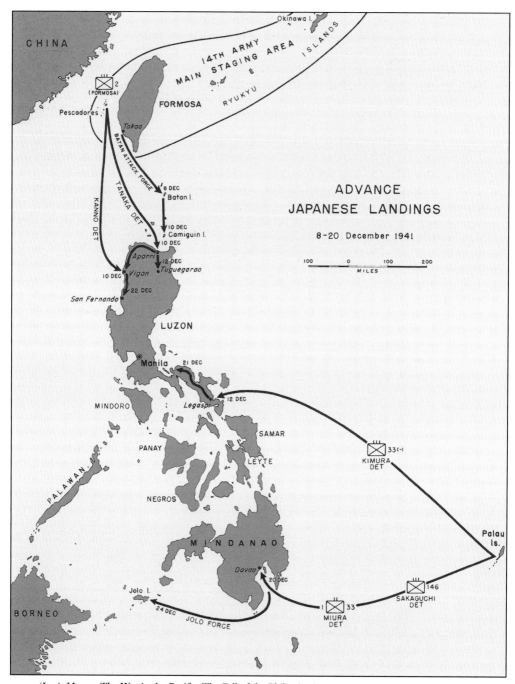

(*Louis Morton*, The War in the Pacific: The Fall of the Philippines)

to 'production difficulties'. His new divisions had, at best, 20 per cent of their artillery needs and although steps were in train to fill this gap, MacArthur had run out of time.

The initial landings were made on 8 December: 14th Army landed on and took Batan Island (not to be confused with the Bataan Peninsula), about 120 miles (193km) north of Luzon. It followed up by landing on North Luzon at three points – Vigan, Aparri and Gonzaga. Brereton sent a small force of his remaining precious B-17s to attack the landing at Gonzaga and Vigan. Two Japanese transports were damaged but not sunk. The landings in North Luzon faced little opposition and moved south towards Manila.

On 12 December, Homma put 2,500 men ashore at Legazpi in southern Luzon. (See map on page 96.) The landing was unopposed as the nearest opposition was about 150 miles (240km) away. It advanced on Manila from the south. The capital was in an ever-tightening vice. A week later, Mindanao was the target and here troops from 16th Army were deployed to allow 14th Army to concentrate on the taking of Luzon. The map on page 100 shows the progressive nature of the invasion.

Numerically the American/Filipino forces were superior to the invaders by a ratio of 3:2. However, in any war it is not 'how many', it's 'how good are they?' The defending troops were a mixture of non-combatant, experienced, regular, national guard, constabulary, and newly created Commonwealth units. Although in total they numbered 130,000, they were no match for the Japanese. The latter became complacent and, by early January 1942, decided to extract some of their units from the Philippines to fast track operations in Borneo and the Dutch East Indies (Indonesia).[6]

Homma was pressing on towards Manila and his advance units ran up against a Filipino unit blocking his route to the capital. The Filipinos were no more than civilians in uniform. They were untrained and many could not master their obsolescent firearms. After first contact with the Japanese, they broke and fled and, in so doing, left their precious artillery unprotected. Major General Jonathan Wainwright, who was commanding all forces in North Luzon, asked for permission to withdraw behind the Agno River.[7]

MacArthur had by now neither an air force nor a powerful navy. The survivors of his air force had flown to Australia and Admiral Thomas Hart commanded his only viable asset, the Asiatic Fleet and ABDA fleets. Thomas Hart was a four-star Admiral and had briefly outranked Lieutenant General MacArthur. Their relationship, although of long-standing, was becoming very strained.

In the closing months of 1941, Hart began to write in his diary of his increasing frustration with the lack of cooperation from MacArthur and the army. Hart was one of the few people in the world who would call MacArthur by his first name.

In Hart's official correspondence and war diary, he noted that there was no cooperation from MacArthur on critical issues; MacArthur repeatedly ignored what the navy knew to be proper procedures and capabilities. MacArthur was convinced that the Japanese could not attack the Philippines prior to 1945, or 1946 at the earliest. MacArthur made it clear that he intended for there to be no cooperation between the army and the navy. MacArthur was openly disparaging of Admiral Hart, resenting Hart's four stars to his three. MacArthur described the situation as a 'small fleet, big admiral'.[8]

Hart sent MacArthur a memorandum explaining why he intended to remove his remaining seaplanes – not an unreasonable decision as General Brereton had been given permission on 12 December to fly his surviving B-17s to Australia. Hart did not need permission; he was being courteous and professional.

Hart developed a deep-seated irritation with the general, despite his long friendship with him. Hart wrote to his wife: 'The truth of the matter is that Douglas is, I think, no longer altogether sane ... he may not have been for a long time.' Hart wrote to Admiral Stark, Chief of Naval Operations, that Stark should keep MacArthur's personality and mental issues in mind when selecting the next commander of the Asiatic Fleet, and that Hart expected further trouble from MacArthur and from his supporters in Washington.[9] The personality and vanity of MacArthur was to become an issue later in the war.

MacArthur, sane or not, had a large but predominantly untrained army. This had no capability to resist further invasions; the initiative lay with the invaders and the only viable course of action was to go into defensive mode. Accordingly, and as the Japanese net tightened, MacArthur withdrew all his forces and decided to concentrate on the Bataan Peninsula. The general established his headquarters in the Malinta Tunnel, which was cut deep into the rocky heart of the island of Corregidor. He took with him President Manuel Quezon and Vice President Sergio Osmeña of the Philippines.

Corregidor is about 30 miles (48km) from Manila but only 2 miles (3.2km) from the coast of Bataan. It is 4 miles (6.4km) long and about 1.2 miles (2km) wide. The island had always been one of the guardians of Manila Bay and was equipped with formidable artillery and hardened shelters. It was a small but very effective fortress.

The move into the Bataan Peninsula was chaotic. The roads were jammed as panicked civilians on foot, in ox carts or old cars, and on bicycles contested the passage to safety with Wainwright's soldiers. His small band of regular soldiers stiffened the resolve of some, but not all, his Filipino troops. The retreat into Bataan was through a series of five defensive lines and progressively 184 bridges were destroyed along the way.

Wainwright's skilful tactics delayed Homma for long enough to allow General Parker to get his 15,000 men of the South Luzon force west of Manila and to the relative, but temporary, safety of the peninsula. The Japanese General Staff would pay tribute to this manoeuvre as 'a great strategic move'.[10] The predetermined and defence arrangements for Bataan were contained in the detail of War Plan Orange (WPO-3). However, the plan had never been implemented (shades of Percival's plans for Johore in 1938). The trench lines and hard defences specified in the plan existed only on paper; the evacuation of the civilian occupants of Bataan was never implemented. They were part of the maelstrom ahead. The paper plan called for sufficient food for six months to be stockpiled; in practice, there was barely enough for a month. Wainwright's task was to keep lines of communication open so that appropriate logistic arrangements could be made.

Admiral Hart recognised the vulnerability of his fleet, now part of the ABDA Force, and dispersed most of his American surface ships but retained his submarine capability. However, these submarines were only safe from air attack when they were submerged or camouflaged.

MacArthur received repeated promises from Washington that help was on the way but by the second week of January these promises lost credibility when nothing materialised. Little wonder, as the nearest American base was Midway Island, and that was 4,500 miles (7,242km) away. Japanese bombing increased and propaganda leaflets were added to the ordnance – both served to damage morale. What MacArthur did not know was that, pragmatically, the Joint Chiefs of Staff and President Roosevelt had decided to leave the Philippines to their fate. There was to be no relief. As the Secretary of State for War, Henry Lewis Stimson, remarked, 'There are times when men have to die.'[11] By most measurements the treatment of MacArthur was dishonourable and reflects little credit on Roosevelt, Stimson or Marshall.

The defenders of Bataan – 80,000 troops and 26,000 civilians – held out for three arduous, hungry, uncomfortable months, during which both sides sustained heavy losses. The Filipino-American force was at a major disadvantage in that Wainwright had been unable to establish a line of logistic support, attempts to bring in supplies by sea having failed.

The US War Department wanted Quezon to be evacuated from Corregidor to avoid capture, but General Douglas MacArthur believed it to be too hazardous to attempt. On 3 January 1942, Quezon directed that $640,000 from the Philippine treasury be conveyed to the personal bank accounts of MacArthur and three members of his staff. This was 'in recognition of

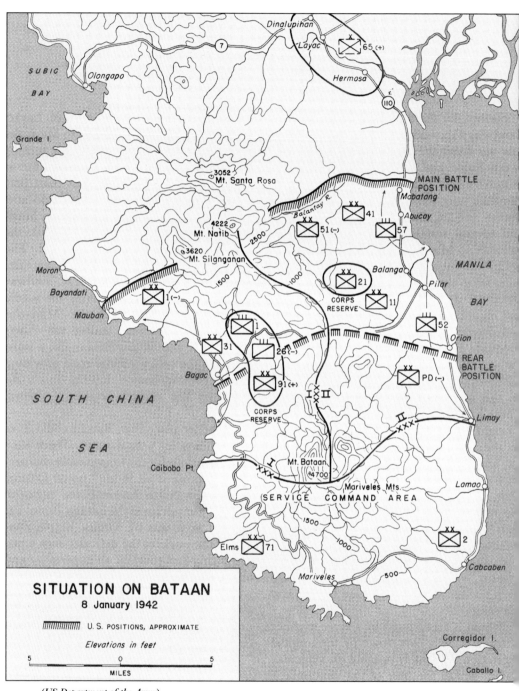

SUBIC BAY

BAY

Grande I.

Dinalupihan

Layac

65 (+)

Hermosa

110

Olongapo

Moron

Mt. Santa Rosa
3052

MAIN BATTLE POSITION

Mabatang

Balantay R.

41

Abucay

51 (-)

57

4222
Mt. Natib

2500

MANILA

3620
Mt. Silanganan

1500

1000

Balanga

21

CORPS RESERVE

Pilar

BAY

Bayandati

1 (-)

11

Mauban

52

Orion

REAR BATTLE POSITION

31

26 (-)

Bagac

91 (+)

PD (-)

SOUTH   CHINA

I   II

CORPS RESERVE

II

Limay

SEA

Caibobo Pt.

Mt. Bataan
4700

I

Lamao

Mariveles Mts.

SERVICE   COMMAND   AREA

1500

Elms

71

2

1000

Mariveles

500

Cabcaben

SITUATION ON BATAAN
8 January 1942

U. S. POSITIONS, APPROXIMATE

Elevations in feet

5   0   5
MILES

Corregidor I.

Caballo I.

(*US Department of the Army*)

outstanding service to the Philippines between 15 November 1935 and 30 December 1941'. The gratuitous gift of $500,000 from the Philippine treasury to MacArthur is worth $8,897,364 at 2021 values.

He was not the only recipient of Quezon's largess. Several transactions, made by radiograms from Corregidor to the Chase National Bank of the City of New York, favoured (newly promoted) Major General Richard K. Sutherland, MacArthur's chief of staff, who received $75,000. Brigadier General Richard J. Marshall Jr., the Deputy Chief of Staff, received $45,000, and Lieutenant Colonel Sidney L. Huff, MacArthur's personal aide, received $20,000.

Carol M. Petillo uncovered the evidence of these payments and wrote about them in *The Pacific Historical Review*, published by the University of California Press. According to Petillo's research, orders for the transfers of funds were not transmitted to the War Department until 15 February 1942. Petillo comments:

> It is significant that after several statements arguing that Quezon could not safely be evacuated, MacArthur, one day after the transfer of funds was ordered, reversed his position and decided that the president's evacuation indeed could be achieved. On Feb. 20, just after he received verification of the transfer, this decision was carried out and Quezon headed south toward the unoccupied islands.[12]

There was nothing illegal about these gifts and MacArthur had been given permission to accept his. However, the culture of most Western armies, including the US Army, is that large cash gifts are never sought and generally never offered by a host country. In this case, the sum involved was so very large and its juxtaposition with Quezon's departure so close, that the implication that it was a bribe is germane.

*   *   *

As Quezon sailed away to safety, elsewhere in Singapore the Japanese were imposing their own version of hell on its inhabitants. When the whole of Singapore had been secured, General Yamashita split it up and allocated responsibility to Lieutenant General Nishimura Takuma, Major General Kawamura Takeshi, Lieutenant General Matsui Takurō, and Lieutenant General Mutaguchi Renya. Yamashita issued orders to these four officers that all Chinese residents in the areas of their concern in Singapore were to be assembled and screened by 23 February. 'Undesirable elements' were to be killed; the where and how of these murders was left to the discretion of the commanders. The total number of innocent Chinese citizens who were killed was about 5,000 – according to evidence later given by Colonel Sugita Ichiji.[13] This became known as 'The Chinese Massacre'.

The Japanese were innovative and not every victim was shot; some were bayoneted, and others beheaded or drowned. This latter method was widely employed in Singapore as hundreds were bound and pushed into the water off Blakang Mati island. The British Military Hospital (now known as Alexandra Hospital) had a normal capacity for 550 patients, but the battle for Singapore had swelled the numbers to 900. The men of the 32 Company, Royal Army Medical Corps were running the hospital under difficult conditions. Water was rationed, torches and lights were used only for medical procedures, and corpses wrapped in blankets remained unburied.[14]

The hospital had been under heavy Japanese shelling since the morning of 14 February 1942. At about 1300 hrs that day, the first Japanese soldier was sighted approaching the building. A British officer walked out to meet him while pointing to his Red Cross armband, the internationally recognised symbol of medical personnel. The soldier opened fire but missed.

Soon after, and for about one hour, three large groups of Japanese soldiers attacked the hospital. They went from room to room, shooting, bayoneting and beating doctors, orderlies and patients indiscriminately. They even killed an anaesthetised patient who was still lying on the operating table. About fifty men were killed in this first round. Around 1530 hrs, 200 men were rounded up, tied into groups of eight and forced to march towards a row of buildings some distance from the hospital. The gravely injured were not spared and were killed if they fell along the way.[15]

Upon reaching their destination, which was a row of outhouses, the men were divided into groups of fifty to seventy people and crammed into three small rooms. There was no ventilation and they lacked water. They neither had the space to sit nor to lie down. Under these terrible conditions, some men died during the night. The following morning, the remaining men were told that they would receive water. By 1100 hrs, the Japanese captors allowed the prisoners to leave the rooms in groups of two on the pretext of their fetching water. However, as the screams and cries of those who had left the rooms could be heard by those still inside, it became clear that the Japanese were executing the prisoners when they went out. The Japanese returned the next day and slaughtered another 150 people. In all, the death toll numbered about 200.[16]

This was a war crime, typical of so many in Singapore – unthinking, brutal and largely unpunished. The men who bayoneted hospital patients and murdered Mr Tan's officers at Sembawang Officers' Mess (see pages 1–2) went on to murder many thousands more elsewhere in Asia over the next four bloody years. To chronicle the full story of the Japanese occupation of

Singapore would fill a book. Suffice it to say that the above serves to illustrate the obscene behaviour of Japanese troops in, what was then, a lovely island.

* * *

Wavell had not relished his appointment to command ABDA forces and, when told of his selection, had commented: 'I've heard of men having to hold the baby, but this is quadruplets.'[17] Malaya, Singapore and Guam were lost, and the Philippines would soon go the same way. From his headquarters in Bandung, in the mountains of central Java, Wavell judged that Java would be the next Japanese objective. He was to be proved right because two invasion forces were on their way. The troopships were under the protection of powerful warships and had air cover.

Wavell's ABDA naval assets were commanded by US Admiral Thomas Hart, whose opinion was that the Dutch East Indies were a lost cause. This view was roundly rejected by Vice Admiral C.E.L. Helfrich, a Dutch officer. Helfrich persuaded the Americans to confront the Japanese fleet that was escorting a convoy of troopships making passage through the Makassar Strait. The significance of the strait is that to the north it enters the Celebes Sea and to the south the Java Sea. It is a strategically important shipping lane.[18]

On 24 January 1942, the passage of the Japanese convoy through the strait was contested by four destroyers of the US Navy: USS *John D. Ford*, *Pope*, *Parrot* and *Paul Jones*. In the engagement, later to be termed the Battle of Balikpapan, six Japanese transport ships and a patrol boat were sunk. It was a less than satisfactory result and American torpedoes were either defective or ill-aimed. Given that the transports were not escorted, the American bag should have been much bigger, although the action was heralded in the USN camp as a major victory.

Nevertheless, it did underscore Helfrich's view that the Japanese should be stopped at sea. However, despite the losses, the Japanese were still able to land sufficient troops to take Balikpapan, a port on the east coast of Borneo with extensive oil facilities. Wavell signalled to Churchill, saying, 'I am afraid that the defence of Java cannot now last long. Anything put into Java can now do little to prolong [the] struggle … I see little further usefulness for this headquarters.'[19]

The reluctance of Hart to engage the enemy had baffled Helfrich as it did the Japanese.[20] The RAF had been destroyed in Malaya and the Dutch were reduced to a handful of old aircraft. Of the 111 American aircraft that had been sent to Java, only twenty-three bombers and a few fighters remained airworthy. Wavell passed the defence of the Dutch East Indies to the Dutch Governor and Helfrich assumed command of ABDA naval forces.

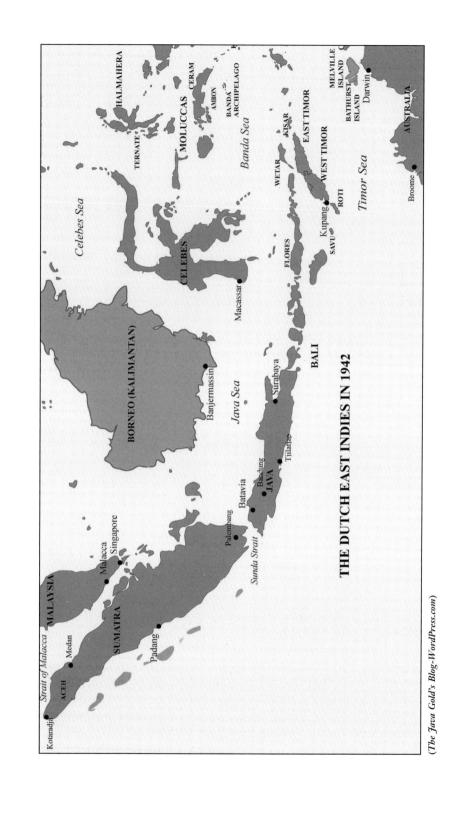

THE DUTCH EAST INDIES IN 1942

(The Java Gold's Blog-WordPress.com)

The Japanese advance was inexorable: they took Pambang on 13 February, and its strategically important oil installations. Spreading its wings even further and employing land and carrier-based aircraft, the Japanese forces mounted two attacks on Darwin, where they did serious damage: 236 were killed, 300–400 wounded, 30 aircraft destroyed, 11 vessels sunk, and 28 ships damaged.[21] All this at a loss of two killed and thirty-four aircraft damaged. Darwin's use as a supply and naval base was vastly degraded.

* * *

Just as Wavell predicted, Java was the next target for Japanese amphibious forces and to this end the Eastern Assault Convoy (EAC) intended to force a passage through the Makassar Strait. Helfrich, the ABDA commander, signalled his countryman Rear Admiral W.F.M. Doorman to sail with fourteen ships and attack the EAC. Doorman's fleet sailed from Surabaya. His command was a collection of ships from all four ABDA nations without any commonality of signal procedure or tactics. It was then that Helfrich became aware of the threat posed by Western Assault Convoy (WAC). Doorman was unable to contact his enemy and about thirty-six hours later he returned to Surabaya.

There was no rest as the Japanese had been sighted. In lieu of a common code book, Doorman signalled his fleet in plain English, saying, 'Follow me. Enemy is 90 miles away.' Doorman's ships were the cruisers HMS *Exeter*, HMAS *Perth*, USS *Houston*, Dutch cruisers HNLMS *De Ruyter* and *Java*, and nine destroyers – three RN, four USN and two Dutch. This was the only force available to confront the Japanese. The WAC of fifty-six ships was 250 miles (400km) from the western tip of Java. The EAC with forty troopships and a very powerful escort was 200 miles (320km) away from its target, the eastern end of Java.

The Battle of the Java Sea, fought on 27 February 1942, was a comprehensive victory for the Imperial Japanese Navy; it outgunned and outnumbered Doormans's flotilla. It also outmanoeuvred Doorman, who could not communicate with his ships effectively. The IJN sank two cruisers, damaged a third and sank three destroyers; 2,300 men were lost. The Japanese only suffered damage to three destroyers and a light cruiser – thirty-six men were killed. The battle was notable for the fusillades of torpedoes launched unsuccessfully by each side. At one point the Japanese launched a salvo of ninety-two torpedoes but had only one hit. That said, it did sink the Dutch destroyer *Kortenaer*.

The ABDA flotilla broke off the engagement at 1800 hrs, covered by a smokescreen laid by the USN destroyers. Doorman turned south towards Java and, when night fell, he turned again, first west and then north. The

USN contingent, on its own initiative, left the formation and returned to Surabaya – a graphic example of the difficulties of command and control in a mixed nation force.

Later that night, at 2115 hrs, the J-class destroyer HMS *Jupiter* hit a mine and sank. Forty-five minutes later, the ABDA Flotilla was engaged by a group of IJN ships. Both sides opened fire and the Japanese were more effective; the two Dutch ships – the light cruiser NLMS *De Ruyter* and the cruiser *Java* – were both torpedoed and sunk; 367 men died in *de Ruyter* and 512 in *Java*, and Doorman went down with his ship. Of the two ships' companies, only 111 survived.

ABDA was now in disarray. HMAS *Perth* and USS *Houston*, in accordance with orders to sail through the Sunda Strait to Tjilatjap, had not had time to fully refuel or re-arm. Thus, when they ran into the main Japanese invasion fleet in Bantam Bay, they were at an immediate disadvantage. The action was fought in the dark and once again the IJN came out on top. Both ABDA cruisers were sunk. HNLMS *Evertsen* was attempting to catch up with *Houston* and *Perth* and managed to slip around the Japanese force. However, *Evertsen* was then engaged by two Japanese destroyers in the strait and, on fire and in a sinking condition, grounded herself on a reef near Sebuku Island. The aft magazine exploded and blew off the stern; survivors were taken prisoner by the Japanese on 9–10 March 1942. The ageing USS carrier *Langley* (the first in the USN), a converted collier, had been part of a convoy but was spotted and sunk on 27 February as she ferried in thirty-two vital P-40 fighter aircraft to Tjilatjap in Central Java.

After repairs, HMS *Exeter*, in company with HMS *Encounter* and USS *Pope*, left Surabaya on 28 February heading for Ceylon (Sri Lanka). However, they ran into a powerful Japanese force and all three ships were sunk. The naval situation was now so dire that the destroyers HNLMS *Witte de With*, USS *Pillsbury*, *Edsall* and *Asheville* were all scuttled.

Allied naval power in the theatre was now extinguished and the Japanese had control of all surface and aerial movement. The IJA conquests had spread its assets widely over Southeast Asia. The navy provided the means of logistic support needed. Japanese expansion did not end here, and it should be borne in mind that there were concurrent invasions elsewhere.

*　*　*

Wake Island is a coral atoll isolated in the Western Pacific. It is 1,501 miles (2,416km) east of Guam and 2,298 miles (3,698km) west of Honolulu. Tokyo lies 1,991 miles (3,204km) to the north-west. It was taken by the USA in 1899 at the conclusion of the Spanish-American war and the annexation of Hawaii and the Philippines. The merits of Wake were just like those of Guam. It was

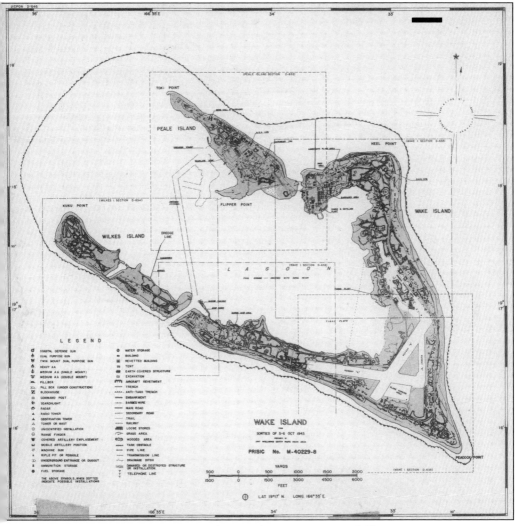

US Navy map showing the two-runway airfield.

ideally located for use as a telegraph cable and coaling station. In 1934, its value as an airhead was recognised by Pan American Airways, which sought permission to build a runway.

Subsequently, in January 1941, the United States Navy started to build the infrastructure for a military base. It was then garrisoned by 449 officers and men of the US Marine Corps with a Marine Corps Fighter squadron of twelve F4F Wildcat fighters. In addition, they were supported by sixty-eight members of the US Navy. The population in December 1941 was completed by 1,221 civilian employees of the American civil engineering company Morrison-Knudsen.

The Japanese launched an attack on Wake in great strength on 8 December and allocated to the task three light cruisers, six destroyers and three submarines, all guarding two troop transport ships packed with infantry. On the face of it there was surfeit of force available to the Japanese, but they had not reckoned on the spirited and courageous defence put up by the small marine force opposing them. The initial landings were repulsed, with heavy Japanese losses. Two destroyers were sunk by the six 5″ guns on the island – some 340 Japanese were killed and sixty-five wounded.

The stoic defence of this rocky atoll surprised the Japanese, who then regrouped. They reinforced for their second attempt and, incredibly, two aircraft carriers, two heavy cruisers, two destroyers and another 2,500 infantrymen were added to the order of battle. It was significant overkill to tackle the very courageous American Marines and civilians.

The outcome was inevitable, and Wake Island surrendered on 23 December, but not until its Marine defenders had sunk two patrol craft and shot down ten Japanese aircraft, and caused a further 144 casualties. In the great order of things, Wake Island was not vital, but the heroics of its defenders lifted American morale that had been damaged by news from the Philippines. The defence cost fifty-four military and seventy civilians killed. In addition, 1,537 military and civilians were made prisoner. The determined and courageous defence of Wake set a benchmark for multiple battles to come.

*   *   *

Hong Kong was particularly vulnerable to Japanese aggression. It was only 446 miles (718km) from Formosa and defended by a mixed army of 14,564 troops. The garrison had been reinforced in September 1941 when the British Government accepted an offer from the Canadian Government to send two battalions of infantry. The Canadian force totalled ninety-six officers and 1,877 other ranks.

Its naval defence was vested in one old destroyer, four small gunboats, a minelayer and eight motor torpedo boats (MTB). In much the same way that they had employed overwhelming force in Guam and Wake, so in Hong Kong the Japanese committed 29,700 soldiers, forty-seven assorted aircraft, a cruiser, three destroyers, four torpedo boats and three gunboats. Major General C.M. Maltby had orders to 'resist for as long as possible'.

There was no question of reinforcement. Maltby managed his amateur, untrained forces sufficiently well that the commander of the invading force, General Sakai Takashi, was vastly discommoded by the obdurate resistance of the garrison and people of the colony.

A Victoria Cross was won by Company Sergeant Major John Osborne of the Winnipeg Grenadiers and George Crosses were won by Lanceray Newnham, Douglas Ford and Bertram Gray. The recipients of the GC were all murdered. The colony held out for eighteen days but was finally forced to

Lieutenant General Sakai Takashi (1887–1946), executed for war crimes by the Chinese.

surrender on Christmas Day 1941. Like all Japanese, Sakai held the Chinese in low regard and his frustration at the prolonged battle is cited as the reason for the murder of at least 10,000 Chinese citizens.

The battle cost 2,113 British, Canadian, Indian and Chinese lives; a further 2,300 were wounded and 10,947 captured. Many of the prisoners died in Japanese hands. Japanese losses were 675 killed and 2,079 wounded.[22] The killing did not stop with the surrender and the Japanese committed any number of atrocities. General Sakai had been a participant in the massacre in Nanjing and after the war he was extradited to China and tried for war crimes. He was found guilty and shot on 30 September 1946.

In a most unusual gesture, in December 2011, Toshiyuki Kato, Japan's parliamentary Deputy Minister for Foreign Affairs, apologised for the mistreatment to a group of Canadian veterans of the Battle of Hong Kong.[23]

* * *

For the defenders in the Philippines, the three-month battle in Bataan from 7 January 1942 was not just against the Japanese, but also against the hostile climate, rugged terrain and malnutrition. The effects of malnutrition were many and serious. They included chronic fatigue, malaria, scurvy, amoebic dysentery, beriberi, night blindness and oedema. A complete dearth of medication meant that sufferers could not be treated. By early March, 35 per cent had malaria. The cavalry horses and mules were progressively eaten, and soon after it was the turn of cats and dogs. In the foothills of the Mariveles Mountains the defenders ate anything with a pulse. Uniforms were hanging in rags.

Homma had his problems too. His soldiers were as vulnerable to malaria as the Filipino-Americans they faced. In addition, his logistic chain was faltering; food supplies were short.[24] On 8 February, he suspended operations and made his immediate priority a reorganisation of his force, which had suffered debilitating casualties.

The Imperial General Headquarters in Tokyo was displeased with Homma, who had not conquered the Philippines in the anticipated time frame. Tōjō was losing faith in him. A further division was deployed to the Philippines, and, on its arrival, Homma had 75,000 men under command.

MacArthur departed from the Corregidor on 12 March. He endured a lengthy and uncomfortable journey to Australia and then made a highly publicised statement to the press. He said, 'I will return.' Advised that 'We will return' would be more appropriate, he rejected the suggestion. Wainwright, promoted to lieutenant general, took over command, but MacArthur was not consulted on Wainwright's promotion and, loath to leave the spotlight, he expressed doubt in Wainwright's ability to fill his shoes. From his new headquarters in Australia, he issued a stream of commands to his erstwhile soldiers, insisting that they not surrender. It was at this point that Roosevelt ordered General Marshall, the Chief of the Combined Staff, to write a citation that would support the award of the Congressional Medal of Honour to MacArthur.

Marshal demurred, as MacArthur had done nothing remotely to justify the supreme award for bravery. He was overruled. It was a purely political decision and award of the medal was accompanied by a propaganda campaign. Roosevelt's actions fed the ego of an egomaniac. The British equivalent would have been the VC for Percival.

Wainwright moved out to the island redoubt and was left to convince his men that the absence of MacArthur was by presidential order but, nevertheless, the evacuation of the general was a clear signal that the battle for the Philippines was lost. Notwithstanding the strategic situation, there were countless acts of individual great bravery. However, even courage could not deny access to the heights of the Mariveles Mountains. Although thought to be impenetrable, the high ground was taken and held by the Japanese. Wainwright signalled to Washington that unless he got food by 15 April, his force would be starved into submission. General Marshall shared this signal with MacArthur in Australia. The great man responded curtly, saying, 'It is of course possible that with my departure the vigour of application of conservation may have been relaxed.'[25] This was a cheap snipe at Wainwright and it did MacArthur no credit.

Meanwhile, Wainwright was subject to constant orders from the Australian-based MacArthur. In one signal he wrote: 'When the supply situation becomes impossible, there must be no thoughts of surrender, you must attack.' Wainwright, in the face of common sense and from the relative safety of Corregidor, ordered his subordinate, commanding forces in Bataan, to do just that. Major General Edward King knew that this was military nonsense and took it on himself to disobey MacArthur and Wainwright's order; he would not waste any more lives.

He chose to surrender with his 76,000 men on 9 April 1942. This left Wainwright, and the 10,000 men with him on Corregidor, out on a limb. They eventually surrendered on 6 May. In Bataan, the Filipino-American force lost 10,000 killed and 20,000 wounded. The Japanese lost 3,347 killed and missing, and 5,069 wounded.[26]

The Japanese were nonplussed. They had anticipated taking 25,000 prisoners, but they had three times as many on their hands and their fragile

A memorial that marks the start point of the Death March. (*Ramon Velasquez*)

logistic system broke under the strain. They had neither the food to feed nor the trucks and coaches to transport their charges to POW cages. The men would have to march, to be more accurate, shuffle and stumble into the deeper captivity that awaited them.

The battle was lost but now the horror began. It was the Japanese intention to concentrate all prisoners at Camp O'Donnell, about 66 miles (106km) from Bataan. The prisoners were to be loaded onto trains at San Fernando, Pampanga, and taken on to Capas. The march, which started on 9 April, was notable for the cruelty displayed by the captors. Estimates vary widely and Filipino deaths were between 5,000 and an improbable 18,000. Between 500 and 650 Americans died. The prisoners, who were already starving, were given little food and water. A request for water could cause the summary shooting of the supplicant. 'Stragglers were mercilessly clubbed, those dying of disease and malnutrition were left by the wayside and men who appeared to be succumbing were buried alive by their comrades at gunpoint.'[27] Men who fell were bayoneted. Those who survived the march had now to cope with a train journey in unventilated metal boxcars to Capas. Staff Sergeant Alfred Larson recalled:

> The train consisted of six or seven World War I-era boxcars ... They packed us in the cars like sardines, so tight you couldn't sit down. Then they shut the door. If you passed out, you couldn't fall down. If someone had to go to the toilet, you went right there where you were. It was close to summer and the weather was hot and humid, hotter than Billy Blazes! We were on the train from early morning to late afternoon without getting out. People died in the railroad cars.[28]

The Philippines, and the people who lived there, were to endure a further three years of egregious brutality and then a liberation campaign that would cost many more lives. The Japanese imposed their standards and culture across their captured territories. In several instances these were abhorrent to the people they now held captive. The next chapter gives a graphic example.

Notes

1. Toland, J., *The Rising Sun: The Decline and Fall of the Japanese Empire, 1936–45* [1970] (Modern Library, New York, 2003), p. 246.
2. https://corregidor.org/chs_wpo-3/wpo-3.htm.
3. Bartsch, W.H., *December 8, 1941* (Texas, A&M University Press, 2003), pp. 283–324, 409, 427, 442.
4. Correll, J.T., 'Disaster in the Philippines' (*Air Force Magazine*, 2019).
5. Ibid.
6. MacArthur, Gen. D., *Japanese Operations in the Southwest Pacific Area* (Reports, Vol. 2), p. 104.
7. Toland, p. 251.

8. Leutze, J., *A Different Kind of Victory: A Biography of Admiral Thomas C. Hart* (Annapolis, MD: Naval Institute Press, 1981), p. 218.

9. Ibid.

10. Jones, F.G., *Japan's New Order in East Asia: Its Rise and Fall 1937–45* (London, 1954, Vol. 11), p. 16.

11. Manchester, W.R., *America Caesar: Douglas MacArthur 1880–1964* (Boston, 1968), p. 241.

12. Petillo, C.M., 'MacArthur, Quezon, and Executive Order Number One' (*Pacific Historical Review*, February 1979). *See also* Petillo, *Douglas MacArthur: The Philippine Years* (Bloomington, Indiana University Press, 1981).

13. Russell, Lord of Liverpool, *The Knights of Bushido* (London, Cassell, 1958), p. 244.

14. Partridge, J., *Alexandra Hospital: From British Military to Civilian Institution* (Singapore Alexandra Hospital, 1998), pp. 58–60.

15. Bruton, P., *The matter of a massacre: Alexandra Hospital Singapore 14th/15th February 1942* (Singapore Infopedia, 1989), p. 23.

16. Partridge, pp. 64–6.

17. Carver, M., *The War Lords: Military Commanders of the Twentieth Century* (Boston, Little Brown & Company, 1976), p. 224.

18. Klemen, L., *Forgotten Campaign: The Dutch East Indies Campaign 1941–42* (http://www.dutcheastindies.webs.com).

19. Toland, p. 278.

20. Ibid.

21. Lewis, T. & Ingman, P., *Carrier Attack Darwin 1942: the complete guide to Australia's own Pearl Harbor* (South Australia, Avonmore Books, 2013).

22. Ishiwari, Heizō (1956), Army Operations in China December 1941–December 1943 (PDF). Japanese Monograph. IV 17807.71–2. Washington, DC: Office of the Chief of Military History, Department of the Army.

23. (Associated Press) 'Japan Apologizes to Canadian POWs from H. K. Battle' (*Japan Times*, 10 December 2011), p. 2.

24. Costello, J., *The Pacific War 1941–45* [1981] (New York, Harper Collins, 2009), p. 227.

25. Toland, p. 288.

26. Alexander, I., *Surviving Bataan and Beyond* (Stackpole Books, 2005), p. 272.

27. Costello, p. 228.

28. Greenberger, R., *The Bataan Death March: World War II Prisoners in the Pacific* (Compass Point Books, 2009), p. 96.

Chapter Ten

1931–45
Comfort Woman

In any army, at any time in history, when a young soldier joins, he does not hand in his libido at the guardroom. Armies are full of young men with powerful sexual needs, and the Imperial Japanese Army was no exception.

To cater for the sexual needs of its soldiers, military brothels have been set up by any number of governments. The first to be recorded was during the Third Crusade, of 1189–92, when Philip II of France, appalled by the sodomy that was rife in his army, imported a shipload of 'girls of joy'.[1] Thereafter, and certainly from about 1830, in Algeria, the French Army maintained military brothels in its African stations until 1995. The girls staffing these establishments were recruited and the sex was consensual.

The provision of brothels was not a moral issue but rather a combination of medical necessity and an aid to morale. The control of venereal diseases (VD) by establishing medically inspected brothels made for a more battle-ready army – any army.

In 1933, Lieutenant Colonel Bernard Montgomery, then commanding a battalion in Egypt, saw to it that his soldiers took their 'horizonal refreshment' in clean, well-regulated brothels run by the garrison adjutant in Alexandria and, as a result, VD rates were very low.[2] Typically, Montgomery took a realistic view and later, in 1940, when commanding the 3rd Division in the British Expeditionary Force (BEF) in France, he was aggrieved to learn that his men were eschewing the well-run establishments in Lille. Instead, they were consorting with self-employed, amateur ladies in the fields and hedges of northern France. There were forty cases of VD and Montgomery addressed the issue directly. In a letter to his commanding officers he wrote: 'We must face up to the problem, be perfectly frank about it and do all we can to help the soldier in this very difficult matter.'[3]

There were serious repercussions from Montgomery's letter, and he was subject to a major dressing down by his corps commander, later to be Lord Alanbrooke. Brooke represented a blinkered, Victorian-era view and Montgomery came close to being sacked for his pragmatic concern for his soldiers.

By the middle 1930s, the IJA recognised that the wholesale rape of women in captured territory was the cause of very negative publicity and international

Comfort women, one of whom is demonstrably pregnant. Photographed at Lameng, Yunnan, on 3 September 1945. (*US National Archive*)

revulsion. It realised that its soldiers had to be provided with non-violent, easily accessible sex, without the risk of being infected with a sexually transmitted disease (STD). Initially, Japanese military brothels were staffed by volunteer prostitutes. However, demand outstripped supply as the army was 5 million strong – the navy and the air force in addition.

Historically, the Japanese had embraced a system known as *karayuki-san* – the name applied to Japanese girls and women in the late nineteenth and early twentieth centuries who were trafficked from poverty-stricken agricultural prefectures in Japan to destinations across the Southern Hemisphere. In 1918, there was a policy change in the 'Yellow Slave Traffic'. Thereafter the women were limited to providing a service to Japanese men only.

> The *karayuki-san* system was undoubtedly a repressive system of sexual exploitation. The methods of procuring young women were clearly unlawful and morally unjustifiable. In this sense, they were little different from the methods that were used for the later procurement of comfort women. In both cases, serious criminal acts were involved.[4]

Many, if not all, the *karayuki-san* came from an impoverished family background and were sold by their parents to procurers and employed in various places in the Asia-Pacific region. From 1922 onwards, the Japanese *karayuki-san* in China began to be supplemented by Korean women. The protocols in place for the *karayuki-san* and the Second World War comfort women were in many ways similar.

> Whenever they engaged a client, the *karayuki-san*, just like the WWII comfort women, received a ticket indicating that a payment had been made. Approximately 50 per cent of the fee for this ticket went to the *karayuki-san*. Although the 'comfort women' were theoretically also to receive a portion of the fee paid for their time and services, that was often not the case because of alleged debts that the comfort women were expected to amortise and because of injustices and graft within the system itself.[5]

The Japanese had a culture of employing women to provide sexual services and if that could only be achieved by supplementing the ranks of the professionals with unwilling but coerced amateurs, then so be it. It is at this point that the provision of consensual sex provided by prostitutes changed into compulsory, state-managed sex slavery. The expression 'a fate worse than death' applies here.

The number of women lured or abducted into the role of comfort woman varies according to the source. The Japanese historian Hata Ikuhiko puts it at 20,000 and, in contrast, the Chinese historian Hua-Lun Huang estimates between 360,000 and 410,000. This writer favours something towards the upper end of the scale, if only because even 20,000 very enthusiastic ladies would be unable to meet the continuous and recurring needs of 5 million men.

A Korean woman or girl who applied for an advertised post as a nurse, a waitress, or even an entertainer rarely had any idea of what awaited her when she arrived at a military camp in the Pacific War theatre. Upon arrival, these women and girls were introduced to a routine where they were coerced into having multiple sexual encounters daily, even several each hour, in some cases.

A Chinese girl, Chen Jinyu, when interviewed by Max Hastings, averred that, aged 16 she was told that she was to be moved from her job, planting rice for Japanese consumption, and employed in 'battlefront rear service group'. She had no idea what this new job entailed but found out soon enough when she was gang-raped by a group of Japanese soldiers. She ran away to her home but when she was found, an interpreter told her that her family would suffer dire consequences if she did not return to her duties. She worked as a comfort woman until June 1945, when, once again, she absconded, this time successfully.[6]

Japan's military medical corps closely monitored these women through check-ups to detect STDs, but military doctors and medical workers frequently raped the women during these examinations.[7] The comfort women felt threatened and were forced to perform sexually every day, even during their menstrual cycle. Their military 'johns' could punish them if they left a session unsatisfied. When women resisted having sex, they could be sharply disciplined through various means, including severe beatings.[8] Because they serviced troops along the IJA's front lines, many comfort women perished as Allied forces eventually overwhelmed Japan's Pacific defence and annihilated their troop encampments.[9] In the Battle of Saipan, comfort women, along with many other Japanese soldiers and civilians, reportedly chose suicide rather than surrender to the Allied forces.[10] As they say in Yorkshire, 'There's nowt so queer as folk.' In some cases, the Japanese military executed the Korean comfort women when they retreated from losing battles with Allied forces.[11]

These so-called comfort women were subject to continuous rape for several years – if they did not succumb to disease or violence. There is precious little poetry in sex of this type: no human contact, no conversation, no emotion and absolutely no humanity. There were queues outside the 'comfort stations' and so these women were raped perhaps twenty, perhaps fifty times a day, *every day*. They were often tortured, beaten and killed by their clients/customers/masters, all of whom were in the service of the Emperor. War crimes are usually focused on murder and especially mass murder. It is argued that the treatment of the comfort women was, in each individual case, a war crime.

Multiple comfort stations were established in every territory under Japanese control. It was clearly a priority, and Singapore, for example, had about five such 'stations'. A world-famous Singaporean recorded that, as a boy:

> within two weeks of the surrender, I heard that the Japanese had put up wooden fencing around town houses in Cairnhill Road ... It had been an upper middle-class area. I cycled past and saw long queues of Japanese soldiers snaking along Cairnhill Circle outside the fence. I heard from nearby residents that inside there were Japanese and Korean women who followed the Army to service the soldiers. It was an amazing sight, one or two hundred men queuing up, waiting their turn ... There was a notice board with Chinese characters on it which neighbours said referred to a 'Comfort House'. Such Comfort Houses had been set up in China, now they had come to Singapore. There were at least four others.[12]

By May 1942, they were operating widely in the newly expanded Japanese Empire. There must have been a form of central management for what was a major activity employing tens or hundreds of thousands of women. To the Japanese imbued with a fallacious sense of ethnic superiority, these women were lesser beings. They were culled from Korea, Burma, Thailand, French Indochina, the Dutch East Indies (Indonesia), Malaya (Malaysia), Manchukuo, Formosa (Taiwan), Portuguese Timor and New Guinea. A few unfortunate European and Australian women fell into Japanese hands, about 400 of whom were Dutch. One of the latter was Ellen van der Ploeg, who survived, and died aged 90 in 2013.

Ellen van der Ploeg (1923–2013), the face of just one of the hundreds of thousands of comfort women abused by the Japanese. (*Jan Banning*)

There is an extensive bibliography dealing with the issues around comfort women and an abundance of harrowing reminiscences of survivors. It is not intended to linger over this ghastly matter and one account is typical of the treatment these women received at the hands of the Japanese.

> Kim Dae-il recalled three instances, one time a soldier sat on top of the stomach of a pregnant 'comfort woman' who was almost full term. Apparently, this act induced labour. As a baby started to appear, he stabbed both the infant and the mother and exclaimed, 'Hey, these *senjing* (dirty Koreans) are dead. Come and see. The soldier in line came in, holding a lighted cigarette close to my nose, made me inhale the smoke to wake me up. He then stuck the lit cigarette into my vagina spreading my two legs apart. He laughed and clapped his hands for having done this.
>
> One time another drunk came in and continued drinking in my cubicle. He then stabbed the lower part of my body and shouted, 'Hey, this *senjing* is dying.' He screamed, '*Kono yaro*' (Damn you!) and he then stabbed a few more times on my lower abdomen.[13]

A curiosity of the system was that, in some cases, the women identified with their abusers and committed suicide with them later in the Pacific War. However, the majority of these unfortunate women, not unreasonably, hated their oppressors with a passion. Their misery is remembered and commemorated in many places in Southeast Asia. Not the least is a modest memorial of a seated comfort woman, located outside the Japanese Embassy in Seoul – a permanent reminder to latter generations of Japanese of their nation's

The Daily Telegraph Saturday 9 January 2021

Japan must compensate sex slaves, says S Korean court

By Julian Ryall *in Tokyo*

A SOUTH Korean court yesterday ordered the Japanese government to pay compensation to 12 Second World War sex slaves or their families, in an unprecedented ruling that prompted an immediate denunciation by Tokyo.

The Seoul Central District Court ruled that Japan should pay the victims 100 million won (£67,000) each.

It is the first civilian legal case in South Korea against Tokyo by wartime sex slaves for Japanese troops, who were euphemistically labelled "comfort women". The ruling comes despite a 1965 treaty between Seoul and Tokyo which declared claims between them and their nationals had been settled.

Yoshihide Suga, the Japanese prime minister, said the ruling was contrary to the June 1965 agreement that also provided $300 million in order to settle all claims to compensation linked to Japan's colonial rule of the Korean Peninsula from 1910 to 1945.

"I strongly urge the South Korean government to correct this violation of international law," Mr Suga said.

The ruling stated that Imperial Japan "violated international norms by committing intentional, systematic and wide-ranging criminal acts against humanity".

After yesterday's hearing, Lee Na-young, head of the Korean Council for Justice and Remembrance for the Issues of Military Sexual Slavery by Japan, said: "This was a pioneering ruling."

A spokesman for Japan's foreign ministry said "the Japanese government cannot accept it". Another ruling in a case involving 20 more former "comfort women" is due on Wednesday.

inhuman behaviour. The Japanese have been protesting for years, but their demands that the statue be removed have been ignored by South Korea. The women who survived had ruined lives. Usually rejected by their families, very, very few married and had children. Their plight and restitution for that is still being resisted by the Japanese, nearly eighty years later, as the cutting demonstrates.

Notes

1. Reynaert, F., *'Dans les bordels de l'armée française'* (L'Obs.com, 2014).
2. Hamilton, N., *Monty: The Making of a General* (London, Hamilton Hamilton, 1981), p. 222.
3. Ibid., p. 315.
4. Tanaka, Yuki, *Japan's Comfort Women: Sexual Slavery and Prostitution during World War II and the US Occupation* (Routledge, 2001), p. 173.
5. Yoshiaki Yoshimi, *Comfort Women: Sexual Slavery in the Japanese Military during WWII* (New York, Columbia University Press, 2002), pp. 142–4.
6. Hastings, Sir M., *Nemesis: The Battle for Japan 1944–45* (2007) (London, Collins, 2016), p. 13.
7. Statement by Jan Ruff O' Herne AO, Friends of 'Comfort Women' in Australia, 15 February 2007.
8. Yoshiaki, p. 151.
9. George Hicks, *The Comfort Women: Japan's Brutal Regime of Enforced Prostitution in the Second World War* (New York, W.W. Norton & Company, 1995), pp. 153–5.
10. Bartlit, N., 'Japanese Mass Suicides' (Atomic Heritage Foundation, July 2016).
11. Hicks, p. 154.
12. Lee Kuan Yew, *The Singapore Story* (Singapore, Straits Time Press, 1998).
13. Sangmie Choi Schellstede, *Comfort Women Speak: Testimony by Sex Slaves of the Japanese Military* (New York, Holmes & Meier, 2000), p. 26.

Chapter Eleven

15 December 1941–8 May 1942 Burma, Battles of Ceylon and the Coral Sea

Burma is a large country surrounded on three sides by mountain ranges covered in thick rainforest. Four great rivers flow from north to south and disgorge into the Bay of Bengal. Two of these rivers rise in the Himalayas – the Irrawaddy, and its tributary, the Chindwin. Rangoon, the capital of Burma, sits astride the Sittang River and further to the east, the Salween River reaches the sea near Moulmein (now Mawlamyine). (See map on page 123.)

The Japanese made their intention towards Burma clear on 15 December 1941 when they made an air raid on Victoria Point (now Kawthaung) at the southernmost tip of Burma on the Kra Isthmus. The attack was no more than a warning shot, but sufficient to alarm Lieutenant General Thomas Hutton, the GOC-in-C of the Burma Army. The Burma Army was no more than a weak corps of two divisions – 17 Indian Infantry Division and 1 Burma Division. This later division had been raised as an armed quasi-police force for internal security duties. It was neither equipped nor trained to meet a modern, fast-moving Japanese army. In fact, 'They proved to be unreliable and even treacherous when subject to the test of battle.'[1]

For practical purposes Burma was indefensible and undefended. The only possible source of reinforcement was the Chinese troops of Chiang Kai-shek – if he could be persuaded to assist.

Burma has a border with Thailand, a country that had declared war on Great Britain and which readily offered the Japanese access to Burma's raw materials and its oil wells. Hutton had not only to face a rampant Japan but also the growing hostility of the Burmese. In the early twentieth century, Britain sought to govern Burma by making it a province of India. However, the amalgamation of two disparate cultures was not harmonious. This was despite the significant constitutional change, made in 1937, when Burma became a separate colony with a largely autonomous government and with a fully elected assembly. This democratisation was viewed by the political hierarchy in Burma as a divisive issue and judged to be no more than a manipulation designed to exclude them from any wider reforms that might be accorded to India. On 10 January, Thailand invaded French Indochina – specifically Vietnam – and two weeks later, on 25 January, opportunistically it declared war on Britain and the USA.

Burmese public opinion was not singular because there was, throughout Britain's Far East empire, an increasing demand for independence and self-determination. In 2022 that seems to be entirely reasonable but, eighty years earlier, the world was a vastly different place. British colonies were not full-blown, independent democracies, but then the potential rulers of an independent Burma were not wedded to democracy either.

Hutton did not think that he could defend Rangoon (now Yangon) and when General Wavell visited Hutton in his headquarters, he berated him publicly 'for defeatism'. Churchill, realising that he could not provide more troops, decided that he could at least send an outstanding general. General Sir Harold Alexander was despatched to replace Hutton, who was retained as Chief of Staff (more humiliation for Hutton). As it was, Alexander concurred with Hutton's view and a full-scale retreat to the Indian border was ordered. It was to be 'a grim race against the Japanese and the approaching rains'.[2]

On 22 January, the Japanese launched a ground attack when its 55 Division breached the Thai/Burma border about halfway up the isthmus at the Kawkareik Pass. 16 Indian Brigade, which was blocking this obvious access point, recognised that it was massively outnumbered, and withdrew to the west.

At Moulmein, 2 Indian Brigade was positioned at the delta of the very wide Salween River. This river was a formidable obstacle at 1.5 miles (2.4km) wide. The brigade slowed the Japanese advance, but as one young British officer commented:

> We were staked out there like a goat for the Japanese tiger and sacrificed for no reason. The CO was killed, and we lost over sixty percent of our officers. Only about half the battalion got away ... with the exception of one officer, the Japs butchered all of our wounded. News got back to us, and this conditioned my, and the whole battalion's attitude toward the Japs. We were not merciful to them and for the rest of the war we didn't take any prisoners.[3]

Eventually, on 31 January, the brigade commandeered all available ferries and withdrew across the river. This was not a crisp, clean disengagement and several soldiers of the brigade were left behind and had to swim – inevitably, some drowned.[4]

Throughout the Second World War, the ever-present issue between the USA and Great Britain was the future of the British Empire. Roosevelt held strong anti-colonial views and his aim was to hasten the end of the British,

Dutch, Belgian and French empires. He was a capable, shrewd and pragmatic statesman but although allied to Great Britain he was not an admirer of things British, and nor was he 'a friend'. The situation did not improve as the war rolled on and 'it is hard to overstate the mutual suspicion and indeed antagonism which prevailed between the Western Allies in Asia in 1944–45.'[5]

Roosevelt wanted China to be treated as an equal Allied partner in the war against Japan. The hope was that China would, over time, develop into a great power, well disposed to the West. On a more immediate and practical note, keeping China in the war would also keep a large contingent of Japanese ground forces occupied on the Asian mainland and out of the way of future American operations in the Pacific.[6]

Initially, many Burmese welcomed the Japanese, who, on arrival, made it clear that it was their aim to create an Independent State of Burma. 'Independence' was the political tool employed by the Japanese in most of the territories they captured up to mid-1942. Before the war they had encouraged, entertained and trained potential subversive elements. In Burma, one of these was Aung San who, on 28 December 1941, along with 226 other Burmese supplemented by seventy-four Japanese, formed the Burma Independence Army.[7] In Burma, subsequent Japanese behaviour took the icing off the political cake.

The Allies recognised the difficulty in holding Burma but the Japanese leadership, in contrast, was prepared to do more, and viewed Burma as critical to their overall strategy for the war. They believed that the occupation of Burma would protect gains already secured in the Southwest Pacific and set the stage for a possible invasion of India.[8]

17 Indian Division, commanded by Major General John Smyth, VC, MC, retreated to the north, pursued by four Japanese divisions. Only limited delaying operations were possible, as the Japanese tide was inexorable. The division, now in some disarray, reached the Sittang River at a point where there was a strategically important, single-track railway bridge constructed with huge steel girders. There were eleven spans, and each span was 140 feet long. The bridge was seen as a prime route to Rangoon, and the retention of Rangoon was key to the defence of Burma.

As it was a single-track railway bridge, wheeled transport had difficulty in crossing it on an improvised surface. One truck slipped off the track and blocked the bridge for several hours. The Japanese were, by now, approaching the east bank of the Sittang and it was decided to wire the bridge for demolition. Major. R.C. Orgill, RE, who was in command of the Malerkotla Field Company, gave the task to Lieutenant (later Major) E.R.B. Hudson RE, an officer of the Royal Bombay Sappers and Miners and attached to the Field Company.

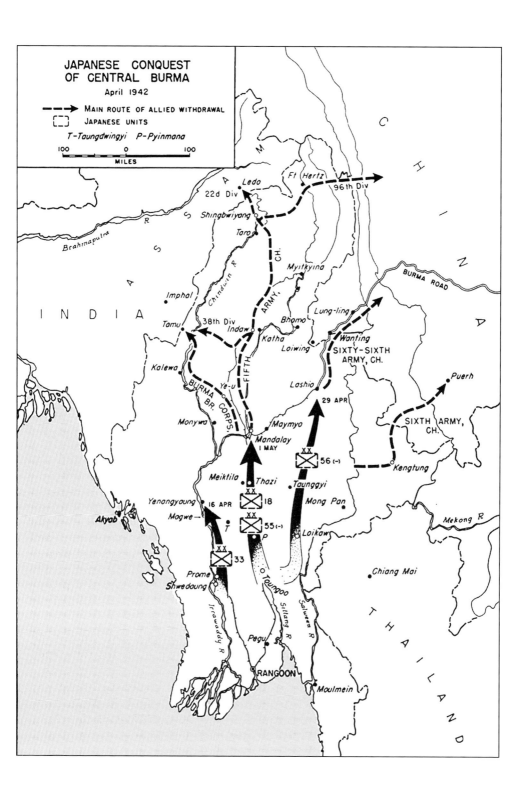

JAPANESE CONQUEST
OF CENTRAL BURMA

April 1942

▶ MAIN ROUTE OF ALLIED WITHDRAWAL
☐ JAPANESE UNITS

T-Taungdwingyi P-Pyinmana

100   0   100
MILES

The fixing of the demolition charges was very hazardous and only completed under continuous Japanese fire. In any other circumstance, Hudson would have been decorated for his courage and perseverance. Brigadier Noel Hugh-Jones was in local command as the divisional commander was about 8 miles (13km) from the bridge. The general was a very sick man, and in Roy Hudson's opinion, now shared by others, Smyth's health was a factor that affected his judgment:

> He was in almost constant pain from an anal fissure. His health problems started earlier that year, while he was still in India. He was scheduled to go to the Middle East and was suddenly given command of 17 Indian Division on its way to Burma. In February, when 17 Division was already fighting in Burma, the Senior Medical Officer in Burma insisted that Smyth go before a medical board. The board was held, and as it turned out, Smyth's own medical officer headed it, and Smyth had 'had a word with him beforehand'. It was no surprise that the board pronounced Smyth fit but recommended two months' rest at the first opportunity. Smyth's pain continued and it was difficult for him to sit in a jeep. He was given injections of arsenic and strychnine to keep him going.[9]

Hudson completed his demolition arrangements and, as a very junior officer, his job was done. 17 Division was widely spread, with two brigades on the east bank and in close contact with the enemy. Hudson's recollection was that:

> They had found some more electric wire and Lieutenant Bashir Ahmed Khan, who everyone called 'BAK', was able to run it off the bridge. He had dug a deep foxhole in the riverbank near a bridge abutment and set up the exploder box there. Brigadier Hugh-Jones became nervous about the Japanese capturing the bridge intact. Enemy pressure had increased; the bridge was continuously being swept by fire. He thought the Japanese could land a raiding party behind us and take the bridge.
>
> He rang the divisional commander; Smyth was miles away when he should have been up front. Before making the call, Hugh-Jones asked if Major Orgill could guarantee to blow up the bridge if the Japanese took the bridgehead after daylight. Orgill said he could not make any guarantees; Orgill said he was ready now, but he could not say he would still be able to do it tomorrow. That was when Hugh-Jones decided to phone for permission to blow the bridge. His phone call was taken by Brig. D.T. Cowan, who woke Smyth. It took five minutes to get a decision. Smyth had two options. He could say 'no' and risk the bridge being taken. The way to Rangoon would be open then, and reinforcements still landing in Rangoon would be cut off. Option two was to blow the bridge. This

would deny it to the Japanese but would cost Smyth the loss of two of his brigades on the east bank.[10]

Smyth, remote from the site and in great pain, was confronted with a difficult decision but, after the event, he was not without support. Field Marshal Slim said later, 'It is easy to criticise this decision; only those who have been faced with the immediate choice of similar grim alternatives can understand the weight of decision that presses on a commander.'[11] In the event, Smyth gave the order to blow the bridge at 0530 hrs on 22 February. It was to be a controversial decision, taken by the wrong man, and perhaps at the wrong time. The effect was calamitous. Hudson watched his handiwork and reported that:

> two of the spans went down immediately. The third was badly damaged but did not collapse completely. Once the bridge was blown, the Japanese took no further interest in it. They went up-river and looked for another place to cross. 16 and 46 Indian Brigades that had been withdrawing toward the Sittang were now left on the east bank, encircled by the Japanese. Because the Japanese broke off the battle when the bridge was blown, many of our troops on the east bank were able to cross the river.
>
> A party of Malerkotla sappers from the Punjab, still on the east bank, helped by making flotation devices out of bamboo, petrol tins, or anything that floated. Some of the troops got across, but many drowned trying. Some were able to clamber over broken bits of the bridge with the help of rope strung between the downed sections.

The Japanese could have eliminated the two brigades stranded on the east bank, but they had greater aspirations, and Rangoon was more important. Brigadier Noel Hugh-Jones was tortured by the decision to blow the bridge and its aftermath. His hair turned white almost overnight. He was put on a hospital ship and eventually evacuated. After the war, allegedly, he asked repeatedly to be court-martialled. Hudson claims that, 'One day, he went to the seaside, took off his clothes, walked into the sea and never came back.'[12]

Wavell visited the area and sacked Smyth on the spot. The two generals travelled back to Calcutta together, with Smyth in the back of the plane, where Wavell never spoke with him. Smyth paid a high price for refusing to report sick and clearly his health and extreme discomfort were factors in his decision-making. Smyth was proud of never having reported sick in the whole of his service, a bad decision made with the best of motives. After he left Burma, Smyth spent eight months in hospital in India. He returned to England in disgrace and was retired in his substantive rank of colonel and granted the honorary rank of brigadier.[13]

After Sittang, 17 Division was reduced to 3,484 men – about 40 per cent of its established size. It had lost most of its artillery and heavy equipment. The survivors were not a viable force as they had only 550 rifles, ten Bren light machine guns and twelve Thompson (tommy) guns between them. Not all of them had boots; they had been lost swimming the river.[14]

In the weeks that followed the Sittang disaster, 17 Division was reinforced with 63 Indian Brigade and 7 Armoured Brigade. Command of the division was given to the former Chief of Staff, on promotion, Major General David 'Punch' Cowan, CB, CBE, DSO*, MC, and he remained in command for the rest of the war.

Wavell impressed upon Alexander the absolute imperative of holding Rangoon, for without the port there would be no means to resupply British/ Indian forces in Burma. Wavell's strictures were unreasonable, but Alexander had his orders and, 'despite the frantically proffered advice of Hutton, Brigadier Davies (Hutton's chief of staff) and Cowan, he countermanded Hutton's order for withdrawal and ordered both 17 and 1 Burma Division to launch attacks between Pegu (now Bago) and Waw.'[15] The battle for Rangoon started on 3 March and lasted four days but in the opening stages, Brigadier Wickham, commanding the newly arrived 63 Brigade and with three of his battalion commanders, was ambushed and all were killed. The untried and now leaderless brigade was 'virtually helpless'.[16]

At midnight on 6 March, Alexander accepted that, although he would suffer Wavell's disapproval, extending the battle would not only lose Rangoon but the remains of the two divisions as well. On 7 March, Alexander ordered the destruction of the port and the oil refinery, and then a 'withdrawal'. However, this was nothing less than full-blown, abject retreat.

The remains of the Burma Army did not find an easy route from the city of Rangoon and ran into a roadblock manned by the Japanese 214 Infantry Regiment. The block resisted an assault and there was a high possibility that Alexander and his men might be encircled and captured. In the event, the commander of 214 Regiment misinterpreted his instructions, withdrew the block and Alexander lived to fight another day. The Japanese 33 Division took an undefended Rangoon, although it was in flames – the first demonstration of the 'scorched earth' policy that Alexander would henceforth employ. Major Michael Calvert, RE, commented on that period and wrote:

> After the fall of Rangoon, I was given orders to keep any Jap forces on the western bank of the Irrawaddy occupied. I got hold of a paddle steamer which had a Goanese crew and a British Army captain in charge. To support us there was one launch, with a Vickers medium machine gun manned by Major Johnson and some of his Royal Marines ... We were

ordered to raid down the Irrawaddy, destroy the railway in places and anything else that would be useful to the Japanese. We finished up in Henzada.

I went into town, leaving two lay back positions behind me. In the dry season the banks of the river were forty feet or so high, so the boat was out of sight. I began to give a speech in the town square. I had three men with me including Corporal Dermott, all armed with Thompson sub-machine guns. As I was talking someone said, 'You are surrounded. Lay down your arms.'

It was a party of Japanese plus Burmese dissidents. I am a slow thinker. But Corporal Dermott shouted 'Bollocks' and opened up with his tommy-gun, as we all did. We jumped off the dais and ran down the street to my first lay back position. We fought a withdrawal battle across the paddy fields. Major Johnson told his Vickers machine gunner to give us some covering fire. As we started to cast off, I discovered that we had a left a party behind and so we had to circle round, beach with the boat pointing upstream and land again. While we were recovering the party, my batman and I climbed up the bank and saw about thirty Japs all looking down at something on the ground. I don't know what they were looking at, a corpse perhaps. They were about twenty yards away. We opened up with our tommy-guns into the bunch each using the full [magazine of] thirty-eight rounds. I think we killed most of them. We then slid down into the sticky mud of the bank, got into the boat and with the Royal Marine fast launch giving us covering fire we steamed upstream.[17]

A key player in the war in Burma from February 1942 was Lieutenant General Joseph Stilwell, USA, appointed by Roosevelt to become the Chief of Staff to Generalissimo Chiang Kai-shek and soon the commander of the Chinese Expeditionary Force (CEF).[18] Stilwell was a shrewd staff officer, but he had never had a field command. He was a very abrasive, antagonistic personality. Not for nothing was he accorded the sobriquet 'Vinegar Joe'. He demonstrated, daily, the characteristics that earned the unaffectionate nickname, which he relished. Like MacArthur, Patton, Admiral Ernest King (Chief of the USN) and Roosevelt, among many others, he was Anglophobic and that was deleterious to his relationship with his British allies, whom he, publicly, held in contempt. He was not the best choice for a quasi-diplomatic appointment – being able to speak Mandarin was perhaps his greatest gift but it did not offset his personality traits.

'Wavell was incensed that his orders to defend Rangoon had been disregarded and he sent Alexander a terse telegram demanding to know whether battle had taken place.'[19] Alexander's riposte was robust and not in the least bit apologetic. Wavell never did acknowledge the potentially catastrophic effects on the Burma Army had his instructions been observed.

The Burma Corps (BURCORPS) was created on 13 March and Wavell gave its command to Major General William Slim in the belief that, with the right leadership, the situation in Burma could be retrieved. It was wishful thinking; but Slim was appointed acting lieutenant general and was to prove to be, arguably, the greatest British general of the Second World War.

However, he started from a very low point. BURCORPS was logistically strong, had ample food stocks and access to the still functioning oil fields of central Burma. However, that logistic situation was temporary, as resupply was going to be difficult, bordering impossible, without the port of Rangoon.

Slim was obliged to retreat further in the face of renewed Japanese pressure, as two further divisions, 18 and 56, had been transferred from the now pacified Malaya and Dutch East Indies. The Burma Independence Army exploited Slim's precarious position and raised the tempo of its assaults on BURCORPS. Burmese soldiers of 1 Burma Division were deserting in increasing numbers and the civilian population was broadly hostile. To add to Slim's burden, the Japanese had aerial supremacy from

Lieutenant General (later Field Marshal) William Slim, KG, GCB, GCMG, GCVO, GBE, DSO, MC, KSTJ (1891–1970).

late March as RAF radar units were withdrawn.[20] The future looked very bleak, a fact that did not escape the civilian population, as hundreds of thousands fled ahead of the Japanese and were heading for India. The roads were choked, and civil administration broke down.

On 18 April, the USA launched what is generally called the 'Doolittle Raid', named after the commander of the sixteen B-25B Mitchell medium bombers that flew from USS carrier *Hornet* and attacked Tokyo. Militarily it was no more than a token, but politically it was of enormous importance as it demonstrated to the Japanese that they were vulnerable to US air power. Most of the aircraft crash-landed in China and the surviving crews were helped by the Chinese. One unexpected consequence was the mass execution of Chinese families as a reprisal. A second consequence was that the raid generated a great deal of extra radio traffic between ships of the Imperial Japanese Army and their base. This traffic was closely monitored, and its analysis led in turn to the breaking of the IJN code. It was a substantial intelligence breakthrough.

The impact of the Doolittle Raid was to spur on General Iida Shōjirō, who was commanding 15th Army, 35,000 strong. His aim was to cut the Burma Road and by so doing halt the resupply of Chiang Kai-shek's Nationalist Army. The speed of his advance had given encouragement to the Indian independence movement, led by Gandhi, who said that Britain's presence on the sub-continent was 'an invitation to Japan'.[21] The threat to the Burma Road caused consternation in Chiang's headquarters. However, he resisted the recently arrived Stilwell's insistence that he be given command of the only possible salvation for Burma – the Chinese Expeditionary Force, which consisted of the 5th, 6th and 66th armies. In manpower terms this force equated to a strong British corps of three divisions, although it was deficient in equipment.

Stillwell had been given responsibility for the Lend-Lease supplies being channelled to the Chinese Nationalist forces and to his credit he was single-minded in protecting American interests at all costs. He fought the ingrained corruption in the Nationalist Army, but later involved himself in political issues beyond his remit. This included Chinese political sectarianism and later, in November 1943, proposals to incorporate Chinese and US forces in the 11th Army Group under British command.

BURCORPS established a defence line at Prome, on the lower Irrawaddy, about 150 miles (241km) north of Rangoon. From here Slim could deny access to the oilfields. Stilwell agreed to deploy his 5th Army to set up a parallel defence line from Toungoo (not shown on map) on the Sittang River, west across Burma from the Salween River. It all made sense but, in practice, the Chinese generals found every reason not to commit their forces. They pleaded transport difficulties and the activity of the Japanese Air Force. Stilwell was appalled and angered, and noted in his diary: 'The pusillanimous bastards, I can't shoot them, I can't relieve them and just talking to them does no good.'[22] The upshot was that the Japanese drove through the middle of the line and the effective defence of Burma was at an end. The oilfields were put to the torch, and Slim led his defeated corps north and to the sanctuary of India.

Stilwell had intended to bring 100,000 Chinese soldiers to the defence of India but his decision to speed the evacuation by train was frustrated when 'General Lo Choying commandeered an engine at gunpoint to make his own escape. It crashed into an incoming train blocking the single track.'[23] Stilwell's personal journey into India was an epic that merits admiration. At age 60, the general led his own command party, 114 strong, to cross the Chindwin River and for five days they marched along elephant trails, with little to eat. They rafted part way down the Chindwin and then completed a 50-mile (80km) trek through jungle-clad mountains into India. Only 10,000 of Stilwell's original 100,000 reached India.

In the five-and-a-half-month campaign in Burma that led to a 1,000-mile (1,600km) retreat, the British suffered 10,036 casualties, of which 3,670 were killed. The Burmese Army lost a further 3,400 men killed and wounded. Slim and his depleted corps took up positions around Imphal and Kohima in India. The conquest of Burma cost 2,000 Japanese lives but, ere long, it was to cost them twenty times that number to try to hold it.

*   *   *

A perusal of the map will reveal that the new, much expanded Japanese Empire covered vast areas of sea, since its comprehensive success at the Battle of the Java Sea in late February. It further strengthened its hand by expelling the RN from the Indian Ocean in the Battle of Ceylon (31 March–10 April). The Japanese fleet contained five carriers: *Akagi*, *Shōkaku*, *Zuikaku*, *Sōryū* and *Hiryū*. In company were four Kongō-class battleships and two cruisers. Admiral Sir James Somerville, commanding the Far East Fleet, completely underestimated the capability of the IJN air arm, and it cost him dearly.

At the modest cost of twenty aircraft, the Japanese sank HMS *Dorsetshire*, *Cornwall*, *Hermes* and twenty-three merchant ships (totalling 112,312 tons).[24] The carrier-borne aircraft of Admiral Nagumo were led by Captain Fuchida Mitsuo, who had also led at Pearl Harbor. The airstrike was not limited to Admiral Somerville's fleet; it also directed its attention to the port of Colombo. This was not a surprise as preparations for an anticipated attack had been made for several weeks beforehand. Allied reconnaissance aircraft had discovered the proximity of the Japanese fleet on the previous afternoon, 4 April, and had tracked it during the night. On that basis the defences were fully alerted, and radar kept updating the situation. Inexplicably and unforgivably, the defending fighters were still on the ground when the Japanese aircraft arrived, and they were not scrambled until the pilots themselves saw the attackers overhead.

Ninety-one bombers and thirty-six fighters wreaked havoc. The armed merchant cruiser HMS *Hector* and the destroyer *Tenedos* were sunk, as was the Norwegian tanker *Soli*. The most damaging result of the raid was the destruction of British aircraft. Twenty of the forty-one British fighters that managed to get airborne were shot down, as were six Swordfish of 788 Naval Air

Squadron.[25] The incompetence exhibited in Colombo that day was on a par with that of four months earlier at Pearl Harbor.

Ceylon was an important British base in the Far East, and it remained in British hands throughout the war. The RAF base (RAF China Bay) was the site of fuel storage and support facilities for the British Eastern Fleet, as well as the submarines of the Dutch Navy. Trincomalee was the base for all RN operations in the Far East during 1944–5.

However, in April 1942 the IJN had command on the Indian and Pacific oceans and the South China Sea. The IJA held swathes of conquered territory. It had imposed its brand of martial law over millions of Asiatic people and installed its own brand of administration, which included comfort stations, throughout its territory. Japan was master of all it surveyed, and its empire was at its zenith. Churchill described the situation as 'a cataract of disaster'.[26]

From this time on, the war waged by Japan would be a war of logistics and from a position of great vulnerability it was taking on the logistically best equipped country on earth. In every war, without exception, it is logistic support that is the single most crucial issue. The quality of the commanders, numerical strength, climate and terrain are all incidental. Without food, fuel, ammunition, medical supplies and transport in all its many forms, no military formation can survive. Food was not the least item in the vital Japanese logistic inventory and, in this theatre, for the indigenous population and their conquerors, rice was king. This is a matter to be addressed on page 178.

Japan's conquests were very widely spread and, only to some limited extent, were self-sufficient. However, captured oil and its distribution to the home islands was needed to fuel the politico/military complex and that movement was about to be challenged.

On 24 March 1942, the US/British combined chiefs of staff agreed that operations in the Pacific area were to be the responsibility of the USA. It was on that basis that the theatre was divided into the 'Pacific Ocean Area', commanded by Admiral Chester Nimitz. The 'Southwest Pacific Area' was to be commanded by General MacArthur (still isolated in Australia) and the 'Southeast Pacific Area' was the responsibility of Rear Admiral Abel T. Bidwell, USN. Nimitz was one of the outstanding commanders to emerge from the Second World War. He shared with General Slim many of the same characteristics and was the antithesis of the self-serving egotistical MacArthur. It was Nimitz who had operational control over all Allied units, air land and sea.

The first sign of the ebbing of the tide of Japanese expansion was on 7 May 1942 in the first of a series of epic sea battles. The United States Navy was outmatched by the Imperial Japanese Navy at this point, but its capacity to read IJN signals in the JN25B fleet code gave Admiral Nimitz a massive strategic advantage. An early example was that the reading of signals showed that a Japanese ship had re-fuelled the seaplanes that had parti-cipated in the Pearl Harbor attack, in an area around the French Frigate Shoals, located between Hawaii and Midway Island. The USN mined the location. This provided an unwel-come surprise to any IJN ships visit-ing in future. However, there were much bigger fish to fry in the Coral Sea, which separated Queensland in the north-east of Australia from the Solomon Islands and New Guinea.[27]

In early May 1942, it was the inten-tion of the Japanese to take and hold New Guinea and the small island of Tulagi, the capital of the British Solomon Islands Protectorate. It was less than 25 miles (40km) from Guadalcanal. The only non-British islands in the group were Bougain-ville and Buka.

Fleet Admiral Chester W. Nimitz (1885–1966).

The object, for the Japanese, was to enhance their overall defensive posi-tion, and to this end, Tulagi was thought to be suitable for use as a seaplane base. The island was bombed, was clearly indefensible and the Resident Com-missioner, William Marchant, sagely ordered the evacuation of the British/ Australian residents to Australia.

On 3 May, a powerful fleet of the IJN consisting of one light carrier, one seaplane carrier, nine cruisers and thirteen destroyers covered an invasion force aimed at both Port Moresby in New Guinea and Tulagi. Tulagi was occupied without difficulty. However, unbeknown to the IJN, the USN was able to read its signals and plot the movement of its ships. Reconnaissance aircraft from a combined American-Australian Task Force 17, commanded by Admiral Jack Fletcher, confirmed the presence of Japanese forces on Tulagi and ninety-nine aircraft from the USS *Yorktown* attacked on 4 May and sank several vessels.

The consequence was that Vice Admiral Takagi Takeo, the victor of the Battle of the Java Sea, was alerted to the presence of carrier-borne US aircraft. This air attack was the prelude to the Battle of the Coral Sea, fought on

4–8 May. The battle made military history in that it was the first sea battle in which the adversaries did not have sight of and did not fire directly upon each other. The battle was between carrier-borne aircraft. The result was numerically slightly in favour of the USN, which sank a light carrier, a destroyer and three minesweepers. Damage was inflicted on a fleet carrier and three smaller ships. The IJN lost seventy-seven aircraft and had 1,074 killed.[28] On the other side of the balance sheet the USN suffered the loss of one of its four carriers, USS *Lexington*, and severe damage to another, USS *Yorktown*. Two small ships were also sunk, 543 men were killed, and sixty-six aircraft lost.[29]

Strategically this was a first and very welcome Allied success. Admiral Inoue Shigeyoshi realised that he no longer had the air cover he needed to invade Port Moresby and so he withdrew. This eventually cost him his command and in October he was replaced and moved to command the Naval Academy.

The Battle of the Coral Sea did not mark the turning of the military tide, but it did mark the beginning of the logistic supremacy of the USA. After the Battle of the Coral Sea, the USA was deficient in aircraft carriers. Three years

USS *Lexington* in sinking condition on 8 May 1942. It is presumed that a bomb initiated a catastrophic explosion of stored torpedo warheads. USS *Yorktown* is on the horizon, left centre. (*USN Photograph*)

later, by mid-1945, it had built and manned 105 carriers. In the same period, the RN had commissioned eighty-seven and, tellingly, the IJN only twenty-four. The writing was on the mess deck bulkhead. It said the age of the aircraft carrier had dawned back in November 1940, when the RN carrier HMS *Illustrious* had attacked the Italian fleet at Taranto and incapacitated three Italian battleships for the loss of only two aircraft. The Japanese noted this action at the time, and it was the model for Pearl Harbor a year later. However, the Japanese Empire was about to be paid back in its own coin.

By way of clarification, not all the aircraft carriers after 1941 were purpose-built. In the case of the two Allied navies, a significant number were converted merchantmen, with a bolted-on flight deck but able to launch and recover aircraft.

Any success in the Coral Sea was in part offset by the news of the surrender at Bataan. Nimitz perceived the Solomons to be a two-way street and, just as the enemy could leapfrog up the chain, so too could the Allies in the opposite direction. He intended to establish USN bases on Efate (previously Sandwich Island) and Nouméa, a French territory. From the secure bases in the Pacific, Nimitz planned to attack Japan's southern perimeter.

An overriding priority for Nimitz was the security of the signal intelligence material being obtained on Japanese operations, now in an increasing volume. That, and the safeguarding of USN carriers. USS *Wasp* and *Ranger* were in the Atlantic, *Yorktown* was being refitted, *Lexington* was with Task Force 17, and *Saratoga* was in reserve until the Essex class of carriers were completed in 1943.

For Britain, the war was going very badly on all fronts. Singapore, Hong Kong, Malaya, Burma and Borneo were all lost. In Europe, there was no British presence, and in North Africa, the defence of the Suez Canal was problematic. British generalship was lacklustre and only the rising star of

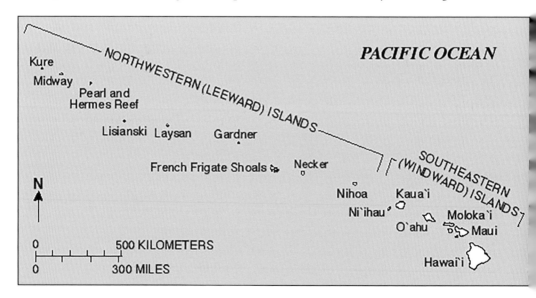

young Lieutenant General 'Strafer' Gott provided the least hope of containing the brilliant Erwin Rommel.

Notes

1. Thompson, J., *Forgotten Voices of Burma* (London, Ebury Press, 2010), p. 3.
2. Toland, J., *The Rising Sun: The Decline and Fall of the Japanese Empire, 1936–45* [1970] (Modern Library, New York, 2003), p. 147.
3. Randle, 2/Lt J., OC B Company, 7th/10th Baluch Regiment, Thompson, p. 14.
4. Allen, L., *Burma: The Longest War* (London, Orion Publishing, 1986), pp. 24–35.
5. Hastings, Sir M., *Nemesis: The Battle for Japan 1944–45* (2007) (London, Collins, 2016), p. 63.
6. *Burma: 1942* (US Army Centre of Military History, www. history.army.mil).
7. Bayly, C. & Harper, T., *Forgotten Armies* (London, Penguin, 2005), p. 174.
8. Ibid.
9. Allen, p. 3.
10. Hudson E.R.B., 'A Close View of the Disaster at the Sittang Bridge' (*Michigan War Studies Review*, 2018).
11. Slim, FM W., *Defeat into Victory* (Four Square Books, 1958), p. 17.
12. This is Hudson's opinion. The coroner decided that his death, in 1952, was accidental.
13. When retired from the army, Smyth adopted the title of major general. He was only ever, briefly, an acting major general but, perhaps in recognition of his VC, he was not challenged. He became an MP (1956–66), a Privy Counsellor (1962), a baronet (1966), and was chairman (1957–71) and then president of the VC & GC Association (1966–83). He died in 1983, aged 89.
14. Slim, p.18.
15. Lyman, R., *Slim, Master of War* (London, Constable & Robinson, 2004), p. 15.
16. Ibid.
17. Thompson, pp. 24–5.
18. Newell, C.R., 'Burma 1942' (Washington, US Army Centre of Military History, 1995), p. 16.
19. Lyman, p. 16.
20. Bayly & Harper, p. 174.
21. Churchill, W.S., Vol. IV, p. 191.
22. Tuchman, B., *Stilwell and the American Experience in China 1911–1945* (New York, Macmillan, 1971), p. 355.
23. Costello, J., *The Pacific War 1941–45* [1981] (New York, Harper Collins, 2009), p. 243.
24. Boyd, A., *The Royal Navy in Eastern Waters* (Seaforth Publishing, 2017), p. 384.
25. Stuart, R., 'Air raid, Colombo 5 April 1942: The fully expected surprise attack' (*Royal Canadian Air Force Journal*, 2014).
26. Churchill, Vol. IV, p. 125.
27. Costello, p. 248.
28. Ibid., p. 263.
29. Gillison, D., *Coral Sea and Midway* (RAAF 1939–42, Chapter 26, Australian War Memorial, 1962).

Chapter Twelve

June–July 1942
The Ebb of the Tide – The Battle of Midway

The Battle of the Coral Sea had shaken the Japanese and although it was celebrated as a great victory in Tokyo, the reality was that it had been, marginally, a strategic defeat. In Tokyo and Washington, it was recognised that the outcome of the Pacific War would depend on naval capability and specifically the use of naval air power. In May 1942, it was Japan that had the upper hand.

This was the high-water mark of the Japanese Empire. It had control over millions of people, and vast expanses of territory and ocean. This vast empire had to be serviced and the early victories did generate logistic pressures. However, Japan moved quickly to exploit its territorial advantage and the United States Navy noted that intercepted signals made frequent reference to an objective termed 'AF'.

This appellation was tentatively thought, by some, to refer to Midway Island, a small, bleak atoll about halfway between North America and Asia. It was not part of the US State of Hawaii, although it is close to the Hawaiian archipelago. Its value in 1942 was that it was the home of a US naval air station centred on an airstrip.

On 18 May, Admiral King, recognising his parlous carrier assets, signalled London and asked: 'Will Admiralty entertain request for carrier from Eastern fleets to join up with [Admiral H.F.] Leary temporarily, if so, the move must be made at once.'[1] King would have been very loath to ask for British help, but it was an indicator of the seriousness of his problem. The Admiralty declined to help. In retrospect it seems to have been a churlish response, particularly as King had sent a carrier to assist in the battle of the Atlantic. Later, when Churchill was made aware of the degree to which the decision had fuelled King's raging Anglophobia, he regretted the decision.

Admiral Ernest King was a disagreeable man. He was respected but not admired by his officers. He was described as 'perhaps the most disliked Allied leader of World War II'.[2] General Dwight Eisenhower complained to his private diary that Admiral King 'is an arbitrary, stubborn type, with not too

**Fleet Admiral Ernest King
(1878–1956).**

much brain and a tendency toward bullying his juniors'.[3] One of his daughters alleged that 'he is the most even-tempered person in the United States Navy. He is always in a rage.' This was a man thought by the British to be an ally but, in fact, he was only barely neutral.

Nimitz had all the admirable characteristics that King lacked, and he had to manage his superior with skill, especially when it came to deploying naval assets. Nimitz was able to convince King that Japan was massing its forces for further action in the Central Pacific Area and got him to agree to the redeployment of his forces to thwart any Japanese attack on Port Moresby. Notwithstanding his acquiescence to Nimitz's plan, King insisted on extreme caution and ordered that there be 'no decisive action that would be likely to incur heavy losses in carriers and cruisers'.[4] Nimitz was sufficiently able that he did not need such a patronising order.

The objective of the gathering Imperial Japanese Navy force was not known, but Nimitz was one of those who believed it to be Midway. On 20 May, he flew to the island to review its defences. As a result of that visit, and with alacrity, the garrison was strengthened to 2,000 men, every aircraft available was sent to the island, three submarine patrol arcs were established, and additional anti-aircraft batteries were installed. However, there was still an urgent need to identify Japanese intentions towards the anonymous 'AF'.

A member of Nimitz's staff, Lieutenant Commander Wilfred Holmes, hit upon a simple ruse and he caused an uncoded radio message to be sent from Midway saying that the garrison was experiencing a water shortage as its desalination plant had broken down. Two days later, a Japanese signal was intercepted saying, 'AF is short of water.' This confirmed the objective and gave the USN an advantage. It is a matter of surprise that the Japanese radio operators who intercepted the message did not appreciate the significance that the Americans were broadcasting, in clear speech, the important information that a major naval installation, of interest to the IJN, was having a

Midway Atoll, Eastern Island, in 1942 the site of Midway's airfield, is in the foreground. Sand Island, the location of most facilities, is in the background.
(*USN photograph, 1941*)

water shortage. No one showed any suspicion that there was any deception intended.[5]

The Main Force of the IJN was commanded by Admiral Yamamoto. It consisted of eleven battleships, eight carriers, twenty-three cruisers, sixty-five destroyers and about ninety auxiliary ships. This was, at the time, the largest maritime operation in history. 'More oil would be used in this single operation than the peacetime IJN consumed in a year.'[6]

Yamamoto had organised his fleet into several components. The first of these was dedicated to Operation AL, which was to be a diversionary attack and invasion of the Aleutian Islands. It was commanded by Vice Admiral Hosogaya Boshirō, who had a force of two non-fleet carriers, five cruisers, twelve destroyers, six submarines, and four troop transports, along with supporting auxiliary ships. Hosogaya was charged to take the island of Adak after an air attack on Dutch Harbor. However, the Japanese did not know the island was undefended. The result was to be something of a military anti-climax.

The remaining components were all directed at Midway in Operation MI and they left home waters separately. The First Carrier Strike Force commanded by Admiral Nagumo led the way. Vice Admiral Kondō Nobutake was in command of the Second Fleet, the Midway Invasion Force, with two battleships, one carrier, four cruisers and eight destroyers. The Occupation Force of 5,000 men was embarked in twelve transports, with all the logistic support required for the invasion of Midway. The IJN had decided to stow additional water for its Occupation Force based on the earlier subterfuge. The Occupation Force was well protected by four cruisers, two destroyers and a host of smaller vessels such as minesweepers and patrol boats. Ten submarines formed the Advance Fleet, commanded by Vice Admiral Komatsu Teruhisa, ashore in Kwajalein.

Yamamoto's aim was to widen his country's defensive perimeter – a direct requirement consequent to the Doolittle Raid. The taking of Midway would provide an airstrip from which attacks could be launched against Fiji, Samoa and even Hawaii. To achieve this aim he had to engage an unprepared USN in a battle, fought on his terms, in the Midway area. He reasoned that the battle would be fought outside the range of US land-based aircraft.

To bait his trap, Yamamoto deployed his fleets widely to conceal them from his enemy. Accordingly, his battleships sailed hundreds of miles behind the four carriers of Admiral Nagumo. The master plan was that the battleships would join the battle only after Nagumo's aircraft had crippled the USN.[7] The capacity of the Americans to read Japanese signal traffic was a huge advantage. Nimitz was aware that the Japanese had divided their powerful fleet into four groups that were not mutually supporting and Nagumo would be unable to concentrate his force on any single objective.[8] The USN had three carriers, but also a significant bomber force stationed on Midway. Nimitz believed that, on that basis, he could match the four carriers that opposed him. In contrast, Japanese intelligence was sparse and the IJN was unaware of their enemy's strength and knew nothing of its disposition.

The American fleet under Nimitz was to operate as two separate Task Forces, commanded by Rear Admiral Raymond Spruance and Admiral Frank

Fletcher. The presence of *Yorktown* in Fletcher's order of battle was a minor miracle. She had been very badly damaged in the Coral Sea, and it was thought that it would take all of three months to repair the ship and make it fit for sea, once she was dry docked in Hawaii. Given the urgency of the situation, the commander-in-chief said flatly, 'We must have the ship back in three days.'[9] All other work stopped, and 1,400 men worked day and night on the *Yorktown*. The measure of the activity level in the dockyard was that locally, Honolulu suffered from the overload on the electricity supply and the lights went out. Incredibly, USS *Yorktown* was able to sail with Fletcher's Strike Force, albeit with work on her structure continuing unabated.

The map below shows the manoeuvres of the three fleets on 4–5 July in what was a resounding victory for the USN. The feature of the battle was the great heroism of the naval aviators on both sides. They all attacked their targets tenaciously despite ferocious and very effective anti-aircraft fire. The USN lost 150 aircraft and the IJN 248.[10] Those Japanese losses were crucial, amounting to three quarters of the IJN Carrier Strike Force. At a stroke, the cream of its IJN air arm was lost, and those skilled and experienced pilots proved impossible to replace with men of the same quality. It could be argued that this and subsequent engagements gave rise to the kamikaze philosophy.

The USN sank four fleet carriers, *Akagi*, *Kaga*, *Sōryū* and *Hiryū*, and a heavy cruiser, and killed 3,057. In comparison, American losses were slight. The carrier *Yorktown* and a destroyer, *Hammann*, were sunk, and 307 men were killed. The victory had three prime constituents. These were: first, the superb performance of the USN intelligence arm and its capacity for secrecy; second, the outstanding bravery and tenacity of USN pilots; and third, the strategic vision of Nimitz complemented by the well-judged tactics of admirals Fletcher and Spruance.

Nimitz not only had to worry about *Yorktown*, but also deal with his boss, Admiral King. King, in Washington, had decided that Fletcher had not commanded his Task Force in the Battle of the Coral Sea with enough aggression. On that premise, he wanted him to be sacked. Nimitz persuaded King that Fletcher 'had done a fine job and had exercised superior judgement'. There can be no doubt that 'Midway changed the course of the war and arrested the Japanese advance across the Pacific.'[11] It was 'the most stunning and decisive blow in the history of naval warfare'.[12] Symonds went further in describing it as 'one of the most consequential naval engagements in world history ranking alongside Salamis (480 BC), Trafalgar (1805) and Tsushima Strait (1905) as both tactically decisive and strategically influential'.[13]

The tide had turned and from this time on, the Japanese Empire was in decline. It would take three long, arduous years, the disruption of millions of

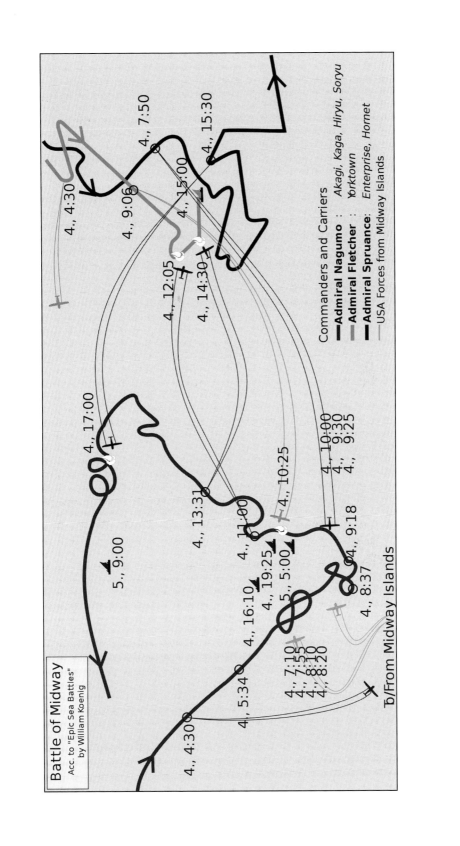

Battle of Midway
Acc. to "Epic Sea Battles"
by William Koenig

Commanders and Carriers
Admiral Nagumo :   Akagi, Kaga, Hiryu, Soryu
Admiral Fletcher :   Yorktown
Admiral Spruance: Enterprise, Hornet
USA Forces from Midway Islands

To/From Midway Islands

4., 7:50
4., 15:30
4., 4:30
4., 9:06
4., 15:00
4., 12:05
4., 14:30
4., 17:00
5., 9:00
4., 13:31
4., 11:00
4., 10:25
4., 10:00
4., 9:30
4., 9:25
4., 9:18
4., 16:10
4., 19:25
5., 5:00
4., 8:37
4., 5:34
4., 7:10
4., 7:55
4., 8:10
4., 8:20
4., 4:30

lives and the killing of hundreds of thousands before its malign presence was eliminated.

In the meantime, in mid-1942 there was one product of conquest that had to be addressed – that of prisoners of war.

Notes

1. US NGA COMINCH signal log, 18 May 1942.
2. Skates, J.R., *The Invasion of Japan: Alternative to the Bomb* (University of South Carolina Press, 2000), p. 303.
3. Wukovits, J., *Eisenhower: A Biography* (St Martin's Press, 2015), p. 66.
4. Costello, J., *The Pacific War 1941–45* [1981] (New York, Harper Collins, 2009), p. 275.
5. Baker, B.D., 'What if Japan had won The Battle of Midway?' (*The Diplomat*, 2016).
6. Toland, J., *The Rising Sun: The Decline and Fall of the Japanese Empire, 1936–45* [1970] (Modern Library, New York, 2003), p. 326.
7. Parshall, J. & Tully, A., *Shattered Sword: The Untold Story of the Battle of Midway* (Virginia, Potomac Books, 2005), pp. 51, 55.
8. Ibid, p. 409.
9. Potter, E.B., *Nimitz* (Annapolis, 1976) p. 85.
10. Parshall, p. 524.
11. Hastings, Sir M., *Nemesis: The Battle for Japan 1944–45* (2007) (London, Collins, 2016), p. 27.
12. Keegan, J., *The Second World War* (New York, Penguin, 2005), p. 275.
13. Symonds, C.L., *World War Two at Sea: A Global History* (Oxford University Press, 2018), p. 293.

Chapter Thirteen

1415–1945
Inconvenient Guests and their Treatment

In its march across Asia, Japan had taken thousands of prisoners by mid-1942. It had a responsibility to house and feed its captives. In many respects it failed to meet even the most basic standards of humanity; but the conduct of the Japanese in respect of their prisoners cannot be considered in isolation. To establish a measure of balance it would be useful to place it in its historical context and offer comparisons.

In Singapore, General Yamashita had about 130,000 prisoners on his hands. They were a security and logistic burden. Prisoners were taken from Malaya, Singapore, Burma, Wake, Guam and Hong Kong, and another 70,000 when the Philippines finally fell. The Imperial Japanese Army was not equipped psychologically or logistically for the problems that victories had brought.

The treatment of POWs is, in effect, bound only by what might be considered the norms of humanity. The Geneva Convention, first promulgated in 1864, was intended to regulate the treatment of the wounded in war. The Convention was refined in 1907 and again in 1929. Japan signed up to the 1929 Convention, in principle, but did not ratify it. The Geneva Convention is, at best, a statement of good intentions. It cannot be effectively enforced, nor can it be imposed on any belligerents. Over the last century it has been broken frequently, often by 'civilised' Western nations. In the Second World War, the Convention was very widely disregarded, and the conduct of adversaries was more a reflection of their culture than an adherence to the treaty. However, post-conflict, and when the shooting stops, the Geneva Convention provides the benchmark for the measurement of war crimes.

In any armed confrontation, the victor inflicts casualties on his opponent and the probability is that he will also take custody of enemy soldiers, some wounded. The responsibility for these, now unarmed but still hostile, men make them the *inconvenient guests* of the chapter title.

Soldiers are not homogeneous; quite the reverse. They are an infinitely varied in ethnicity, culture, education, training, moral values, political beliefs and commitment to their countries' cause. On that basis it is unrealistic to expect, or even hope, that any two countries that take up arms against each other will conduct war in accordance with some sort of rule book. It is naïve to suppose otherwise. War is not fair, there are no rules, there are no boundaries and there certainly is no referee.

In north-eastern France there is a small hamlet called Agincourt (sometimes Azincourt) and it was here, on 25 October 1415, that perhaps one of the most significant battles in British/French history was fought. The English Army, under the command of King Henry V, was in bad order. It had landed in Normandy, 12,000 strong, ten weeks earlier and taken the port of Harfleur. The hard campaigning that followed had reduced its strength to about 6,000 and Henry was now intent on reaching the safety of Calais, an English-held fortress. A French Army of between 24,000 and 36,000 blocked the route.[1] The English Army was unwashed, verminous and very tired. It was daunted by the strength of the opposition and only Henry's leadership kept it together.

King Henry V (1386–1422).

The composition of the army was unbalanced. Over 5,000 of its men were English and Welsh archers and only about 900 were armoured men-at-arms. Each of these bowmen was capable of firing ten aimed arrows a minute and the combined firepower of about 5,000 experienced bowmen was overwhelming. It was a fifteenth-century version of 'shock and awe' and, on 25 October, it was devastating and conclusive.

At what Henry thought was the end of the battle, several thousand French prisoners, having been disarmed, were assembled in the general area of the baggage train, close to the hamlet of Maisoncelles. The prisoners outnumbered their guards by about 20:1. Victory having been won, the English busied themselves adding to their bag of prisoners. Suddenly, it appeared that a fresh assault was about to be mounted on the English position and Henry recognised that the growing collection of unwounded prisoners in his rear constituted a significant threat. He gave an order that the prisoners were to be killed – executed or, to be more precise, murdered. Was that a war crime?

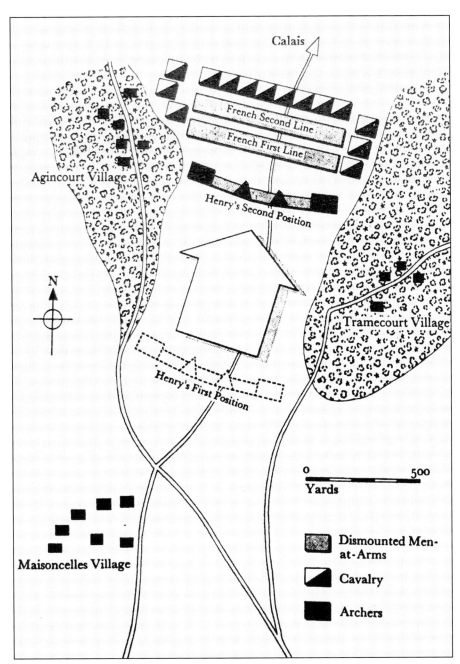

The battlefield at Agincourt (25 October, 1415). The killing of French prisoners was near the village of Maisoncelles. (*Howard*)

That order, its legality, practicality and the magnitude of the killing has been debated by historians for the last 600 years. One view was that Henry's decision 'was entirely justified, the safety of his men was his overriding priority'.[2] Another historian opined that 'a prince had the right to execute an opponent who had been captured and handed to him if he was convinced that great harm would befall himself and his people if he allowed him to go free.'[3] Despite these two endorsements, Henry's decision flew in the face of that expected of 'a Christian king who was also an experienced soldier and versed in the elaborate code of international law covering relations between prisoner and his captor'.[4] In the event, the expected French attack did not materialise and Henry at once stopped the killing.

The incident outlined above is a graphic illustration of a dilemma that has been faced by countless commanders, of all nationalities, over the ages. It begs the fundamental and oft asked question, 'Does military necessity take precedence over all moral, or legal constraints?' Whether it should or should not, there are countless examples when military necessity *was* accorded priority in the period 1942–5, and by all participants.

However, for Lieutenant General Baba Masao, tried by court-martial in Rabaul in June 1947, his 'not guilty' plea rested on his defence that the events for which he was charged were 'operationally necessary'.[5] Nevertheless, he was charged for failing 'to discharge his duty as a ... commander to control the conduct of the members of his command whereby they committed brutal atrocities and other high crimes'. He was found guilty, and duly hanged.

*   *   *

It was over 400 years after Agincourt that the Crimean War caused dreadful suffering when the soldiers of Great Britain, France and Russia fought without adequate logistic or medical support. The Battle of Solferino (1859) was much more of the same. A far-sighted Swiss, Henry Dunant, was appalled when he visited the Solferino battlefield and observed the plight of the soldiery. Three years later, Dunant wrote a book titled *A Memory of Solferino*, and it proved to be one of the most influential tracts of the nineteenth century. In his text Dunant posed several questions. He asked, quite reasonably: 'Would it not be possible, in time of

Henry Dunant.

Lieutenant General Baba Masao (1892–1947), the Japanese commander in Labuan, Borneo, on his way to sign the surrender document, 10 September 1945.
(*John Thomas Harrison*)

peace and quiet, to form relief societies for the purpose of having care given to the wounded in wartime by zealous, devoted and thoroughly qualified volunteers?'[6]

Dunant's book attracted wide attention and was instrumental in the formation of the International Red Cross, and subsequently, the drafting of the Geneva Convention in 1864. This was designed to provide a permanent relief agency for humanitarian aid in time of war and, in addition, international recognition of the completely neutral status of the Red Cross, giving it access to war zones for the purpose of giving succour where needed.

The original Convention went through a series of tortuous amendments, clarifications and additions, but it is the third Convention that is of interest here. *'Relative to the Treatment of Prisoners of War'*. This was first adopted in 1929 and revised in August 1949. In brief, that made provision for 'persons taking no active part in the hostilities including members of armed forces who have laid down their arms and those placed *hors de combat* by sickness, wounds, detention, or any other cause'. It went on to specify what the captor should not do to any captive.

Any regulation or law, to be effective, must have the means to enforce it. Without enforcement, the law, or in this case Convention, is no more than well-meaning words and, for practical purposes, quite useless. Every nation that has taken prisoners of war since 1864 has disregarded the Convention and this book identifies many examples.

*   *   *

The moment of capture is the most hazardous in any captive's life. As he raises his hands, he is confronted by a captor who is excited, triumphant and affected by a surfeit of adrenaline. To add to the mix there is the probability that the captor has no incentive to take a prisoner – indeed, he may have been told explicitly not to take a prisoner. It is in the first five or ten minutes after an engagement that the victor, on a martial high, suspends rational behaviour and is liable to exact summary vengeance on anyone who has been resisting him, and who may have killed some of his comrades.

The killing of prisoners immediately after an action is commonplace. The cards are stacked against the captive, who is dejected, despairing and very apprehensive. In short, he is frightened. Fear can be communicated and the captor's attitude is influenced by the knowledge that he has complete mastery over his opponent. Given that the victor has the initiative, the captive has somehow to prevent him from being violent. He must make clear that he is no longer a threat and to this end must discard his helmet and arms. He must open his arms and, by his body language, exude empathy for his foe. There is a need to encourage the victor to view him in human terms and, like him, just a family man – the swift display of a photograph of a wife and children and perhaps the brandishing of a crucifix (not recommended if the captor is a Muslim or Jap).

Time is short and the offer of the contents of his pockets is no more than a supplicatory gesture. An offer to shake hands may be rejected but, in these very stressing few minutes, it is worth trying anything. Single captives are usually more vulnerable than larger groups and especially so if the prisoner is a sniper. If the sniper's position is overrun, his life expectancy is very low indeed, and his only chance of survival is to rid himself of any weapon or equipment that would reveal his employment. Killing, at the moment of surrender, can be initiated by ignorance.

Although fictitious, a sequence in the film *Saving Private Ryan* illustrates the point. Two soldiers emerge from a bunker, repeating, 'Please don't shoot me! I am not German, I am Czech. I didn't kill anyone! I am Czech!' Except they weren't speaking German, they were speaking Czech. The Americans, who did not understand, shot both dead. It makes for compelling, uncomfortable cinema.

Vietnam, *c.*1948. This man, perhaps Vietminh, encapsulates the apprehension at the point of capture. How the French soldiers responded is unknown.

It is suggested that all soldiers are liable to commit out and out barbarity, and spontaneous acts, in hot blood, are at one end of the scale and cold-blooded murder is at the other. There remains the gap between the two.

If the prisoner survives those critical first few minutes, he must then make the hazardous journey back to the enemy rear area and the relative safety of a holding pen. Prisoners are invariably marched off, under escort. The hope is that the escort will not take advantage of the situation and shoot prisoners 'whilst attempting to escape' – a frequently reported incident and rarely the subject of any investigation. The issue of escaping and the treatment of escapees was addressed by Article 42 of the third Geneva Convention, which optimistically again laid down a reasonable protocol; one readily and frequently ignored.

*   *   *

Prisoners of war have been confined in all manner of conditions and under varied situations. There is no consistent pattern of treatment; nevertheless, the most recurrent theme is one of starvation and, in places, this was deliberately imposed, such as by the Turks in 1916–18 and the Japanese, German and Russians during the Second World War. However, often the captors were themselves starving.

After Sédan fell to the Prussians in 1870, 104,000 French prisoners and 6,000 horses were marched just about 2 miles (3.2km) to a loop in the Meuse River, where it forms the peninsula of Iges. The canal of Villette, in effect, turned the peninsula into an island. This bleak, empty tract – about 988 acres (400 hectares), was ideal for cattle and sheep, but not for men. It had no facilities whatsoever. The French were dumped here in unpleasant weather, without shelter, food or medical support. Little wonder that this spot became known as *camp de misère* (camp of misery). It was no more than a reflection of the inadequacy of the captors.

The Prussians were not malicious, but they were overwhelmed by the vast host of *inconvenient guests*. They did not have the logistic capacity to feed another army and, predictably, they gave their own men priority. Frenchmen started to die of exposure, malnutrition and all the diseases that occur when large groups are confined together. The need to dig latrines, hundreds of them, was a priority, but shovels, picks and barrows were needed. Tentage, clothing, cooking equipment . . . the list was a quartermaster's nightmare. The battlefield, just a mile away, was full of the suppurating corpses of men and horses, a breeding ground for disease.

The dreadful situation at Iges was exacerbated when Marshal Bazaine surrendered his Army of the Rhine and the Fortress of Metz six weeks later,

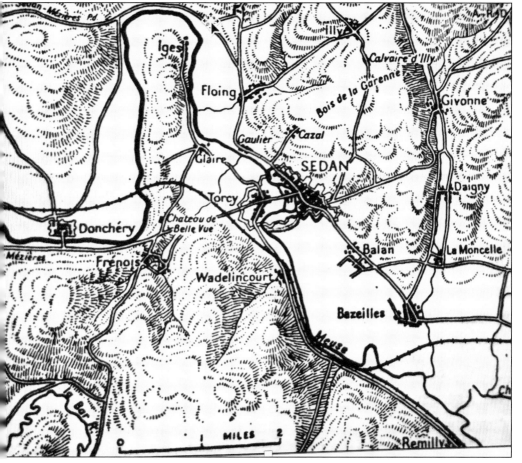

The peninsula of Iges and the site of a Prussian POW camp after the Battle of Sédan.
(*Howard*)

on 27 October. The Prussians' victory was sweet but offset by the need to cope with a further 167,000 soldiers and 6,000 officers, all of whom were on the edge of starvation. The 20,000 French sick and wounded left behind in the fortress of Metz were an added and unwelcome burden.

The Prussians were relatively benign captors but, at the other end of the scale, the same could not be said about the Japanese. The Sino-Japanese War (1931–45) was notable for the ferocious brutality of the invading Japanese. Their treatment of all prisoners, combatant and non-combatant, was unremittingly criminal – at least it was by Western standards. Japanese soldiers habitually beheaded prisoners and individuals competed to inflict the most deaths. In turn they suffered about 2,500,000 military casualties between 1937 and 1945. The Chinese casualties in that same period were of the order of 3,237,000.[7]

The nature of this war was such that accounts of Japanese or Chinese prisoner of war camps are difficult to find but what is clear is that the culture of the captor is the single key factor in POW management. In the Far East and the Pacific, the well-deserved reputation for extreme brutality had preceded the Japanese.

In Singapore, the British forces performed badly; they outnumbered the enemy by 3:1 yet were soundly beaten in February 1942. Some 80,000 men were taken prisoner and they were joined by 50,000 other Indian, Australian and British troops captured earlier, as the Japanese swept south through Malaya. This capitulation by the British earned them the unbridled contempt of the Japanese, in whose culture surrender is a disgrace.

The civilian prison at Changi, built for 600 inmates, was used by the Japanese to house about 3,000 civilians. Fifty thousand military prisoners were held in Selarang Barracks close by, where about 850 died. Conditions for the POWs in both places were appalling and their captors did nothing to ameliorate the situation. Eventually, from 14 May 1942, the surviving military prisoners from Singapore were moved to Burma and Thailand and, from there, they went to work, as slave labour, on the notorious Burma Railway. In modern military history there is probably no more egregious example of the misuse and abuse of POWs than those in Japanese hands. The use of POWs as a labour force is permitted in some restricted circumstances. One unacceptable use of POW labour is in direct support of a military aim. The Burma Railway had a quite clear military purpose.

It was 258 miles (415km) long and ran from Ban Pong in Thailand to Thanbyuzayat in Burma. The aim was to connect to the existing line between Bangkok and Rangoon. Much of the line has now fallen into disrepair but at the Thai end it is still in use. Thanbyuzayat was the site of a POW camp for those working on the railway and today a military cemetery holds the bodies of 3,000 of the Australian and British soldiers killed in the construction. When this line was completed, the workforce was moved on to build the Kra Isthmus and the Sumatra railways – under equally awful conditions. Nevertheless, an estimated 61,000 Allied POWs were put to work on this project, of whom 16,000 died.[8] This number, however, pales when compared to the 250,000 or more Asian civilians forced to toil under Japanese direction. The forced labour of Burmese civilians was a factor in the changing attitude of the Burmese towards their 'liberators' – in contrast, perhaps the British were not too bad!

No reference is made in this chapter to Japanese prisoners and that is because, by May 1942, there were less than 100, probably less than fifty Japs in Allied hands. Right up to 1944, only 1,990 Japanese prisoners had been taken.

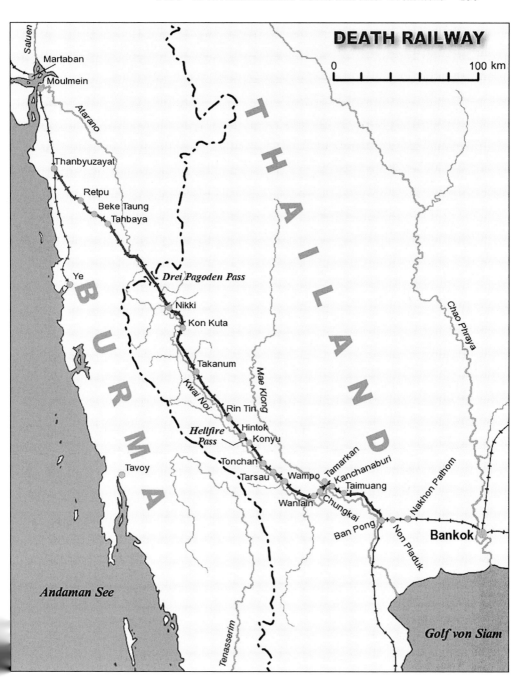

Notes

1. Barker, B., *Agincourt* [2005] (London, Abacus, 2007), p. ix.
2. Ibid., p. 303.
3. de Pizan, C., *The Writings of Christine de Pizan*, selected and ed. by Charity Willard (New York, Persea Books, 1994). Quoted by Barker.
4. Keegan, J., *The Face of Battle* [1976] (London, Jonathan Cape, 1995), p. 109.
5. Russell, Lord of Liverpool, *The Knights of Bushido* (London, Cassell, 1958), p. 320.
6. Dunant, H., *Un Souvenir de Solférino* (Genève, Imprimerie Jules-Guillaume Fick, 1862).
7. Clodfelter, M., *Warfare and Armed Conflicts: A Statistical Reference* (McFarland & Co, 1992), Vol. 2, p. 956.
8. Coast, J., Noszlopy, L. & Nash, J., *Railroad of Death: The Original, Classic Account of the River Kwai Railway* (Newcastle, Myrmidon, 2014).

Chapter Fourteen

August 1942–February 1943
The Kokoda Trail, Guadalcanal,
the Battle of Savo Island and
the Battle of the Bismarck Sea

The considerable reverse suffered at Midway in July 1942 did not curb Japanese ambitions. Despite its continuing, deep, bloody, 1 million-men involvement in China, and in the face of military reason, it pressed on with its plans to take Port Moresby in New Guinea.

Lieutenant General Hyakutake Harukichi was appointed to command the Imperial Japanese Army's 17th Division at Rabaul and given orders to accomplish in Papua that which Admiral Inouye had failed to do. Naval support would be limited, with the commensurate logistic implications. Hyakutake deputed command of the invasion force to Major General Horii Tomitarō, who decided to land and establish beachheads at Gona and Buna. From there he would march, by way of the Kokoda Trail, across the formidable Owen Stanley mountain range and capture Port Moresby. Air cover would be provided by Admiral Mikawa's 11th Air Fleet, based in Rabaul.

That was the plan.

The Allies, aware of the importance of the Papuan Peninsula and its vulnerability, had plans to reinforce the area and construct an airstrip at Buna, which lay on the coast at the end of the 100-mile (161km) Kokoda Trail. MacArthur was in the process of planning Operation PROVIDENCE, in which some 3,000 Australian troops would be sent to support the local militia. In the meantime, on 10 July, a six-man team was inserted to survey the ground around Buna.

The Japanese beat the Allies to the punch and, on 21 July 1942, landed 13,000 men at Gona and Buna. However, they were operating under a serious misapprehension, having been assured, by their intelligence sources, that there was a trafficable road from Buna to Port Moresby. It came as an unwelcome shock to discover that the trail giving access to their objective was a narrow, very steep, rutted track that ran through rainforest and across a mountain range.

Progress along this track would be fought for yard-by-yard. Initially, the only opposition was one company (100 men) of the Australian 29th Infantry Battalion and a few hundred men of the lightly armed Papuan militia. However, the defenders had one very effective asset and that was the Owen Stanley Range. The Kokoda Trail wound its way over, arguably, the most hostile environment on earth. The Trail found its way up 10,000-foot mountains, and across cavernous ravines and raging rivers. The jungle was thick, matted, and infested with ticks and mosquitoes. It was very hot and humid, and torrential rain fell every day. Swarms of trillions of flies, ever-present, added to the torment. It was a deeply unpleasant place to be. On that basis the defenders could not believe that the Japanese would, from choice, seek to fight in these conditions. However, to the considerable credit of General Horii Tomitarō and his soldiers, they cut their way by hand through the thickest jungle and up the most precipitous of mountainsides.

The fighting was savage, often at close quarters and when the weapon of choice was the machete. The Japanese frequently bypassed Australian positions by abandoning the trail and cutting through the jungle, thought to be impenetrable – much as they had done in Malay. These were very tough, resourceful and courageous soldiers. Men on both sides recorded the wretchedness of this campaign,

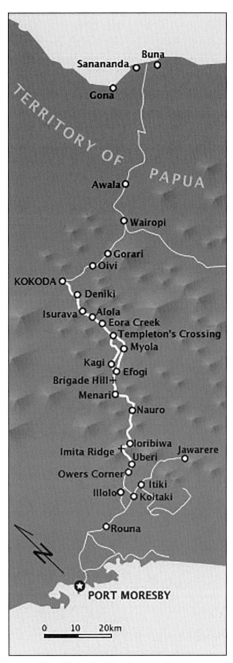

The Kokoda Trail, an arduous 100 miles (161km). (*Chris Rees*)

but it was only a sideshow in the greater panoply of the Second World War. By mid-August, and despite determined Australian delaying tactics, the Japanese had reached beyond the halfway mark and were at 'The Gap', the steepest part of the trail. 'The thin air and blazing sun increased the misery of the ordeal.'[1]

Concurrently with operations in Papua, a much bigger operation in the British Solomon Islands Protectorate, specifically Guadalcanal, started on 7 August. This was not just a battle. It was to be a six-month-long land, sea and air campaign, conducted at great cost to both sides in men, materiel and treasure.

In Papua, the 7th Australian Division had arrived and by now a new command chain had been established. A key appointment was that of General George Kenney, who assumed command of the Allied Air Forces in the Southwest Pacific Area. Kenney developed innovative command structures, weapons, and tactics that reflected his preference for what he termed 'attack

Australians of the 3rd Battalion AIF on the trail. This is not flat terrain – note the mule front centre. (*Australian Army*)

aviation'. He interdicted the Japanese as they toiled over the mountains. The further the Japanese advanced, the more elongated became their logistic chain and the less effective the cutting edge of their operations. By now the Allies held a numerical advantage. Casualties were mounting and the removal of sick and wounded was a problem for both sides. For the Japanese, the evacuation of wounded was a particular burden. Nevertheless, by 16 September, advance units of Horii's force had reached Ioribaiwa, from which heights Port Moresby could be seen in the distance below.[2] Horii was obliged to halt here as his resupply system faltered and then failed. The porters struggling to bring forward ammunition and food were faced with an increasingly lengthy round trip upon which they consumed a high proportion of the food they were carrying.

General Hori had anticipated a swift advance in which enemy food stocks would be captured. His optimism was misplaced as increasingly, and then most urgently, Japanese operations were entirely aimed at obtaining food – any food. The Australians were aware of the Japanese plight and observed them fighting among themselves: 'In the scramble for punctured tins and mud-stained rice, the warrior spirit evaporated, and the Australian rearguard went unmolested.'[3] The Australians made it a practice to leave damaged or contaminated food behind and their enemy suffered from the consequent gastric complaints.

On 23 September, Horii was ordered to withdraw as Japan was now fighting a major engagement on Guadalcanal and was unable to support both forces. Withdrawal is one of the most difficult phases of war and a clean separation, although desired, is often not achieved. In this case the Japanese had to fight a rearguard action all the way back down the trail and, initially, they did it as well as starving soldiers might.[4] However, at the battle at Oivi-Gorari, on 4–11 November, Horii's men were routed and discipline collapsed. This breakdown in good order was accompanied by amoebic dysentery and a powerful strain of malaria, which devastated the undernourished soldiers. It caused the death of many as they sat in their foxholes. In the Buna area, further retreat was inhibited by the flooded Kumusi River. Horii decided to raft down the river with a few of his personal staff. Later he took to a canoe but was swept out to sea and drowned.[5]

The campaign along the Kokoda Trail, although involving relatively small forces, was disproportionately important because it was the first time that the Japanese had suffered a defeat on land. They lost 2,050 killed and about 4,500 incapacitated by sickness and wounds. The Australians and Papuans had 625 killed, 1,055 wounded and over 4,000 sick.[6] They had demonstrated that, good though the Japanese soldiers were, they were not supermen and could be beaten. Allied morale rose as a result.

However, Buna and Gona held out and were to prove a tough nut to crack. Allied casualties were rising. MacArthur was impatient and, on 22 November 1942, he ordered Major General Edwin Harding, commanding 32 Infantry Division, to take Buna 'regardless of cost'. This division was ill-equipped, poorly trained and struggling against the determined and skilful Japanese. Nevertheless, Harding eventually penetrated Buna on 30 November 1942, at great cost.

Meanwhile, an increasingly frustrated MacArthur sent for Lieutenant General Robert Eichelberger, and told him:

> I'm putting you in command at Buna. Relieve Harding ... I want you to remove all officers who won't fight. Relieve regimental and battalion commanders; if necessary, put sergeants in charge of battalions and corporals in charge of companies ... Bob, I want you to take Buna, or not come back alive ... And that goes for your chief of staff, too.[7]

The new commander found that his men were unfed and ill-disciplined. The battle was far from won and the condition and morale of 32 Division did not auger well. Eichelberger took very positive action. He suspended operations for two days and having re-established a chain of command, on 5 December, 32 Division tried again but with scant results and further casualties. Around 10 miles (16km) further north, the Australians were encountering similarly obdurate opposition and on both fronts the conditions were as difficult and unpleasant as anywhere on the globe. One Australian described the fighting in the swamps outside Gona as:

> the wildest, maddest, bloodiest fighting I have ever seen, grenades were bursting among the Japs as we stabbed them with our bayonets from the parapets. Some of our fellows were rolling on the swamp with Japs locked against them in wrestling grips. It was all over within a few minutes. Some Japs had escaped but the bodies of thirty were tangled among their captured guns.[8]

The fighting in New Guinea, Papua and the Dutch East Indies continued into 1945. It was a particularly bloody campaign fought in a very unpleasant part of the world. The battle for Gona and Buna was but just a part of a much wider campaign. Japanese resistance on this enormous, jungle-clad island was resolute. On 28 February 1943, the Japanese determined to reinforce its garrison at Lae, by now the capital of New Guinea.

Despatched, from Rabaul, were 6,900 troops in a convoy of eight transports sailing under the protection of eight destroyers. The IJA code having been broken, the movements of the convoy were known to the 5th US Air Force and it mustered an overwhelming force of 160 aircraft to fight what came to be known as the Battle of the Bismarck Sea, fought in the first week of March 1943.

The US won a complete victory and lost only six aircraft and thirteen men. For the Japanese, the engagement was a disaster. They lost all eight of their transports, four of their destroyers and 2,890 men.[9] About 2,700 survivors were taken to Rabaul by Japanese rescue destroyers. However, on 4–5 March, about 1,000 or so survivors were still at sea either swimming for their lives or on rafts. 'American PT boats and planes strafed those in the sea and attacked Japanese rescue vessels.'[10] Admiral Samuel Morison, USN, wrote in defence of this action: 'It was a grisly task but a military necessity since Japanese soldiers do not surrender and those within swimming of distance of the shore could not be allowed to land and join the garrison.'

This incident has a parallel with Henry V's dilemma at Agincourt in 1415 (see page 146) but the validity of the 'military necessity' was not tested in this case – unlike that of Lieutenant General Baba Masao (see page 146).

The campaign in Papua and New Guinea was described by the historian John Laffin as 'arguably the most arduous fought by any Allied troops during World War II'. The participants would concur. The human cost was enormous. The Australian and Americans suffered about 42,000 casualties. Australian dead numbered about 7,000 and American 4,684. The Japanese had 127,600 killed, but the great majority died of disease and starvation.[11]

During the Second World War, Japanese war dead are estimated at 1.74 million. Of these, about 1 million died in action, and the balance of either starvation or disease. The New Guinea experience was to be repeated all over the Pacific and Southeast Asia. Australian and American troops had taken Gona and Buna on the north Papuan coast – an important but not decisive victory in an exhausting campaign. General George Kenney USA observed presciently, 'There are hundreds of Bunas ahead of us.' He went on to predict, 'The awful cost in time, effort, blood and money may run to proportions beyond all perception.'[12]

The IJA mounted an investigation to analyse the reasons for their unsatisfactory performance in Papua New Guinea. The conclusion was that 'malnutrition' was the cause because it led to a loss of morale, generated despair and had a deleterious effect on discipline. The report sketched over the heavy losses in shipping that severely inhibited the logistic chain and instead determined that Horii's men had been unable to 'live off the land' because New Guinea was 'a barren wasteland'. The immediate response to the 'live off the land' policy had been a third of the Japanese 20th Division being directed into gardening tasks and several thousand others being tasked to forage for food and steal it when necessary. Military equipment was exchanged with villagers

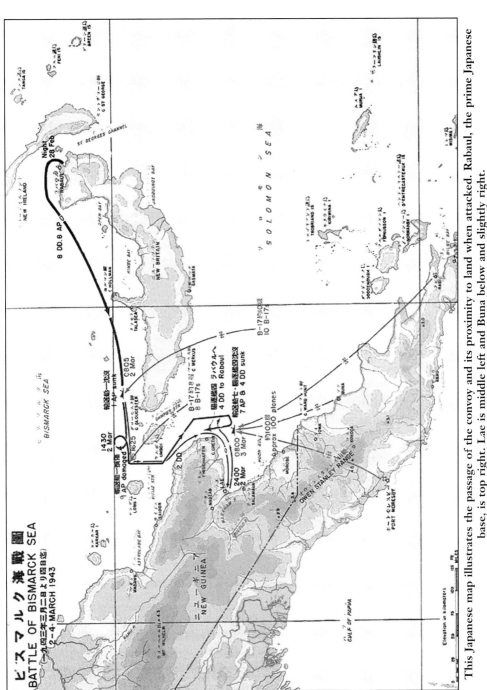

This Japanese map illustrates the passage of the convoy and its proximity to land when attacked. Rabaul, the prime Japanese base, is top right. Lae is middle left and Buna below and slightly right.

for food and operations were conducted with the sole aim of capturing Allied rations.[13]

Allied interrogation of the very few prisoners revealed an army disintegrating from hunger. This hunger was increasingly exacerbated across the Pacific by the American command of the air and sea. An intelligence report reached the conclusion that:

> officers and men alike, in forward areas are preoccupied almost to the exclusion of everything else with the shortage of food ... Bitterness and resentment, reaching at times a homicidal level, are generated by this life-or-death competition, especially towards officers who are, or appear to be, abusing the privileges of rank. Comparison of their own plight with the enemy's comparative affluence, especially brought home by the capture of our parachute dropped supplies or of our ration dumps reminds the Japanese soldier again to the extent of their abandonment.[14]

A measure of the pressure on the Japanese supply system was that for both Guadalcanal and New Guinea, supplies were floated ashore from small, fast ships in oil drums. The USN sank fifty-eight such vessels and, as a consequence, submarines later towed rubber bales towards the coast and released them in the hope that they would be recovered by their countrymen. By this system each submarine could discharge enough food for 30,000 men for two days – unfortunately, about 65 per cent fell into American hands.

* * *

A feature of the American war in the Pacific was the discord between the United States Navy and the Army, and specifically between senior officers.

The primary Allied efforts in the Pacific War were prosecuted along two axes, within two independent theatres under the direction of theatre commanders General Douglas MacArthur in Australia and Admiral Chester Nimitz in Hawaii. MacArthur and Nimitz each reported directly to the chief of their respective service in Washington. General George Marshall, Chief of Staff of the Army, allowed MacArthur considerable freedom and generally supported his strategic recommendations, essentially allowing MacArthur to run the war in his theatre as he saw fit. On the other hand, Admiral Ernest King, Chief of Naval Operations and Commander-in-Chief, US Fleet, took a much more personal interest in Pacific strategy and essentially dictated the course of operations to Nimitz. Therefore, the two men who really shaped Allied strategy in the Pacific were MacArthur and King.[15]

MacArthur and King differed over the strategy to be used against Japan and, whatever strategy *was* adopted, both men wanted their service to have supremacy. Admiral King was an aggressive, unlikeable man, as was General

MacArthur. It fell to General Marshall in Washington to referee the philosophical conflict between the two. The geographic demarcation of responsibility between Army and Navy was a matter for debate. Although much of the fighting between 1942 and 1945 was conducted on land, a high proportion was directed by the USN as Marines were often the dominant force employed. It is worth noting that the USMC was 142,613 strong in 1942 and 308,523 the following year. It peaked in 1944 at 475,604. However, it was dwarfed by the US Army, which, in 1943, was 6,994,472 strong. The Army may have had many more men; however, it was the USN that had the ships and the capacity to move those men and their materiel.

In July 1942, the command of operations to be centred on Tulagi was unsettled. The island lay in MacArthur's area, but the adjacent Santa Cruz islands were in the Pacific Ocean Area and the responsibility of Admiral Nimitz, who would provide the manpower. General Marshall gave the operation his full support, even if MacArthur's command could not lend support and the Navy had to take full responsibility. In practical terms, that called for a redrawing of the boundary between MacArthur's Southwest Pacific Area and Nimitz's Pacific Ocean Area, which was shifted 60 miles (97km) to 360 miles (579km) to the west to be effective from 1 August 1942.[16]

The American Joint Chiefs of Staff determined that their strategic aim was to take Guadalcanal, activate its airfield and then to take and hold the Admiralty Islands and Bismarck Archipelago, and specifically the Japanese base on Rabaul. The liberation of the Philippines was at this stage not considered – although to MacArthur it was his highest and overwhelming priority. Beckman commented:

> Regarding the liberation of the Philippines, MacArthur was an unwavering, almost fanatical, advocate of this course of action from the moment he left Corregidor. King, on the other hand, opposed the islands as a primary objective from the beginning, and remained steadfast in his opposition long after all other key decision-makers had been convinced of the desirability of invading Luzon. This case serves to illustrate the effects of two dominant personalities pursuing diametrically opposed courses of action.[17]

*   *   *

Nimitz appointed Vice Admiral Robert Ghormley, with the concurrence of King, to command of the South Pacific Area (COMSOPA). He was to prove a poor choice, and it may well have been that his appointment to the post, over other more experienced commanders with aviation expertise, was because of his close relationship with President Roosevelt. However, Ghormley's first task was to execute Operation WATCHTOWER – in which his force was to attack and hold two islands of the British Solomon Islands Protectorate. The first target was the tiny islet of Tulagi, 3.42 miles (5.5km) long and 0.62 miles (1km) wide. In all, it was just 0.80 square miles (2.1km²). Tulagi sheltered in the shadow of Florida Island and was where the Japanese had established a seaplane base. It provided accommodation for the workforce constructing an airstrip on the adjacent, and very much larger, island of Guadalcanal. That airstrip had been identified as a key strategic objective and its use had to be denied to the Japanese as a priority.

Admiral Ghormley intended to conduct his command over the coming battle from his headquarters ship USS *Argonne*, which lay at anchor in Auckland Harbour, New Zealand – an example of 'hands off' command.

During the early summer of 1942, the United States was putting together the invasion force which primarily consisted of the 1st Marine Division commanded by Major General Alexander Vandegrift. Not the least of the difficulties facing Vandegrift was the dearth of knowledge of the ground over which he was to fight. All conceivable sources were explored: past editions of *National Geographic*, retired missionaries, sea captains, copra planters. All were consulted but, nevertheless, the intelligence was still sparse. What was clear was that whilst Tulagi was a storybook island with only light vegetation:

> it was considered healthy enough for the white settlers and adminis-
> trators who managed the copra plantations and governed the Solomons'
> scattered territory from a one-street town of bungalows which boasted
> that indispensable symbol of British colonialism – a cricket pitch.[18]

In August 1942, Tulagi was home to a large force of Japanese marines and about 1,400 members of the IJN's Airfield Construction Unit. Every day this workforce was ferried across to labour on the airstrip on Guadalcanal. Three thousand yards (2.7 km) east of Tulagi are the small islets of Gavutu and Tanambogo. They are joined by a 500-yard-long causeway. Gavutu Harbor, on the north-east end of the island, and Purvis Bay, to the south-east of Gavutu and Tanambogo, formed the finest deep-water anchorage in the Solomons.

The detail for WATCHTOWER was confirmed. Admiral Turner would command the nineteen transports and their escort of four destroyers. Prior to the landing, three cruisers and six destroyers in Turner's fleet would bombard the landing areas on Tulagi and Guadalcanal. Close at hand, but uncom-mitted, was 'MacArthur's Navy', commanded by Rear Admiral Sir Victor Crutchley, who had under command three Australian cruisers and five destroyers, complemented by USS *Chicago* and four Pacific Fleet destroyers.

Tulagi. (*USN photograph*)

To gild the lily, three of Nimitz's four carrier task forces and the new fast battleship *North Carolina* would be in close support.

Before a shot had been fired, Americans were calling their landing Operation SHOESTRING. The arrangements had not gone well and a rehearsed beach landing in Fiji was a disaster. Rations available to the invading troops had been reduced and there was an atmosphere of 'make do' about the whole exercise. It was as well that the American force did not face a bigger and better prepared enemy.

Japanese intelligence did not provide any warning until US Marines were storming ashore on the two target islands. The 1st US Marine Division landed on Tulagi, Florida and Guadalcanal almost unopposed on 7 August 1942. The landing at Lunga Point on the north coast of the main island was close to the unfinished airstrip, which was swiftly secured. Immediately, US Navy Seabees commenced work to complete the job. At the initial landing the Japanese had been massively outnumbered, but Guadalcanal is a large land mass about 140 miles long (225km) and 39 miles (63km) wide. It was quite the opposite to its tiny neighbour, densely covered in very thick jungle with the smell of decaying vegetation ever-present. For the Japanese, access to its lengthy coastline was easy and rapid reinforcements and supplies were quickly delivered, always at night, by fast ships. This process became known as the Tokyo Express.

The Americans always had numerical superiority and in the six long months that stretched ahead they had 20,000 Marines and 40,000 soldiers deployed on the island at different times.[19] The Japanese opposition amounted to 36,200, of whom 4,800 were sailors. These thousands of men had only one thing in common, and that was to have possession of the airstrip that was now called Henderson Field. It was the focus of all the major fighting and a measure of its importance.

The apparently unopposed invasion of Tulagi, Gavutu and Tanambogo proved to be a temporary illusion. There were, in fact, 2,000 determined Japanese in residence on Tulagi and they emerged from shelter and took on the 2nd Raider Battalion and 2nd/5th Marine Battalion, who may have had control of the small town but were not masters of all they surveyed.

The battle that ensued could only have one result and the Japanese, although outnumbered, sold their lives with commendable bravery. The casualties incurred in this battle were one-sided, but all agree that Japanese killed were in a ratio of about 7:1 to Americans, who lost 122. A feature of the fighting was that the very few Japanese taken prisoner were all wounded – twenty-three is suggested by Costello. The obdurate resistance of an enemy, with no hope, fighting to the death on these obscure islets, gave an indication of what would follow as the US land forces tracked across the Pacific.

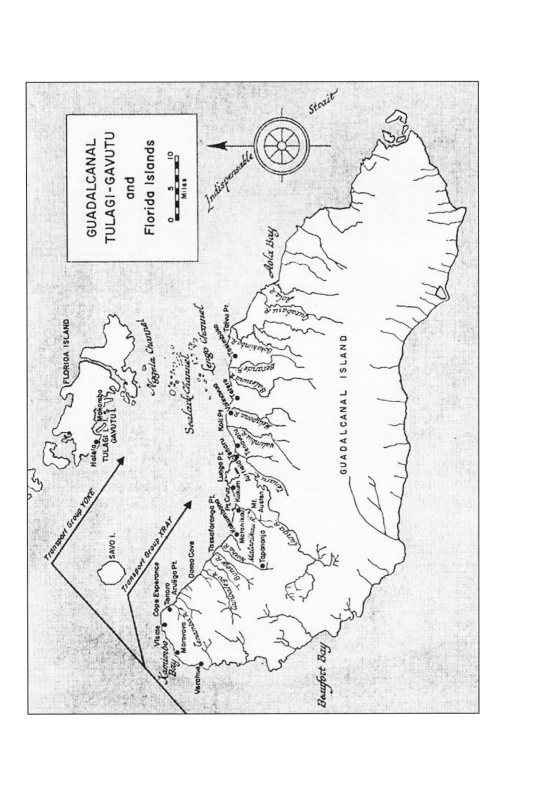

Although the whole island of Guadalcanal could not be secured, a beach-head was established. This was attacked by aircraft based at Rabaul on 7–9 August, of which thirty-six were destroyed. The Japanese did have some success, inflicting serious damage to the destroyer USS *Jarvis* and the transport *George F. Elliott*, which eventually sank on 10 August.[20] The US lost nineteen aircraft and of these, fourteen were carrier based. Notable in this campaign was the relative caution, perhaps timidity, of the American admirals Fletcher and Turner and the detached, ineffective leadership of Ghormley, their superior.

After this initial clash, Fletcher was sufficiently perturbed by his carrier losses and the prospect of further bombing that, on the afternoon of 8 August, he signalled Ghormley. He recommended the immediate withdrawal of his carriers, citing, as he often did, concerns about his fuel state. He did not wait for a response and promptly sailed away from the danger area. This discommoded Turner, who, at a meeting later that day with his commanders,

The route chosen by Admiral Mikawa Gunichi to attack the anchorage at Lunga Point on 8–9 August 1942. His fleet sailed from Rabaul and Kavieng (upper left), pausing off the east coast of Bougainville (centre) and then travelling down 'The Slot' to attack Allied naval forces off Guadalcanal and Tulagi (lower right).

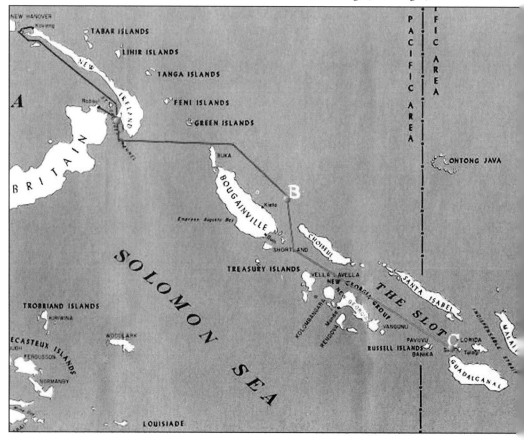

made clear that the loss of air cover obliged him to withdraw the cruisers and transports early on 9 August. This was a dreadful decision because the 16,000-strong invasion force now established ashore was depending on the transports to unload their logistic needs, a task less than half completed.[21] It was an acrimonious meeting and Rear Admiral Turner's assertion that unloading would continue all night did not assuage all the bad feeling. Turner was not everyone's cup of tea. He was described by Marine General Nathan Twining as:

> a loud, strident, arrogant person who enjoyed settling all matters by simply raising his voice and roaring like a bull captain in the old navy ... [His] peers understood this and valued him for what he was, a good and determined leader with a fine mind – when he chose to use it.

Meanwhile, Vice Admiral Mikawa Gunichi, in command of the newly designated 8th Fleet of seven cruisers and a destroyer, was en route to Guadalcanal. His captains were all skilled in night operations and Mikawa intended to assault Allied shipping during the night of 8/9 August, when he knew that he would not be at risk from air attack.

Mikawa's approach was not entirely covert, and the US submarine *S-38* sighted the Japanese force in St George's Channel. The submarine radioed the sighting of the ships, but no action was taken. At 1020 hrs and 1110 hrs, two RAAF Hudson aircraft based in Milne Bay, New Guinea, spotted the Japanese fleet, but each misidentified the size of the ships and the number in the Japanese force. This was because, shrewdly, Mikawa had dispersed his ships over a wide area.

The first Hudson's crew tried to report the sighting to the Allied radio station at Fall River, New Guinea. Receiving no acknowledgement, they returned to Milne Bay at 1242 hrs to ensure that the report was received as soon as possible. The second Hudson also failed to report its sighting by radio but completed its patrol and landed at Milne Bay at 1500 hrs. The second Hudson reported sighting 'two heavy cruisers, two light cruisers, and one unknown type'. Inexplicably, these reports were not relayed to the Allied fleet off Guadalcanal until 1845 hrs and 2130 hrs respectively, on 8 August.[22] The first Hudson's report was not received by radio because the Fall River station was shut down at that time for an air raid alert. When the second Hudson tried to radio its sighting of Mikawa's force, Fall River refused to receive the report and rebuked the Hudson's crew for breaking radio silence.[23] The Allied screen, protecting the transports, was under command of Rear Admiral Victor Crutchley, VC, KCB, DSC, RN, who flew his flag in the cruiser *Australia*. To give protection to the transports, busy unloading in support of the invasion force, Crutchley sent two American destroyers, USS *Blue* and USS *Ralph*

Talbot, to guard the entrance to the anchorage. The remainder of his ships he divided into three flotillas (shown on the map as 'Forces'). A 'Southern' flotilla consisted of the Australian cruisers HMAS *Australia*, HMAS *Canberra*, the cruiser USS *Chicago* and the destroyers USS *Patterson* and USS *Bagley*. The role of the flotilla was to patrol between Lunga Point and Savo Island. This was to block the gap between Savo Island and Cape Esperance, the northernmost point of Guadalcanal. Crutchley deployed a 'Northern' flotilla composed of the cruisers USS *Vincennes*, *Astoria* and *Quincy*. The destroyers USS *Helm* and *Wilson* patrolled a box-shaped area to defend against any incursion between Saco and Florida islands. Finally, the 'Eastern' flotilla of cruisers, USS *San Juan*, HMAS *Hobart* and the destroyers USS *Buchanan* and USS *Monssen* gave protection from any approach to the sound between Florida and Guadalcanal.

Crutchley was a perfectly capable officer, and the disposition of his fleet was entirely reasonable. All he required was some warning of an approaching enemy. Unaware of Mikawa's intentions, at 2055 hrs, Crutchley left the Southern group in *Australia* to attend the conference, leaving Captain Howard D. Bode of *Chicago* in command of the group. After the meeting Crutchley re-joined his ship but did not take up his previous station with the Southern flotilla and did not advise his subordinate commanders of his position in the transport anchorage. On this basis, Captain Bode remained in command.

Mikawa had little difficulty in avoiding USS *Blue* and *Ralph Talbot* because in their peregrinations they were up to 8 miles (13km) apart. However, stressingly, at one stage *Blue* closed to within a mile (1.6km) of the intruders. With many Japanese guns trained on her, *Blue* apparently reached the end of her beat and suddenly reversed course and sailed away from Mikawa's force, apparently oblivious to the long column of large ships sailing close by her.[24] Seeing that his ships were still undetected, Mikawa turned back to a course south of Savo Island and increased speed, first to 26 knots (48km/h), and then to 30 knots (56km/h). At 0125 hrs, Mikawa released his ships to operate independently of his flagship, and at 0131, he ordered, 'Every ship attack.'[25]

What followed was like the chaos that ensues when a fox gets into a chicken coop. Mikawa's ships turned on searchlights to illuminate targets, and float-planes dropped flares for the same purpose. The still burning *George F. Elliott*, mortally damaged the previous day, aided the Japanese gunnery, which was highly effective. USS *Chicago* and HMAS *Canberra* were both hit in a fusillade. *Chicago*'s captain, Howard Bode, steamed his ship west for forty minutes, leaving behind the transports he was assigned to protect.[26] The cruiser fired her secondary batteries at the trailing ships in the Japanese column and may have hit *Tenryū*, causing slight damage. Captain Bode did not try to assert

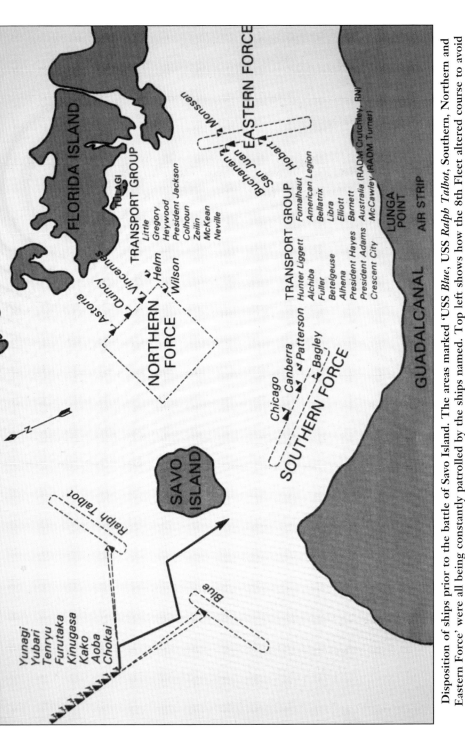

Disposition of ships prior to the battle of Savo Island. The areas marked 'USS *Blue*, USS *Ralph Talbot*, Southern, Northern and Eastern Force' were all being constantly patrolled by the ships named. Top left shows how the 8th Fleet altered course to avoid 'USS *Blue*' and was able to attack by squeezing through the gap to the left of Savo Island. Initially, *Australia* was clearly not able to influence events.

control over any of the other Allied ships in the Southern force, of which he was still in command. More significantly, Captain Bode made no attempt to warn any of the other Allied ships or personnel in the Guadalcanal region as his ship headed away from the battle area.[27]

Mikawa turned his attention to the Northern flotilla. *Astoria* took incoming fire from 0152 hrs and shortly after, *Vincennes* was hit by two torpedoes fired from *Chōkai*. *Vincennes* was hit seventy-four times but another torpedo strike at 0203 was fatal and she sank at 0250 hrs. At 0216 hrs, Admiral Mikawa, on the brink of a major victory, consulted his staff as to whether they should turn back and attack the defenceless merchant transports. The consensus was to be cautious and so, at 0220 hrs, Mikawa gave the order to retire. He left his enemy in serious disarray.

USS *Quincy* had been engaged simultaneously by *Aoba*, *Furutaka* and *Tenryū*, took heavy punishment, was set ablaze and sank at 0238 hrs. HMAS *Canberra* was fighting her fires with the assistance of USS *Patterson* and *Blue*. The fires were under control when Admiral Turner decided that, if *Canberra* was unable to accompany his fleet when it made its planned withdrawal at 0630 hrs, she was to be scuttled. It took 300 shells and five torpedoes, and then *Canberra* joined others at the bottom of Iron Bottom Sound. USS *Astoria* succumbed to her wounds and sank at 1215 hrs.

The Battle of Savo Island was a resounding Japanese victory. However, Admiral Mikawa missed an opportunity to make it greater, and one that could have altered the course of the war. Military historians are much given to speculating 'what if', and this author is no exception. What if Mikawa had turned his guns on the transports unloading at Lunga Point? By so doing he could have caused the isolation of the American invasion force and perhaps been instrumental in the Japanese retention of Guadalcanal and its all-important airstrip.

As it was, he inflicted the heaviest defeat in the USN's history: 1,077 men were killed, three heavy cruisers were sunk (*Quincy*, *Vincennes* and *Astoria*) and one was scuttled (*Canberra*). One heavy cruiser was damaged (*Chicago*), as were two destroyers (*Ralph Talbot* and *Patterson*). Japanese losses were 129 killed, two heavy and one light cruiser damaged (*Chōkai*, *Tenryū* and *Kinugasa*).

Turner had evacuated the anchorage on 9 August in view of 'impending heavy air attacks'.[28] He took with him 'the unlanded Marine Division's 1,000-man reserve, most of its heavy artillery and equipment as well as half its food supplies'.[29] It could be argued that his first priority had to be the safety of his ships. His decision may have been challenged in Marine circles but otherwise Turner was never called to account. Kelly Turner ended the war as a full, four-star admiral and died, much honoured, in 1961.

It is worth noting that only a small proportion of the Allied fleet, five cruisers and seven destroyers, were engaged in the battle, and that emphasises the margin of defeat. Inevitably there was a Board of Enquiry into the conduct of the Allied fleet. The subsequent report criticised only one officer, and that was Captain Howard Bode, USN, of the USS *Chicago*. Distressed at the findings of the Board, Captain Bode shot himself on 19 April 1943.

Admiral Turner, who was in overall command of the Allied naval forces and, by definition, responsible for the defeat, attributed it less to his own significant deficiencies and concluded that it was because:

> the Navy was still obsessed with a strong feeling of technical and mental superiority over the enemy. In spite of ample evidence as to enemy capabilities, most of our officers and men despised the enemy and felt themselves sure victors in all encounters under any circumstances. The net result of all this was a fatal lethargy of mind which induced a confidence without readiness, and a routine acceptance of outworn peacetime standards of conduct. I believe that this psychological factor, as a cause of our defeat, was even more important than the element of surprise.[30]

On Guadalcanal the marines toiled to hold and develop Henderson Field. The constant torrential rain produced a quagmire of sticky black mud. The Seabees had only one bulldozer – the others were on the high seas with the absent Turner. Captured Japanese vehicles were put into use, as was the veritable mountain of food left behind. These produced a menu foreign to marine tastes, but rice and fish was better than nothing.

The naval success at Savo Island spurred the Japanese to reinforce its hold in Guadalcanal and the 28th Infantry Regiment, commanded by Colonel Ichiki Kiyonao, was in the van of this reinforcement. On 19 August, 917 soldiers of the 28th landed from destroyers at Taivu Point. This was about 9 miles (14km) east of Henderson Field, well beyond the defended perimeter. The unopposed landing was uneventful but Japanese intelligence had failed to provide Ichiki with an accurate estimate of American strength and optimistically he determined to make an attack on the American eastern perimeter during the night of 20/21 August.[31]

A Solomon Islands Coastwatcher, Jacob Vouza, had been sent with a small patrol to investigate the landing. He found the Japanese force and moved in closer – too close, and he was captured. While being interrogated, a tiny American flag, given to him as a souvenir, fell from his loincloth, and revealed his loyalties. He gave the Japanese no information, despite being brutally beaten and tortured. He was tied to a tree and left to die from three bayonet wounds. Vouza managed to free himself and, despite his wounds, reached

Sir Jacob Charles Vouza, KBE, GM –
Coastwatcher, brave man, and later
distinguished public servant, and an
honorary sergeant major in the USMC
(*c.*1892–15 March 1984).

the American lines, where he issued a warning about the forthcoming attack. Jacob Vouza survived and was decorated with the George Medal and the American Silver Star.

The brief notice given by Vouza allowed the marines to repulse the assault when it came in and heavy losses were inflicted on the Japanese around Alligator Creek. This was later known as the Battle of Tenaru. After dawn the marines counter-attacked and savaged the demoralised enemy. Ichiki was killed, possibly by his own hand. A total of 789 Japanese corpses were counted and only around thirty of the original 917 survived unwounded. They withdrew to join a rearguard at Taivu Point.

The Battle of Tenaru was but the first of many engagements over the following five months when the balance swung slowly and expensively towards the Americans. The aim of the campaign was not to secure and garrison on the large island, but to hold, maintain and operate Henderson Field. The American success in doing so was not solely due to its land-based operations, bloody and savage though they were. In large measure, the USN was fully committed and fiercely engaged throughout. In September 1942, Admiral Nimitz appointed Vice Admiral William 'Bull' Halsey as Commander, South Pacific Area. He replaced the uninspiring and exhausted Vice Admiral Robert Ghormley. This was a critical appointment at a critical time. The 1st Marine Division was holding on to Henderson Field only by its fingernails. The arrival of a new, dynamic, energetic and aggressive commander was a significant boost to morale. Halsey's leadership during the latter part of the campaign and especially at the Battle of Cape Esperance, also known as the Second Battle of Savo Island, on 11–12 October 1942, underscored the increasing American naval superiority.

It was not a conclusive engagement but nevertheless a clear victory for the United States Navy. Overall, during those five months the cost to the USN was twenty-nine ships, including two fleet carriers, six cruisers and fourteen destroyers. Not least of the cost was the 615 aircraft destroyed.[32] The

Dead Japanese soldiers on the sandbar at the mouth of Alligator Creek, Guadalcanal, after the Battle of Tenaru. (*USMC photograph*)

Japanese lost thirty-eight ships and 683 aircraft, so it is little wonder that, when the sea floor around northern Guadalcanal was paved with the remains of sixty-seven ships, it was called 'Iron Bottom Sound'. Japanese casualties were 24,600–25,600; of these, 2,300 were invaluable aircrew.[33]

The campaign came to an end when it became apparent to the Japanese high command that the position on Guadalcanal was no longer tenable. On 28 December 1942, General Sugiyama Hajime and Admiral Nagano Osami had the task of telling Hirohito and advising him that his troops on the island should be evacuated. Hirohito had no option but agree. The evacuation of Japanese ground forces was accomplished with skill. On 14 January, the Tokyo Express delivered a battalion of fresh troops to act as a rearguard and warships were moved into locations from which they could give support. As it was, the Americans had no idea of the evacuation and Major General Alexander Patch, who had replaced Major General Alexander Vandegrift as the land force commander, was very cautious as he was expecting to face an offensive.

The IJA disengaged and concentrated on the west coast of Guadalcanal, leaving a screen to warn of any American advance. By 1 February, the IJN had assembled twenty destroyers, in an initial operation, and successfully evacuated 4,935 men. This exercise did not go unopposed and both sides lost a destroyer to air attacks.[34]

It was now evident to the Americans that an evacuation was underway, and it might be supposed that the time was ripe to launch an offensive and destroy an enemy who had already acknowledged defeat. However, Patch did not attack, and his caution allowed a further 10,652 Japanese to be lifted out of harm's way on 4–7 February. This was not Dunkirk, but it was still a very successful operation, and it took until 9 February for General Patch to realise that he no longer had any opposition.[35] The battle for Guadalcanal had been won.

This was a campaign in which quarter was neither asked for nor given. The death toll, modest by that of the Sino-Japanese conflict, was nevertheless high by the standards set early in this war. The Americans had 1,592 killed and about 8,000 wounded. Eighty-five Australians were killed at the Battle of Savo Island, but the number of Solomon Islanders killed is unknown. For the Japanese, the latter stages of the campaign were notable for the deaths from malnutrition, neglect and disease. They had 19,200 killed, but over half of their fatalities (10,700) were attributed to medical causes, and that is, in part, a reflection of the logistic deficiencies in this part of the campaign. The attrition among Japanese aviators continued as they lost 683 aircraft.[36]

To put those 683 aircraft into a wider context: from the second half of 1942 until mid-1943, Japanese pilots flying land-based aircraft suffered 87 per cent casualties and those that were carrier-based, a calamitous 98 per cent. These elite pilots were irreplaceable.[37]

The Americans had grown wary about taking prisoners and had noted the proclivity of wounded Japanese to commit suicide or to clasp a grenade to detonate when a captor approached. On this basis, many Japs were not given the option of surrender. The 1,000 taken were dishonoured by their society and for the great majority it was only the severity of their wounds that caused them to capitulate.

Notes

1. Costello, J., *The Pacific War 1941–45* [1981] (New York, Harper Collins, 2009), p. 317.
2. McAulay, L., *To the Bitter End: The Japanese Defeat at Buna and Gona, 1942–43* (Sydney, Random House, 1992), p. 12.
3. Grey, J., *A Military History of Australia* (Cambridge, Cambridge University Press, 1999), p. 171.
4. Harries, M. & Harries, S., *Soldiers of the Sun* (London, Heinemann, 1991), p. 343.

5. Bullard, S. (trans.), *Japanese Army Operations in the South Pacific Area 1942–43* (Canberra, Australian War Memorial, 2007), pp. 173–5.
6. Williams, P., *The Kokoda Campaign 1942* (Melbourne, Victoria, Cambridge University Press, 2012), p. 235.
7. James, D.C., *The Years of MacArthur*, Vol. 2 (Boston, 1970–5), p. 241.
8. Combined Arms Research Library, C&GSC, US Army Archive, Eichelberger.
9. Gillison, D., *Australia in the War of 1939–1945* (Canberra, Australian War Memorial, 1962), p. 696.
10. Ibid., p. 697.
11. Fenton, D., *How many Died?* (Australian War Memorial, 2004), retrieved June 1920.
12. Kenney's Post Action Report, quoted by Costello, p. 381.
13. Richmond, K., *The Japanese in New Guinea* (Curtin ACT, 2003), pp. 185–6.
14. *Antagonism between Officers and Men in the Japanese Armed Forces* (Research Report No. 122, AWM 55 12/94), p. 4.
15. Beckman, K.B., *Personality and Strategy: How the personalities of Gen. MacArthur and Adm. King shaped Allied strategy in the Pacific* (Fort Leavenworth, US Army C&GSC, 2002), p. 3.
16. Dyer, G.C., *The Amphibians came to Conquer: The Story of Admiral Richmond Turner* (Washington DC: Department of the Navy, 1972), pp. 259–60.
17. Beckman, pp. 53–4.
18. Costello, p. 320.
19. Frank, R., *Guadalcanal: The Definitive Account of the Landmark Battle* (New York, Random House, 1990), pp. 57, 619–21.
20. Loxton, B. & Coulthard-Clark, C., *The Shame of Savo: Anatomy of a Naval Disaster* (St Leonards, NSW, Allen & Unwin, 1997), pp. 99–103.
21. Hammel, E., *Guadalcanal: Decision at Sea: The Naval Battle of Guadalcanal, November 13–15, 1942* (New York, Crown, 1988), p. 100.
22. Loxton, pp. 139–50.
23. Ibid.
24. Ibid., pp. 171–3.
25. Dull, P.S., *A Battle History of the Japanese Navy, 1941–45* (Annapolis, Naval Institute Press, 1978), p. 197.
26. Loxton, p. 213.
27. Frank, R.B., pp. 105–106.
28. Morison, S.E., *The Struggle for Guadalcanal*, Vol. V (Boston, Little, Brown, 1948), p. 19.
29. Costello, p. 326.
30. Frank, p. 123.
31. Ibid., p. 147.
32. Ibid., pp. 589–618.
33. Ibid.
34. Ibid., pp. 589–97.
35. Ibid.
36. Ibid.
37. Paine, S.C.M., *The Wars for Asia 1911–1949* (New York, Cambridge University Press, 2012), p. 194.

Chapter Fifteen

November 1942–3
Food, the Bengal Famine and
the First Chindit Operation

From the mid-1930s, Japan had pursued autarky and the expanded empire was to be a key component of that as it would be the fount of riches in many forms. However, the capability of the existing Japanese merchant marine to serve the needs of a larger empire was doubtful. Accordingly, it was important that, from 1941, the merchant fleet should be enlarged to a size commensurate with the territorial expansion. A programme to build these ships and armed escorts to protect them was a top strategic priority – incredibly, that was fatally ignored.

In the spring of 1943, the effects of three Japanese policies, or courses of action, all started to bear fruit – and it was far from sweet. First, the decision to focus all shipbuilding on warships left a merchant marine without any replacement vessels in the building chain and the attrition of Japanese shipping to the United States Navy submarines had begun to have a deleterious effect on the logistic system. Hence the decision to abandon logistic support to Papua New Guinea.

Second, the Government had made inadequate contingency provision for the import of food into the home islands. Japanese were going hungry everywhere, and the situation worsened day by day. Domestically, farmers toiled manfully but were unable to fill the gap. Exacerbating the problem, home-based military forces grew from 1 to 3.5 million from 1941 to 1945. These men had absolute priority in food distribution and their consumption of rice rose from 161,000 tons in 1941 to 744,000 tons, which, in 1943, equalled the entire amount of rice that had been filtered through the blockade.[1] The voracious demands of the military accelerated the food crisis and pushed Japan's population towards starvation by mid-1945.[2]

Pre-war Japan's imported foodstuffs may have only accounted for 20 per cent of its consumption, but that 20 per cent was critical because it included all its salt, 92 per cent of its sugar and most of its soya beans, which provided important protein when processed into miso.[3] About 35 per cent of rice was imported from Formosa and Korea. There was a huge gap between the domestic production of rice and its consumption. A deficiency in any of these products would lead to inexorable dietary ailments. Salt is a fundamental element in any diet, and for the Japanese, sugar was the source of 7 per cent of the national calorific intake.

Third, the Imperial Japanese Army was expected to feed itself from the larder of its conquered territory and the IJA sat astride the Asian rice bowls of Indochina, Malaya and Burma. Nevertheless, given this bounty, it managed its asset very badly indeed. Under Japanese occupation, rice production fell and the merciless requisition of supplies created widespread civilian depriva- tion and hunger. There was famine in Burma and Vietnam. Japanese hatred of the Chinese was manifest in Malaya, where about 50,000 Chinese were murdered. These were the very people that farmed the rice paddies and who would have fed the IJA. This was the law of unintended consequence in action.

With all the facts to hand, the modern historian can see that from, say, February 1943, the awesome power and wealth of the USA was bound to prevail over the logistically bereft Japan. The American policy of bypassing Japanese-held islands, garrisons and bases such as Rabaul was saving Ameri- can lives. However, in the longer term it would cost the deaths of many enemy soldiers and indigenous people marooned with them.

In this war, the need for logistic support was not confined to the Japanese front line; it was needed in the home islands as well. Japanese industry was dependent upon imported iron ore, aluminium, steel and oil. The product of its factories had then to be transported, somehow, to the empire's soldiers spread across the Pacific and Southeast Asia.

Japan's merchant marine had been greatly degraded during the blockade to date and whilst hitherto the domestic transport around the Japanese island had been by sea, this capability was much reduced. The Japanese shipbuild- ing industry was entirely focused on the construction of warships, and it was not able, at relatively short notice, to fill the gap in its civilian fleet and the knock-on impact upon its soldiers in distant islands was catastrophic.

The American victory at Guadalcanal was but one of a series of successes as the tide started to flow in favour of the Allies. In North Africa, Montgomery's 8th Army had turned its massive logistic advantage to good effect and had vanquished Rommel's Africa Corps. Operation TORCH followed, and the invasion of Vichy French colonies in North Africa introduced American soldiers into the Western theatre for the first time. The Battle for Stalingrad was won on 2 February 1943 as the Russian winter started to bite. German losses were enormous.

Churchill was exultant after the victory at El Alamein, and famously he pronounced, with characteristic sagacity and eloquence: 'Now is not the end, it is not even the beginning of the end, but it is perhaps the end of the beginning.'[4]

However, it was not all roses, and as 1943 dawned, the world was a very complicated place. There was a host of apparently disconnected issues that when taken together shaped the way the war was to be fought.

These issues included the Bengal Famine in which it is estimated that between 2.1 and 3 million died. The trigger for this catastrophe was the fall of Rangoon in March of the previous year. Consequent to that defeat, the Japanese were able to stop the routine export of Burmese rice to India and Ceylon. This, in turn, caused an unachievable demand on locally grown rice

Australians cross a stream during their advance on Gona. (*Australian War Memorial*)

and afforded Indian entrepreneurs an opportunity to exploit the market. Across Southeast Asia, the price of rice rose to unprecedented levels; inflation followed, and civil unrest was the result. This unrest was exacerbated by the 'Free India Movement', directed by Subhas Chandra Bose, and troops had to be diverted from Burma to help maintain order.

There is no doubt that the Government of India had a responsibility, but it did not help the situation with some earlier flawed decision-making. For example, it had imposed a scorched earth policy to deny foodstuffs to the Japanese Army should it invade India. It established a Foodstuffs Scheme to manage the distribution of food, ensuring that those in high priority roles such as the civil service, police and armed forces were given priority. To compound the problem, local rice crops were infected by brown spot disease and then, on 16–17 October, Bengal was hit by a massive cyclone; 14,500 died, as did 190,000 of their cattle. The cyclone created three tsunami waves which overwhelmed the sea walls and flooded 450 square miles (1,200km^2). The abject misery and destitution of 2.5 million people worsened. Bose exploited the political situation, enthusiastically supported by the Japanese.

In early 1943 in Burma, a British offensive in the Arakan was being conducted by 14th Indian Division, commanded by Major General Wilfred Lloyd, DSO*, MC. This force, at one point, was composed of nine brigades. Nevertheless, it had achieved nothing, and at the end of February, Wavell decided to withdraw. However, Churchill was adamant that the operations against the invaders should continue. It was against this backdrop that Lieutenant Colonel, Acting Brigadier Orde Wingate convinced Wavell that operations, by a relatively small force, behind Japanese lines would be disproportionately productive, and he was authorised to form a Long-Range Penetration Group. These men were always referred to as 'Chindits'. The Chindit aim was to attack Japanese troops and installations, cut communications and spread confusion in enemy ranks.

Wingate was an unusual man. 'Messianic and unbalanced' was one description, 'ruthless and eccentric' was a second.[5] Lieutenant Denis Gudgeon, of 3 Column, 3rd Bn/2nd Gurkha Rifles, remarked:

> he carried a Flit gun with him everywhere, which was a bit disconcerting when you were eating lunch and he puffed Flit about the place. He also carried an alarm clock about with him. We thought he was mad. I did not like him. Not many of the Gurkha officers liked him. You couldn't have a rapport with him, he was aloof never said very much.[6]

On 8 February 1943, Wingate led 3,000 men, designated 77 Indian Brigade, from Imphal into Burma on Operation LONGCLOTH. They first contacted the enemy on 15 February, having crossed the Chindwin River. The force was split into seven columns and allotted territory and objectives. They were all to be resupplied from the air and they sought to convince the Japanese that they were a much larger force. The fortitude and courage of the Chindits is not challenged but the reality is that their successes were insufficient to be more than an irritant to the enemy. For example, the destruction of the north–south railway line in seventy separate places, by a column commanded by Michael Calvert, should have been a crippling blow but the Japanese had the line operable again within a week.

The nature of jungle operations was such that evacuation of the wounded was all but impossible and a disabling wound was tantamount to death. Where possible the wounded were left in Burmese villages, but

Major General Orde Wingate, DSO*
**(1903–44), commander of the
Chindit Force.**

their survival was dependent upon the very doubtful loyalty of the villagers. Others were left with a water bottle and a grenade or pistol. They all died.

After three months of the most arduous activity, the Chindits were, by now, pursued by three Japanese divisions. They withdrew to the north towards India, but the initiative was with the Japanese, who patrolled the rivers and removed all river craft. The columns split into small groups, and each made its way across the Chindwin and trickled back to Imphal.[7] They left behind 818 of their number. The surviving 2,182 were in poor health and 'about 600' were so debilitated that they were unfit for further service.[8] For practical purposes, Operation LONGCLOTH incurred 47 per cent losses in dead and disabled. Notwithstanding the lack of military success, the Chindits gave British morale a boost and their sally into Japanese-held territory was a propaganda victory if nothing else.

One of the consequences of Wingate's first foray was that the Japanese commander-in-chief in Burma, Lieutenant General Kawabe Masakazu, was determined to thwart any further incursions from India. To this end he identified that he had to occupy the Imphal plain and take Kohima, and he planned to mount an offensive in 1944. It also hastened the construction of a railway link between Bangkok and Rangoon. This railway was to be the cause of the most abject misery and death of thousands of Allied prisoners employed in its building.

A Major General William Slim was sent to the Arakan to review the unsatisfactory situation there and he quickly identified the reasons for failure. Lloyd had concentrated on all his movement by road and paid a high price. Slim was sent back in April 1943 to take command and to extricate the 14th Division. Slim initiated a fighting withdrawal, but he left 2,500 of his soldiers' bodies decomposing in the rainforest and in roadside ditches. This was another low for British arms. Chindit operations were suspended for almost a year and these latter operations are addressed in their chronological order in Chapter 20.

Notes

1. Frank, R., *Guadalcanal: The Definitive Account of the Landmark Battle* (New York, Random House, 1990), pp. 129–30.
2. Collingham, L., *The Taste of War* (Penguin, 2011), p. 230.
3. Johnston, B.E., *Japanese Food Management* (Stanford University Press, 1953), pp. 43, 87.
4. Churchill, W.S., in a speech at the Mansion House, London, November 1942.
5. Thompson, J., *Forgotten Voices of Burma* (London, Ebury Press, 2010), p. 67; Hastings, Sir M., *Nemesis: The Battle for Japan 1944–45* [2007] (London, Collins, 2016), p. 65.
6. Thompson, p. 67.
7. Rooney, D., [1994] *Wingate and the Chindits* (London, Cassell, 2000), p. 91.
8. Brayley, M., *The British Army 1939–45 (3): The Far East* (Osprey Publishing, 2002), p. 19.

Chapter Sixteen

January–December 1943 Yamamoto, Attu, Casablanca, Cairo, Quebec and Teheran

The British recognised that its campaign in the Arakan had failed, but on the upside, it had a considerable success in the signal intelligence field (SIGINT), when it participated in the breaking of the Imperial Japanese Army code in March 1943. A 'Wireless Experimental Centre' had been established in New Delhi and it was from here that the crucial breakthrough was made. The penetration of that code thereafter provided British and American commanders with accurate, pre-emptive intelligence of Japanese intentions. However, just as this success was being celebrated, the German Navy revised its Enigma codes and, for some weeks, the U-boats in the Atlantic were able to ravage the convoys supporting the British Isles. This was a situation described as being of 'extreme gravity'.[1] The U-boats were on the cusp of a victory in the Battle of the Atlantic and Churchill admitted later that 'the only thing that ever really frightened me during the war was the U-boat peril.'

The breaking of the IJN code led directly to the death of Admiral Yamamoto, who was, by some measure, the most able of the Japanese commanders. His staff had signalled to all concerned his itinerary for a morale-boosting tour of airfields in the Pacific, including one on the island of Bougainville.

The message was intercepted and the chance to assassinate Yamamoto was evident. The killing of an enemy combatant would not normally raise any issues, but in this case, there were concerns that the Japanese would suspect that their codes had been breached. The Americans were unsure of what they should do and referred a decision ever upwards. Eventually, it fell to Roosevelt, and his decision was to shoot down Yamamoto's aircraft. On 18 April, at Henderson Field on Guadalcanal, a squadron of seventeen P-38 Lightnings were fitted with extra fuel tanks for Operation VENGEANCE.

Yamamoto and his entourage filled two Mitsubishi 'T' type bombers and the pair were easy meat when they arrived, precisely on time, above Bougainville. Both bombers were shot down and later the admiral's body was found in the wreckage. He had been killed in the air; a bullet had hit him in the jaw and exited through his temple.

The death of Yamamoto was a serious blow to the Japanese, who initially suppressed the news of his death; thereafter, he was deeply mourned. The USA had to quell any suggestion that the assassination was anything other than the result of a chance encounter, and it was successful.

This episode in the Pacific has a parallel with the assassination of Lieutenant General William 'Strafer' Gott, CB, CBE, DSO, MC**, in North Africa on 7 August 1942. Gott had been appointed to command the 8th Army by Churchill only the day before and it was his intention to enjoy a few days' leave in Cairo before taking up his new command. A message to the airstrip, sent by an incompetent staff officer, 'to hold the aircraft because the general is delayed' was sent in clear speech over the radio. Predictably, the message was intercepted by the Germans, who sent six ME-109s to shoot down Gott's unarmed transport plane. He died, along with seventeen others.[2]

On 7 June 1942, Japan had invaded the Aleutian chain of islands, American possessions, 1,700 miles (2,736km) from the south-west coast of Alaska. Of the seventy islands, Attu and Kiska, the most important, were also the most western. The Kurile Islands were within 650 miles (1,046km). Since purchasing the Aleutians from Russia in 1867, the United States had done little to develop the area, and most of the islands had not even been fully mapped.

The loss of these obscure, rarely visited, bleak islands was nevertheless an embarrassment to the USA. Japanese planners believed that control of the Aleutians would prevent any possible US attacks from Alaska. The reality was that the Aleutians afforded the invaders precious little advantage, as the extreme weather restricted air movement and a threat to shipping lanes between Seattle and Russia was never more than . . . just a threat.

By early 1943, however, the Joint Chiefs of Staff decided that it was time to dislodge the Japanese from the Aleutians once and for all. Attu was chosen as the first objective, since reconnaissance seemed to show that it was less heavily fortified than Kiska. After Attu was taken, the plan was for the invading troops from that island and Amchitka to move on and jointly invade Kiska.

Attu is a disagreeable place; it has a cold, hostile climate and although the initial American landings were not contested, nevertheless there were 1,200 casualties from frostbite alone. The logistic support of the invading force was inadequate both in quantity and portability.

The Japanese commander in Attu was Colonel Yamasaki Yasuyo, and he was to prove an obdurate foe. Yamasaki and his 2,650 soldiers entrenched themselves on the high ground and from this advantageous position they were able to resist for over two weeks, during which they took a toll of the American force in the most extreme conditions of snow, fog, freezing temperatures and 120mph winds. Their logistic chain had broken down and the Japanese were starving. Nevertheless, they gave a good account of themselves until

29 May, when they swept down from their well-established defensive positions, led by Yamasaki, with sword in hand, in a human wave, frontal, mass attack. This is now termed a '*banzai*' charge, and, in this case, it was the first and last on US soil: 2,351 Japanese were killed and just twenty-eight taken prisoner. The site of this hopeless charge is now called Massacre Bay. US casualties in the Attu campaign were 867 killed, 1,148 wounded and 614 incapacitated by infection. This was a US victory, but a high price was paid for this worthless island. The Japanese realised that their possession of Kiska was now militarily untenable and, in August

Colonel Yamasaki Yasuyo (1891–1943).

1943, they withdrew. The conduct of Colonel Yamasaki and his soldiers was so bizarre by Western standards that some sort of explanation is needed.

Central to Japanese military culture was the 'code of bushido'. It was inculcated in Japanese servicemen during their earliest days in uniform. The code promulgated the philosophy that it was cowardly to show one's back to the enemy and to do so dishonoured the family. Inouye Jukichi, in 1910, wrote:

> Japanese warriors looked upon it as a shame to themselves not to die when their Lord was hard pressed … their own shame was the shame upon the parents, their family, their house, and their whole clan. And with this idea deeply impressed upon their minds the Samurai, no matter what rank, held their lives light as feathers when compared with the weight they attached to the maintenance of their good name.[3]

Thus it was that the youth of Japan, now engaged in bitter fighting with the Americans and having been raised in this bushido atmosphere, believed that the greatest honour open to them was to die for their emperor. Surrender was ignominious and offended the military code. For this reason, Japan never ratified the Geneva Prisoner of War Convention of 1929. The mass suicide on Attu was to be repeated elsewhere and individual suicide was to be commonplace throughout the Pacific War. It should be noted that many of the atrocities committed by the Japanese 'were in the sacred name of Bushido'.[4]

*   *   *

During 1943, differences between the Allies polarised and the USA assumed, quite correctly, that its massive reserve of manpower, materiel and money were, in combination, all it needed to take control of Allied strategy in all theatres except Burma. There it merely applied its influence but limited its physical support. Roosevelt and his senior commanders were bordering obsessional in their secondary aim, which was the dissolution of the British Empire. In effect, America shared a similar aim with Tokyo in this respect. American concern for the colonial populations in Asia and their social and political freedom was laudable though it was not matched by the domestic treatment they accorded their own indigenous, black Americans or, for that matter, those Americans of Japanese heritage. Churchill, on the other hand, unreasonably expected a return to the pre-war colonial arrangements, but that was never going to happen, and the demise of the empire was already underway without American assistance.

In January 1943, the Combined Chiefs of Staff and their political masters met in Casablanca. Stalin did not attend, as he had the ongoing Battle of Stalingrad to deal with, and de Gaulle was a reluctant attendee. There was no disguising the fundamental disagreement along national lines of future strategy. For the British, the ongoing Battle of the Atlantic was critical to survival and of the highest priority. Consequently, Churchill could not support an invasion of mainland Europe in 1943 – a measure that Stalin was insisting upon. Churchill favoured a thrust into the 'soft underbelly' of the Axis from the Mediterranean. Admiral King, true to form, opposed any British suggestion, and there existed the possibility that King could sway American commitment from 'Europe first' in favour of an expanded Pacific campaign.

The British came to the Casablanca Conference well prepared and with their position polished. The Americans less so, other than with a shared determination to thwart any imperialistic ambitions that their principal ally might entertain. It was on this basis that they opposed 'any major expansion of the Mediterranean offensive believing it to be tainted by imperial designs'.[5]

Marshall made it clear that, for many of his countrymen, the principal aim was the defeat of Japan and not that of Germany – with whom American soldiers had engaged for the first time only a few weeks before. General Sir Alan Brooke nailed his colours to the mast of legend when he averred, 'Unless we can effectively combat the U-boat menace, we might not be able to win the war.'[6] Brooke kept a diary and in it he recorded a meeting, on 14 May 1943, in the USA. He noted that:

We lunched with the American Chiefs of Staff and went on to the White House where we met the President and PM and again discussed the whole of Burma. First president and PM made statements. Then Wavell was called upon followed by [Admiral Sir James] Somervell [*sic*] who contradicted him! Then Stilwell, who disagreed with both Somervell and with himself as far as I could see! He is a small man with no conception of strategy. The whole problem seemed to hinge on the necessity of keeping Chiang Kai-shek in the war. Chennault was then called upon followed by more Stilwell and more confusion ... by the time we left a simple problem had become a tangled mass of confusion.[7]

The priority of the Western theatre over the Far East/Pacific had been confirmed and British interests in the Far East would not attract US support. Prior to the meeting of the great men the two sets of military commanders met in acrimonious debate about strategy. The USA played their logistic card ruthlessly and General Sir Alan Brooke was obliged to make concessions.

Once the military men had come to a measure of agreement, Churchill and Roosevelt found common cause. After the meeting and while chatting to the press, without any preliminaries, Roosevelt made an announcement. He said, 'The elimination of German, Japanese and Italian war power means the *unconditional surrender* [author's emphasis] of Germany, Japan and Italy.'[8] This was political and military dynamite and although Churchill was caught off balance, he endorsed the statement later – he really had no other option. The knock-on effect of Roosevelt's pronouncement was to provide the Axis with a powerful propaganda tool that they could use 'to incite their people to resist to the end'.[9] How many lives this cost cannot be measured.

From 17 to 24 August, Roosevelt and Churchill and the Canadian Prime Minister, Mackenzie King, met in Quebec, although King was not much more than a gracious host. There were two issues to debate and the first of these was setting the date for the invasion of France, to be called Operation OVERLORD – 1 May 1944 was selected. Churchill still aspired to wider operations in the Mediterranean and the elimination of Italy from the war. It was agreed to invade on 3 September 1943 but, on that very day, Italy surrendered. The three Western Allies did not have the inhibiting presence of Stalin and so they could discuss the development of the atomic bomb.

Churchill and Roosevelt, without Canadian input, signed the Quebec Agreement, stating that the nuclear technology would never be used against one another and that they would not use it against third parties without the consent of one another, but also that 'Tube Alloy' would not be discussed with third parties.[10] Canada, although not being represented at the meeting, played a key role in this agreement as it was a major source of uranium and heavy water, both essential in the atomic bomb.[11]

The next conference was held on 22–26 November, when Roosevelt, Churchill and Chiang Kai-shek met in Cairo. The attendance of Chiang was the reason Stalin did not attend. Had he done so, it would have exacerbated Russia's relations with Japan as, at the time, the two countries were not at war. On 27 November, a statement was released that endorsed the earlier aspiration to seek unconditional surrender and emphasised that the three major Allied powers were intent, in the case of Japan, to punish its aggression:

> Japan would be stripped of all the islands in the Pacific, which she has seized or occupied since the beginning of the First World War in 1914. All the territories Japan has stolen from the Chinese, including Manchuria, Formosa and the Pescadores Islands, will be restored to China. Japan will also be expelled from all other territories which she has taken by violence and greed and that in due course Korea shall become free and independent.[12]

Roosevelt, with remarkable insouciance, offered Chiang Kai-shek control of the whole of the Vietnamese Peninsula to thwart any return by the French, an American ally, to their colony. Chiang declined. The presidencies of three of Roosevelt's successors were to founder on the hidden reef of Vietnam.

On 28 November, Roosevelt and Churchill met Stalin in Tehran and they spent three days together. This conference debated issues of worldwide significance and were in broad agreement, not least on the launching of Operation OVERLORD in May 1944. Stalin, having got his way on this issue, and apparently without any persuasion, agreed to enter the war against Japan once Germany was defeated.[13] This was a hugely important commitment although there was nothing altruistic about it, as history would show.

Notes

1. N.A.R.G. 457, *History of US Ultra intelligence* (Washington, 1946).
2. Nash, N.S., *Strafer: Desert General* (Barnsley, Pen & Sword, 2013), pp. 211–19.
3. Inouye Jukichi, *Introduction to Chushingura*, 4th edition (Maruzen Company Ltd., 1910).
4. Russell, Lord of Liverpool, *The Knights of Bushido* (London, Cassell, 1958), pp. 56, 210.
5. Costello, J., *The Pacific War 1941–45* [1981] (New York, Harper Collins, 2009), p. 386.
6. Bryant, A., *Triumph in the West 1943–46* (London, 1959), p. 450.
7. Alanbrooke, FM Lord, *War Diaries 1939–45*, eds Danchev & Todman (London, Weidenfeld & Nicolson, 2001), p. 403.
8. Toland, J., *The Rising Sun: The Decline and Fall of the Japanese Empire, 1936–45* [1970] (Modern Library, New York, 2003), p. 437.
9. Ibid., p. 438.
10. 'Tube Alloys' was the programme initiated by the United Kingdom, with participation from Canada, to develop nuclear weapons. The programme preceded the American version of the same research. The British efforts were highly classified and treated accordingly.
11. Reardon, T., *Winston Churchill and Mackenzie King: So Similar, So Different* (Toronto, Dundurn Press, 2012) pp. 249–50.
12. *Cairo Communique 1 December 1943* (Japan National Diet Library, 1 December 1943).
13. *The Tehran Conference 1943. Milestones 1937–1945* (US Department of State, Office of the Historian, 2016).

Chapter Seventeen

April–December 1943
Operation CARTWHEEL,
Bougainville and Rabaul

Hirohito was not a general. However, he was deeply involved in his country's affairs and increasingly so as the war progressed. He voiced his opinion, as was his constitutional right, a right that he had previously exercised very infrequently. Following the loss of Attu he instructed General Sugiyama, 'In future please see to it that you have a reasonable chance of success before launching any operation.'[1] This mild remark would have cut Sugiyama to the quick, as royal disapproval had a hugely disproportionate impact. Hirohito encouraged the IJN and the IJA to coordinate their operations and voiced disapproval of the friction between the two. There is no doubt that the Emperor was a frustrated player in his nation's affairs, and he was aware that the loss of Attu and Yamamoto had sharpened inter-service rivalry and damaged morale.

Eight months into this war, Japan's crippling lack of war materials was starting to have a deleterious effect. Ships and planes that were lost could not readily be replaced and the highly effective American submarine force was exacting a toll on the rapidly degrading merchant marine. Japan's manufacturing capacity was only about 35 per cent of that of the USA and so the logistic gap could only widen. 'More significant, Japan's gross national product (using 1940 as an index basis of 100) had gone up two points by January 1943. That of the USA by 136.'[2]

The loss of the Aleutian Islands had highlighted the importance of the Japanese Kurile Islands, which would now have to be fortified, garrisoned and supplied. The fortification of the Kuriles would call for the redirection of already scarce raw materials and exacerbate the logistic burden.

The scene of operations moved to the Solomon Islands and Admiral William Halsey, designated Commander, Air Force, Pacific Fleet, led the US force. Halsey was an aggressive, blunt, determined and talented man. To the surprise of many, he and MacArthur became firm friends and held each other in mutual regard.

Although Japanese carrier-based aircraft had suffered grievous attrition at Midway and Guadalcanal, they still posed a threat. Halsey appointed Rear

Admiral Marc Mitscher, in April 1943, to be Commander Air, Solomon Islands (COMAIRSOLS) and allocated to him a mixture of aircraft, from all sources, as the United States Navy fought its way up the Solomon chain.

Operation CARTWHEEL, which was launched on 30 June 1943, was the all-enveloping strategic plan to advance on the Japanese home islands by successively taking Japanese possessions and establishing landing strips ever closer to Japan. In August 1943, the Allies had yet to establish complete control of the air. Nevertheless, its aircraft ranged widely over the Bismarck Sea and New Guinea. ULTRA-intelligence alerted MacArthur to the Japanese build-up of 200 aircraft at Wewak in New Guinea and General Kenney struck at this enemy base on 17 August. He caught the enemy air fleet on the ground. The effect was devastating and the Japanese Air Force in this theatre had been very severely degraded. It was an important victory.

The major Japanese port and base at Rabaul was of such importance that its neutralisation was a high priority. Although MacArthur had directed his force composed of Australian, Dutch, New Zealand and American soldiers along the north-east coast of New Guinea, and they had eventually taken Gona and Buna and the Japanese offshore islands on the way, it was not enough to secure the area, and in October 1943, Rabaul remained as a Japanese fortress and port. It was the command centre for Japanese operations and now a prime target for Allied aggression.

Fleet Admiral William Halsey Jr (1882–1959).

Admiral William Halsey, with the agreement of his superior, Admiral Nimitz, had moved through the Solomon Islands and advanced on Bougainville. The taking of this island, part of Operation CARTWHEEL, was a lengthy process.

In the first phase, American marines established a bridgehead at Torokina on 1–3 November 1943. The Japanese response was an attempt to reinforce Bougainville from Rabaul but, during the ensuing battle of Empress Augusta Bay, the IJN lost two ships sunk, four badly damaged and twenty-five aircraft shot down. The reinforcement did not take place.

There was no strategic reason to take and hold the entire island – all that was needed was enough suitable terrain upon which to build an airstrip. The US Marines were successful in capturing a suitable piece of ground and the airstrip quickly followed, a prerequisite for the bombing of Rabaul. Ground operations were later passed into Australian hands to free American forces to invade the Philippines. The US lost 727 men fighting in Bougainville.

The Japanese force on Bougainville was never entirely defeated and was still resisting up to 15 August 1945, when their country finally surrendered. By then the Australians controlled about two thirds of the island. During the offensive against the Japanese on Bougainville, the Australians experienced 516 fatalities and a further 1,572 men were wounded. Disease and starvation had reduced Japanese numbers from an initial 65,000 to about 23,800 at surrender in August 1945.[3]

The Japanese were painfully aware of American intentions for Rabaul, and the port became the first target for the American, Australian and New Zealand aircraft, commanded by General George Kenney. Rabaul was a well-defended target; it bristled with anti-aircraft guns. Nevertheless, on 12 October 1943, 349 aircraft made the first assault, although bad weather delayed a second wave until 18 October. There were further raids on 23 October and 2 November.[4] Meanwhile, a strong Japanese force of ten cruisers and eleven destroyers sailed from Truk to defend Rabaul.

Halsey had a part to play but his assets were much diminished as his biggest ships had been diverted to the central Pacific to assist in the invasion of Tarawa. He was left with the two carriers *Saratoga* and *Princeton*, together with their embarked air arms. Until this point, carrier-borne aircraft, Pearl Harbor apart, had not been employed on the interdiction of powerful land targets. If Halsey committed his aircraft to an attack on Rabaul he was taking a very serious risk. His carriers would be unprotected, and he was courting heavy losses at the hands of Rabaul's formidable defences, which were now supplemented by the cruiser force. On 4–5 November, Halsey moved his carriers closer to the target and then, under cover of a weather front, he launched all ninety-seven of his available aircraft. Their attack was supplemented by Kenney's bomber force of twenty-seven B-24 Liberators, protected by fifty-eight P-38s.[5] This combination overwhelmed Rabaul and caused very serious damage to six of the seven ships in the Japanese cruiser force. Fifty-six Japanese planes were destroyed. Allied losses were twenty-seven, of which only ten were carrier-based.

To underscore this victory, on 11 November Halsey attacked again, having been reinforced by elements of the 5th Fleet. He now had under command the carriers *Essex*, *Bunker Hill* and *Independence*. The Japanese then made the error of reinforcing failure and flew in hundreds of aircraft from Truk and an unconfirmed number between 200 and 300 were annihilated. The port of

The Japanese cruiser *Haguro* under attack, Rabaul, November 1943.

Rabaul was in ruins; it was no longer a base for offensive operations and in February 1944 the Japanese recognised the reality and evacuated its remaining aircraft back to Truk. Rabaul had no further part to play, and it was isolated for the remainder of the war.

Notes

1. Toland, J., *The Rising Sun: The Decline and Fall of the Japanese Empire, 1936–45* [1970] (Modern Library, New York, 2003), p. 444.
2. Ibid., p. 445.
3. Veterans.sa.gov.au, *The Bougainville Offensive*, 2019.
4. Mortensen, B.L, *Rabaul and Cape Gloucester* (Hyper-War Foundation, Army Air Forces in World War II: Vol. IV, 1953), p. 333.
5. Ibid.

Chapter Eighteen

November 1942–August 1943 Co-prosperity, Tarawa, Makin and Mountbatten

The foundation stone of Japan's political and military expansion was initially propagated in 1938 by the first Konoye government, which declared an aim to create a 'Greater East Asia Co-prosperity Sphere' (GEACS). The attendant propaganda emphasised that it sought to 'unite Asia in the spirit of universal brotherhood'. This would, of course, be under the enlightened leadership of Japan. It was political idealists who created the policy to free Asia from exploitation by white men, but it was the militarists and realists who were the practitioners.

This latter group saw Asia's wealth in natural resources as the panacea for Japan's economic ills and the invasion of Manchuria had, some years before, supported that view. The noble idea of GEACS was embraced by many in Japan's captured territories. On the face of it, and quite reasonably, the Imperial Japanese Army was greeted as a liberator from the colonial yoke. Not so in Singapore/Malaya, where multiple murder had been public and widely witnessed.

Burma was the most fertile ground for Japanese propaganda to flourish and here Dr Ba Maw became the leading advocate for Burmese independence, a perfectly understandable aspiration. Before the war he had served in ministerial posts in the Burmese Legislature and for two years from 1937, he was premier. His background in government made him a powerful voice in Burmese affairs, even after the country was invaded. Prior to that, in 1940, he opposed Britain's likely participation in the Second World War and resigned from the Legislature. He was arrested for sedition on 6 August 1940 and jailed, but little more than a year later, the Japanese invaders freed him from jail and invited him to lead the Executive Administration of Burma on their behalf.

Ba Maw busied himself and, on 8 May 1943, he formed and headed the 'Burma Independence Preparatory Committee'. This was the precursor to the declaration of an Independent State of Burma on 1 August 1943, of which he was the first Naingandaw Adipadi (head of state), effectively, the president.

Principal GEACS conference attendees, left to right: Ba Maw (Burma); Zhang Jinghui, Wang Jingwei (China); Hideki Tōjō (Prime Minister of Japan); Wan Waithayakon (Thailand); José P. Laurel (Philippines); Subhas Chandra Bose (India).

He moved swiftly to declare war on Great Britain and the USA and entered a formal alliance with Japan.

Another opponent of British rule encouraged into active, armed opposition, this time in India, was Chandra Bose. He was an intellectually gifted man with an Anglocentric education and a passionate ambition for Indian independence. He was for some years allied to Gandhi, who shared his views but not his methods, and they went their separate ways. When the war broke out, Bose sought to foster a campaign of civil disobedience in India as a protest at Britain's declaration of war on India's behalf, but without any democratic mandate to do so. He was briefly jailed and then made a covert journey to Germany in the spring of 1941. He met Hitler and, predictably, enjoyed support for his cause.[1] Moving on to Russia, he was disappointed at the lukewarm greeting and lack of enthusiasm for his bid for independence.

Bose enjoyed modest success in recruiting Indian soldiers captured in North Africa and Asia and formed them into the Indian Legion – about 4,500 strong and placed under German command in the Waffen SS. He repeated the movement, and recruited about 50,000 Indian soldiers captured in Burma, Malaya and Singapore into the Indian National Army (INA). The birth of this army was beset with difficulties but eventually it took its place alongside the IJA, and many died in Japanese colours.

The INA and its significance should be viewed against the wider canvas of recruitment of volunteers for the Indian Army when 2.5 million came forward to form the largest volunteer force in the world. The overwhelming majority served the Crown bravely and honourably; 87,000 were killed. 'British and Commonwealth troops viewed the INA recruits as traitors and collaborators.'[2] About 40,000 Indian soldiers captured in Malaya and Singapore rejected the INA and remained as POWs. For many, the oath of allegiance they had taken to the king was prime among reasons not to join a Japanese-supporting orga-nisation. These men paid a high price for their loyalty as they were then singled out for particularly harsh treatment to persuade them to reconsider their position and join the INA.

The Japanese mounted a conference in Tokyo on 5–6 November 1943, to which it invited representatives of this new-found Co-prosperity Sphere and latent independence movement. The principal attendees posed for the obligatory photograph.

The creation of GEACS was, in principle, a shrewd political strategy upon which the Japanese could have built a mutually supportive commonwealth. However, the IJA and its millions of soldiers spread across Southeast Asia were not imbued with the political nous that was required to make it all work. Instead, they continued to abuse the residents whose country they now occupied and GEACS was reduced to pie in the sky.

* * *

In late 1943, the Americans thwarted British attempts to be more proactive in the war against Japan. Churchill's plan for Operation CULVERIN to seize air bases in Sumatra from which Japanese forces in Singapore and Rangoon could be bombed could not be launched without American support. They viewed it as yet another ploy by Britain to regain its imperial possessions – which, of course, was one of the unstated aims. The USA favoured the reopening of the Burma Road to facilitate the logistic support of Chiang Kai-shek and improve and increase Chinese Nationalist operations against the Japanese. The Quebec Conference code named QUADRANT had been held in August and, at that meeting, Major General Orde Wingate was given the floor to expound on his plans for Long-Range Penetration (LRP). It was a masterly presentation and, as a result, General Arnold agreed to provide air support. Marshall was sufficiently impressed that within six months the US Army had formed its own 5307th Composite Unit (later christened Merrill's Marauders) to specialise in the same guerrilla tactics.[3]

It was at this meeting that it was agreed that Admiral Louis Mountbatten should be appointed the Supreme Allied Commander, Southeast Asia Com-mand (SEAC). He was only 42, an age when most officers were of lieutenant colonel rank. In the opinion of his critics, Mountbatten was grossly over-promoted. His chief of staff, Lieutenant General Sir Henry Pownall, however, was an admirer. He drew attention to Mountbatten's charm, which he thought to be one of his greatest assets, but commented on his almost wilful disregard for common sense and sound advice. Mountbatten was impulsive and was prone to hold meetings at which he talked at very great length. There was something of the poseur about him and he made constant reference to his relationship with King George VI, his cousin.[4] He was ruthlessly ambitious but did not have the intellectual depth to function as a commander-in-chief. Field Marshal Sir Alan Brooke recorded witheringly:

> A long COS meeting attended by Mountbatten I find it very difficult to remain pleasant when he turns up! He is the most crashing bore . . . is always fiddling about with unimportant matters and wasting other people's time.[5]

It was probably as well that Mountbatten did not have practical command of anything and was, in effect, nothing more than a figurehead. To be fair, as perhaps the only man to match MacArthur's ego, he was nevertheless an accomplished diplomat. He was very pro-American, sympathetic to Asian aspirations for independence and an excellent ambassador for Britain. Although he did not achieve any military success in SEAC, he excelled diplomatically.

Just ten days after marines stormed ashore on Bougainville, the United States initiated Operation GALVANIC, under the overall command of Admiral Spruance. On 11 November 1943, sixteen transports, protected by three battleships, five carriers, five cruisers and twenty-two destroyers, carried the 2nd US Marine Division to their objective, which was the small island of Betio. This lay off the south-western side of Tarawa Atoll, one of the Gilbert Islands.

The 5th Fleet Amphibious Command was headed by Admiral Turner and the logistic effort to support this vast force of 53,000 men was the responsibility of Vice Admiral William Calhoun, who:

> had assembled an armada of transports repair and supply vessels and a collection of 300-foot concrete oil barges. He had established a floating naval base at Funafuti Lagoon, in the Ellice Islands. Everything this 5th Fleet would need to sustain its 200 ships and 20,000 sailors, from bandages to bombs, strawberry ice cream to spare aircraft parts, was ready and waiting. The thirteen fleet oilers, the flotilla of minesweepers and repair vessels was only at the beginning of a massive naval housekeeping operation that was to grow as the 5th Fleet expanded.[6]

For this operation, Calhoun had also to arrange for the feeding of the host embarked for GALVANIC. The division, commanded by Major General

Julian Smith, was well rested having been withdrawn from Guadalcanal to recuperate in New Zealand. Its men were fit, well fed, and had high morale.

American strategy called for the acquisition of airfields in the strongly garrisoned and defended Mariana Islands, from where bombers could reach the Japanese home islands. However, before the Marianas could be attacked a firm base was needed and Tarawa/Betio to the west filled the bill.

The small island of Betio is 2 miles (3.2km) long and only 800 yards (739m) wide. It is featureless, flat, and surrounded by a coral reef about 550 yards (500m) wide, which, when exposed at low tide, is a formidable obstacle.

A significant asset was the lengthy pier that had been built out over the reef to service ships anchored in deeper water. To the north of Betio lay the

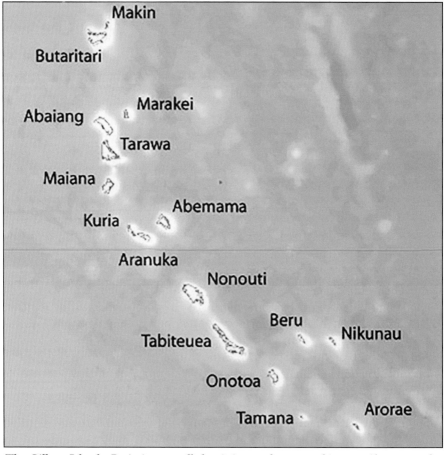

The Gilbert Islands. Betio is so small that it is not shown on this map. Shown are the targeted islands of Makin and Tarawa.

Tarawa lagoon while to the south and west was the deep water of the Pacific Ocean.

Betio and Tarawa had been heavily fortified by 6th Yokosuka Naval Landing Force. The islands bristled with pillboxes and gun positions. Fields of fire had been cleared of vegetation, range cards constructed, and ammunition and food distributed. The sons of Bushido were well prepared, and it was their intention to defeat any American invasion on the water's edge; 4,836 troops from several different formations formed the garrison and they operated fourteen tanks and forty-four heavy guns. The American force was vast: 35,000 soldiers, 18,000 marines, five carriers, three battleships, four cruisers, twenty-two destroyers, two mine sweepers, eighteen landing ships and transports. This looked to be 'a walk in the park'.

But it was not.

The landing was to be made by infantry soldiers carried to the beaches in Higgins boats and Amphibious Tracked Vehicles. To traverse the reef, 5 feet of water was required, and an expert warned this was a period for the neap tides and there would be only 3 feet of water – insufficient to float the Higgins boats. The expert was ignored.[7] Clearly the reconnaissance and planning for this operation was flawed. However, to postpone an invasion on this scale, waiting for the tide to turn was firmly in the 'too difficult' category and the landings went ahead.

The attack started with a blistering naval bombardment of all the landing beaches but when the assaulting troops went in, their boats, predictably, beached on the reef. They were then faced with a 500-yard hike through thigh-high water in the face of withering fire. Casualties mounted quickly but some of the tracked vehicles got through, and fragile beachheads were established. The taking of Tarawa/Betio took three days of savage fighting.

The Japanese had demonstrated at Buna and Guadalcanal their tenacity and courage, and so they did again in Tarawa: 1,009 Americans were killed and 2,101 were wounded.[8] The Japanese were simply wiped out and only seventeen were captured, as were 129 Korean labourers; 4,690 Japanese were killed and the balance of 129 Japanese was never found. Tarawa was an emphatic American victory brought about by massive force and unrivalled logistic support. It was the first time that the USA had made an opposed landing, but more were to follow. Newspaper photographs of the devastated Tarawan landscape and of the American soldiers and marines after the battle had shocked the American public, as did the casualty list. It seemed to be a very heavy price to pay for such an insignificant little island in the middle of nowhere.

There was a review of Operation GALVANIC and, quite correctly, it was acknowledged that the tides had been an important factor that reconnaissance

Betio Island with Tarawa in the distance. The reef and strategically important airstrip can be clearly seen.

had failed to identify. That was not true, but the uncomfortable facts were swept aside. The review also noted the survivability of Japanese defences and the need for accurate and sustained bombardment before similar landings.[9] Nimitz had visited Betio and had been appalled by what he saw. He had replicas of Japanese bunkers built on a Hawaiian island and tested them with different forms of artillery, concluding that flat-trajectory ordnance was more effective than plunging fire. Better waterproof radios, more tank landing craft, and amphibious craft were added to his shopping list and his vastly wealthy country moved swiftly to accommodate his needs.

With the airstrip on Betio secured, the US moved north to Makin Atoll, where the enemy had established a seaplane base in December 1941. At that time a garrison of about 160 served the base, which became the focus of American attention much earlier, on 17 August 1942, with the intention of destabilising and confusing the Japanese about American intentions in the Gilbert Islands. Some 211 US Marines of the 2nd Raider Battalion were landed from submarines on that day.

The Japanese garrison was surprised, outnumbered and outfought; about eighty-three were killed. American losses were twenty-one killed and nine captured. The nine men became the victims of a war crime when they were moved to Kwajalein Atoll and decapitated. Although the Makin raid was a short-term military success, nevertheless it was counterproductive as it alerted the Japanese to American interest in the Gilbert Islands and accelerated the fortification of, not least, Betio and Tarawa.

The island-hopping philosophy of Nimitz identified Makin as the next objective. Its garrison was 806 strong and, of these, at best only 400 were infantry. The balance was composed of aviation specialists of one sort or another, and by Korean labourers with no military skills. The largest atoll was Butaritari, incorrectly identified by the USA as Makin Atoll, although Makin Atoll is about 1.9 miles (3km) away to the north-east.

Two days after the invasion of Tarawa, on 13 November 1943, the USA commenced air attacks and opened a naval bombardment that targeted the limited military facilities on both coral atolls. The Japanese had no chance. They were outgunned, outnumbered and had no possibility of reinforcement or aerial support. Their only option was to resist and inflict as many casualties as possible. This they did, displaying enormous courage; the island was not taken until 23 November. By then, 395 Japanese had been killed and seventeen captured. American ground losses were only sixty-six. However, the sinking of the USS *Liscome Bay*, just off Makin, by the Japanese submarine *I-175* on 24 November, changed the balance: 644 USN personnel were lost as the escort carrier and flagship succumbed to a single torpedo and sank quickly. The loss of this ship was avoidable, but two of her anti-submarine escorts left a gap in their defensive screen and *I-175* took full advantage of the opportunity offered.

Notes

1. Hayes, R., *Subhas Chandra Bose in Nazi Germany: Intelligence and Propaganda 1941–43* (Oxford University Press, 2011), pp. 65–7.

2. Fay, P.W., *The Forgotten Army: India's Armed Struggle for Independence, 1942–1945* (University of Michigan Press, 1993), p. 417.
3. Costello, J., *The Pacific War 1941–45* [1981] (New York, Harper Collins, 2009), p. 417.
4. Pownall, Gen H., *Diaries*, Vol. 2., ed. Bond, B. (London, Leo Cooper, 1972–74), p. 201.
5. Alanbrooke, FM Lord, *War Diaries 1939–45*, eds. Danchev & Todman (London, Weidenfeld & Nicolson, 2001), p. 716.
6. Morison, S.E., *History of United States Naval Operations in World War II*, Vol. 3, quoted by Costello, p. 429.
7. *Major Francis Holland* (The Oxford Companion to New Zealand Military History, McGibbon ed.), p. 220.
8. Wright, D., *Tarawa 1943: The Turning of the Tide* (Oxford, Osprey, 2004), p. 93.
9. Costello, p. 419.

Chapter Nineteen

January 1944
Kwajalein, Roi-Namur, Truk, Food
and Eniwetok

The battle of Tarawa set a pattern for future American operations in the Pacific as Nimitz hopped from island to island and ever closer to Japan. The targets were usually small coral islands that were fortified and garrisoned. Individually these target islands were inconsequential, but the whole formed the defensive perimeter of the homeland. Their piecemeal acquisition by the US did not call for either brilliant generalship or innovative tactics. However, there was a need for massive logistic support for the aerial and naval bombardments that preceded an invasion over defended beaches.

The necessary courage and tenacity from US ground forces was readily available as, time and time again, soldiers and marines excelled in the face of suicidal opposition. The swift evacuation of casualties was needed to maintain morale in this morale-sapping campaign when every engagement was just like the one before. No other nation on earth had the wealth, industrial capacity and will to mount and support a campaign such as that of the USA in the Pacific.

Kwajalein Atoll, in the Marshall Island group, was the next object in Nimitz's plan. It is composed of ninety-three small coral islands that surround one of the largest lagoons in the world, measuring 324 square miles (839km^2). The two largest islands in the atoll are Kwajalein, in the south, and the linked islands of Roi-Namur in the north. By 1941, the Japanese had established the atoll as part of their defensive perimeter and had installed the appropriate facilities and fortifications. Rear Admiral Akiyama Monzo commanded the garrison of about 5,000. He and his men were willing to die to defend their patch of coral, sand and palm trees when the US attacked on 31 January.

Nimitz moved his forces on, and the next very fruitful objective was to be the large and seemingly secure Japanese naval base at Truk, an atoll in the Marshall Islands surrounded by coral reefs, with a large lagoon having only a few points of entry. It was in this lagoon that the Japanese had assembled a fleet of military and priceless merchant ships. Protection was afforded by shore batteries and anti-aircraft artillery. A landing strip was key to its aerial defence. The Imperial Japanese Navy had boasted that Truk was its 'Gibraltar of the Pacific'. The Japanese anticipated an invasion of Truk and planned accordingly. The garrison had constructed copious concrete bunkers and was well prepared to repel a cross-beach invasion.

MacArthur was making progress in Southwest Pacific and isolating some Japanese-held islands and capturing others. This was in accord with Operation CARTWHEEL, which planned to bypass the eastern Marshall Islands. The IJN had recognised the possible isolation of Truk and moved most of its fleet out of the lagoon to the relative safety of the Palau Islands. The US had no need to capture Truk; it could now be neutralised by aerial bombardment and those remaining, firmly anchored ships provided a target-rich environment.

Operation HAILSTONE commenced on 17 February 1944, in a demonstration of the growing military power of the USA. For two days, the idyllic Truk lagoon erupted in a maelstrom of bombardment from US ships and persistent bombing from its aircraft. Admiral Spruance had selected Vice Admiral Marc Mitscher's Fast Carrier Force (TF-58) to conduct the assault on Truk. TF-58 was well equipped for the job. Three of Mitscher's carrier groups were allocated to the mission. The fleet carriers *Enterprise*, *Yorktown*, *Essex*, *Intrepid* and *Bunker Hill*, together with four light carriers, *Belleau Wood*, *Cabot*, *Monterey* and *Cowpens*, carried over 500 aircraft. They were supported by seven battleships and an assortment of cruisers, destroyers and submarines.[1] This was probably a case of overkill.

The Japanese had no answer and their losses were immense: 250 aircraft and irreplaceable pilots. More than 4,500, mostly seamen, were killed, and 17,000 tons of stored fuel oil was destroyed. Despite attempts to get out of the lagoon, all but one ship failed to do so. Japanese naval losses were:

Sunk
2 Cruisers: *Katori* (5,800 tons), *Naka* (5,195 tons)
4 Destroyers: *Maikaze* (2,000 tons), *Fumizuki* (1,320 tons), *Oite* (1,270 tons), *Tachikaze* (1,215 tons)
2 Submarine chasers: *CH-29* (440 tons), *CH-24* (440 tons)
1 Auxiliary submarine chaser: *Shōnan Maru* (355 tons)
1 Motor torpedo boat: *No. 10* (85 tons)

Damaged
1 Repair ship: *Akashi* (10,500 tons)
1 Seaplane tender: *Akitsushima* (4,650 tons)
2 Destroyers: *Matsukaze* (1,400 tons), *Shigure* (1,685 tons)
2 Submarines: *I-10* (2,919 tons), *RO-42* (1,115 tons)

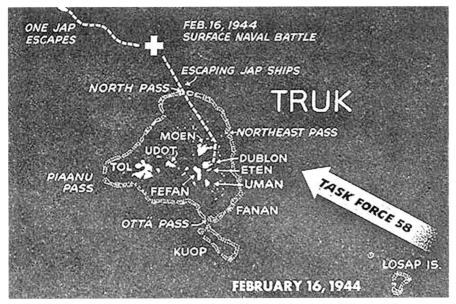

The Battle of Truk Lagoon (Our Navy Neutralizes the Pacific Truk Atoll, February 1944). (*Lieutenant Oliver Jensen, USNR*)

1 Submarine chaser: *CHa-20*
1 Target ship: *Hakachi* (1,641 tons)

These IJN losses paled into insignificance when weighed against the sinking of thirty-two merchant vessels – about 200,000 tons in total. These ships had been the lifeline to any number of Japanese outposts and their loss was a major factor in the later isolation of Japanese in the Pacific and starvation in the home islands. The US did lose twenty-five aircraft and forty killed, but it was a modest price to pay.

Truk was not occupied, the concrete defences were never tested, and the Japanese survivors were left to their own devices. They were never resupplied, and at war's end, they were starving. Truk was like many other Japanese outposts; it became, by default, a prison camp. The Japanese-held islands in the Bismarck Archipelago, the Caroline Islands, the Marshalls and the Palaus were all bypassed and their resupply, or lack of, rested with the US Navy.

As the USN advanced it built new naval bases and airstrips, such as those on Majuro. The lagoon at Majuro gave the USN a massive anchorage in the Central Pacific and it was a major asset until the war moved on and the same building process was repeated on Ulithi Atoll.

At this time, an issue was the efficiency of the USN submarine service, which was hopelessly inhibited by its use of the Mark XIV torpedo. As

Theodore Roscoe, author of the official naval history of submarine opera-tions, put it, 'The only reliable feature of the torpedo was its unreliability.' After two years' wartime use and innumerable alterations, the torpedo still failed to explode 70 per cent of the time. Nevertheless, and despite the unreliable torpedo, USN submariners, who were only 2 per cent of US naval personnel, sank more than 1,178 merchant vessels and 214 warships, totalling more than 5,600,000 tons. Fifty-two submarines were lost, together with 374 officers and 3,131 men.[2]

*   *   *

Of all the material that falls under the generic 'logistics', food is arguably the most important. Without it no society, military or civilian, can function. Food supply in the Japanese home islands was becoming increasingly scarce. The cessation of rice imports obliged the Government to supplement rice with 10–20 per cent of unpopular substitutes. Meat was practically unobtain-able, fish was limited, and milk was only available for children and sick people. Malnutrition breeds illness and both have a deleterious effect on morale.

'By mid-1943, even generally law-abiding citizens were resorting to the Black Market to buy food.'[3] If life was difficult for civilians, for Japanese soldiers it was harder, much harder. Guadalcanal had fallen to the Americans in January 1943, by which time 200 Japanese were dying each day from starvation. Those who had survived this far were skin and bone. 'Their teeth were falling out, their eyebrows and lashes too. For three weeks none of these men had a bowel movement. Their bodies were so starved of salt that sea water tasted sweet.'[4]

In New Guinea, the Japanese were confronted by perhaps the most hostile environment on earth and they were in desperate straits. Resupply had been by the dropping, into the sea, of oil drums filled with food, ammunition and medical stores. The ship would signal to alert the troops on or near the beach. The signal also alerted Allied artillery, which would then bring fire down on the unfortunates detailed to collect the drums. The next device was for submerged submarines to release submerged containers that they had towed close to shore. The idea was feasible, and it worked as each successful delivery would feed 30,000 men for two days. Unfortunately, only one third of these deliveries reached the intended recipients.[5] The bulk was lost, adding further to Japan's food deficit.

Allied interrogations of Japanese prisoners made clear the disintegrating state of discipline in the IJA brought about by their 'preoccupation with food ... Bitterness and resentment, reaching at times a homicidal level, are generated by this life or death competition (for food), especially towards officers who are, or appear to be, abusing the privileges of their rank.'[6]

By the middle of 1944, the Japanese were so stretched that they were obliged to feed their soldiers *sacsac*.

> This was a tasteless, brown starch made from sago palms. Water was passed through the fibre hollowed out of palm trunks to produce a glutinous mass which was wrapped in leaves and cooked. This sticky mess was even sent up to front-line troops. At first, they mixed it with rice or wheat but eventually they ate plain *sacsac*. In the Sepik River area the men in combat were given dried grasses to eat. Aware of how hungry the Japanese were, the Allies bombed supply bases and even strafed palm trees to deny them coconuts and *sacsac*.[7]

The measure of the dire straits into which the Japanese had plunged is best demonstrated by the orders issued by Lieutenant General Adachi Hatazō on

10 December 1944. He proclaimed that 'whilst troops were permitted to eat the flesh of Allied dead, they must not eat their own.' Reports of Japanese cannibalism were made from various sources. For example, Hatam Ali, an Indian soldier taken prisoner and sent to New Guinea to help build an airfield in 1943, recorded that when the Japanese ran out of food, the guards would select one prisoner each day who was taken out, killed, and eaten. He said, 'I personally saw this happen.'[8]

Lord Russell records, in ghastly and graphic detail, examples of Japanese cannibalism, which was often accompanied by the most extreme torture – such as the extraction of organs from a living victim.[9] This is human behaviour that simply beggars belief.

Lieutenant General Adachi Hatazo (1890–1947).

* * *

The island-hopping continued and, on 16–24 February 1944, the US attacked and took Eniwetok Atoll and its three main islands of Eniwetok, Engebi and Parry. Engebi had an airstrip and that was an initial target for the aerial component of Task Group 58.4, which swiftly destroyed fourteen aircraft on the ground and a coastal defence emplacement. The two small undefended islets of Canna and Camelia were occupied. Then, on 17 February, the combined firepower of the battleships *Colorado*, *Tennessee* and *Philadelphia*, and the cruiser *Louisville*, was directed on the beaches as the prelude to the landing the following day. Eighty-five men of the 22 US Marine Regiment were killed in the operation, but as was now the pattern, Japanese losses were vastly higher: 1,276 killed and only sixteen captured.[10]

The other two islands were invaded and taken after obdurate defence by the hopelessly outnumbered Japanese. In all, and over the three islands, the defenders had 3,380 men killed and 144 captured. The Americans had 390 killed and missing. The kill ratio was down to 1:8.6 – an early indication of the price that would have to be paid when any of the Home Islands were assaulted.

Notes

1. Rems, A., 'Two Birds with One Hailstone' (*Naval History Magazine*, Vol. 28, 2014).
2. History.net
3. Ibid., p. 289.
4. Harries, M. & Harries, S., *Soldiers of the Sun* (New York, Random House, 1991) p. 341.
5. Collingham, L., *The Taste of War* (Penguin, 2011), p. 296.
6. Research report No. 122, AWM 55 12/94, p. 4, quoted by Collingham, p. 297.
7. Richmond, K., *Japanese Forces in New Guinea* (Australian War Memorial, 2003), p. 181.
8. Tanaka, Y., *Hidden Horrors: Japanese War Crimes in WWII* (Oxford, Westview Press, 1996), pp. 115–16.
9. Russell, Lord of Liverpool, *The Knights of Bushido* (London, Cassell, 1958), pp. 233–40.
10. Rottman, G. & Gerrard, H., *The Marshall Islands 1944* (Oxford, Osprey Publishing, 2004).

Chapter Twenty

February 1944–August 1945 Kohima, Imphal, the Second Chindit Operation, Marauders and the Recapture of Burma

In the war against Japan, the ruthlessly effective march of the seaborne US Forces through the Pacific in 1942–5 had all but decided the outcome. That was until the US Army Air Corps delivered its bombs on Hiroshima and Nagasaki to settle the issue. There were, however, three campaigns that although individually important did not materially contribute to the defeat of Japan. Arguably, and perhaps simplistically, these were that of the Australian/ US in New Guinea, the US in the Philippines, and the British/Indian/West African Army in Burma.

The Allies could not avoid battle in Burma and New Guinea as they had to respond to Japanese activity, but they *could* have bypassed the Philippines. However, in that case, MacArthur's titanic ego got in the way, and he insisted on the invasion of the islands. Allied success in all three places was hard-fought and well won, but had no strategic value and cost hundreds of thousands of lives and the destruction of the beautiful city of Manila.

In early 1944, although the Chinese and Japanese had established an informal truce, Lieutenant General Joseph Stilwell, Chiang Kai-shek's chief of staff, was anxious to stir the Chinese back into action. Stilwell, who seemed to dislike everyone, had at least a working relationship with Lieutenant General William (known as 'Bill') Slim, the commander of the 14th Army – composed of British, Indian and African soldiers.

A consistent American aim was to boost the Chinese Nationalists, to save China from communism, and to establish China as a world power. Chiang was to be the tool in this enterprise. However, Chiang was an uncomfortable bedfellow who was intent on pressing the USA into even greater largesse than that hitherto freely and generously given. The situation was not helped by Stilwell's ill-concealed dislike for his Chinese leader. Chiang's forces were sustained by American logistic support, directed by Stilwell, and delivered by air over the Himalayas to Kunming in the province of Yunnan. This route was known as 'the hump'. Stilwell intended to supplement this supply route by extending the Ledo Road, to connect India and China, but the British did not share American faith in Chiang Kai-shek and were unenthused about the Ledo Road.

The Cairo Conference (22–26 November 1943) had agreed that an assault would be made on southern France and available resources would be diverted to that cause. This had the effect of downgrading the priority of operations in Burma, where the major Allied effort was intended to be in the north by American-trained Chinese troops of Stilwell's 'Northern Combat Area Command'. Cairo thwarted Mountbatten's aim for amphibious assaults on Rangoon and Singapore – for which he had not the ships, the landing craft or the soldiers. The US Chiefs of Staff identified, quite correctly, Mountbatten's undeclared imperial aim. Operations in Burma during 1944 were a complex amalgam of many moving parts, involving several players, and accounting for thousands of deaths. The battles were fought in dreadful conditions and the attrition, on both sides, caused by disease outnumbered those suffered 'in action'.

The reconquest of Burma, a country from which the British/Indian/East and West African Army had been humiliatingly ejected in May 1942, was an important goal for the British, whose aspirations for empire were undimmed. In February 1944, intelligence reports from several sources indicated that Lieutenant General Kawabe Masakazu, the commander of the Burma Area Army, had designs on British bases in Assam, Northeast India. Observation Posts (OPs) along the Chindwin River surmised that 15th Army, commanded by Lieutenant General Mutaguchi Renya, would cross the river and cut the rail link between Dimapur and Imphal. The latter was strategically important, just 50 miles (80km) west of the Burmese border and perceived to be the gateway to India.

The small town was located on a plain about 40 miles (64km) long and 20 miles (32km) wide. Just south of the town was an area of swamp dignified by the name Loktak Lake. This lake varied in size depending on the season. It is a sizeable feature, about 20 miles (32km) long and about 12 miles (19km) wide. Imphal was the base from which 14th Army was supplied. It housed all the facilities that were needed ranging from hospitals and ammunition dumps to engineering shops and airstrips. Imphal was, and is, a communications hub; five roads join at the town. Its importance to Slim was very clear to Mutaguchi, and he planned accordingly.

'Were Imphal to fall to the Japanese it would be of massive propaganda value and would, perhaps, kindle into flame the aspirations of all anti-imperialists.'[1] The Japanese aim would be to attack and take Kohima, then turn south and address Imphal. A product of this strategy would be to capture the airfields being used to resupply Chiang Kai-shek's Nationalist Army over 'the hump' by Major General Claire Chennault's 'Flying Tigers'. This organisation was incorporated into the USAAF in 1942 and Chennault's status was regularised when he advanced from mercenary to commissioned officer in the rank of brigadier general and later, major general.

Mutaguchi had been impressed by Wingate's first Chindit expedition and he reasoned that if an Englishman could navigate through and survive in the rainforest, surmount mountains, and bring down effective fire, then so too could his Japanese soldiers. The differences were that Wingate's men were specially trained in guerrilla tactics, and they also had ample logistic support. Brigadier Bernard Fergusson, who commanded 16th Brigade in Wingate's second expedition, observed:

> Wingate had the ability to make us believe in ourselves and to be confident that we could achieve what we had set out to do. One day he wanted to send a patrol into an area of jungle, which I knew to be impenetrable, and I said so. He rolled a contemptuous eye on me and added to his orders, 'No patrol will report any jungle impenetrable until it has penetrated it.'[2]

It was Mutaguchi who had been commanding the regiment of the Kwantung Army at the Marco Polo Bridge. He was an opportunist and was waiting for the British XV Corps, advancing down the Arakan Peninsula, 'to be hanging

Lieutenant General Mutaguchi Renya (1866–1966).

like a bunch of grapes before launching his *Ha-Go* offensive', which would sever their logistic line.[3]

In the area of his likely advance, Mutaguchi was faced by the IV Corps (Scoones), comprising 17, 20 and 23 divisions. The commander of the British 14th Indian Army, Lieutenant General Bill Slim, decided to retain IV Corps on the Imphal plain and Kohima and fight Mutaguchi on ground of his choosing. Slim was shrewd and he could see that, as ever, logistic supply would be an issue. By shortening his lines of communication he extended those of Mutaguchi into difficult country west of the Chindwin. The monsoon would arrive in a couple of months and that would exacerbate Mutaguchi's resupply difficulties.

In a decision of breathtaking folly, the Japanese general based his operation on the taking of British food stocks to feed his army. Until he had achieved that aim his soldiers would have to live on what they could carry. The contents of their packs would be supplemented by eating their pack animals and a few cattle injected into their columns. This was logistic madness, doomed to fail.

Mutaguchi's aim was unclear, but the probability is that he had wildly ambitious plans to pass through Assam and once into India provoke a mass uprising against British rule. To this end he included in his order of battle the 1st Indian National Army. 'The INA was ineffective in battle so Mutaguchi's motives for saddling himself with 7,000 useless mouths could only have been to use them for propaganda on arrival in India.'[4]

The battle for Imphal started on 15 March, when the Japanese 33rd Division, which Slim recognised as 'living up to its reputation of being the toughest division in Burma', advanced up the Tiddim road towards Imphal, necessitating a fighting withdrawal by 17th Division. 'The battles ... on the Tiddim Road were some of the fiercest of the whole Burma war and were to have a profound influence on its outcome.'[5] The withdrawal to the Imphal plain was delayed by Slim, one of his rare errors of judgement, and as a consequence, 17th Division was threatened by an attempt to encircle it. The Japanese aim was to cut the division's communications with Kohima. Major General 'Punch' Cowan would have none of this and in 'a series of brilliant battles the 17th Division utterly defeated the Japanese attempts to cut them off and withdrew safely to the Imphal plain'.[6]

* * *

If British IV Corps was obstructing and distracting the Japanese, there was more distraction to come in the shape of Long-Range Penetration (LRP), the brainchild of Major General Orde Wingate, who was mounting his second Chindit expedition (Operation THURSDAY). His masterly presentation at the Quebec conference had won his Chindits the support of the US 1st Air Commando Group, who would provide the aircraft for resupply and casualty evacuation (CASEVAC). Wingate prepared his men with rigorous and intensive training. They were tough, fit, young soldiers capable of living in the jungle and coping with its multiple hazards. Elsewhere, the US 5307th Composite Unit (provisional) was undergoing similar training and preparation. The unit title was widely ridiculed and likened to a street address in Los Angeles. It adopted the title 'Merrill's Marauders' after its commanding officer, Brigadier General Frank Merrill. The incursions behind Japanese lines by these two deep penetration formations were bold but required a high level of logistic and air support.

Lieutenant General Stilwell, typically, made it his business to ensure that these US troops should not serve under a British officer. His Anglophobia was such that it adversely affected his decision-making and cost Chindit lives. A fundamental element in the culture of Western armies is that an officer spends the lives of his soldiers frugally and cares for their well-being. Stilwell displayed disinterest in the survival of the Marauders, a brigade-sized unit that was the only US infantry force under his command. '[He] treated them like dirt by running them into the ground and by breaking every promise he made them.'[7] He committed the unit to the point of its complete destruction. Stilwell was loathed by British and American soldiers alike and one commented: 'I had him in my rifle sights, no one would have known it wasn't a jap that got the son-of-a-bitch.'[8] The future of LRP was to be placed in the hands of this man.

Initially, there were six brigades employed in Operation THURSDAY: the 77th, 111th Indian Infantry Brigade, 14th, 16th and 23rd brigades – formed from 70th Division – and 3rd (West African) Brigade. It was the intention that these brigades should be reordered into columns, each of 400–450 men, provided with around sixty mules and with a few casualty-carrying ponies. Columns could, and would, act independently but would join occasionally to confront the enemy and then disperse back into the jungle before the Japanese could concentrate against them.

This was Wingate's original LRP philosophy. It was the availability of No. 1 Air Commando's aircraft that gave Wingate flexibility to adapt his plan and, for example, agree a static 'block' across the main south-north supply road and railway feeding enemy forces in the north.

On 5 February, Brigadier Fergusson's 16th Brigade left its base in Ledo and marched into Burma. Fergusson chose a rugged and difficult route to avoid contact with the enemy. It was planned that the rest of the force would be flown into three jungle airstrips codenamed Piccadilly, Chowringhee and Broadway. However, last-minute information revealed that Piccadilly was covered in logs and was unusable. The indications were that the Japanese had anticipated the incursion and that the other two landing sites might be ambushed.

Brigadier Mike Calvert, commanding 77th Brigade, was prepared to take the risk, but the decision was left to Slim. As always, the epitome of measured calm, Bill Slim decided that 77th Brigade should be diverted to Broadway.[9] In the event, this was not a soft option because the landing there was hazardous.

> of the sixty-one gliders that set out for Broadway that night only thirty-five reached it. Tow ropes broke, aircraft engines overheated, fuel ran out. The gliders crash-landed all over Burma causing the Japanese great

confusion. Of those that did reach Broadway some crashed into the trees. As one of the missing gliders contained the ground control organisation there was no way of controlling other landings. Twenty-three men were killed and thirty injured in the landing.[10]

The twenty-six missing gliders caused the loss of a mass of equipment and mules, but above all else, the lives of a further sixty-six intrepid men. Later, it was discovered that the logs laid out over Piccadilly, and the cause of much soul-searching, had been put there by Burmese loggers to dry out. Thereafter, further landings on Chowringhee were successful and 9,000 men were inserted 200 miles (320km) behind the Japanese front line. The landing strips were improved and regular flights by Dakota aircraft were introduced.

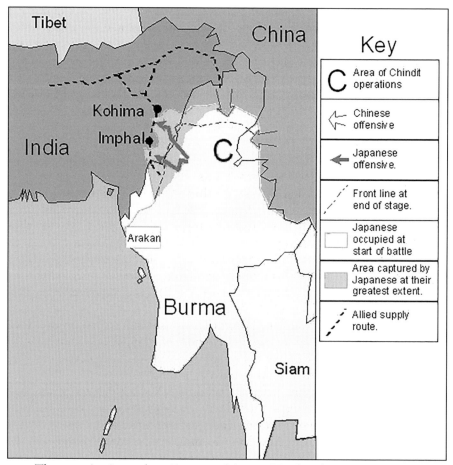

The campaign in northern Burma and Assam. March–July 1944. (*Mike Young*)

Logistics and CASEVAC were secure. Broadway became the base of operations. It was garrisoned, and provided with anti-aircraft and field artillery. Six Spitfires of 81st Squadron RAF were flown in. However, on 17 March, a Japanese air strike, twenty strong, destroyed five for the loss of two. 16th Brigade established a firm base around Indaw, which it named Aberdeen. Similarly, 77th Brigade established its firm base at White City, near Mawlu, from where it dominated both road and rail links to the north. 111th Brigade blocked the road south of Indaw and set up ambushes on likely lines of Japanese approach.

*   *   *

As the Chindits flew in, Mutaguchi launched his *Ha-Go* offensive. On 8 March 1944, three strong Japanese divisions and one of the Indian National Army – 155,000 troops in all, crossed the Chindwin and advanced north towards Kohima. The 31st Division, commanded by Lieutenant General Satō Kōtoku, was directed to Kohima and the remainder of the 15th Army moved on Imphal, the transport hub. The army commander had declared: 'The Army has now reached a state of invincibility, and the day when the Rising Sun shall proclaim our definite victory in India is not far off.'[11] Slim left IV Corps and its three divisions in forward position and sought to draw the Japanese onto the Imphal plain, where his superiority in armour and aircraft would be decisive.

In the event, Mutaguchi's advance was quicker and more flexible than anticipated and 17th Indian Division was threatened with encirclement by the 33rd Division. The 28th Indian Division was outflanked by the 15 Japanese Division. This was a crisis and it called for a bold response. Mutaguchi's attempt to cut off and destroy the British XV Corps in the Arakan had failed and, in part, the corps could be redeployed. Mountbatten took the initiative and, 'In a spectacular feat of military logistics the entire 5th Indian Division with its mules and artillery were air lifted 400 miles (644km) from the Arakan to secure the rear of Scoones's IV Corps.'[12] XXXIII Corps, commanded by Lieutenant General Montague Stopford, was swiftly moved from India, where it had been training for the now abandoned amphibious operations, to relieve the garrison at Kohima. The plan was that when Kohima was safe, Stopford would then move south to relieve Imphal.

However, by 5 March the Japanese had established a block across the road at Kohima, cutting its link to Imphal 50 miles (80km) to the south-west. Kohima was 5,000 feet up in the hills and its ad hoc garrison consisted of only 1,500 men. This small force held the Kohima ridge, which dominated the road to Imphal, now blocked by the Japanese. Possession of the ridge was fiercely contested between 4 April and 22 June.

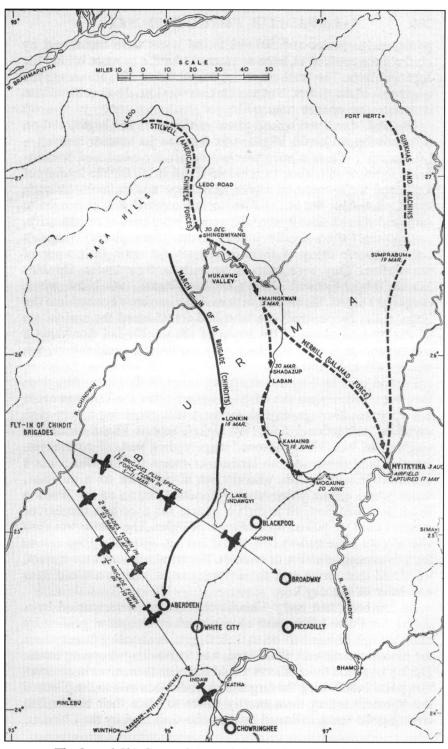

The Second Chindit expedition and the Northern Front in Burma,
December 1943–August 1944. This map illustrates the area in which
the LRP activities of both Allies were conducted.

Piccadilly. The landing ground covered in logs. (*The Chindit Society*)

The Chindit presence in the Japanese rear had the desired effect and the enemy were attracted to White City, and a much-improved Broadway, like wasps to a honeypot, where ferocious hand-to-hand fighting ensued in both places. The Japanese were eventually repulsed with heavy losses.

Fergusson, recognising the priceless value of the airstrip at Indaw, resolved to take it, and the town with it. However, his brigade was exhausted, and the Japanese defences were being reinforced. It was a further blow to discover that the only local water source was firmly under Japanese control. 14th Brigade had been flown into *Aberdeen* and Fergusson anticipated incorporating it into his assault on Indaw, but 14th Brigade had moved out of the area and so 16th Brigade made some despairing and piecemeal attacks that achieved nothing, except more casualties. Severely depleted, 16th Brigade, or its survivors, were then withdrawn.

On 21 March, Wingate decided to move his headquarters from Imphal to Sylhet in India, which caused some interruption in communications during the attack on Indaw (bottom centre of map on page 216). Just as that administrative issue was being resolved, on 24 March 1944, Wingate flew to review the situation in three of his Chindit-held bases. On his return to Imphal he resolved to go to Lalaghat and agreed to allow two British war correspondents to fly with him. The pilot protested that the weather conditions were dangerous, and that the plane was overloaded. Wingate, at his imperious best, overruled the pilot. The USAAF B-25 of 1st Air Commando Group took off but, soon thereafter, it crashed into a jungle-covered hill. All ten passengers aboard, including Wingate, were incinerated.

Brigadier (later Lieutenant General) Walter Lentaigne (always known as 'Joe') was appointed to overall command of British LRP forces. His appointment caused a degree of consternation as Mike Calvert (77th Brigade) was a popular, respected and much-favoured candidate. However, the British Army is not a democracy and Lentaigne assumed command just as Japanese forces began their assault on Imphal. 23rd Brigade was moved to assist in the defence of Imphal and Kohima. This left five brigades of Chindits for Operation THURSDAY.

Lentaigne proved to be a forceful senior commander and among his early decisions was the abandonment of Broadway and White City and the establishment of a new operating base called Blackpool (centre of the map on page 216). This redoubt was attacked by the Japanese on 24 May. They penetrated the perimeter defences and the Chindit occupiers, of 111th Brigade, were obliged to evacuate the site the following day. This brigade was commanded by captain/acting major/local Brigadier Jack Masters.

Masters was in the thick of the savage fighting at Blackpool and commenting on the bravery of Japanese soldiers. It was reported that the Cameronians had inflicted very heavy losses on an attacking Japanese force and 'over 200 hundred enemy' lay in front of their position. 'One Japanese continued to charge alone. He arrived finally at the muzzle of a Cameronian machine gun, which cut him to pieces. His bayonet was not fixed, and his rifle was not loaded.'[13]

*　　*　　*

Slim had other matters to concern him in the defence of Kohima/Imphal/Dimapur and so he happily passed overall command of LRP operations to Stilwell, who focused on support for the American/Chinese operations in north Burma. Stilwell's performance in overall command of LRP forces was pedestrian and, in part, self-serving. The ad hoc defence of Kohima was in the hands of the 4th Battalion, Queen's Own West Kent Regiment, and a battalion of the Assam Regiment. The commander of this scratch force was Colonel Hugh Richards, a former Chindit. He was faced by 15,000 Japanese who had taken the town but not the dominating ridge above it. Sixty-four days of intense, close-quarter fighting ensued.

In 1956, Slim commenting in *Defeat into Victory* on operations around Imphal, said that they:

> swayed back and forth through great stretches of wild country, one day its focal point was a hill named on no maps, the next a miserable unpronounceable village a hundred miles away. Columns, brigades, divisions marched and counter-marched, met in bloody clashes and reeled apart, weaving a confused pattern hard to unravel.

If it was confusing to the general soon after the battle, the reader will understand the reluctance of this author to seek to unravel the pattern other than to summarise the result.

Satō was unable to move onto Imphal until he had quelled those resolute defenders although Chandra Bose and the INA Division did advance on Imphal. Bose had the new Indian currency packed in bales ready for distribution, but he never got the chance to do so because Satō ordered the INA to return to the Kohima battle. Bose interpreted this as a conspiracy to deny Indian soldiers the chance to win a significant victory in their own country.

The British-Indian troops held a small defensive perimeter that centred on Garrison Hill. On 5–18 April, Kohima saw some of the most bitter fighting of the war. In one sector, only the width of the town's tennis court separated the two sides.

Satō's force had minimal logistic support and food quickly became a problem. The British food stocks were not taken and so his men went hungry. Hunger becomes debilitating after three or four days and not long after, the indications of starvation become manifest. Satō was always unhappy with his role, having been excluded from the planning process for the offensive; thereafter, he had voiced doubts about the possibility of success. He was painfully aware of his operational deficiencies, and he had already told his staff that they might all starve to death, as Mutaguchi had made no provision for resupply.[14]

Garrison Hill, Kohima. The scene of some of the bloodiest fighting in the Burma campaign.

The tennis court today.

The British defence of Kohima was dogged and firm. Elsewhere, the attack on Imphal was bogged down and, in April, Satō was incensed when he was ordered to reinforce the attackers at Imphal with all or at least part of his division. This at a time when he was sorely pressed in the siege of Kohima. On 18 April, the relief forces of the British 2nd Division arrived, by which time Richards's defensive perimeter was reduced to a shell-shattered area only 418 square yards (350m²).[15] Today, a memorial stands on what was the tennis court, its lines still marked. From 22 April, the British garrison in Kohima, now reinforced by two divisions – 23rd Chindit Brigade and a motor brigade – allowed Slim to move onto the offensive.

For Satō, committed to an operation that was starting to fail, the situation worsened day by day and, by mid-May, he was at odds with his commander, Mutaguchi, whose orders were unclear and sometimes even contradictory. 15th Army was not providing any support and Satō's men were starving.

On 25 May, Satō warned Mutaguchi that it was his intention to withdraw from Kohima on 1 June unless he was resupplied. Issuing an ultimatum to one's commander does not go down very well in any army; indeed, it is seriously career inhibiting in the British Army. Similarly, it was beyond the pale and totally unacceptable in the IJA. Satō did not receive any supplies and accordingly he withdrew. He paid for his insubordination and was sacked on 7 July.

The part played by Merrill's Marauders was equally as effective as that played by the Chindits. On 24 February, Merrill led 2,750 men over the Patkai mountains and into Japanese-occupied north Burma. Each of the three battalions was divided into two combat teams (about the same size as a Chindit column). During their operations they faced the Japanese 18th Division, upon whom they inflicted many more casualties than they suffered. They excelled in engagements at Maingkwan and Walawbum, where their skill at arms with automatic weapons was a factor. In March 1944, they cut the Japanese logistic line in the Hukaung valley in Thailand.

Meanwhile, Stilwell directed his Chinese Expeditionary Force under Wei Lihuang, and with the Marauders in company, to advance on Myitkyina and take the airstrip and town. The attack went in on 17 May. Merrill's force, severely depleted by myriad causes of ill health, was reduced to only 1,310 fit men. They reached the town after an arduous 65-mile (105km) trudge through thick rainforest and were exhausted when they reached the objective.

Calvert's 77th Brigade, under Stilwell's command, was directed towards Mogaung to relieve some of the pressure on the CEF around Myitkyina. The approach march was over the most difficult country, but on the way, on 2 June the village of Lakum, about 2 miles (3.2km) south-west of the objective, was taken. The Japanese responded vigorously but were unable to stem the advance and the Gurkhas of 77th Brigade, who took a small settlement. Here, they not only eliminated the forty-strong garrison but also captured an ammunition dump, fifteen trucks and a field hospital. The brigade was not equipped to take large numbers of the wounded patients prisoner; fortuitously, many of these fled into the jungle and others committed suicide.

It was at this point that the monsoon broke and conditions for those living in the jungle bordered unbearable. The wounded were extracted, and the fighting strength of the brigade was down to 750 – no more than that of a battalion. Calvert advised Stilwell of his position but received scant sympathy, although he did direct the 1st/114th Chinese Infantry Regiment to support 77th Brigade. Calvert launched his attack on 25 June, took the town and repulsed several counter-attacks. The Japanese withdrew the next day, but that became a rout and many of the fleeing Japs were killed as they headed for the doubtful sanctuary of Myitkyina.

77th Brigade was no longer a viable formation; it was reduced to only 550 fit men, and these garrisoned the town in the short term. Mogaung was the first major town in Burma to be liberated from the Japanese and it was a significant victory. Michael Calvert commented:

> When we captured Mogaung we heard on the BBC that the Americans and Chinese had captured the town. So, I sent a message saying 'the Americans and Chinese have captured Mogaung. 77th Brigade is proceeding to take umbrage.'
>
> When I was ordered to move to Myitkyina, still in Japanese hands, I closed my wireless for fourteen days and marched out. I was summoned to Stilwell's HQ at Shaduzup to explain my insubordination.
>
> He said, 'You send very strong signals Calvert.'
>
> I said, 'You should see the ones my brigade major won't let me send.'
>
> I hit the right note because he roared with laughter. From then on, we got on very well. He didn't realise that we had done a glider-borne invasion, didn't realise that we'd blocked the railway at White City for almost five weeks, four of them against repeated Japanese attacks. He didn't realise that my brigade had not only been decimated but had had other bits taken off to help other brigades. We had no artillery; he didn't realise these things.
>
> He kept saying, 'Why wasn't I told? Is this true?'
>
> His staff admitted it was.[16]

Apparently, thereafter, Stilwell's American staff officers spent several fruitless hours searching for Umbrage on the map. The attack on Myitkyina was a confused affair with Chinese battalions firing on other Chinese troops. The airstrip was taken on 26 July, but the fighting around the town lasted until

Brigadier General Frank Merrill (1903–55) and
Lieutenant General Joseph Stilwell (1883–1946).

3 August. Then the Japanese commander, General Mizukami Genzo, having ordered his troops to abandon the town, committed suicide. Mountbatten radioed congratulations and declared it to be 'a feat that will live in military history'. He was right – as this text testifies. Stilwell, exhalant in victory, confided in his dairy that 'this will burn up the Limeys'.[17] He obviously saw the operation as some sort of competition.

The result at Myitkyina was an Allied success and although Merrill's Marauders were present, it was a Chinese victory. Chinese losses were 972 killed, 3,184 wounded and 188 sick. Japanese losses were estimated at 2,400 killed, wounded or captured. Depressingly, Stilwell, to whom all credit is due for his part in these operations, was a general who seemed incapable of empathising with his own troops, and he pushed the Marauders to extinction. By 10 August, and barely a week after the fall of Myitkyina, the 5307th (Marauder) force, had been reduced to only 130 fit men of the original 2,997. The Marauders were disbanded.

Stilwell's conduct, attitude and inability to relate to either friend or foe had been the subject of innumerable reports, complaints and negative observations over the previous two years. It was inevitable that there would be a denouement. Although he was recalled to the United States on 19 October 1944, to the relief of many, he was not disciplined but promoted to full general. Typically, he had made no arrangements for the briefing of his replacement.

*   *   *

At this distance one might well ask, 'Were the Chindits a success?' Dick Hilder, who soldiered with 14 Brigade's HQ Column, commented:

> At the military level the Chindits disrupted three Japanese divisions and took some of the weight off Imphal and Kohima. We dispelled the notion that the Japanese were invincible in the jungle. Until then, our soldiers really thought that the Japanese were superhuman.[18]

The operation came at a cost and when the dust had settled the casualties could be counted (see table opposite). 'Missing' in this context is a euphemism for killed.

Although it is not shown separately in the table, sickness, caused by the exhausting nature of the operation and the inhospitable environment, by far outnumbered battle casualties. Given the nature of the LRP and the duration of their activities, 944 Chindits were killed (although most of the missing 452 were probably also dead) and 2,343 were wounded or disabled by sickness. Overall, the casualty rate was 41 per cent. That is very high by any yardstick, but Merrill's Marauders suffered higher attrition.

Chindit Casualties, 1944[19]

Brigade	Killed Officers	Killed Other Ranks	Wounded Officers	Wounded Other Ranks	Missing Officers	Missing Other Ranks
14th	14	227	23	191	23	2
16th	13	85	14	164	5	74
77th	46	346	84	1,156	11	168
111th	17	107	24	465	6	130
3rd	11	78	23	290	1	23
Totals	101	843	168	2,266	46	397

The Marauders were a much smaller force, and their casualties were calculated in a different form (see following table).[20] The Americans were particularly susceptible to the multitude of jungle ills. The table below illustrates an overall casualty rate of 80 per cent *up to 30 June 1944* and before the Myitkyina operation. That operation cost a further 272 deaths and poses the question, was it worth it?

Casualties of the 5307th Composite Unit provisional, February to June 1944

		Casualties	Percent of casualties Actual	Percent of casualties Estimated
Battle casualties	Battle deaths	93		
	Non-battle deaths	30		
	Wounded in action	293*		
	Missing in action	8		
	Subtotal	424	14%	35%
Disease casualties	Amoebic dysentery	503		
	Mite typhus fever (usually fatal)	149		
	Malaria	296**		
	Psychoneurosis	72		
	Miscellaneous fevers	950		
	Subtotal	1,970	66%	50%
	Total	2,394	80%	85%

*These are the official figures of the Adjutant General's battle casualty roster for hospitalised wounded. Many cases of light battle casualties were not evacuated but treated by unit surgeons and consequently not reported in hospital returns. Therefore, complete statistics are not obtainable. The actual number of wounded at Nhu Ga alone exceed the official total for the entire campaign.

**296 is the number of malaria cases evacuated. Nearly every member of the force had malaria more than once.

Later, Slim offered a view on LRP. In his opinion:

the Chindits gave a splendid example of courage and hardihood. Yet I came firmly to the conclusion that such formations, trained, equipped, and mentally adjusted for one kind of operation, were wasteful. They did not give, militarily, a worthwhile return for the resources in men, materiel, and time that they absorbed. ... [Special forces] were usually formed by attracting the best men ... The result of these methods was undoubtedly to lower the quality of the rest of the army.[21]

In the war against Japan, the LRP activities in northern Burma set a new benchmark for jungle fighting. They did not win the campaign, but these courageous men did influence it at a critical time. However, in the great tapestry of the Second World War, they are but a footnote to history.

*   *   *

Slim's 14th Army now commenced offensive operations. The British 2 Division led XXXIII Corps, commanded by Stopford. 2 Division, having already ejected the Japanese from Kohima ridge, were a battle-hardened, experienced formation. The point units of IV Corps and XXXIII Corps joined up at milestone 109 on the Dimapur–Imphal road on 22 June and the siege of Imphal was at an end. Satō had withdrawn; his division was exhausted, and a shadow of its former self. The absence of a logistic system had forced the 15th and 31st divisions to the edge of starvation. Their morale was at rock bottom, disease of all sorts was rampant and killing hundreds of soldiers. Medical units were unable to cope, and the medics had no medications to offer. Discipline was at risk in both formations.

Mutaguchi, encouraged by his superior, Kawabe, did not acknowledge the parlous state of his troops, and drove his 33rd Division into further attacks south of Imphal. It was not until early July that the reality of the situation dawned upon him, but he was loath to ask for permission to withdraw. Indeed, Kawabe made it clear that he expected the 15th Army to act zealously and fight harder.[22] Field Marshal Terauchi made the decision for Mutaguchi to break contact with the Indian Army, but it took until 8 July before that decision reached the 15th Army.

The withdrawal of the 15th Army that followed triggered a catastrophic defeat – one of the greatest in Japanese history. Slim's Army pursued the enemy with ruthless energy. They killed the enemy by the thousand, but it was disease and starvation that wreaked the most damage. Dead Japanese were to be found alongside all the tracks and roads; most survivors were summarily shot because no one was going to risk approaching a Jap who might be concealing a grenade.

The wanton behaviour of the enemy in Singapore and Malaya was common knowledge and now they reaped the consequences. Private Peter Hammond, 9th Battalion, The Border Regiment, remarked of the Japanese, 'They would booby-trap their wounded.'[23] The members of the Indian National Army were given short shrift – especially by their opposing countrymen. Despite their unenviable reputation for inhumanity, there was general if grudging admiration for the tenacity and courage of individual Japanese soldiers. Lieutenant Mahesh Sharma, of 70th Independent Field Company, Bengal Sappers and Miners, observed:

> The Japanese were very tough. They stored their rice in old socks tied to their belts. I have seen a Japanese officer with part of his arm missing and maggots crawling all over him still fighting. They are very brave. They had no idea of preserving human life. They lived off the land which was hard on the villagers. They had few medical facilities.[24]

War is an unpleasant business and stomach-turning, as a soldier of 3rd Carabiniers, Malcolm Connolly, recounted:

> during the clearing of the Imphal road we were sent to bury the crew of a tank that had been hit, caught fire, and exploded. There was only one complete body; 'Chick' Henderson had managed to get out of the side door and crawled to the back possibly to cover the retreat of his crew. But the japs must have killed him. He was pretty badly burned by the exploding tank. We had the job of bringing him down and finding the pieces of the crew. The inside of it was derelict; we crawled inside and managed to find a foot here and a hand there … Chick's body was rotting, we rolled him into a blanket and put him on a stretcher. As for the bits and pieces of the others nobody had an idea of which bit belonged to who.[25]

The monsoon had broken but Slim would allow the Japanese no respite as he drove them towards the Chindwin River. 11th East Africa Division made progress down the Kabaw Valley and 5th Indian Division pushed through the mountains following the Tiddim Road. The *London Gazette*, when publishing despatches, noted that, in the destruction of the 15th Army, Japanese losses were huge. 'They had suffered 50–60,000 dead and 100,000 or more casualties.'[26] Most of these losses were the result of disease, malnutrition and exhaustion. 'The Allies suffered 12,500 casualties, including 2,269 killed.'[27] It was a minuscule price to pay and wildly disproportionate.

That is the numerical measurement of Slim's victory, which was the first defeat suffered by the Japanese on the mainland of Asia and it encouraged him to believe that the expulsion of all Japanese forces in Burma was now an achievable aim. Unfortunately, Bill Slim's superiors did not share his vision and 'Mountbatten badgered the Combined Chiefs of Staff for a decision as what to do next.'[28] This does seem to be more than a little wet and eventually Mountbatten was told to 'press advantages against the enemy by exerting maximum ground force particularly during the monsoon season'.[29] That was sufficiently vague as to allow him to order General George Gifford to move the remainder of his 11 Army Group on across the Chindwin in the Yuwa-Tamanthi area.[30]

Personalities were once again an issue. Mountbatten considered Gifford to be negative and pessimistic. The two men did not get on and Gifford, like many others, was the recipient of Stilwell's dislike. Mountbatten sacked Gifford in October 1944 and replaced him with Lieutenant General Sir Oliver Leese. Slim regretted the departure of Gifford, with whom he had worked well and whom he admired. He was less enthused by Leese.

Slim interpreted his orders very loosely and 14th Army continued his pursuit of the Japanese wherever he found them. His successes validated his actions and, aware of the logistic consequences of extending his line of communication, he decided to rely on aerial resupply. He also made structural changes and warmed to the ideas of General Frank Messervy, who had replaced Scoones at IV Corps. A series of advances were made in the latter part of 1944 and through until mid-1945. Successful though they were and crippling to Japanese arms, they did not materially affect the outcome of the war, which was being decided elsewhere. The taking of Rangoon in early May 1945 just preceded the arrival of the monsoon. Japanese resistance continued until August, suffering great losses until the end.

Notes

1. Toland, J., *The Rising Sun: The Decline and Fall of the Japanese Empire, 1936–45* [1970] (Modern Library, New York, 2003), p. 611.
2. IWM Archive, Thompson, p. 368.
3. Costello, J., *The Pacific War 1941–45* [1981] (New York, Harper Collins, 2009), p. 463.
4. IWM Archive, Thompson, p. 208.
5. Lyall Grant, I., *Burma: The Turning Point* (Barnsley, Pen & Sword, 2003).
6. IWM Archive, Thompson, p. 252.
7. Masters, J., *The Road Past Mandalay* [1961] (London, Cassell, 2002), pp. 249–50.
8. Ibid.
9. Slim, Gen. W., *Defeat into Victory* (London, Cassell, 1956) pp. 257–9.
10. Masters, p. 172.
11. Moser, D., *China, Burma, India* (Alexandria, Va., *Time Life*, 1978), p. 148.
12. Costello, p. 465.
13. Masters, p. 213.
14. Allen, L., *Burma: The Longest War 1941–45* [1984] (London, Phoenix Press, 2000), p. 232.
15. National Army Museum website.
16. IWM Archive.

17. Masters, p. 265.
18. thechinditsociety.org.uk
19. 'Medical History of the Second World War', *Army Medical Services, Campaigns*, Vol. 4, HMSO.
20. Marauder.org
21. Slim, Gen. W., *Defeat Into Victory*, (London, Cassell, 1956), pp. 546–9.
22. Toland, p. 614.
23. IWM Archive, Thompson, p. 272.
24. Ibid., p. 293.
25. Ibid., pp. 294–5.
26. Despatch 'Operations in Assam and Burma from 23 June 1944 until 12 November 1944', supplement to *The London Gazette*, 3 March 1951, p. 1,711.
27. Despatch 'Operations in Burma and Northeast India, 16th November 1943 to 22nd June 1944', *London Gazette*, 13 March 1951, p. 1,361.
28. Lyman, R., *Slim, Master of War* [2004] (London, Constable & Robinson, 2005), p. 230.
29. Ibid.
30. General Sir George Gifford, GCB, DSO was GOC-in-C of 11 Army Group, of which 14th Army was a constituent.

Chapter Twenty-One

22 April–19 June 1944
Hollandia, Aitape, Biak Island, Mopping-up, Saipan and the Marianas 'Turkey Shoot'

While the British 14th Army wrestled with its enemy in Burma, the US continued with its campaign in New Guinea. On 22 April, it landed two divisions with the aim of taking Hollandia, a port on the north coast of the island, which provided the Japanese with an anchorage in Humboldt Bay. In the area there were three airstrips in use and a fourth was under construction.[1]

It was the intention of the Japanese to hold Hollandia; its 2nd Army viewed it as unlikely to attract American attention and to be the focus of an amphibious attack. This appreciation was on the assumption that, as Hollandia was beyond the range of US land-based aircraft, any invasion would be without air support. It came as an unwelcome surprise to the 11,000-strong Japanese garrison when, supported by aircraft from eight of the 5th Fleet escort carriers, 29,500 Americans stormed ashore. The defenders were predominately logistic troops, and they were easy meat for the 24th and 41st US Infantry divisions. Hollandia was taken at a cost of 152 killed and 1,057 wounded. As ever, the cost to the Japanese was vastly higher, of whom 3,300 were killed. On 24 April, 78 Wing RAAF flew in twenty-five P-40 aircraft.

Concurrently with the Hollandia operation a further landing was made at Aitape, about 125 miles (200km) south-east of Hollandia, and 22,500 men were allocated to the task. They brushed aside the light resistance that was offered by the 1,000 resident Japanese, of whom 525 were killed. Twenty-five were captured, and the balance of 450 must have fled into the all-consuming jungle. US losses were nineteen killed and forty wounded. These two widely spaced landings contributed towards MacArthur's advance on the Philippines and isolated the Japanese base at Wewak.

At MacArthur's direction, in May 1944 the Australian 6th Division took over from the US troops around Aitape. From then, until the end of the war in August 1945, the Australians fought a limited campaign in the Aitape–Wewak area. This was termed a 'mopping-up' operation.

* * *

During the campaign, the strategic necessity of this mopping-up operation was called into question as it became clear that the fighting would have little impact upon the outcome of the war. In that regard, it was argued that the Japanese forces in Aitape–Wewak posed no strategic threat to the Allies as they advanced towards mainland Japan. The Japanese in New Guinea could be isolated and contained, and then left to 'wither on the vine' as their supplies ran out.[2]

Given the relegation of Australian troops to mopping up, it is germane to consider the circumstances that triggered MacArthur's correct, but politically insensitive, decision. The strength, quality and motivation of Australian soldiers to the Pacific War and the domestic strife in their homeland were factors in his decision.

The relegation, by MacArthur, of Australian troops to mopping up is indicative of the value he placed on their capacity in 1944 and the relative unimportance of Australia to American strategy in this latter part of the war. This rejection, from the strategically important battlefronts, was a bitter pill for Australians. The probability, although not documented, is that the USA recognised that, huge although Australia is, it had a small population and was unable to put in the field the vast armies to match the other antagonists. Australia's worth was as a secure base and a breadbasket to supply the logistic machine supporting the American advance across the Pacific. It has also been suggested that MacArthur did not want to share any of the glory that goes with victory with Allies.

The unrecognised reality was that Australia was a minor player in a very large game. Despite that, back in December 1941 and just after the provocation of Japan by Roosevelt and Hull, John Curtin, the Prime Minister of Australia, made a very significant speech, during which he said:

> The Australian Government, therefore, regards the Pacific struggle as primarily one in which the United States and Australia must have the fullest say in the direction of the democracies' fighting plan. Without any inhibitions of any kind, I make it clear that Australia looks to America, free of any pangs as to our traditional links or kinship with the United Kingdom. We know the problems that the United Kingdom faces . . .[3]

To the UK, this was an unexpected and unwelcome change of stance, but Curtin put all his money, and that of his country, on the USA – as he was perfectly entitled to do. He made it his business to strike up a warm relationship with MacArthur, whom he saw as his conduit to the White House. This approach reduced him to that of a mere supplicant, not an equal of a sovereign partner. Thereafter, Curtin was never invited to the top table. Nevertheless, his biographer took the view that:

> A lesser Australian leader might have grated against MacArthur's vanity, cavilled at his assumption of command, contradicted his grandiloquent claims, satirised his manner. Curtin did not. He seized the chance to share authority with MacArthur, refused to offend his vanity, drew him as close as he could. Of Curtin's military decisions, it was the cleverest, most fruitful, most abidingly successful.[4]

Despite the view of Curtin's biographer, the relationship with MacArthur was unproductive as Curtin realised that MacArthur's aims were not swayed by personal relationships. MacArthur had witnessed the daily disruption in Australia's docks caused by recalcitrant dockers who caused persistent delays on the loading and unloading of vessels. There was no sense of urgency and the workforce seemed to be striving actively to thwart the war effort – and MacArthur's part in it. Quite why this was the case has never been satisfactorily explained. A trawl of the Australian Parliament's archives shows that Curtin was obliged to employ soldiers to fill the manning gap on several occasions.

Australia had been an unhappy place as it fought its way through the Depression, and the outbreak of war in 1939 had added to the gloom. Nevertheless, three divisions of volunteers were raised to support the 'Old Country' and sent to the Middle East. A fourth went to Singapore and was promptly captured. Australian airmen flew in the Battle of Britain and wherever else Britain was fighting. The Royal Australian Navy was incorporated into Nimitz's fleets. These representatives of Australia reflected well on their country, but they were in a minority.

The vast bulk of 691,400 Australians that were conscripted for 'Home Service only' were incorporated into militia units, where they contributed nothing to the war effort. This is in stark contrast to the courage of the volunteer Australians in the Western Desert in 1941–2. By 1941, Australia was in the grip of industrial strife and this was aggravated by communist-led trades union activists. As soon as Russia attacked Germany, the Communist Party, hitherto a proscribed organisation, came out into the light and its 20,000 members, although paying lip service to the war effort, contrived to limit its effect.

> remoteness had made Australia a parochial society, but this is an inadequate explanation for the behaviour of some of its people. The refusal to

adapt to participation in a war of national survival when Japan aspired to make them subjects of the empire was extraordinary.[5]

It took time but eventually the rose-tinted spectacles fell off. Curtin was obliged to face the fact that the all-powerful USA only had need of Australia as a base camp from which it could conduct its affairs and feed its forces. He was not privy to the strategy making forums and, in 1943, he reversed his position when he realised that the threat of Japanese invasion had passed. On that basis, Curtin increasingly returned to a commitment to the British Empire and, in conciliatory mode, said that Australia comprised '7 million Britishers'.

Curtin now saw the United States as a predatory economic and military power that would threaten Australia's own ambitions in the Pacific. Australia moved closer to New Zealand and suggested a lesser role for the US after the war. Washington was rather miffed at this.[6]

The command of Australian land forces was invested in General Thomas Blamey, a singularly unimpressive, corrupt, corpulent drunk. His contemporaries said of him that he was:

'Not an impressive specimen. He looks entirely drink-sodden and somewhat repulsive.' (General Sir Alan Brooke)

'Knowing that Blamey had the reputation of being a crook, they [Australian soldiers] did not serve happily under him.' (Chester Wilmot)

'A rather unpleasant political soldier … a tubby little man with a snub nose and expensive complexion.' (Air Marshal Sir Arthur Tedder)

'He wasn't a general I should have chosen to command an operation.' (Field Marshal Sir Claude Auchinleck)

No doubt senior American officers held Blamey in similar regard. This was the man responsible for the deployment, support and well-being of the Australian Army. His propensity was to commit his soldiers to unimportant operations of the mopping-up persuasion in which lives were needlessly lost. This ensured that he was cordially hated by many who survived his 'leadership'. His retention in high office and his extraordinary eventual elevation to field marshal – the only Australian to reach that pinnacle – was entirely the responsibility of the Australian Government, and Curtin in particular.

Australians had served with courage and distinction along the Kokoda Trail (see Chapter 14), but later, in the campaign in New Guinea, in which conscripted militia were employed, the strategic necessity of the operation was quite reasonably challenged. However, some units refused to fight and those that did were apathetic.

There was dissent in Australia at the loss of life, and Blamey, the commander-in-chief of the Australian Army, was viewed by some as permitting the ongoing campaign for his own aggrandisement. The consensus is that 'politically or strategically, the offensives on Bougainville and at Aitape–Wewak served no useful purpose.'[7] Nevertheless, the Australians lost 442 men killed and 1,141 wounded in battle.[8] In addition, a further 145 died from other causes, and 16,203 men were listed as 'sickness casualties'. Many of these casualties were the result of an Atabrine-resistant strain of malaria that infested the area.

Japanese casualties are estimated at between 7,000 and 9,000 killed, while 269 were captured during the fighting.[9] Following the end of hostilities in New Guinea, approximately 13,000 Japanese surrendered, with about 14,000 having died of starvation and illness during the entire campaign.

Australia lost 7,384 killed in its war with Japan. Nevertheless, and despite this butcher's bill, 'the Pacific War ended in rancour and anti-climax'.[10]

*   *   *

Having taken Aitape, and notwithstanding the availability of the captured airstrips, it was determined that Biak Island was to be preferred – but it would have to be fought for. The defence of Biak Island was different. Its 11,400 men were commanded by Colonel Kuzume Naoyuki, who abandoned the practice of defeating the invaders on the beach because the length of his coastline made that impractical. In anticipation of an American invasion, he made best use of caves west of Mokmer and to the east of Bosnek. This defensive complex was intended to turn the area around the vital airfield into a honeycomb of defended tunnels, caves and bunkers, all manned by riflemen, machine guns, artillery, mortars, and in one place, a company of light tanks. All his positions were supplied with water, ammunition and food. Provision was made for living quarters.[11] Water was to be precious in the engagement that followed, and the oppressive heat and humidity would prove to be a burden to all.

The battle of Biak Island started on 27 May, and Colonel Kuzume's preparations proved to be highly efficient. His men, concealed and well dug in, offered the same resolute defence until death that had been seen on Tarawa and all other Japanese possessions. MacArthur ignored intelligence reports and pronounced that the enemy was 'collapsing' when it most certainly was not. A little later he called operations 'mopping up', and they were not that either. MacArthur would not call for reinforcements because to do so would reveal that he was in difficulties and that might damage his reputation.

The Japanese had plans to reinforce Biak and one arm of that reinforcement was the 23rd Air Flotilla with 184 aircraft, which was moved to

Sorong in Dutch New Guinea. The Imperial Japanese Navy prepared Operation KON and had 2,500 troops embarked for transport from Mindanao (Philippines). That party would be protected by Rear Admiral Sakonju with a force composed of the battleship *Fuso*, three heavy cruisers and eight destroyers. The plan was that they would arrive on 3 June.[12]

These reinforcement attempts were strongly resisted, and the Japanese introduced the battleships *Yamato* and *Musashi* for a third attempt on 13 June, but the bombardment of Saipan had just commenced, and it caused their big guns to be redirected elsewhere in the Marianas. Despite suffering the loss of twenty-three aircraft, about 1,200 troops were landed on Biak during June. The numerical strength of the two sides was about the same, 12,000 to 11,400, but the Americans also had twenty-nine field guns and twelve tanks.

On 17 August, American might finally prevailed and Kuzume, having burned his regimental colours, committed hara-kiri. Of his 11,400 men, only 200 were captured and at least 4,700 were killed. The victory cost the USA 438 dead, 2,361 wounded, and an astonishing 7,234 non-battle casualties. That last figure was the result of scrub typhus, a fatal disease if left untreated.

Admiral Ernest King was a key player in determining American policy in the Pacific War, not least because all Allied operations were entirely dependent on the USN under his overall direction. King had previously acknowledged that the Mariana Islands were a low priority as they were not on a direct line from the United States Navy base at Pearl Harbor to the likely target of the Philippines. However, by 1943 he had moved his position and was able to see that, given the increased range of the B-29 Superfortress, now 3,250 miles (5,230km), bases for these aircraft in the Marianas could provide the means of bombing the Japanese home islands.[13] In addition, communications between the Japanese Government and its conquered territories could be disrupted from the Marianas. To this end, the US had a shortlist of future targets that included Saipan, nearby Tinian, and Guam. It was Saipan at the head of the list and, just before operations on Biak Island, Nimitz moved swiftly. He tasked his V Amphibious Corps (2nd and 4th Marine divisions and 27th Infantry Division) under the command of General Holland Smith, to take Saipan. Naval support was provided by Task Force 52, led by Vice Admiral Richmond Turner. This was to be Operation FORAGER.

The taking of Saipan started on 13 June with the, now routine, naval bombardment by the 5th Fleet, of which overall command was vested in Admiral Raymond Spruance. It included Task Force 58, comprised of seventeen carriers, six battleships, thirteen cruisers, fifty-eight destroyers and about 1,100 aircraft. This vast fleet was under the command of Vice Admiral Marc Mitscher. The separate invasion force element was commanded by Vice

Admiral Richmond Turner, who had fifty-six attack transports, eighty-four landing craft and over 127,571 troops at his disposal.

Recognising that it could not match the power and industrial might of the USA, it was the aim of the Japanese Government to inflict such losses on the USA that peace could then be sued for with some credibility. The Combined Fleet was perceived to be the instrument that could inflict the massive losses that would drive the USA to the negotiating table, and in June 1944, it sought to confront the 5th Fleet in the Philippine Sea.

*   *   *

While American soldiers and marines toiled on Saipan, the two fleets circled each other at a range of several hundred miles. Eventually, when battle was joined, it became a contest between the aerial assets. The American aircraft were all carrier-borne but the Japanese had the advantage of being able to employ aircraft from island bases to supplement their carrier force.

There were only minor differences between the aircraft of the two adversaries. The American Hellcat had a slight edge on the Japanese Zero. It was faster but not quite as manoeuvrable, but had armour plate behind the pilot's seat, and that extended its life (and that of the pilot) in combat. Those advantages were offset by the better manoeuvrability and longer range of the Zero. The major difference was in the personnel who would fly these aeroplanes. The Japanese pilots had only abbreviated training and were, for the most part, much less experienced than their opponents. The previous losses of Japanese pilots had been of such magnitude that the capability of the carrier force was much depleted because there is no substitute for training and experience. On both sides there was ample courage and commitment to their country's cause.

The Japanese fleet was commanded by Admiral Ozawa Jisaburō, an early proponent of naval air power. He had at his disposal about 450 aircraft embarked on his nine assorted carriers and about 300 land-based aircraft. He was faced by those 900 planes on fifteen carriers. Ozawa's plan was to exploit the greater range of his aircraft and engage Mitscher at a maximum distance and, by so doing, shield his carriers from attack. The two fleets made aerial contact on 19 June, four days after the assault on Saipan, which had been covered by the fire support of eleven ships. Beachheads were established and numerical superiority gained.

Spruance, about 200 miles (320km) west of Saipan, was alerted to the position of Ozawa's fleet by the interception of a radio message that made mention of refuelling at Guam. The gap between the two fleets was about 300 miles (483km) and outside the range of the Hellcats. Ozawa's plan was based on the availability of the land-based aircraft under the command of

Admiral Kurita, in command of 1st Air Fleet. However, unknown to Ozawa, Kurita had redeployed his aircraft to Yap and the Palau islands – he then lied, saying his aircraft were in contact with the Americans and 'inflicting heavy damage'.[14] The effect was that Ozawa was not nearly as strong as he thought he was.

Responding to the information that the Japanese – or at least some of them – were in the vicinity of Guam, Mitscher sent aircraft to intercept them. There was a skirmish that was the prelude to the Battle of the Philippine Sea, which was later named 'The Great Marianas Turkey Shoot'.

After the Guam engagement, 5th Fleet's radar picked up incoming hostiles when they were about 150 miles (240km) from the island. Hellcats were scrambled and all anti-aircraft weapons were readied. The first Japanese strike set the pattern for the rest of the battle. Only twenty-eight of the seventy attackers survived this encounter. One bomb hit its target on *South Dakota* but caused no serious damage. Nothing daunted, Ozawa launched a second strike of 130 aircraft. It was obliterated: ninety-nine were shot down.

As that attacking force set off, some from *Taihō*'s flight deck, the carrier was hit with a torpedo from USS *Albacore*. The submarine had fired two torpedoes and, while the second was tracking towards the carrier, a pilot later identified as Warrant Officer Komatsu Sakio, who was just aloft, spotted the torpedo and unhesitatingly dived his plane into the path of the missile. This war in the Pacific was the scene of countless selfless acts of great courage, and this was one of them.

In the event, the single torpedo sealed the fate of *Taihō* because it breached the aviation fuel tanks. The vapours that were released were highly inflammable and, when they were seen to be accumulating, a junior damage control officer ordered all the ventilating ducts to be opened. This made matters worse, and the gasoline fumes permeated the entire ship. Soon thereafter, *Taihō*, the flagship, exploded and Ozawa had to be cajoled into not going down with the ship and accompanying the 1,650 who did.

The submarine USS *Cavalla* moved into an advantageous position and was able to discharge six torpedoes at the carrier *Shōkaku*. Three strikes were observed and one of them, like that on *Taihō*, ruptured the aviation fuel tanks and the result was the same. The ship exploded, was blown apart, and sank 140 miles (225km) north of Yap Island; 1,263 men perished.

The following day, the two fleets shadow-boxed until about 1540 hrs, when a garbled message was received indicating that Ozawa was about 250 miles (400km) away to the north-west. Notwithstanding the limited daylight, Mitscher decided that he would pursue Ozawa and ordered the launch of 116 aircraft to attack at maximum distance. He well knew that his pilots would almost certainly not have sufficient fuel to make the return journey. It was a ruthless decision.

The 116 headed out towards the setting sun and, when Ozawa picked up American radio traffic, he ordered his fleet to withdraw further to the north-west. The US airmen caught up with the Japanese fleet at the extremity of their range. The light carrier *Hiyō* was hit with two torpedoes and sank. The carriers *Zuikaku* and *Jun'yō* were badly damaged. Three tankers were sunk. Eighty-five Japanese aircraft were flown to face this attack and sixty-five of them were shot down at a cost of twenty American planes.

It was now dark, and the ninety-six remaining Americans turned for home, hoping to find their carrier, any carrier, in the stygian gloom. It was a forlorn hope for most and, out of fuel, about sixty had to ditch. A handful of the pilots were rescued. The USN carriers turned on all their lights to assist the landing of the few who had sufficient fuel.

The air battle was hopelessly one-sided, as the arithmetic reveals. Japanese losses mounted to catastrophic heights. The Americans lost 123 aircraft and had 109 men killed. The only damage was that inflicted by the single bomb on *South Dakota*. On the other side of the balance sheet, Japan lost three carriers and two oilers that were sunk. Six other ships were damaged. The butcher's bill is estimated at over 3,400 killed and between 550 and 645 aircraft destroyed.[15] Most of the pilots of those downed aircraft were killed and their deaths exacerbated Japan's already serious shortage of pilots. This battle was the final nail in the coffin of IJN air power. It removed any hope that the defenders of Saipan might have had of reinforcement or of logistic support.

After the event, Spruance was criticised for being overly cautious and by defending the Saipan invasion had missed the chance of obliterating Japan as a naval force. He had, in fact, won a comprehensive victory at very low cost and when the dust had settled it was acknowledged that 'the battle of the Philippine Sea was one of the most complete in the whole Pacific War.'[16]

* * *

On 15 June, the scene was set for the invasion of Saipan by V Amphibious Corps, commanded by Lieutenant General 'Howling Mad' Holland Smith. His corps was composed of 1st and 2nd Marine divisions and 27th Infantry Division.

Ashore he was awaited by 39,000 troops of the 31st Army and about 30,000 Japanese civilians, who had colonised the island of Saipan. General Saito Yoshitsugu was the military commander, and he was well prepared. He had arranged for range markers to be placed in the sea so that he could bring down effective fire on the landing craft. This measure caused the sinking of twenty amphibious tanks on the first morning. Nevertheless, by that evening

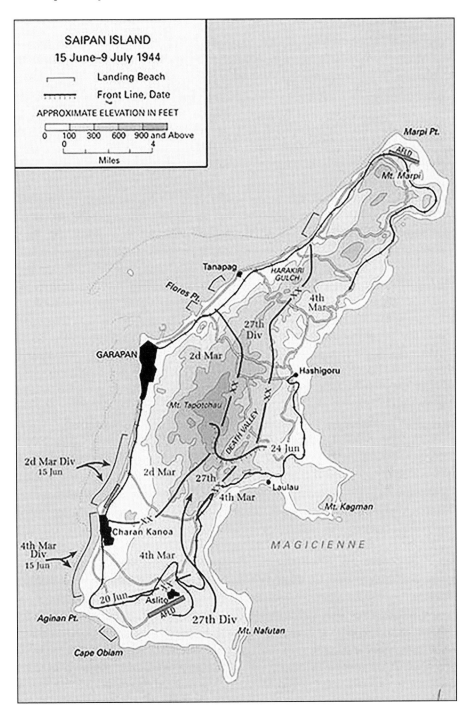

SAIPAN ISLAND
15 June–9 July 1944

⎦⎣ Landing Beach

······· Front Line, Date

APPROXIMATE ELEVATION IN FEET

0   100   300   600   900 and Above

0   4

Miles

Marpi Pt.

Afld

Mt. Marpi

Tanapag

HARAKIRI GULCH

Floras Pt.

4th Mar

27th Div

GARAPAN

2d Mar

Hashigoru

Mt. Tapotchau

24 Jun

DEATH VALLEY

2d Mar Div
15 Jun

2d Mar

27th

Loulau

4th Mar

Mt. Kagman

Charan Kanoa

4th Mar Div
15 Jun

4th Mar

MAGICIENNE

20 Jun

Aslito

Afld

27th Div

Aginan Pt.

Mt. Nafutan

Cape Obiam

the two marine divisions were ashore and had established a beachhead about 6 miles (9.7km) long and half a mile deep; a Japanese attack on the beachhead was repulsed.

The following day, the 27th Infantry Division landed and moved at once to its first objective, which was the airfield at Aslito (bottom centre of map). It was confronted by extremely rugged territory; his line of advance was down a valley dominated by Japanese positions on the heights above, which overlooked the valley. Inevitably, the 27th made slow progress. The advance stalled.

The corps commander, Holland Smith, was irritated and, without visiting the scene, decided to sack Major General Ralph Smith, the 27th Division commander. He discussed the matter with Spruance, who was also nowhere near the scene but who nevertheless concurred. Smith was duly sacked. It was an unfair and precipitous decision. The aftermath of Smith's sacking was serious damage to the relations between the Army and the US Marine Corps. This was exacerbated when the press took sides and publicised the matter. An army investigation concluded that the sacking of Smith 'was not justified by the facts'.[17]

Immediately after Smith's departure, the 27th Division put into operation his plan made earlier. It was successful and, having involved the division in vigorous fighting around the airstrip, it caused Saito to abandon Aslito on 18 June. After his withdrawal Saito mounted a night attack in which he deployed his twenty-five tanks. The Americans, alerted by the clanking of the tanks, called for illumination and when star shells burst overhead, the attackers were caught in the open. The armour was destroyed and with it went Saito's last chance. Tokyo ignored the failure of the attack and radioed to 31st Army the following message:

> Because the fate of the Japanese Empire depends on the result of your operation, inspire the spirit of your officers and men and to the very end continue to destroy the enemy gallantly and persistently, thus assuaging the anxiety of our Emperor.[18]

That fatuous message, delivered to men in an unsupported, impossible situation and facing imminent death, does at least give an indication of the culture and quality of military nous in Tokyo. Nevertheless, it drew a toenail-curling response from General Igeta, who signalled:

> Have received your honourable imperial words and we are grateful for boundless magnanimity of the imperial favour. By becoming the bulwark of the Pacific with 10,000 deaths we hope to requite the imperial favour.[19]

It was during Saipan operations that flamethrowers came into general use. They were an awesome area weapon although they put the operator at extreme risk. He was a prime target for snipers and there were many cases of operators being immolated. Three weeks later, and after that exchange of signals, it was evident even to Saito that he had run out of options. The defence had been stoic, selfless, and effective up to a point, but with only the sea behind him, Saito prepared for a final bloody denouement.

On 6 July, the surviving Japanese soldiers were mustered, many of them on crutches and swathed in bandages. Saito pronounced: 'There is no longer any distinction between civilians and troops. It would be better for them to join in the attack with bamboo spears than be captured.' This call to the civilian population was to have dire consequences.

At dawn on the morning of 7 July, and behind a banner, over 4,000 Japs charged in a mass attack on the American line held by two battalions of the 105th Infantry Regiment. The impetus of the charge was such that, initially, the Americans were overrun and took heavy casualties. It was a crisis, and an 'all hands to the pumps' situation. Ad hoc groups of soldiers and marines slowly halted the charge and overcame the attackers. It was estimated that in this one incident, 4,300 Japanese were killed, as were 650 Americans.

Generals Saito and Igeta committed suicide, as did Vice Admiral Nagumo. That simple statement conceals the pathos of the event. In fact, the three agreed that the ritual disembowelling prescribed in hara-kiri was too protracted and that it would be preferable to be shot by an aide. There was some discussion as to who might carry out this task. A small cave was selected, and the three men sat cross-legged at its mouth. Then, without a further order, and somewhat prematurely, two young officers shot them all in the back of the head.[20]

In the afternoon of 9 July, Admiral Turner announced that Saipan had been taken. But the killing did not stop there. The civilian population had been indoctrinated to believe that the Americans would rape, mutilate and then kill them all. As a direct result, at least 7,000 threw themselves off the heights of Marpi Point and Suicide Cliff at the northern tip of Saipan. There is a memorial there today to mark the utterly fruitless loss of life.

In all, 22,000 civilians died on Saipan, as did 29,000 Japanese soldiers. US losses were 2,949 killed and 10,464 wounded.

*   *   *

In Tokyo, the defeat in Saipan had political consequences. It was a national disaster, and someone had to pay. The blame is usually laid at the door of the most senior, and this was no exception. Prime Minister Tojo had set Japan on its imperialist way and in the early stage of his leadership his ambition knew no bounds. He was viewed both at home and abroad as 'the embodiment of national determination, hard line nationalism and militarism'.[21]

In mid-1944, Japan had a multitude of problems. Strategically, the Aleutian Islands had been lost, garrisons on the Solomons and New Guinea were beyond help and the Central Pacific islands that were the principal defence line had been breached, with the collapse of the Marshalls, Gilberts and Marianas.

Domestically, Japan had had to take strong measures to counter the ever-tighter blockade being imposed by submarines of the USN. During 1944, in 520 war patrols, the USN fired 6,092 torpedoes and the Japanese merchant fleet lost 219,907 tons of shipping in July, 245,348 tons in August, and 181,363 tons in September. Sinkings reduced later in the year – because US submarines could not find targets from the now severely degraded Japanese Merchant Marine. Losses of this magnitude could not be sustained by an island nation as bulk imports fell by 40 per cent during 1944.[22]

The population was obliged to cope with changing circumstances. Many civilian companies had been taken over to produce war materiel. Schools reduced classroom time and student labour was deployed. A seven-day work-week was imposed, internal travel was difficult and subject to police permits, the train service was degraded, and that led to civil unrest in protest. Food was rationed, and so too was clothing. Newspapers were reduced in size and frequency of publication. Fuel, be it gas or charcoal, was in short supply, places of entertainment were closed, and the final straw was the edict that coffins were to be recycled. The country was swept with rumours and the policy of not being honest with the population now started to backfire.

Tojo, and those around him, had fallen victim to 'Victory Disease'. This is a phenomenon that occurs in military history when a combination of complacency and arrogance, generated by a series of early victories, leads to a later crushing defeat. Napoleon, Hitler and Tojo were all so afflicted.

The loss of Saipan had infuriated Hirohito and he called together his senior army and naval officers to consider the possibility of recapturing the island. The Emperor got no comfort from that meeting. Unknown to him, Prince Konoye and Admiral Okada had been working on a plan to unseat Tojo. Unknown to them all, Major Tsunoda Tomoshige was preparing to assassinate the Prime Minister, as was Admiral Takagi Sōkichi. Tojo was on a razor's edge.

He was aware of his increasing unpopularity, and he offered his resignation to Hirohito, which was rejected. Tojo withdrew, and next he suggested a re-shuffle of his cabinet to the Emperor's Privy Seal, Kido Kōichi. Kido, speaking for Hirohito, rejected the suggestion and said that the entire cabinet should resign. At this point, Tojo realised that he had lost the support of Emperor Hirohito, and on 18 July, he resigned.

In July 1944 it would have been rational, intelligent and pragmatic for Japan to take the first steps towards surrender or some other device just short of the unconditional surrender that the Allies demanded. There were a few muted voices that expressed that view but when identified they found themselves on the next boat to China. The pointless, ludicrous killing went on for another year.

Notes

1. Smith, R.S., 'The Approach to the Philippines' (United States Army Centre of Military History, *The United States Army in World War II*, 1953), pp. 16–18.
2. Odgers, G., 'Air War Against Japan 1943–45' (Canberra, *Australia in the War of 1939–1945, Series 3 – Air Force, Vol. II*, Australian War Memorial, 1968), p. 180.
3. 'Australia looks first to US' (*The Daily Telegraph III*, NSW, 28 December 1941).
4. Edwards, J., *John Curtin's War: Vol. II – Triumph and Decline* (Melbourne, Viking, 2018), p. 18.
5. Hastings, Sir M., *Nemesis: The Battle for Japan 1944–45* [2007] (London, Collins, 2016), p. 364.
6. Day, D., *Curtin: A Life* (New South Wales, Harper Collins, 1999), p. 540.
7. Keogh, E., *Southwest Pacific 1941–45* (Melbourne, Grayflower Publications, 1965), p. 428.
8. Ibid., p. 408.
9. Odgers, p. 180.
10. Hastings, p. 372.
11. Keogh, pp. 300–301.
12. Morison, S.E., *New Guinea and the Marianas, March–August 1944, History of US Naval Operations in World War II* (Urbana, University of Illinois Press), p. 227.
13. Toll, I.W., *The Conquering Tide* (USA, WW Norton & Co, 2015), p. 436.
14. Costello, J., *The Pacific War 1941–45* [1981] (New York, Harper Collins, 2009), p. 480.
15. Shores, C., *Duel for the Sky: Ten Crucial Battles of World War II* (London, Grub Street, 1985), p. 205.
16. Costello, p. 481.
17. Toland, J., *The Rising Sun: The Decline and Fall of the Japanese Empire, 1936–45* [1970] (Modern Library, New York, 2003), p. 505.
18. Ibid, p. 495.
19. Ibid.
20. Toland, p. 512.
21. Willmott, H.P., *June 1944* (Poole, UK, Blandford Press, 1984), p. 216.
22. Hastings, p. 291.

Chapter Twenty-Two

19 July–27 November 1944
Trophies, Logistics, Guam, Tinian, Morotai and Peleliu

The capture of each island initiated the building of an airfield, sometimes several. Those airfields had to be maintained and defended. Provision had to be made for fuel and ammunition storage. Personnel with specialist skills or experience were required and they were left behind as the war rolled on. Life on a recently captured island was utterly without incident other than the arrival of an occasional aircraft. It was possibly out of boredom and an ample availability of material that an unpleasant phenomenon was generated among American soldiers and marines. It was the practice of 'skull stewing' – more of that in a moment. On the now abandoned battlefield the taking of Japanese body parts as trophies was becoming commonplace. These trophies were then sold for others to mail them home to family. Gold teeth and ears were the most favoured trophies.

As early as September 1942, 'stern disciplinary action' against human remains souvenir taking was ordered by the Commander-in-Chief of the Pacific Fleet when it was found to be necessary to proscribe the practice of mutilating enemy dead.[1] In the ensuing twelve months the threat had clearly had no effect because, in October 1943, General George Marshall spoke to MacArthur about 'his concern over current reports of atrocities committed by American soldiers'.[2]

Any strictures that followed were ineffective and in early 1944, it fell to the Joint Chiefs of Staff to issue yet a further directive proscribing the taking of body parts. However, although they may have been effective in some areas, 'they seem to have been implemented only partially and unevenly by local commanders'.[3]

Taking trophies from enemy dead is acceptable and a map, binoculars or compass are neither here nor there. American servicemen in the Pacific theatre generally followed that pattern but were also deeply influenced by racial propaganda aimed at the Japanese foe. Anthropologist Simon Harrison argued that the United States military's use of racially graphic posters and pamphlets depicting the Japanese soldier as vermin meant to be exterminated allowed Americans to see them as subhuman.

The taking of body parts as trophies was sufficiently widespread that it proved to be difficult to curb. This is further evidenced when, two years later, *Life* magazine printed a picture of a young woman who was the recipient of a trophy skull. If the image shocked Americans it quite reasonably outraged the Japanese, who reprinted it 'as a symbol of American barbarism'.[4] The *Life* photograph was a propaganda gift to the Japanese. Readers of *Life* were shocked, and their response was overwhelmingly condemnatory. The junior officer who sent the 'gift' was reprimanded – in effect, a slap on the wrist. This trophy mentality was perhaps exemplified by US Representative Francis

Life magazine, 22 May 1944, 'Picture of the Week: Natalie Nickerson, 20, writes her Navy boyfriend a thank you note for the Jap skull he sent her.'

E. Walter, who was crass enough to send, as a gift to President Roosevelt, a letter opener fashioned from the arm of a Japanese soldier.[5] Roosevelt rejected the gift and asked for it to be correctly interred.

The skull photograph stirred the military into taking some belated action. In a memorandum dated 13 June 1944, the US Army Judge Advocate General (JAG) asserted that 'such atrocious and brutal policies', in addition to being repugnant, were also violations of the laws of war. He recommended the distribution of a directive, to all commanders, pointing out that the maltreatment of enemy war dead was a blatant violation of the '1929 Geneva Convention on the Sick and Wounded', which provided that: 'After each engagement, the occupant of the field of battle shall take measures to search for the wounded and dead, and to protect them against pillage and maltreatment.'

The JAG added that such practices were also in violation of the unwritten customary rules of land warfare and could lead to the death penalty. However, and despite official disapproval, the taking of enemy skulls continued and became a cottage industry. A technique was developed to boil the skulls and thereafter to strip away all flesh. The skull was then polished and sold to willing fellow servicemen.

'Skull stewing' was not an activity to be pursued under fire and when in contact with the very live enemy. On that basis it was almost always conducted well away from the action and in locations free from the supervision of responsible officers. The lines of communication troops had the opportunity and the means to operate this grisly business.

The official American reaction to these practices was, in effect, 'If you do this what will the Japanese do in response?' It was fear of retaliation that drove official condemnation of trophy taking but the grotesque, uncivilised behaviour was not pursued. No reference could be found of disciplinary action against the practitioners. Many collected for purely economic purposes and took the valuable gold-capped teeth of their foe. Marine Robert Leckie had a friend who received the telling nickname of 'Souvenirs'.

> the men remembered Souvenirs as the Marine who always carried pliers in his back pocket and a pouch around his neck. He avidly collected Japanese gold capped teeth. He willingly went out on patrols just so that he could scour the area for dead soldiers with gold teeth still intact. Leckie and his comrades took turns estimating how many gold teeth Souvenirs had collected since they arrived on the island. They guessed around seventy-five, but Souvenirs never revealed the actual number. He had good reason to keep the amount a secret. The gold caps fetched money in the United States. Even with seventy-five teeth, Souvenirs

Boiling Japanese heads; 'skull stewing' prior to polishing the skull for later sale.

could receive around $2,000. Keeping the teeth around his neck and never sharing how many he had helped Souvenirs hang on to his expensive prizes.[6]

Most Americans serving in the Pacific had nothing to do with body part trophies and this aberrational behaviour was the exception rather than the norm. Australian soldiers also took body parts, which was just as objectionable, but the Australian presence in the theatre was on a very much lower scale and it did not have the same commercial element. The British did not take trophies of this sort, but one incident is worth quoting. It appears that Lieutenant Colonel Derek Horsford, commanding 4th/1st Gurkhas in Burma, advised his brigade commander of Japanese activity in his area. However, the brigadier did not believe him. Horsford sent out a patrol to gather evidence and, the next morning, he left three Japanese heads strung for convenience on a string by the brigadier's desk. The great man said, 'Never do that again. Next time I'll take your word for it.'[7]

Over time, much energy has been expended seeking an explanation for the extraordinary mindset of the perhaps hundreds of thousands of Japanese who committed war crimes. The mindset of skull stewers also merits attention.

*   *   *

It is suggested that logistic operations in the Pacific theatre were uniquely complex as they were multiple, aimed at a miscellany of targets, sometimes concurrently, and incorporated land, sea and air activity over a vast area and during a period of almost three years in which cross-beach landings were the norm. Notwithstanding the magnitude of D-Day and the invasion of Europe, the logistic operations supporting the war in the Pacific were, arguably, the largest, and most effective in military history. They were also, probably, the most expensive.

The limitless wealth of the USA was the key to its success in both theatres. The USA could produce more ships, planes, tanks, wheeled vehicles and ordnance than any other nation on earth. Its armed forces asked for nothing – well, that is not quite right because the logistic support, although all-embracing, was nevertheless patchy and appallingly profligate. The sailors of the United States Navy lived 'high on the hog', the marines on Saipan less so.

The Pacific War covered about a third of the planet and 1.25 million Americans served there in some capacity or other. Over 40 per cent of these did not hear a shot fired in anger and they manned the vast infrastructure that managed the logistic effort. Of the 1.25 million, perhaps '40% of the officers and 33% of the soldiers/sailors spent some time "in combat" by the most generous interpretation of the word.'[8]

Hastings's slightly negative observation generates the need for a closer study of the logistics of the Pacific War. The storybook Pacific island is warm, filled with palm trees that dip and wave in a cool gentle breeze. The local inhabitants are attractive, generous and friendly. Hot showers, cold beer and ice cream are plentiful.

For the men fighting on those islands the reality was vastly different.

It was very hot and humid, uncomfortable, and very dangerous. The sun was hostile, boots rotted, weapons rusted unless well maintained, water was rationed, and personal hygiene was difficult to maintain. The smell of decaying corpses was a constant. The food in the front line was predominantly tinned and eaten cold. There was continual stress. Sleeping, eating, even defecating was affected by the likelihood of possible mutilating injury or death. To get one man into this unattractive setting and maintain him there took the combined efforts of more than ten, perhaps as many as twenty others in the logistic chain – employed all the way back to the man who made the boots.

Logistics are a bit like taxes – they are necessary if society is to function. In this case, the military society. It is alleged that Admiral Ernest King once said, 'I don't know what the hell this "logistics" is that Marshall is always talking about, but I want some of it.' That quote is at odds with the facts because it was King who was responsible for the supply of his ships and personnel during their advance across the Pacific. He was a master logistician.

Ships of all types were the fundamental tool of King's operations, but the burden of each ship is, of course, limited. The following very tedious passage explains the loading of support ships:

> Gross tonnage is the entire enclosed space of a ship, measured in register tons of 100 cubic feet (2.83 cubic meters). Net tonnage is the space that can be used for cargo, also measured in register tons. Logisticians prefer the 'measurement ton', which is equal to 40 cubic feet (1.13 cubic meters) of cargo or cargo space. The capacity of the average ship in 'measurement tons' was roughly equal to 1.775 times its gross register tonnage.
>
> A ship can be loaded with only so much weight of cargo before it sits dangerously low in the water. A cargo ship has a deadweight tonnage equal to the maximum permissible weight of ship's gear, supply, and personnel as well as cargo, measured in long tons of 2,240 pounds (1.016 metric tons). The deadweight effective lift of a ship is the maximum cargo weight and is typically about 80% of deadweight tonnage. The deadweight lift of the average ship was about 1.2 times its gross register tonnage.
>
> In practice, for typical military cargoes, it was volume rather than weight that limited carrying capacity. For planning purposes, the U.S. Army adopted a figure of 2.56 measurement tons per long ton of average military cargo and compact cargo, such as oil in 55-gallon (208 litre) drums, might take 1.37 measurement tons per long ton.[9]

That helpful quotation will have made the reader's eyes glaze over long before he/she reached the end. However, it does serve to illustrate the highly complex calculations that preceded any operation involving hundreds of thousands of men and hundreds of ships and aircraft.

There had to be some rules of thumb to calculate the needs of, say, an American infantry division. In 1942, 6.8 'measurement tons' per man were required for the initial deployment. That is 105,000 tons for the whole division – and would require six cargo ships. An armoured division required 17.9 tons per man – and fifteen cargo ships. Later in the war these calculations were amended, and the infantry requirement reduced to 4.4 tons and armour to 13.1 tons.

The feeding of soldiers is always problematic. In this author's experience, bulk feeding is usually conducted at night, in the rain and at the junction of four maps. Soldiering is a vigorous business and the US military determined that the ration allowance for an American infantryman in the Pacific was to be a very substantial 4,758 calories per day. This is generous when compared to that of a British civilian, given a ration of about 2,800 calories per day. In Japan, civilians were limited to 2,000 calories, which reduced to 1,680 calories per day in 1945. The American staff had the following scale for guidance. Once overseas, each man required about 45 pounds (20kg) of supplies per day. These were broken down into five categories for planning purposes by the US Army:

6.22lb (2.82kg) of rations and other consumables, termed Class I.

3.11lb (1.41kg) of clothing, replacement vehicles, general supplies, Class II.

10.67lb (4.84kg) of fuel and lubricants, Class III.

15.46lb (7.0kg) of medical motor maintenance, quartermaster, construction, and other miscellaneous supplies, Class IV.

9.58lb (4.35kg) of ammunition, Class V.[10]

The ready availability of food, equipment, ammunition, vehicles and other assorted supplies led to tremendous waste. Every tin, tyre, helmet, rifle bullet and pair of boots was shipped at considerable cost across the face of the earth but 'up to 19% of some categories of food were spoilt in transit by climate, poor packing or careless handling.'[11] Twenty years later, the same situation was replicated in Vietnam. Waste is a privilege that only the very rich can afford.

The Americans who fought on the beaches lived in miserable conditions while those who supported from a distance lived rather better. In any army, officers and men go where they are sent. 'Not hearing a shot fired in anger' is a result of the arbitrary way armies are deployed and should not be an adverse reflection on the courage or commitment of those sent to the logistic chain. The teeth arms (infantry, armour, artillery, engineers, aviation – perhaps signals) always denigrate the logistic tail and they probably always will. It's not fair, but then nor is war.

Enough of logistics, we should return to the Pacific.

*   *   *

Whilst Japan was concerned with events on Saipan and the advance of Smith's V Amphibious Corps, the USA had the capacity to carry out concurrent major operations and had turned its sights on its own territory – the island of Guam. The island, the largest of the Mariana group, is 32 miles (52km) long and between 4 and 12 miles (19km) wide (see map opposite). It had been invaded on 10 December 1941 and taken in a humiliating blow to US pride.

The 'softening up' process started on 11 June and involved 216 carrier-based aircraft and land-based B-24 bombers, which sank twelve Japanese transports in the early stages. From 27 June, and for three weeks, USN big gun ships bombarded the island's defences until 21 July, when III Marine Amphibious Corps, some 59,401 strong, commanded by Major General Roy Geiger, crossed the beaches.[12]

The Japanese defence was led by Lieutenant General Takashina Takeshi, who commanded the 22,554 soldiers and forty tanks of the 29th Division. The general was killed in action on 28 July and command passed to Lieutenant General Obata Hideyoshi. The defenders emulated their countrymen

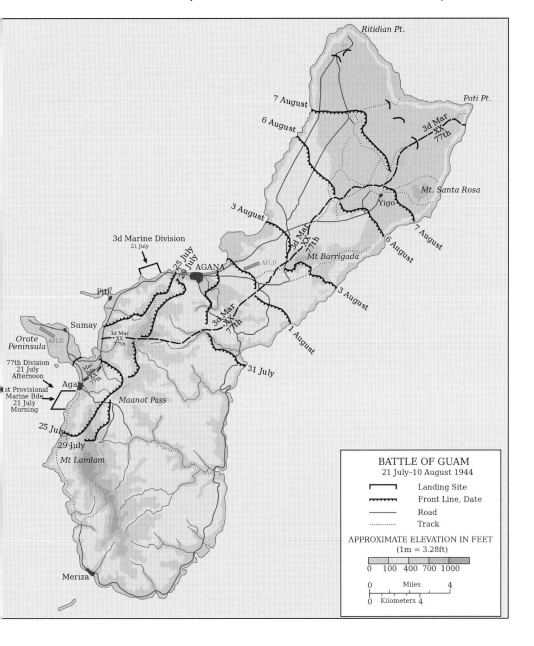

on other Pacific islands by concealing their artillery inland and exploiting natural caves which they adapted for defence. Obata knew that he would be neither reinforced nor resupplied and, like most Japanese, accepted that the battle would end in his death and that of his men. His aim was to kill as many Americans as possible. In the waters of the Pacific, the USN reigned supreme, and it was the US submarine service that was accelerating Japan's demise by denying any hope to officers like Obata.

The common problem experienced by the Americans in several cross-beach operations, such as that at Tarawa, was the difficulty of traversing the coral reefs that ringed each island. The invading force was under fire and very vulnerable as it waded ashore, sometimes hundreds of yards in waist-deep water. This was the case again in Guam, and many Americans died without reaching dry land.

Beachheads had been established on either side of the Orote Peninsula and they joined up on 28 July after the failed Japanese attack in which Takashina had been killed. Thereafter, Geiger directed his 3rd Marine Division to his left flank and the 77th Infantry Division to his right. Both then drove north until, on 2 August, they encountered Obata's defences centred on Mount Barrigada. Japanese resistance was only broken on 4 August and, as the map shows, Obata's brief final defence was on and around Mount Santa Rosa, which fell on 8 August. The general committed ritual suicide on 10 August, just one of 19,587 Japanese deaths. Unusually, there was a bigger bag of prisoners and 1,250 surrendered. American losses were 1,783 killed and 6,010 wounded.

The US declared Guam liberated on 10 August, but those Japs who were neither dead nor wounded decamped into the thick jungle. Initially, around 7,500 were at large, the last of whom, Sergeant Yokoi Shōichi, was captured in 1972, twenty-eight years after the war ended – a considerable demonstration of loyalty to his emperor.

*   *   *

The march across the Pacific continued and swept on over nearby Tinian, just 4 miles (6km) from Saipan. The brief campaign did not follow the general pattern of Tarawa, Saipan and Guam because Tinian posed several differences. One was the Tinian-based artillery that responded to the USN's bombardment, and to some effect. The battleship *Colorado* was hit with twenty-two shells that killed forty-three and wounded a further 198. The destroyer *Norman Scott* was struck six times, killing the captain and eighteen of his crew. Forty-seven were wounded.[13] This modest success drew US artillery fire from Saipan, from across the strait.

Tinian presented only two small landing beaches and most of the island was ringed by coral cliffs about 15 feet (5m) high. Those landing beaches were well defended. With some ingenious, innovative and swift engineering on the part of Commodore Paul Halloran, several ramps were constructed up which troops and vehicles could assault less well-defended parts of the island. The new commander of V Amphibious Corps, Major General Harry Schmidt, insisted on a test of the ramps, which, duly conducted, met all the requirements.

The 4th Marine Division, supported by that artillery in Saipan, landed via the Halloran ramps on the north-west corner of the island on 24 July and the 2nd Division followed a day later. V Corps was 41,364 strong and its opposition only 8,039. Those 8,039 were a miscellany of infantry from 29th Division, marines of 3rd Special Forces, 56th Naval Guards, flight technicians, construction workers and administrative staff. However, every one of these was prepared to give his life. V Corps brought to Tinian twenty-four mechanised flamethrowers. These had been developed following the earlier request from Holland Smith. They were an awesome weapon and ideal for use on Tinian, which was generally flat and suitable for tracked and wheeled vehicles. The island became a training ground for 'Satan' tanks, which were used extensively later in the war. Flame tanks carried much more fuel than the man-portable version and were able to fire longer and more destructive bursts. They were armoured and were able to approach enemy bunkers with relative impunity.

The maximum range of a flamethrower was typically less than 170 yards (150m). This did limit its use and made it vulnerable and ineffective on a wide-open battlefield. However, they had great psychological value and their very presence induced soldiers to surrender, cremation being the other option.

Notwithstanding bad weather on 28 July, which was sufficiently severe to damage some of the landing ramps, V Corps stormed across the island and on 30 July, 4th Marine Division had occupied Tinian town and taken the airfield.

The aftermath of defeat was that 13,000 Japanese citizens were interned but a further 4,000 had either committed suicide or been murdered by their countrymen; 5,522 Japanese soldiers were killed and only 252 taken prisoner; the balance of 2,265 were categorised as 'missing'. The body count ratio was 17:1. A total of 326 Americans were killed and 1,593 wounded.

It was at this time that thought was being given to the eventual invasion of Japan. As a routine part of any military plan an estimate must be made of the likely casualties on both sides. In Japan, civilians were already being schooled in close-quarter combat – albeit only with sharpened bamboo spears. It was anticipated that Allied casualties would be at least 500,000 – perhaps more. The likelihood was that 7 million Japanese would be killed. The Americans

M5A1 Light Flame Tank, a later version of the M3 vehicle used in Tinian.

recognised that they might need the participation of allies, until now excluded as far as possible from Pacific operations.

* * *

Intercepted messages provided intelligence that the Morotai was undefended and that in turn attracted the attention of MacArthur, whose outline plan was to invade Mindanao on 15 November 1944. MacArthur's aim was the liberation of the Philippines and to that end he now identified Morotai, a small island in the Halmahera group of islands, part of the Netherlands East Indies, as suitable for an airbase.

The island did have the Doroeba Plain in its south-west corner that was ostensibly a suitable place for an airfield. Unfortunately, it was very wet, verging on a swamp. The Japanese had taken the island in 1942 but, at the time, it was not of any strategic value and so was occupied only by indigenous people. Nothing ever stays the same and, by 1944, the Japanese were engaged in developing the much larger Halmahera Island, where they built nine airstrips. The importance of Halmahera washed off on Morotai and two battalions were sent to develop a further airstrip on the swampy plain. The conditions were too difficult for the Japanese and the project was abandoned.[14] They left the island to its 9,000 inhabitants, who had no idea what awaited them and their island home.

The attack on Morotai was made on 15 September and was concurrent with the invasion of Peleliu. The Americans did not expect any resistance and their focus was on the flat plain. They planned to hold and defend only the perimeter of the soon to be constructed airstrip.

The American invasion force of Morotai outnumbered the defenders by 100:1. The island was taken with the loss of thirty Americans killed and eighty-five wounded. The defenders had about 300 killed and thirteen captured.[15] The Netherlands reclaimed sovereignty of the island and an administrative cell was established. American plans were grandiose – the aim was to build three long airstrips in a time frame of only forty-five days on very unpromising territory. It did not end there; an anticipated 60,000 personnel from all services were to be based on the island and appropriate facilities built for their professional needs and comfort. A 1,900-bed hospital was a priority. To service the airstrips there were to be fuel tank storage, engineer workshops, air defence positions and ammunition bunkers. This was military engineering on a grand scale.

Work was at a furious and highly commendable pace. The first of those airstrips was known as Warma Drome, all 5,000 feet (1,500m) of it being completed by 4 October, just under three weeks since the invasion. The next strip was the very much larger Pitu Drome, which had two runways and was built parallel to Warma. Pitu was operational from 17 October, and provided B-29 crews with 7,000-foot (2,100m) runways.

By the end of 1944, Morotai was a major US installation in the Pacific. It was developed as a port and used as a launch pad for operations against several small islands, among them Pegun, Bras and the Asia islands. It was a key component in MacArthur's assault on the Philippines – just as he had intended. Not all Japanese surrendered, and they were a minor threat until the end of the war. In 1975, the following appeared in the press:

> Like his predecessors, Private Nakamura Teruo was motivated to hold out both by fear of capture and fidelity to orders. After a final *banzai* charge against invading U.S. troops failed in January 1945, radio contact between Tokyo and Morotai was lost. Nakamura, who was separated from other members of his commando unit, managed to avoid capture and built a grass hut deep in the jungle. He survived by raising potatoes and picking bananas off the trees. 'My commanding officer told me to fight it out,' he explained. Last month (18 December 1974) he was spotted by a Morotai native, who alerted Indonesian authorities. Four airmen lured the naked Nakamura out of hiding by singing the Japanese national anthem and waving the rising sun flag. Then they pounced on him.

Aerial view of Pitu (left) and Wama (right) airfields in 1945. (*Harrison, John Thomas*)

Nakamura would like to return home and join his wife. She has long since remarried but says that she will still be happy to see him. So far, the Japanese government has not sent a jet to take him back to Tokyo nor have the banners been brought out for a grand welcome. The Welfare Ministry, however, did compute Nakamura's back pay. After nearly 30 years alone in the jungle, he is entitled to the princely sum of $227.59.[16]

*   *   *

During the Pacific War, the US fought a lengthy series of battles on isolated islands, and each followed much the same pattern. The islands fought for were each moderately important at the time but, as the advance rolled on, so their degree of importance was degraded. The Japanese logistics system had all but collapsed by September 1944, and Japanese garrisons on isolated islands were, in effect, prisoners. This point was made in Chapter 19, but it is worth reiterating because, on 15 September 1944, the US committed itself to the most futile of its island battles. Peleliu was neither tactically nor strategically of any importance at all. For ten dreadful weeks until 27 November, the Americans fought for something they did not need or want. Peleliu was no

Saipan or Morotai. It was merely the graveyard of thousands of very brave men of both nations.

Generals are best advised not to make predictions and Major General William Rupertus of the US 1st Marine Division stuck his neck out when he said that, following the invasion of Peleliu, the island would be 'secured within four days'. How very wrong he was.

Peleliu was occupied by about 11,000 men of the 14th Infantry Division, commanded by Major General Inoue Sadae. There were, in addition, an unmeasured number of engineers and civilians. Inoue was absent from the island on 15 September having delegated command to Colonel Nakagawa Kunio.

Colonel Nakagawa Kunio (1898–1944).

Inoue and Nakagawa had taken note of previous island battles and planned accordingly. Deep, concealed and tactically well-placed defensive positions were constructed across the island. The advantages offered by the Umurbrogol hills that dominated the centre of Peleliu were exploited, and not least the limestone caves – allegedly about 500, which riddled the terrain. The caves were linked by tunnels and the engineers added sliding armoured doors and developed old mine shafts for defensive purposes.

Nakagawa was fully aware of American tactics for dealing with caves and so he altered cave entrances to reduce the effect of direct fire, flamethrowers and grenades. Provision was made for concealed withdrawal from any position to an alternative. Nakagawa was aware that eventually he would be overwhelmed but planned to kill as many Americans as possible before that happened. *Banzai* charges were not his style, and his men would die where they stood.

The 1st Marine Division and 81st Infantry Division came ashore on 15 September and were at once confronted by concrete pillboxes that overlooked the landing beaches but had not been revealed in reconnaissance photographs. The invading troops were cut down in swathes. By dusk on 15 September, the beachhead was secure, but 1st Division already had 1,000 casualties, 200 of whom were dead.

Those who had fought on other islands later said that operations on Peleliu had been the most demanding. The National Museum of the US Marine Corps described it as 'the bitterest battle of the war for the Marines'. The Japanese fought skilfully, very bravely, and as American casualties rose, they were achieving their commander's aim. The invaders advanced cave by cave and ridge by ridge. One cave alone was found to contain 1,000 enemy dead. A simple statistic gives an indication of the intensity of fighting. It had taken 1,589 rounds of small arms and heavier ordnance to kill each single Japanese soldier. The adjacent outlaying islands in the Palau group were also taken.

Eventually and inevitably, the Americans overcame their adversary but, by 27 November, they had suffered 7,919 casualties. In the USA, 1,460 mothers would morn a lost son. In accordance with their extraordinary culture, 13,600 Japanese were killed or committed suicide, and 400 were captured on Peleliu and those other smaller islands. Vice Admiral J.B. Oldendorf observed: 'If military leaders were gifted with the same accuracy of foresight as they are with hindsight undoubtedly the assault and capture of the Palaus would never have been attempted.'[17]

Notes

1. Harrison, S., 'Skull Trophies of the Pacific War; Transgressive objects of remembrance' (*Journal of the Royal Anthropological Institute*, 12:4, 2006), p. 827.
2. Weingartner, J.J., 'Trophies of War: US Troops and the mutilation of Japanese war dead' (*Pacific Historical Review*, 61.1, 1992), p. 57.
3. Harrison, p. 827.
4. Ibid, pp. 817–36.
5. Weingartner, p. 57.
6. Leckie, R., *Helmet for My Pillow* (New York, Bantam Books, 1957), p. 117.
7. Hastings, Sir M., *Nemesis: The Battle for Japan 1944–45* (2007) (London, Collins, 2016), p. 6.
8. Hastings, p. 9.
9. The Pacific War online Encyclopedia.
10. Ibid.
11. Hastings, p. 9.
12. Rottman, G.L., *Guam 1941 &1944: Loss and Reconquest* (Botley, Osprey, 2004), p. 60.
13. Rottman, G.L. & Gerrard, H., *Saipan & Tinian 1944: Piercing the Japanese Empire* (Oxford, Osprey Publishing, 2004).
14. Willoughby, C.A., *Japanese Operations in the Southwest Pacific Area*, Vol. II (Reports of General MacArthur, United States Government Printing Office, 1966), pp. 348–9.
15. Smith, R.R., *The Approach to the Philippines: United States Army in World War II* (Washington, US Army Centre of Military History, 1996), p. 489.
16. *Time* magazine, 13 January 1975.
17. Heinl, R.D., *Soldiers of the Sea: The US Marine Corps, 1775–1962* (Annapolis, USN, 1962), p. 473.

Chapter Twenty-Three

October–December 1944
Leyte

MacArthur had been summoned to meet President Roosevelt in July 1944 and he conducted himself very badly. He deliberately dressed down and made a point of not greeting the President when he arrived in Hawaii. MacArthur despised Roosevelt and had been toying with the idea of running against him as the Democrat candidate for president. Then, recognising that he was unlikely to beat Thomas Dewey for the nomination, he let the matter die. MacArthur believed, probably correctly, that Roosevelt was determined to be involved in the strategic planning because he saw it as a useful electioneering ruse in his campaign to win his record fourth nomination for the presidency.

MacArthur decided to upstage Roosevelt, arriving in a long, open-top limousine with elaborate motorcycle escort, accepting the welcome from the cheering crowd. Even before he arrived at Hawaii, he was unhappy about being forced to leave his troops to attend this 'picture-taking junket'. A measure of MacArthur's Brobdingnagian ego was that he was discommoded by his president, and ultimately his boss for presuming to address him as 'Douglas'. Nevertheless, the product of the meeting was that MacArthur was given the green light to invade the Philippines, later in 1944.

The successful capture of islands in the Marshall and Gilbert groups had provided airbases from which, by mid-1944, America was bombing the Japanese mainland. In their wake across the Pacific the advancing forces of Nimitz and MacArthur had circumvented unimportant Japanese garrisons which were left in isolation, unsupported and of no military value.

The Imperial Japanese Navy was in something of a quandary. It recognised that the fighting had been shouldered by the army spread across the Pacific and that, to date, the Japanese Army had lost every island outpost and thousands of lives. The IJN was aware that it had to involve itself, but where? The Americans were closing in on the home islands and their next objective could be anywhere – Formosa, the Philippines, perhaps Iwo Jima or Okinawa? The USA had the ships, hundreds of them, the men, and the means to keep both supplied.

On balance, the IJN decided that the Philippines were the most likely target but their geography presented a problem. The archipelago consisted of

7,100 islands and spread 1,150 miles (1,850km) from Mindanao due north through the central island of Cebu and Leyte to Luzon, the largest. Only eleven of the islands had an area greater than 1,000 square miles (2,590km^2) and two, Mindanao and Luzon, made up almost 70 per cent of the Philippines' land mass. Where would the Americans land? They were spoilt for choice. In the meantime, a million Japanese soldiers were fighting and dying in the apparently endless and fruitless war with China, now into its eighth year.

To assist in the liberation of the Philippines, the Australian Government offered to the USA the services of a corps with two infantry divisions. In a churlish response MacArthur agreed, but only on the basis that the divisions would be separated and attached to different American corps and would thus be totally under American command. The Australians would have nothing of this, and the offer was not followed up. This was another example of the American senior military not wanting to allow any ally to share in their private war. The RAAF and RAN were later employed, but in token numbers only.

Tokyo moved General Yamashita Tomoyuki to take command of the Japanese troops in the Philippines. Yamashita had an audience with Hirohito before he left Tokyo, and both understood he was going to his death. In this new post he answered to Field Marshal Terauchi, whose Southern Army was responsible for the defence of a huge area, from New Guinea to Burma and included the Philippines. Yamashita was a very capable soldier, probably the best available, but he was also the man responsible for mass murder in Malaya and Singapore in 1942. Among his tens of thousands of victims were Mr Tan's officers.

In Tokyo, the Government had fallen back on lying to the population and announced entirely fictitious victories – for example, on 15 October, 'Tokyo Rose' announced a major naval victory, a 'second Pearl Harbor', off Formosa. The Emperor declared a public holiday to celebrate. The reality was very different. Halsey's 3rd Fleet had been striking at Okinawa and the adjoining Ryukyu Islands. The Japanese 6th Air Fleet came to engage Halsey but with disastrous results. The Japanese airmen, as always, did not lack either courage or determination, but they did lack training and experience – over 500 were shot down. Halsey then moved his fleet to cover the landings of the 6th Army.

Yamashita intended to fight the decisive battle for the Philippines on the main island of Luzon, but that was counter to the wishes of Field Marshal Terauchi, who had been convinced by the absurd claims made by the IJN that had been endorsed by Tokyo. On that basis he directed that the Americans were to be defeated at the point of their invasion.

The events that follow were concurrent. The naval battle was an epic, whilst on land the loss of life was vast. The eventual victory of the USA came as no surprise, but historians have ever since questioned the need for the

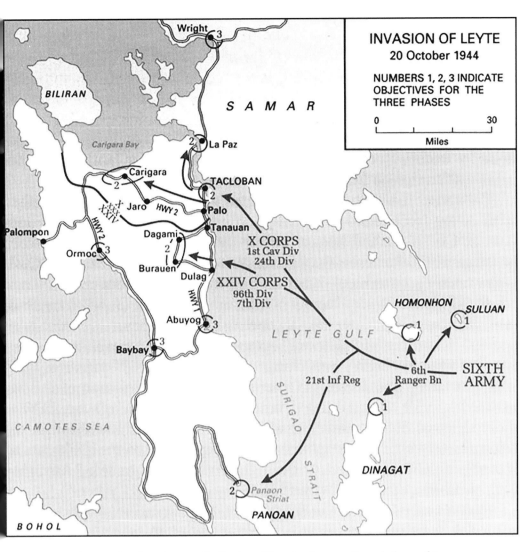

INVASION OF LEYTE
20 October 1944

NUMBERS 1, 2, 3 INDICATE
OBJECTIVES FOR THE
THREE PHASES

0   30
Miles

campaign to be fought at all. Rather like the impending defeat of Japanese forces in Burma, the Philippines campaign did not contribute to the surrender of Japan. Nevertheless, about three quarters of a million lives were lost and it is argued that, just like Truk, but on a larger scale, the Philippines could have been bypassed. That ignores the 4,000 prisoners in Japanese hands and the fact that the battle was for American soil. The burning ambition of MacArthur trumped all contemporary opposition.

It was decided by MacArthur and Nimitz that the invasion of the Philippines should be initiated on the island of Leyte, located around the waist of the country, and where only 20,000 low-grade Japanese soldiers were located. Leyte is an island about 115 miles (185km) long and 45 miles (72km) wide and, in 1944, was home to 915,000 Filipinos who lived a peasant life tending rice paddies and growing corn.

The decision taken to initiate the liberation of the Philippines through Leyte was one of the most ill-judged decisions taken during the Pacific War and presented several obstacles to MacArthur's master plan. There was only one road in Leyte: the circular Route 2. Other routes were narrow, unmade gravelled tracks that were unsuited to the movement of the vehicles that were needed to provide logistic support to the invading army. The general had decided that Leyte's flat central valley would be ideal for yet another airfield. In fact, those parts of the island not under cultivation were low-lying, very wet and swamplike. On 10 August 1944, Colonel William Ely, a senior engineer officer in 6th Army headquarters, produced a survey that dealt with 'soil instability' in the Leyte valley and the difficulty that would impose on all engineering tasks – not least airfield construction. 'With reckless irresponsibility', MacArthur rejected the advice.[1] He also failed to take note of the impending monsoon, which was unfortunate as 24 inches (61cm) of rain fell during November. The decision-making by MacArthur and his staff, prior to the invasion, was incompetent, and it did not improve once battle was joined. The performance of this celebrated general was mediocre and had serious consequences for the men under his command.

Rear Admiral (soon to be promoted) Oldendorf commanded the bombardment force and he operated in the 30-mile wide (48km) Leyte Gulf, where he attacked shore installations previously identified by Filipino guerrillas. Soon thereafter, on 20 October, the US 6th Army, commanded by Lieutenant General Walter Krueger, landed four divisions, and met only sparse resistance. Krueger was an unexpected choice to lead 6th Army. He was an officer who demonstrated a marked lack of empathy with his soldiers and welcomed officer casualties as he considered them to be a sign of unit aggression.

The two opposing forces had one thing in common, and that was that neither had a single overall commander. This was a fundamental organisational error, unexpected this late in a war in which both sides had a surfeit of very experienced officers. Additional American naval support was provided by a mixture of destroyers, amphibious ships and patrol torpedo boats (PT boats) which harassed the increasingly isolated Japanese. The poor weather conditions precluded Japanese air support.

Macarthur had a large and very professional public relations team whose sole task was to publicise the genius of the general. Later, on the afternoon of 20 October, in a freshly pressed uniform, his hat at a fetching angle, with a corncob pipe close to hand and wearing aviator sunglass, the great man left a landing craft that had been run up on a previously constructed sandbank in the shallows. Then in a *very, very* carefully stage-managed few moments he made his dramatic return to the Philippines. The theatre did not end there. By happy chance, of course there was a battery of microphones and cameramen to capture MacArthur's dramatic and self-serving speech. 'People of the Philippines, I have returned,' he intoned gravely. 'Rally to me! Let the indomitable spirit of Bataan and Corregidor lead on.'[2] There was more in the same tone and style, but it was just right for the time and audience. There were, however, those who were repelled by MacArthur assuming ownership of the invasion and, notwithstanding the demonstration of American power, made the whole event a personal triumph for Douglas MacArthur.

By nightfall, his troops were well established ashore in a 17-mile (27km) front. The advance continued on the following day against only patchy resistance. On 23 October, MacArthur assembled all his senior officers to attend a ceremony on the steps of the badly damaged Tacloban Municipal Building to mark the reinstitution of President Osmeña's civil government.

Yamashita, whilst recognising the folly of Terauchi's orders, nevertheless complied and he directed Lieutenant General Suzuki Sōsaku to commit his full force to holding Leyte and 'annihilating' the invading force. Yamashita bent his energy towards the massive reinforcement of Suzuki but the movement of troops, by sea, in the face of American naval supremacy was highly problematic. Nevertheless, and with extraordinary tenacity, some reinforcements did get through. The courage and commitment of Japanese soldiers had been a feature of the Pacific campaign, and on Leyte, the Japanese infantry excelled. They occupied the high ground at the top of vertiginous ridges covered in thick jungle and were difficult to dislodge. The topography was a gift for the defenders and the names given to various key points are indicative. Breakneck Ridge was fought over for several days and Shoestring Ridge so called because of the supply shortage. Kilay Ridge was atop a 900-foot (270m) mountain with steep sides. It was a formidable defensive position and was just as keenly disputed.

The IJN responded to the landings on Leyte at about the same time that MacArthur was holding civil celebrations in Tacloban. Its confrontation with the USN in Leyte Gulf and beyond was the largest naval battle of the war and arguably the largest in human history. The USA 3rd Fleet (Halsey) and 7th Fleet (Kinkaid) had between them 300 ships, including a total of thirty-four aircraft carriers of different types and carrying about 1,500 aircraft. The Japanese mustered sixty-seven, with six carriers and 300 aircraft. Clearly there was a mismatch, and the battle could only end in favour of the United States.

The invaders pushed on to the east but were slowed by the swampy conditions of the ground. The US 3rd and 7th fleets' aircraft dominated the airspace and their vast array of ships frustrated Japanese attempts to reinforce Leyte by sea. By now Filipino guerrillas were increasingly active and they provided intelligence and reconnaissance as well as assisting with the control of the civil population. They were responsible for attacking Japanese supply

Men of 1st Cavalry Division crossing a swamp in Leyte, October 1944.
(US Army Photograph)

lines, disrupting troop movements and the sabotage of enemy installations. They were an important element in MacArthur's force.

The weather became a major factor as the monsoon broke and torrential rain reduced the tracks to unnavigable quagmires and the aforementioned wet ground became impassable. The conditions in Burma were awful but on Leyte, during the monsoon, it was just as bad, if not worse. Men were permanently wet, their boots and their feet rotted, insect bites turned septic, and hot food was difficult to produce and even harder to deliver. Phone lines shorted out, batteries degraded, damp blankets developed mildew, steel rusted, all weapons had to be cleaned and oiled several times a day, and any vehicle that attempted to move was very likely to be quickly bogged down and irrecoverable. Washing in a river exposed men to liver fluke, and the heat was such that white phosphorous in artillery shells melted. The fuel tanks on vehicles had to be kept topped up to deny access to moisture.[3] Life on Leyte was, in British parlance, 'absolutely bloody'. It was, of course, equally bloody for the Japanese.

Any remote hopes of airfield construction were blown away in the monsoon. Men went hungry as priority was given to ammunition. Casualty evacuation was a rugged nightmare both for the wounded man and his bearers. On 8 November, the fury of the monsoon was enhanced by a fierce storm that exacerbated all the manifold difficulties – and, in addition, the Japanese were hostile too.

Field Marshal Terauchi Hisaichi's orders to Yamashita that the Americans were to be defeated on Leyte presupposed that Leyte could readily be reinforced and supplied. Accordingly, a series of attempts to bolster the number of troops on Leyte were made. On 8–9 November, the Japanese sent two convoys from Manila, a day apart, carrying reinforcements to Leyte, and sought to land them in Ormoc Bay. The first convoy was subject to aerial attack by about seventy land-based aircraft, which sank two of the largest transports and severely damaged a third. With great tenacity the convoy ploughed on and succeeded in landing 10,000 fresh troops, albeit with insufficient supplies. On 11 November, Halsey confronted both convoys with 350 carrier aircraft from TF-38. Four of the protective screen destroyers

Logistic support on Leyte, provided by Filipino porters.

were sunk, as were four immensely valuable transports carrying about 4,000 soldiers. They, and 1,000 sailors, perished when their ships went down.

Success in the ongoing Battle of Ormoc Bay, which lasted from 11 November until 21 December, brought Leyte and the entire Gulf area under firm American control. It was an efficient combination of 3rd Fleet carrier planes, fighter-bomber groups, with a well-conducted pincer movement by the Army's 77th Division and 1st Division.

The Filipino people had suffered under a typically brutal Japanese regime and the resistance movement had been kept supplied by USN submarines. With the landing in Leyte, the expectation was that the guerrillas would play a full part in liberating the islands in close support of the Americans. The Philippine Islands were an American colony but there was a very strong movement seeking independence – the Filipino hope was that once the Japanese were ejected, national sovereignty would follow.

General Krueger was not a charismatic leader and the slow progress made by his army was, of course, his responsibility. He was quick to apportion blame and drew attention to his perception of poor junior leadership. However, his troops were living and fighting in the most extreme conditions, with inadequate logistic support. The medical officer of 1/19th Infantry was a

Lieutenant General Suzuki Sōsaku
(1891–1945),
Commander Japanese 35th Army.

Lieutenant General Walter Krueger
(1881–1967),
Commander US 6th Army.

Captain Hostetter, and his unit was in the thick of the action. He noted that when the men came out of the mountains, 'they looked ten to fifteen years older, they spoke little and walked slowly. There was no joking or horseplay.'[4]

The daily sick list rose, and a high proportion of those reporting sick complained of trench foot. Doctors were unable to treat men suffering from combat exhaustion and had to send them to the rear to recover – hopefully. By 12 November, 6th Army was deficient 1,000 officers and 12,000 men. In effect, it was an entire division short.

The nature of the ground limited the Americans' ability to move the heavy weapons upon which they usually depended, and this increased the propensity of American soldiers to be profligate with their small arms fire, which, in turn, added to the resupply difficulties. The Japanese, on the other hand, were frugal in expending fire. The percentage of Americans killed by small arms increased on Leyte. Krueger's headquarters reported:

> the Japanese … displayed superior adeptness and willingness to go into the swamp and stay until rooted out … the most notable characteristics exhibited were the excellent fire discipline and effective control of all arms. Without exception individual soldiers held their fire until it would have the greatest possible effect.[5]

The unspoken judgement was that, man for man, the Japanese, under these adverse conditions, were just better soldiers. Without the usual, comprehensive, logistic support the Americans were under great pressure in Leyte. To put this logistic matter into context, Shoestring Ridge, just inland from Ormoc Bay, was held by about 6,000 Americans who faced about the same number of Japanese. To support this American force there were only twelve available trucks and five DUKWs. Vehicular access to the ridge was by way of a narrow, unmade track. The supply trucks not only had to cope with the unceasing torrential rain, but their journey was across fourteen hazardous bridges and fifty-one fords in which the water level was unpredictable.

The supply line from the beach was labour-intensive and slow. The vast tonnage that had to be moved daily was a major task. It took three days for that new pair of boots to travel from the beach, across country, to the grateful recipient.

The American advance through Leyte was slow, expensive and fiercely contested, and it was not until a landing was made south of Ormoc on 7 December that Breakneck Ridge was isolated from further reinforcement or supply. The Americans moved on to take the port and city and, by 21 December, the west of the Ormoc valley was in their hands. At this point MacArthur chose to announce that he was victorious and that his troops had killed 117,997 enemy soldiers – an absurdly precise figure that bore no relation to the truth. He went on to assert that only 'mopping up' was required. An officer of 17th Infantry wrote: 'We who are on the spot knew we were only beginning the fight when he made his ridiculous announcement that our objectives were secured.'[6] A further 700 Americans were to fall after this 'victory' announcement. MacArthur was losing credibility with his soldiers. It was a high price to pay for fleeting domestic headlines.

The taking of Leyte was to prove to be the decisive operation in the liberation of the Philippines. It had been very costly for the Japanese and although 20,000 remained in Leyte to conduct guerrilla operations, the eventual outcome was not in doubt. Accurate Japanese casualty figures are always difficult to ascertain, and different sources vary. The official US Army figure is 79,261 dead, of whom 80 per cent died of starvation or disease. 'Approaching 50,000' is the view of Hastings (p. 204); Toland opts for '65,000' (p. 607), and Costello favours '56,000' (p. 521). The American losses are more accurate and 3,593 killed and missing, and 11,991 wounded are generally accepted.

With the loss of Leyte, the only avenue open to Yamashita was to use his remaining 250,000 to defend Luzon, the next American objective. Yamashita had no illusions about his position and realised that when the Philippines fell to the Americans it would provide a war-winning base from which to assault the home islands.

* * *

The reader is now invited to consider the very significant naval operations around Leyte and, specifically, the game-changing Battle of Leyte Gulf. There had been a reorganisation in the USN command structure in August 1944. The unusual arrangement was that one of the US fleets was designated the 3rd when commanded by Admiral William Halsey. However, when he and his staff were rested to plan the next operation, the fleet was redesignated 5th Fleet and was commanded by Admiral Raymond Spruance. This arrangement had one positive advantage in that it confused the Japanese (among others), who thought they were dealing with two separate fleets. During the Philippines campaign, Halsey was in command of 3rd Fleet. This naming process extended further down, with, for example, Task Force (TF) 58 becoming TF-38. The US also had its 7th Fleet in place during the campaign under the command of Admiral Thomas Kinkaid.

Vice Admiral Marc Mitscher remained in command of TF-38, and it was one of his spotter planes that, by chance, discovered the Japanese convoy MATA-27. Mitscher fell upon the convoy and sank all eleven ships, one of which was the *Toyofuku Maru*; she sank under a hail of bombs and torpedoes. It was not until after the war that it was revealed that she carried 1,047 Dutch and British POWs. They were locked below decks, and all drowned.

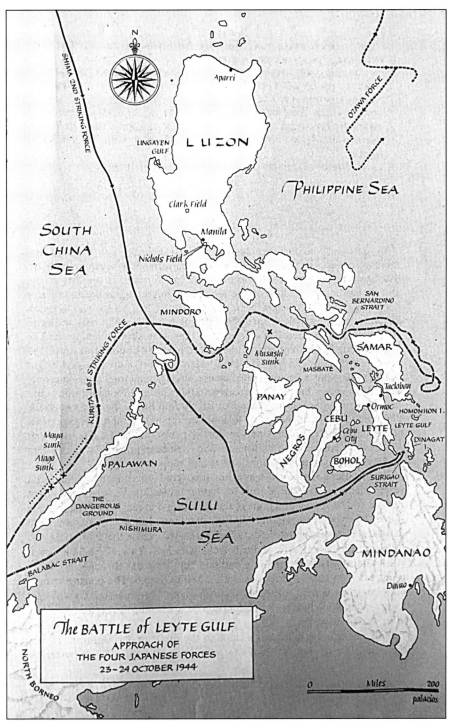

The BATTLE of LEYTE GULF

APPROACH OF
THE FOUR JAPANESE FORCES
23–24 OCTOBER 1944

0   Miles   200

palacios

(*Toland, p. 549.*)

The Japanese naval plan included Operation SHŌ-GŌ. This required Vice Admiral Ozawa Jisaburō's Northern Force to act as a decoy and lure Halsey's 3rd Fleet from its position covering the invasion force on Leyte. Ozawa had four aircraft carriers, but only 117 aircraft, with unskilled pilots. His carrier screen, a mixture of vessels, was about eighteen strong. The hope was that the carriers would be perceived by the USN to be prime targets … as they surely were.

As soon as Halsey was tempted away, two Japanese fleets would attack the landing area. The Southern Force was planned to approach by way of the Surigao Strait and Centre Force would take a route via the San Bernardino Strait into the Philippine Sea. It was this Centre Force that was the most powerful. It was commanded by Vice Admiral Kurita Takeo, and he had at his disposal seventeen capital ships, but no carriers.

Kurita's fleet was on its passage and, as it passed Palawan Island, it was intercepted by the two USN submarines *Dace* and *Darter*. Their torpedo attacks were highly successful and resulted in the sinking of Kurita's flagship, *Atago*. The admiral had to swim to save his life. *Maya*, a heavy cruiser, also sank after four torpedo hits delivered by *Dace*.[7] *Takao*, a sister ship to *Atago*, was hit by two torpedoes and, although disabled, did not sink. Kurita's plans were now in disarray. He was obliged to send the badly damaged *Takao* back to Singapore and allotted two destroyers to escort her.

Meanwhile, on 22 October, Halsey had split his 3rd Fleet and despatched two of his carrier groups to reprovision. However, as soon as he received a radio message from *Darter*, he recalled Rear Admiral Ralph Davidson's Task Group 38-4, but Vice Admiral John McCain's task group, with 40 per cent of Halsey's air power, sailed on, away from the Philippines. On 24 October, Halsey recalled McCain, but events would show that the most powerful element of Halsey's 3rd Fleet was too far away to make significant contribution to the battle soon to follow.

The Battle of Leyte Gulf flared into violent action on 24 October when Vice Admiral Ōnishi Takijirō sent his fifty-plus land-based aircraft in Luzon to attack Task Group (TG) 38-3. This was commanded by Rear Admiral Frederick Sherman, and was one of the three TGs remaining to Halsey. That of Rear Admiral Gerald Bogan, TG 38-2, was the least well-equipped and had only one fleet carrier (*Intrepid*) and two light carriers.[8] The attacks on Sherman failed and USN aircraft from the carrier USS *Essex* wreaked havoc among the attackers. One US naval officer shot down nine enemy aircraft, which probably constitutes some sort of record.

It was not all one way.

A single bomb that hit the carrier USS *Princeton* set off a chain of internal explosions that caused heavy loss of life on the carrier, and even heavier loss

USS *Princeton* explodes on 24 October 1944. Photographed from USS *Essex*.
(US National Museum of Naval Aviation)

aboard the cruiser *Birmingham*, which had come alongside to help. When the carrier exploded, 233 men in *Birmingham* were killed and 426 were wounded. The carrier was sufficiently disabled that, later in the day, she was scuttled; 108 of her crew died but 1,361 lived to fight another day.[9] Subsequently, *Darter* ran aground on an uncharted reef and was a total loss. Notwithstanding the loss of *Princeton* and *Darter*, the first round had been won by the USN.

Vice Admiral Nishimura Shōji and Vice Admiral Shima Kiyohide's fleets were collectively called the 'Southern Force'. During the early morning darkness of 25 October, Nishimura led his Force 'C' into the Surigao Strait. Here he was confronted by elements of the US 7th Fleet and the RAN's Task Force 74. The Japanese fleet was assailed by multiple torpedo attacks from Allied destroyers and PT boats. The Japanese lost the battleship *Fusō*, and three destroyers.

Nishimura pressed on; it was a mistake. Straddling the line of his course were the massive capital ships commanded by Rear Admiral Jesse Oldendorf. USS *California*, *Maryland*, *Mississippi*, *Pennsylvania*, *Tennessee* and *West Virginia* were arrayed in line and, in Nelsonian terms, they 'crossed the T'. They could employ all their main armament and fire broadsides, whilst the approaching Japanese could only engage with their forward-facing guns. In addition to the awesome firepower of the battleships, Nishimura's Force C had also to contend with the fire of USN and RAN cruisers and destroyers that harassed them from the flanks.

The result was inevitable. The flagship, *Yamashiro*, was sunk, taking the admiral down with her. The cruiser *Mogami* was badly damaged and then collided with *Nachi*, of Shima's Second Attack Force. Shima could read the writing on the wall and withdrew.[10] This was a night action, and it was probably the cloak of darkness that saved these two Japanese forces from total elimination.

Halsey, belatedly, recognised the need to concentrate his fleet and he sent orders to achieve this. Rear Admiral Gerald Bogan sent aircraft from his carriers *Intrepid* and *Cabot* to attack the battleships *Nagato*, *Yamato* and *Musashi*, and they scored hits on all three vessels. The heavy cruiser *Myōkō* was badly damaged and limped from the scene. *Musashi* was the focus of further attacks, and she was hit by at least seventeen bombs and eight torpedoes. She capsized and sank at about 1935 hrs on 24 October.

Despite these losses inflicted on Kurita's Centre Force it remained a viable threat because the remaining ships were all battleworthy.[11] Nevertheless, Kurita reversed his fleet and it withdrew out of range of any aircraft, passing the crippled *Musashi*. Halsey assumed that Kurita's withdrawal was evidence that he no longer posed a threat, but the Japanese admiral, under the cover of darkness, turned about to traverse the San Bernardino Strait. He had completely outfoxed Halsey and arrived off the Leyte coast of Samar the next morning. Here, he was a potent threat to the US forces ashore.

Halsey, unaware that he had been outmanoeuvred, prepared a contingency plan. He decided to reorganise his assets to counter any return by Kurita and cover the San Bernardino Strait with a powerful force, which he designated Task Force (TF) 34. Thereafter he issued an ambiguous signal that confused most of those who read it. TF 34 was only provisional at this stage and was only to be formed on Halsey's command.

Content that he had covered all eventualities, Halsey sailed north, with his 3rd Fleet, in pursuit of the toothless Japanese decoy force and by so doing left the San Bernardino Strait wide open. The only barrier between Kurita's Centre Force and the American logistic dumps and supply vessels was Kinkaid's escort carrier group located off the Samar coast.

Halsey was deploying overwhelming force against the decoy force. He had five fleet carriers, five light carriers, six battleships, eight cruisers and forty-one destroyers. He was faced by only a single fleet carrier, three light carriers, a pair of obsolete carrier-battleship hybrids, five destroyers, four destroyer escorts and three cruisers. Halsey also held an overwhelming advantage in air power. The ensuing engagement was a one-sided affair as waves of Halsey's planes descended on the Japanese carriers, and all four – *Chitose*, *Chiyoda*, *Zuihō* and *Zuikaku* – were promptly sunk. Carrier aircraft and naval gunnery also destroyed several destroyers and escort ships throughout the morning and early afternoon.

It was only in late afternoon, and when he was 400 miles (644 km) north of Leyte, that Halsey became aware of the events unfolding to his south. The reader will not be troubled with the detail of the confusion when it was assumed by the key players that TF 34 was already in place – a mythical formation that existed only in Halsey's mind. There can be no doubt that Halsey and his staff performed badly on the night of 24 October. They ignored intelligence from reconnaissance aircraft that the Kurita had turned back. TG 38-2 radioed the same information, but a staff officer blandly rejected it. Vice Admiral Lee had deduced that Ozawa's fleet was a decoy and personally signalled Halsey – he also got a dusty answer.

Vice Admiral Marc Mitscher's staff were sufficiently concerned that they woke their admiral to tell him of the developing situation. Mitscher asked, 'Does Admiral Halsey have the report'? Assured that he did, Mitscher responded by saying, 'If he wants my advice, he'll ask for it,' and went back to sleep.[12]

The 7th Fleet was engaged with Nishimura at Surigao Strait and so all that stood between Kurita and the landing beaches were the ships of TF 'Taffy' 3 – a naval task force that consisted of six escort carriers, three destroyers and four destroyer escorts under the command of Rear Admiral Clifton Sprague.

Kurita's fleet had been reduced but, nevertheless, it remained a powerful force that included four battleships, one of which was the awesome *Yamato*. In addition, he had eight cruisers and about twelve destroyers. The much less powerful American opposition made up for its deficiency by displaying extraordinary aggression and made a series of successful torpedo attacks that damaged the cruiser *Kumano*, forced *Yamato* to take evasive action and, in the process, removed the Japanese admiral from the immediate scene. Taffy 3 controlled the airspace above Kurita's fleet and for two hours inflicted an incessant bombardment.[13]

Kurita did not have the capacity to make any aerial reconnaissance. The aggression of the Americans led him to believe that he was facing the might of Halsey's 3rd Fleet and he mistook his enemy's assets to include fleet carriers. The cruisers *Chikuma*, *Chōkai* and *Suzuya* were all sunk and *Kumano* was heavily damaged. Kurita withdrew, unaware of how close he had come to a decisive breach of the defensive screen around the landing area.

The USN did sustain losses. Three destroyers, *Johnston*, *Hoel* and *Samuel B. Roberts*, were sunk, as was the escort carrier *Gambier Bay*. The latter was sunk by naval gunfire. A little after the battle, the escort carrier *St Lo* became the first USN ship to be sunk by a kamikaze.

The naval battle of Leyte Gulf was concluded, but Nimitz was displeased with Halsey's performance, and said so in a personal message to Admiral King, the Chief of Naval Staff:

It never occurred to me that Halsey, knowing the composition of the ships in the Sibuyan Sea, would leave the San Bernardino Strait unguarded . . . That the San Bernardino detachment of the Japanese fleet, which included the YAMATO and the MUSASHI, did not destroy all the escort carriers and their accompanying screen is nothing short of special dispensation from the Lord Almighty.[14]

The Battle of Leyte Gulf was a crushing American victory in which the residual power of the Imperial Japanese Navy was extinguished. It lost twenty-eight ships, of which four were carriers, 300 aircraft, and had about 12,500 casualties. US losses were modest: six ships, three of which were carriers, over 200 planes and 3,000 casualties. The war at sea having been won, the emphasis was now on MacArthur and the land war in Leyte.

Notes

1. Hastings, Sir M., *Nemesis: The Battle for Japan 1944–45* (2007) (London, Collins, 2016), p. 201.
2. James, D.C., *The Years of MacArthur*, Vol. 2 (Boston, MA, Houghton Mifflin, 1970) p. 557.
3. Hastings, p. 190.
4. US Army Military History Institute, Hostetter MS, p. 89. Newman Papers.
5. Verbeck, Col. W., 6th Army Operations Report, Leyte, pp. 204–12.
6. USAMHI Rodman papers, Box 5.
7. Morison, pp. 170–2.
8. Ibid., pp. 175, 184.
9. Ibid.
10. 'Battle of Leyte Gulf' (*Encyclopaedia Britannica*, 2020).
11. Morison., p. 186.
12. Ibid., p. 196.
13. *Encyclopaedia Britannica*.
14. Wukovits, J.F, *Devotion to Duty* (Naval Institute Press, 2008) p. 190.

Chapter Twenty-Four

October 1944–August 1945
Kamikaze

Although here it is a little out of chronological order, it is necessary to consider a new form of warfare that was initiated by Vice Admiral Ōnishi Takijirō when he arrived in Manila, on 17 October. He had been appointed to command of the air fleet for the anticipated battle and the admiral was appalled to discover that he had fewer than 100 aircraft in the entire Philippine archipelago.

Ōnishi was of an academic bent, with an interest in psychology and, in 1938, had written a book about the responses of servicemen to stressful situations. It was called *War Ethics of the Imperial Navy*. The situation Ōnishi faced in Manila was difficult, but then the overall Japanese position was bleak. Since mid-1942, its military operations had been a succession of defeats, which had killed the best of its pilots, an attrition that continued with losses exceeding the capacity to train new aviators. American aircraft were developing and outdating those in use by Japan. The vast American industrial base dwarfed Japanese industrial output and the gap between the two was widening. Professional Japanese officers had no illusions as to the future, other than that Japan would never surrender.

Ōnishi responded to his current crisis and the impending invasion by taking the most extreme measure. He averred, 'The only way of assuring our meagre strength will be effective to a maximum degree is for our bomb-laden fighter planes to crash-dive into the decks of enemy carriers.'[1] He called for volunteers from his young, unskilled pilots to make the one-way flight to their death.

Initially, there was no shortage of volunteers and they have entered military history as kamikaze. The name is a translation of 'divine wind' – a weather freak that scattered the Mongol fleet on its way to invade Japan in 1281.

This text has made mention of Japanese brutality and inhumanity that sullied the name of Japan – and still does today. However, these young aviators serving under Ōnishi were cut from a different cloth, and they merit respect. They were not planning to kill unarmed women and children. They were going to fly into a maelstrom of fire from Allied warships to give their lives in the service of their emperor. This called for cold courage of the highest order. In Britain the sacrifice of life has frequently been recognised by the award of the Victoria Cross and, in the USA, by the Medal of Honor. The only award given to these kamikaze was the honour of dying in the service of the Emperor. They judged that to be sufficient. The number of volunteer pilots was finite and there is a view that pressure was brought to bear on those who were reluctant to step forward. Peer pressure was a compelling force and difficult to resist.

Kamikaze operations were preceded by a degree of ceremony and the observance of a ritual in which the pilots shared cups of *sake*. They would don a *senninbari*, 'a belt of a thousand stitches', given to them by their mothers, and many composed and read a death poem, much as samurai warriors from a different age once did. Pilots carried keepsakes from their families. Army officers took their swords. On take-off, spectators waved branches from cherry trees. It was all very stoic but with deep emotional undercurrents.

Kamikaze tactics were first employed just before the battle of Leyte Gulf. Rear Admiral Arima Masafumi was, arguably, the first kamikaze and he led an attack on the US carrier *Franklin* on 15 October. His attack failed because he dived into the sea and missed his target. Nevertheless, the Imperial Japanese Navy played up his sacrifice and he received posthumous promotion to vice admiral for his trouble.

The use of suicide tactics was a subject of discussion in Japanese aviation circles and there had already been several cases of Japanese fighter aircraft ramming American bombers, in what were termed *tai-atari* attacks. There is no doubt that the Japanese situation was dire, and Ōnishi was aware that the skills gap between the aviators of the two combatants was growing. US pilots had received two years' training and had at least 300 hours of flying experience, the Japanese pilot was down to forty hours and all his navigational training had been abandoned. The order was, 'follow your leader'.[2]

The hope of Ōnishi and others was that the sacrifice of aircraft and young lives would bring rich tactical gains. The concept had an appeal to the Japanese psyche in which giving one's life for the Emperor was a desirable aim, particularly if that death had a meaningful effect. It is an attitude vastly at odds with Western culture, but then this war was all about different cultural values.

By 20 October, a 'Special Attack' Unit had been formed and Admiral Ōnishi addressed its members, saying:

> Japan is in great danger. The salvation of our country is now beyond the power of the ministers of state, the general staff and humble commanders like myself. It can come only from spirited young men like you. Thus, on behalf of your hundred million countrymen I ask this sacrifice.[3]

Ensign Ogawa Kiyoshi (1922–45). This kamikaze pilot attacked and disabled USS *Bunker Hill* during the battle for Okinawa in April 1945. He caused 393 deaths and wounded 264 others.

This was stirring stuff and on 21 October, the first kamikaze took off from a field in Luzon but was unable to find a target. However, a flight from another field found HMAS *Australia* and killed thirty men. Significant kamikaze successes followed the naval battle of Leyte Gulf, when the carrier USS *St Lo* was sunk and the two escort carriers *Santee* and *Suwanee* were both badly damaged. The carrier USS *Intrepid* was hit a few days later. Ōnishi now had the evidence that kamikaze worked, and he was able to propagate his ideas widely. The support of a propaganda campaign gave the programme an ennobling status.

The attacks continued to reap rewards and an assault on the carrier *Franklin* put her out of action and killed fifty-six men. The strike was observed from *Belleau Wood*, which then suffered a similar hit. Twelve aircraft were destroyed, ninety-two men killed and fifty-four wounded. Both carriers limped away to Ulithi atoll, 850 miles (1,370km) east of the Philippines in the Carolinas, for a lengthy stay in the dockyard.

Ōnishi was reinforced by aircraft from Formosa and Kyushu, and although not all aircraft managed to thread their way through anti-aircraft fire, those that did caused havoc – especially so when their target was one of the smaller ships, such as a destroyer. Then the damage was usually fatal for all concerned. The vast amounts of aviation fuel and ordnance on board the carriers were, in combination, their Achilles' heel.

Ships under kamikaze attack manoeuvred, often wildly, and there were several collisions in the US fleet. Similarly, gunners engaging low-flying aircraft sometimes sprayed other ships, with lethal results. There was no doubt that the kamikaze had altered the balance and although they would not, and could not, win the war, they could make American progress slower and much more painful. In the latter stages of the war, ships burnt oil to produce a smokescreen and that did deter attacks. Combat Air Patrols (CAP) were flown greater distance from the fleet – about 50 miles (80km) to give early warning.

Japanese tactics were polished. Initially, flights of three were despatched with two fighters to escort them to the target area and to observe the results. The arrival of more aircraft permitted the mass attack that was designed to overwhelm the fleet's defences. Morison, the distinguished naval historian, opined, 'The Japanese had perfected a new and effective type of aerial warfare that was hard for the Western mind to comprehend and difficult to counteract.'[4]

The Royal Navy, which had experienced kamikaze tactics during the Okinawa campaign, studied the phenomenon and, fifty year later, published a paper in which it concluded:

> Logically suicide attacks of any form, air or sea, practised by the Japanese differed only in kind from the last-ditch defence enjoined upon the British after Dunkirk, and only in degree from such missions as the RAF attack on the Möhne dam.[5]

This judgement is challenged. In both the British examples quoted the participants made every possible attempt to survive and their conduct cannot be equated to kamikaze. There is no Allied parallel. The only distant Japanese comparisons were the suicidal *banzai* charges on Attu and Guadalcanal.

Between October 1944 and August 1945, 3,193 kamikaze attacks were made and 456 hit a ship, killing about 3,000 Americans and Allies. The success rate is very low and 2,737 young men died for little return. It was not unusual for a pilot to return if he could not find a target. However, one man who returned nine times was summarily shot![6]

The product of this suicide tactic was that it generated fear and fuelled the hatred for Japan in American hearts. Admiral Halsey declared, 'Kamikaze was the only weapon I feared in war.' Mercy was already in short supply during the Pacific War and the USN did not go to great lengths to pick up Japanese survivors in the early stages. After October 1944, it made no effort at all.

Inevitably, the whole concept of kamikaze has been scrutinised by Japanese analysts. The pilots' reputation as courageous and noble was challenged, in 2006, by Watanabe Tsuneo, the editor-in-chief of *Yomiuri Shimbun*, one of Japan's national newspapers, who was critical of the glorification of kamikaze. Sixty years after the event, and without naming a source, he wrote:

> It's all a lie that they left filled with braveness and joy crying, 'long live the emperor!' They were sheep at a slaughterhouse. Everybody was looking down and tottering. Some were unable to stand and were carried and pushed into their aircraft by maintenance soldiers.[7]

It may well be true that some men showed fear and reluctance. Is that unreasonable? But it would be unbalanced to allow this negative view to be the final word. Most military men have a grudging admiration for all kamikaze pilots. Even more for those who did not want to go but, nevertheless, still gave their lives. Very, very few people would have wanted to be in a kamikaze's flying boots.

Notes

1. Baldwin, H.W., *Battles Lost and Won: Great Campaigns of World War II* (New York, Harper & Row, 1966), p. 291.
2. Hastings, Sir M., *Nemesis: The Battle for Japan 1944–45* (2007) (London, Collins, 2016), p. 178.
3. Sakai, S., *Samurai* (Four Square, 1974), p. 179.
4. Morison, S.E., *New Guinea and the Marianas, March–August 1944, History of US Naval Operations in World War II* (Urbana, University of Illinois Press), Vol. XII, p. 367.
5. 'War with Japan', Vol. VI (RN Staff History, MoD, 1995), p. 196.
6. Ohnuki-Tierney, E., *Kamikaze Diaries: Reflections of Japanese Student Soldiers* (University of Chicago Press, 2007), p. 10.
7. 'The Saturday Profile: Shadow Shogun steps into the light to change Japan' (*New York Times*, 11 February 2006).

Chapter Twenty-Five

December 1944–March 1945 Mindoro, Luzon and Massacre

MacArthur's 6th Army, commanded by 63-year-old General Walter Krueger, having subdued opposition on the island of Leyte sought to establish an airfield and, with that purpose, made landings on the island of Mindoro on 15 December 1944.

The island was lightly defended by only 1,200 soldiers and although the beaches most suitable for landings were on the north-east coast, nevertheless it was decided to assault the island near the town of San Jose on the south-west corner. 24th Infantry Division, with 19th Infantry Regiment and 503rd Parachute Regimental Combat Team, were tasked, giving the invading force a massive numerical superiority.

On 13 December, two days before the operation, a kamikaze attack on the light cruiser *Nashville* killed 130 men and wounded about 190 more of the assault forces, including Brigadier William Dunkel, who was to command the landing. Other kamikaze attacks disabled two Landing Ships, Tank (LST) but the invasion was not delayed, and on 15 December, the weight of American aerial and naval power was unleashed on the unfortunate 1,200. Inside two days the island was in American hands at a cost of eighteen dead and eighty-one wounded. The Japanese lost 200 killed and 375 wounded. The survivors fled into the jungle and saw the war out on the very edge of starvation. They did not interfere with the construction of two airstrips that were up and running within two weeks.

If the taking of Mindoro was 'a walk in the park', the next operation – the capture of Luzon – was anything but. The new air bases on Mindoro were soon in action, not least as home to a series of deception flights over southern Luzon. These were designed to convince the Japanese that the assaulting Americans would be taking the shortest sea route from Mindoro. In fact, it was MacArthur's intention to land in the Lingayen Gulf in the north of Luzon that would allow him to access roads and railways and hasten his advance the 100 miles (160km) to Manila. However, he did not fool Yamashita, who had already concluded that Lingayen Gulf would be the target, and centred on the town of Dagupan.

The invasion of Luzon was accomplished by a massive display of force; over 875 warships and transports carried 175,000 soldiers to their designated beach. There had been 200 kamikaze attacks between 13 December and 13 January on Allied ships and in that period, twenty-four Allied ships were sunk and another sixty-seven were damaged. These attacks did not delay the invasion, with a landing area and beachhead about 20 miles (32km) wide. The usual bombardment of coastal defences was carried out, on 6 January 1945, at massive cost, but found to be unnecessary as there were no coastal defences. The landings were unopposed.

The American strategy was to outflank Japanese defences and two further landings were made. The first cut off the Bataan Peninsula, 45 miles (72km) south-west of Manila, and isolated the Japanese forces located there, and the second was a parachute insertion by 11th Airborne Division, just south of Manila, where the important bridge across the Tullahan River was taken and held.

By 23 January 1945, Clark Field, the principal airbase in the Philippines, was overrun but fighting around the perimeter lasted for another seven days. With the airbase secure, XIV Corps, commanded by Major General Oscar Griswold, was able to move on to the prime target, Manila. The American noose was tightening around the capital city. The Airborne Division moved towards the southern edge of the city but on 4 February was halted by well-sited defences, fully manned. Elsewhere it took two months of bitter fighting before the 6th Army forced Yamashita to withdraw into the eastern Sierra Madre mountains, with 260,000 men to an area around Baguio, from where he was able to exercise control over the dams that provided the water supply to Manila. MacArthur knew it was imperative that he control Manila's water source. US Forces had taken the Novaliches Reservoir, 10 miles (16km) north-east of Manila, on 5 February. This was fed via an aqueduct from Ipo Dam, which straddled the Angat River a further 15 miles (24km) north-east. Ten miles south of this was Wawa Dam, near the village of Montalban. With these dams in the hands of the Japanese, the situation would be precarious because the reservoir could not suffice for long without water from the mountains. The dams were strategically important, and their capture was central to a campaign that lasted until late June, when both were taken undamaged.

Meanwhile, in Washington, analysts were trying to put numbers on the human cost of invading Japan whilst in other places, and in the greatest secrecy, work was progressing on the production of the atom bomb. MacArthur's priority, as always, was his aggrandisement. He had taken to publicly criticising Nimitz and 'the awful way' in which he was sacrificing thousands of lives. MacArthur's solution was his immediate appointment as overall commander-in-chief of all operations in the war against Japan. He did not get his wish but, on 3 January, was given command of all ground forces in the theatre and Nimitz was confirmed in command of all naval forces.

* * *

In early 1945, Roosevelt had been re-elected, but was ailing. In Burma, the 14th Army was moving south and inflicting heavy losses on the retreating Japanese. Akyab (now Sittwe), located on an estuarial island in the Bay of Bengal, was occupied on 4 January. Later that month, the Burma Road reopened and logistic support for the Nationalist Chinese started to flow along it. The Battle of the Bulge, in the Ardennes, was almost won. Hitler was on the back foot, as was Hirohito. The hope was that the war would be concluded in 1945, but the great unknown was the cost of an invasion of Japan.

* * *

11th Airborne broke through the southern defences of Manila on 11 February and the battle for the city began. Manila, known as 'the pearl of the Orient', was beautiful, filled with gracious old buildings and Spanish charm. The American aim at this point was to free the 4,000 prisoners of war and citizens who had been held in captivity for almost three years, and to preserve the city if possible.

It was not.

Yamashita gave orders for all Japanese troops to leave Manila and Rear Admiral Iwabuchi Sanji was ordered to destroy the port, harbour and bridges. To accomplish this task, Yamashita put all army forces in Manila under his command. Yamashita was functioning in the mountain town of Baguio, 125 miles (200km) north of Manila. Distancing of himself from Manila was later to be his defence against charges of war crimes that took place there.

Iwabuchi had under his command 12,500 sailors and 4,500 soldiers, and in wilful defiance of his orders from Yamashita, he made the decision to defend Manila house-to-house. His

Rear Admiral Iwabuchi Sanji (1895–1945).

soldiers constructed barricades out of cars and trucks, built pillboxes, laid mines along roads, and barricaded streets at intersections. They also filled windows with reinforced concrete, made gun slits in walls, and stashed ammunition in strategic places. The Japanese press wrote: 'Here on these islands in the vast Pacific Ocean, a great tragedy is about to occur. This is going to be a fight to the death.'[1]

The tragedy was not what the Japanese press envisaged. The tragedy was, in fact, the wholesale slaughter of civilian Filipinos that stemmed from an order published just before the arrival of the Americans on the outskirts of the city. The order read:

> The Americans who have penetrated Manila have about 1,000 troops, and there are several thousand Filipino soldiers under the Commonwealth Army and the organized guerrillas. Even women and children have become guerrillas. All people on the battlefield with the exception of Japanese military personnel, Japanese civilians, and special construction units will be put to death.[2]

This ruthless and illegal order gave Japanese soldiers free rein to kill at will and they exercised this liberty to the full. But mere killing was not enough to sate the bloodlust of the defenders of Manila; they also indulged in grotesque torture and the most extreme rapine behaviour. They acted like unrestrained wild animals. They were a disgrace to their country and to the whole human race. It is not the intention to chronicle in detail the inhuman atrocities committed by those in the service of the Emperor but for one example.

The Bayview Hotel was used as a designated 'rape centre'. The testimony at Yamashita's war crimes trial revealed that 400 women and girls were rounded up from Manila's wealthy Ermita district, and submitted to a selection board that picked out the twenty-five women who were considered most beautiful. These women and girls, many of them 12 to 14 years old, were then taken to the hotel, where Japanese soldiers and officers took turns raping them.[3] For many Japanese it was not enough to rape a woman; there was a need to cut off her breasts and to mutilate her before killing her.

The death toll in the mindless massacre of Manila is generally accepted as being of the order of 100,000. These were old men, women and children who just happened to live in Manila. They were no threat to the Japanese. It is impossible to understand the mindset of the thousands of Japanese mass murderers who participated in the massacre. There was no military expedient, no strategic advantage. All the evidence indicated that the Japs were just enjoying themselves – it was 'fun'. Many of the perpetrators were killed in later battles, but not all, and the survivors were never held to account. The psychopathic behaviour displayed in Manila set a new benchmark in military atrocities.

Iwabuchi shot himself at the end of the battle, which was probably as well, because had he not done so, he would have joined Yamashita and his chief of staff, General Mutō Akira, on the scaffold.

1st Cavalry Division reached the northern outskirts of Manila on 3 February and their arrival triggered fierce fighting for a month. Japanese resistance lasted until 3 March and, in the process, largely destroyed Manila.

The prisoners were liberated having suffered great privation and brutality. Male prisoners lost on average 53 pounds in weight, almost 4 stone, during their imprisonment and were all on the edge of starvation. The prisoners were a mixed bag of nationalities: 3,200 American, 900 British and Commonwealth, 100 Filipino, 40 Polish, 30 Dutch, and representatives of Spain, Mexico, Nicaragua, Cuba, Russia, Belgium, Norway, Sweden, Denmark, China and Burma. Included in those numbers were 400 children.

Corregidor, the site of MacArthur's last stand, was assaulted and taken. To ensure complete American control over the entrance to Manila Bay, Fort Drum, a reinforced concrete sea fort, was also assaulted, and the sixty-eight-strong garrison was cremated when a mixture of petroleum and gasoline was pumped into the defences and ignited.

The loss of life in the Philippines campaign was greater than in any other in the Pacific. The Japanese had held the archipelago in great strength. They fielded 529,802 regular troops and about 6,000 militia.[4] Of these, 420,000 were either dead or missing by June 1945 and about 80 per cent of those deaths were the result of either starvation or disease.[5]

It is germane to pause for a moment and consider the impact of 100,000 dead Filipinos and 420,000 dead Japanese, albeit spread over a wide area. In the tropics a cadaver starts to decompose within a couple of hours. It attracts flies, maggots and birds. The body smells and pollutes any nearby watercourse. If one body is a hazard to health, 520,000 are a serious problem. They must be disposed of quickly. They can be buried but that requires many very large graves, or they can be burned. The stench of death must have been all-pervading and the quality of life in the Philippines, for the survivors of Japanese occupation, must have been very low.

Sporadic low-tempo fighting continued until the Japanese surrender in August, but the surviving Japanese were living in the jungle and starving; they were not a serious threat.

The Allied deaths were lower in number but still significant. The US Army lost 16,233, the USN 7,270 dead and wounded. The Filipino Army had many but uncounted killed; in addition, there were eighty-two Mexicans killed.

Notes

1. Scott, J.M., *Rampage: MacArthur, Yamashita, and the battle for Manila* (London, W.W. Norton, 2018).
2. Perry, M., *The Most Dangerous Man in America: The Making of Douglas MacArthur* (New York, Basic Books, 2014), p. 320
3. 'Manila Girls Relate Horror of Mass Rape' (*The Milwaukee Journal*, 1 November 1945).
4. Jowett, P., *Japan's Asian Allies 1941–45* (London, Osprey Publishing, 2020), pp. 37–9.
5. Dower, J., *Lessons from Iwo Jima* (American Historical Association, 2007), note 1.

Chapter Twenty-Six

February–June 1945
Iwo Jima

There were two remaining Japanese strongholds in the Southwest Pacific. Both were strongly garrisoned, and if taken, would provide the Americans with yet more airfields. The first of these was the small island of Iwo Jima, located about 625 miles (1,005km) north of Saipan, 660 miles (1,062km) south of Tokyo, and one of the Japanese Volcano Islands. It is dominated by the still active volcano, Mount Suribachi. As recently as 6 October 2020, the mountain expelled a volcanic plume up to 3,500 feet (1km) in height. Iwo Jima is almost 5 miles (8km) long and 2½ miles (4km) wide.

The determination of the Japanese to defend Iwo Jima was acknowledged and the probable cost in American lives was calculated – always an exercise that precedes any major military operation. The garrison was between 20,530 and 21,060 strong, all of whom were willing to die in place.[1]

The United States Navy blockade of islands like Iwo Jima was highly effective and the residents could not expect reinforcement or resupply. This begs the question, why invade? Were the two airfields so desirable and vital that lives had to be spent to win them? Why not bypass Iwo Jima?

These were the questions posed by retired Chief of Naval Operations Admiral William Pratt, who opined: 'The island was useless to the Army as a staging post and equally useless to the Navy as a fleet base.'[2] In the event, once captured, the airfield on Iwo Jima was little used – and that alone fully justified Pratt's criticism.

The counterargument was that Iwo Jima provided the Japanese with the means to intercept B-29 bombers flying to and from raids on mainland Japan. They were also still capable of harassing the Marianas Islands. It was on the basis that these two relatively minor threats had to be eliminated that the decision to invade was taken. American intelligence reports gave every reason to suppose that Iwo Jima would not present an obstacle on the route to Japan and Admiral Nimitz, a man of previously sound judgement, went as far as pronouncing: 'Well, this will be easy. The Japanese will surrender Iwo Jima without a fight.'[3]

The Japanese had been allowed plenty of time to prepare their defences on Iwo Jima as the American focus, in early 1945, had been on the Philippines.

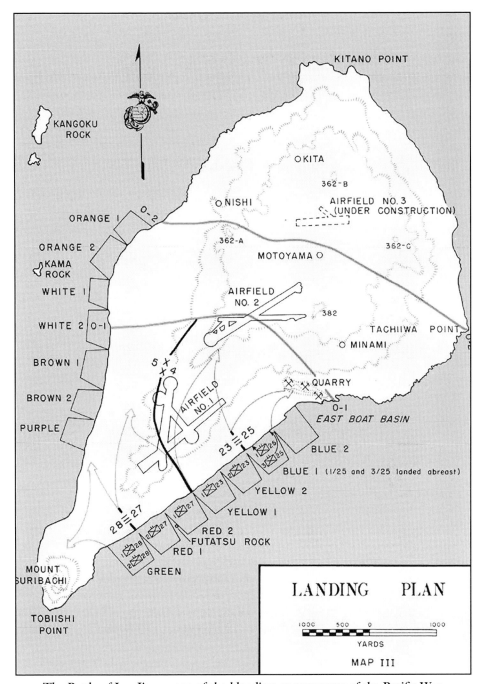

KITANO POINT

KANGOKU ROCK

OKITA

O NISHI

362-B

AIRFIELD NO. 3
(UNDER CONSTRUCTION)

ORANGE I   O-2

362-A

362-C

ORANGE 2

KAMA ROCK

MOTOYAMA O

WHITE I

AIRFIELD NO. 2

382

WHITE 2 O-I

BROWN I

5

TACHIIWA POINT

O MINAMI

QUARRY

BROWN 2

AIRFIELD NO. I

PURPLE

O-I
EAST BOAT BASIN

23 ≡ 25

26
2 25
3 25

BLUE 2

BLUE I (1/25 and 3/25 landed abreast)

23
23

YELLOW 2

YELLOW I

28 ≡ 27

27

27

RED 2
FUTATSU ROCK

1 28
2 28

RED I

MOUNT SURIBACHI

GREEN

LANDING   PLAN

TOBIISHI POINT

1000   500   0   1000
YARDS

MAP III

The Battle of Iwo Jima – one of the bloodiest engagements of the Pacific War.

The volcano, Mount Suribachi, dominating the island of Iwo Jima.

By the time that the invasion force, under the overall command of Admiral Spruance, led by V Amphibious Corps, was ready to crack the Iwo Jima nut on 19 February, it faced formidable defences. The corps was commanded by Major General Harry Schmidt, USMC, and was composed of three marine divisions, the 3rd, 4th and 5th. In total, Schmidt had 69,993 officers and men. He outnumbered his enemy by about 3:1.

Lieutenant General Kuribayashi Tadamichi had been appointed as the commander on Iwo Jima and he had no illusions as to his fate. Tojo had told him, 'The entire army and the nation will depend on you for the defence of that key island.'[4] In the time available he supervised the construction of 11 miles (18km) of tunnels that linked bunkers, command posts, mortar pits,

Lieutenant General Kuribayashi Tadamichi (1891–1945).

artillery positions, machine-gun posts, hospitals, dormitories and storage areas.

Mount Suribachi, at the southern tip of the island, is only 554 feet (169m) high, but it was a heavily armoured honeycomb. Water was stockpiled but food was already scarce when the invasion commenced. Kuribayashi camouflaged all external features of his defences and laid landmines to his front, and he tasked his snipers to target flamethrower personnel. On the morning of 19 February, the routine pre-invasion bombardment of 21,926 naval shells lifted as Kuribayashi waited patiently for the first of the invaders to arrive on his shores. The American reconnaissance of the landing beaches on the south of the island had been inadequate; there was an air of complacency. It came as a most unwelcome surprise to the 9,000 marines, in the first wave, to discover that the soft volcanic ash beaches were all edged with a 15-foot (4.6m) shelf. This was a formidable barrier and successive waves of troops piled up as the beaches became more crowded. Equipment, rations and ammunition were offloaded and dumped on the beach.

Kuribayashi allowed this chaos to continue for about an hour, by which time he had a concentrated and very vulnerable target. At this point he opened fire. His artillery and mortars were all zeroed onto the beach and every round inflicted damage. It was carnage. Some of the Japanese artillery was located behind reinforced steel doors, making American counterbombardment fire ineffective. The tempest proportions of Japanese fire:

> at first came as a ragged rattle of machine-gun bullets, growing gradually lower and fiercer until at last all the pent-up fury of a hundred hurricanes seemed to be breaking upon the heads of the Americans. Shells screeched and crashed, every hummock spat automatic fire and the very soft soil underfoot erupted with hundreds of exploding land mines ... Marines walking erect crumpled and fell. Concussion lifted them and slammed them down or tore them apart.[5]

It was not until several bulldozers and men of the 31st and 133rd Naval Construction Battalions were landed that it was possible to clear a path off the beach. Then the surviving, and much battered, marines were able to move inland. At 1130 hrs, a group of marines reached the airfield at the foot of Suribachi. They were overlooked from the heights but managed to hold what had been previously identified as a priority target. 28th Marine Battalion achieved another aim by crossing the island and thus isolated Suribachi from the rest of the island. This was rather like taking a tiger by the tail, and of debateable value.

The attrition among the marines was such that 25th Battalion had landed with 900 men but, by day's end, only 150 were still fit to fight. There were 30,000 marines on Iwo Jima at the end of the first day – many of the 2,000 casualties were dead.

General Holland Smith, the commander of Task Force 56 and General Schmidt's superior, was a long-distance spectator, from USS *El Dorado*, of the bloody efforts of his men. He is reported to have said, among other things, 'I don't know who he is, but the Japanese general running this show is one smart bastard.'[6] He got that right; there was no doubt that Kuribayashi had won the opening rounds.

28th Battalion was advancing very painfully and slowly towards the lower slopes of the mountain. 'It was preceded by three combat teams who used flamethrowers, grenades, and satchel charges to burn, blast and bomb the Japanese out of their pillboxes and caves.'[7] By 23 February, they had reached the base of the daunting volcanic peak. The following day, Lieutenant Harold Schrier led forty men to the summit of the mountain and, on a length of pipe, they raised a small Stars and Stripes flag. A Japanese officer, armed with a sword, was killed as he tried to remove the flag. The raising of this flag has been the subject of almost religious fervour ever since. As Secretary of the Navy, James Forrestal sagely remarked, 'The raising of the flag on Suribachi means a Marine Corps for the next 500 years.'

Not unlike MacArthur's wade ashore on Leyte, this flag raising was the subject of a later, rehearsed flag raising with a larger flag and with a photographer present. The resulting picture has been reproduced around the world and is the model for a stunning monument standing in Arlington National Cemetery, Washington DC. The image is, quite rightly, treasured by Americans.

The most effective weapons used by the Americans on Iwo Jima were the eight Sherman M4A3R3 tanks with flame equipment, termed by the marines as 'zippo' tanks. The Japanese were obliged to come out of cover to attack these tanks and, when they did, so they fell to the fire of accompanying marines.[8]

The summit of Suribachi was in US hands but inside the mountain tunnel system there remained obdurate Japanese soldiers, now very hungry. It would

A flamethrower operator of 3rd Marine Division advances, under fire, on Iwo Jima, February 1945. He was a prime target for the defenders, and was, in effect, carrying an incendiary bomb on his back.

take several days before all were eliminated. The US controlled southern Iwo Jima but had already suffered 6,000 casualties, of whom 1,600 had been killed. The grinding attritional combat continued while Seabee construction teams made a start on repairing the southern airstrip (of three).

The island was declared to be secured on 16 March, but that was wildly premature, because 5th Marine Division had not taken Kuribayashi's final redoubt in the north-western tip of the island. It was in a deep valley and very strongly reinforced. On 21 March, he signalled Tokyo and said, 'We have not eaten or drunk for five days but our fighting spirit is still high.' This was well received, and Hirohito promoted him to general.

Kuribayashi held out for a further three days. Then, the very gallant and courageous general sent one final message of farewell and is thought to have committed suicide. His body was not found, but this is not surprising as his bunker was breached by a combination of artillery and flame weapons. It took 4 tons of explosives to raze the citadel and thereafter the nearby cave complex was sealed, entombing the occupants. On 25 March, about 300 Japanese emerged from hidden bunkers and attacked the mixed body of Americans around airfield No. 2 in the middle of the island. All the attackers were killed, but they inflicted fifty-three deaths and wounded 120 more.

The six-week battle had seen the fiercest fighting in the Pacific War so far and the human losses were enormous. The marines had 6,821 killed and the USN 539. Japanese losses were 17,845 to 18,375 dead.[9] Only 216 Japanese were taken prisoner. During the Pacific War thus far, the body count had been in favour of the United States. At times it was as high as 8:1 (Saipan), 5:1 (Tarawa), but later in the campaign it was closer to parity. On Iwo Jima it was 2.4:1. The arithmetic, if extrapolated, made any invasion of Japan a very unattractive proposition.

Notes

1. Burrell, R.S., 'Breaking the Cycle of Iwo Jima Mythology: A Strategic Study of Operation Detachment' (*Journal of Military History*, 2004), p. 83.
2. Pratt, W.N., 'What makes Iwo Jima Worth the Price?' (*Newsweek*, 2 April 1945), p. 36.
3. Wright, D., [1999] *The Battle for Iwo Jima, 1945* (Stroud, Sutton Publishing, 2007), p. 51.
4. Toland, J., *The Rising Sun: The Decline and Fall of the Japanese Empire, 1936–45* [1970] (Modern Library, New York, 2003), p. 641.
5. Pratt, p. 36.
6. Wright, p. 33.
7. Costello, J., *The Pacific War 1941–45* [1981] (New York, Harper Collins, 2009), p. 545.
8. Allen, R.E., *The First Battalion of the 28th Marines on Iwo Jima* (Jefferson, North Carolina, McFarland & Company, 2004).
9. Burrell, p. 83.

Chapter Twenty-Seven

April–June 1945
Okinawa

Tokyo was firebombed on 9–10 March and much of the city laid waste. This did not generate any significant reduction in Japan's commitment to the war. Mandalay was taken by the British on 20 March as Slim's 14th Army swept all before it in Burma. President Roosevelt died on 13 April and was replaced by Harry Truman. In late May the repatriation of Japanese troops in China commenced but, in the Pacific, there remained the last of the Japanese fortresses yet unconquered – Okinawa.

* * *

The American Joint Chiefs of Staff had determined that that Okinawa, 400 miles (644km) from the Japanese home island of Kyushu, would be the springboard for an invasion of Japan. To take and hold this bastion, the USA assembled the largest and most powerful fleet that the world had ever seen. Admiral Spruance's 5th Fleet had 1,500 vessels that would accompany and protect Admiral Turner's invasion armada of 1,200 ships. The coordination of these two vast fleets started by the concentration of various element across the entire Pacific region.

The land element of the invasion force, a mixture of US Army and US Marine corps designated 10th Army, was to be commanded by Lieutenant General Simon Buckner. He was a surprising choice, but General Holland Smith, USMC, had generated very bad feeling between the US Army and the USMC, by his premature sacking of Army Major General Ralph Smith. His continuation as commander of a mixed force was untenable. The assault was to be led by 3rd Marine Corps under Major General Roy Geiger. XIV Army Corps, whose units had fought on Leyte, would share the assault. There was a reserve of three divisions.

American planners calculated that their complement of soldiers and marines would be sufficient to defeat the 70,000 defenders. In fact, there were 76,000 of them, supplemented by 30,000 conscripted Okinawans. These two groups, designated 32nd Army, were commanded by Lieutenant General Ushijima Mitsuru. He had made his appreciation of the situation and realised that he could not prevent any landings on the wide beaches below Hagushi (see map on page 296). The flat terrain in northern Okinawa would favour American armour, which he could not match. He drew the conclusion that he should fight the battle in the hills and valleys in the south of the island. Accordingly, he concentrated his artillery and mortar assets in well-prepared positions that he centred on Shuri, an ancient fortification that dominated the '6-mile (9.6km) wide neck of the southern third of the island'.[1] Ushijima's plan was, 'not to resist the landing but allow the invaders to press on inland until they had been lured into a position where he cannot receive cover and support from naval gunfire and aerial bombardment, we must patiently and prudently hold our fire. Then leaping into action, we shall destroy the enemy.'[2]

Ushijima's expectation, having tied down the assault force, was that the US Navy would be obliged to remain in Okinawan waters and become excellent targets for kamikaze. The threat posed by kamikaze had been recognised in American plans and Admiral Mitscher's TF 58, with sixteen fast carriers, had carried out saturation bombing of kamikaze airfields on Kyushu and the naval base at Kure on Honshu. In these raids over 400 Japanese aircraft were destroyed. The kamikaze were not eliminated, and in the ensuing campaign they were a constant threat. As a preamble to the landing on Okinawa, on 26 March, the US 77th Division occupied the Kerama Islands, which surround Okinawa.

The US 10th Army was huge; it had a complement of 182,181 soldiers and a long logistic tail. General Buckner reported to Admiral Turner until the amphibious phase was completed. Thereafter, he answered to Admiral Spruance. A feature of the US armed forces in the Pacific was that frequently, officers reported to a superior, but of the same rank. For example, Buckner was a three-star general, and Turner was a three-star admiral. It seems to have worked.

The 32nd Army, although outnumbered, sought to boost its strength by recruiting schoolboys aged 14 to 17. They were described as 'volunteers' but the reality was that they were conscripted. Girls were conscripted as nurses. In the ensuing battle about 2,000 boys were killed, many acting as suicide bombers against tanks.

The land battle, which was to last for eighty-one long, painful days, started on 1 April, when XXIV Corps and III Amphibious Corps came ashore on the beaches north and south of Hagushi. During late March and April, landings were made on several offshore islands, such as Tokashiki (shown incorrectly on the map as Toshashiki), Ie Shima and Tsugen Shima. In all of them, men of both nations died for possession of a few acres of worthless scrub.

Tokashiki Island lies 19 miles (31km) west of Naha, the capital of Okinawa. Here, on 27 March, just after a landing by US troops, in an act of utter futility, 394 men, women and children were obliged to immolate themselves. This was apparently on the direction of the military garrison.

The beauty of Okinawa was in stark contrast to Saipan and Tarawa. There was no jungle, just lush subtropical vegetation. The island was terraced and cultivated. The sun was pleasant, the ground was dry, and there was no hostility. Quite the reverse. The people, who were not ethnic Japanese but colonial subjects, were silent observers as American soldiers passed on their way.

Ushijima had concentrated his resistance on two areas. The first of these and the principal position was in the southernmost 6 miles (9.6km) of the island, around Naha. Here he built the Shuri Line of fortresses and crowded in 97,000 defenders. No defensive position is permanently inviolate, but the Shuri Line came close. Buckner was not the man to tackle the problem. He had relatively little experience and had had the embarrassment of the Kiska landings in the Aleutian Islands – onto unoccupied objectives. He was a physical fitness enthusiast, and he imposed his regime on all around him. That was all well and good, but he was also inflexible and of poor judgement.

Buckner's force met no opposition, and their impetus was such that they swiftly overran the Kadena and Yomitan airbases. He capitalised on the lack of opposition and moved to occupy as much of northern Okinawa as possible. By 13 April, US troops had reached the northern tip of the island.

Progress was fast and, by way of the Ishikawa Isthmus, the Motobu Peninsula was sealed off. It was here that Ushijima had placed his second, small, 2,000-strong defensive force. This feature is surrounded by Nago Bay to the south and the Haneda Inland Sea to the north. The defenders were bottled up but well placed because the peninsula was ideal for defence. It was broken country with a host of ridges, ravines and caves, all cloaked in thick vegetation. There was a similarity to the topography of Leyte. In Motobu, the Japanese centred their defence on Mount Yaedake, the tallest mountain on the peninsula – at 1,487 feet (453m). It had been the scene of fighting for centuries and Nakijin and Nago castles had been witness since the fourteenth century. The mountain redoubt was formidable, and it took until 18 April to subdue the defenders, all of whom died.

In the south of the island, Buckner's force ran up against the Shuri Line and the general's deficiencies became clear. He ordered frontal assaults on bunkers, armed with automatic weapons, and paid the very heavy and entirely expected price. The Shuri Line was constructed to give line of sight from the high ground and artillery observers were able to call down fire at will. A marine officer commented: 'The enemy tactic which impressed most deeply was the intensity and effectiveness of artillery and the fact that this fire

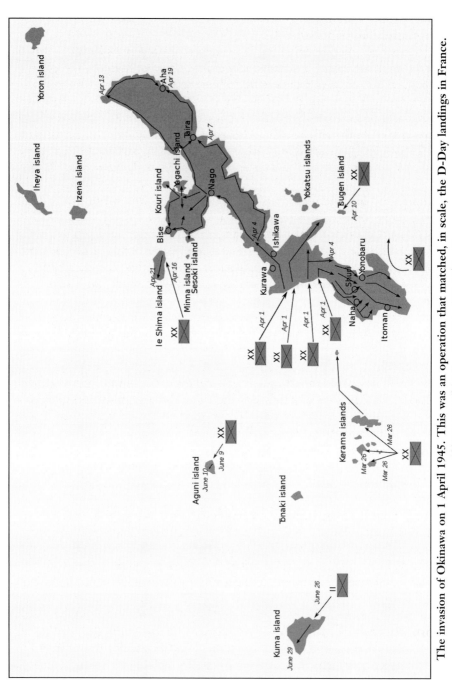

The invasion of Okinawa on 1 April 1945. This was an operation that matched, in scale, the **D-Day landings in France**.

(Okinawa.svg / John Keegan's Atlas of World War II)

covered not only our frontline area but also well back into our rear areas, quartermaster dumps and the like.'[3]

Any numerical advantage that the US had was negated by its inability to get to grips with its adversary. Ushijima held a front of about 3 miles (4.8km) and his concentration of force was proving to be very effective. The frontal attack into machine-gun fire fell out of favour in 1916, but thirty years later on Okinawa, Bruckner reproduced the tactics of the Somme. Just as on the Somme, it started to rain, heavily. The ground, torn up by artillery, turned into a knee-deep quagmire filled with excrement, body parts and abandoned ordnance. Buckner, bereft of ideas, persisted and the body count rose. In the USA, news of the stalemate and of the losses generated domestic anger.

When night fell, the Americans retired in their wet weapon pits; the Japanese came out of the darkness to kill them. The anxiety generated by Japanese night operation was palpable and any movement was likely to cause someone, somewhere, to open fire at an unseen but perceived target. Several US soldiers were killed by accident as a result. The weather, the casualty rate, the lack of success and the constant presence of mosquitos all led to a drop in American morale.

The Japanese were in a worse state and their losses were much greater. The introduction of American tanks was the game changer. Ushijima had only two anti-tank guns and they were quickly disabled. The only anti-tank defence left was for suicide attacks by individuals. These volunteers, clasping a mine or artillery shell, detonated their burden against a tank. These were the tactics of desperation, but then the attrition was such that these were desperate times. Twenty-two tanks were knocked out by this method. Flamethrower tanks, so successful in earlier campaigns, were employed in Okinawa to great effect. Despite this, Ushijima's order for his men to stay in their bunkers was ignored, and several Japanese counter-attacks were mounted, each of which played into American hands. The attackers were wiped out, to a man, on each occasion.

Criticism of Buckner became commonplace and Major General Oliver Smith, his deputy chief of staff, tortured by his commander's weakness, was nevertheless moved to an act of disloyalty and discussed his commander's performance with Vice Admiral Turner. Turner said that it was impossible for him to intervene. The onerous and continuing combat led to an increasing number of cases of 'psychoneurosis anxiety state', or combat fatigue, among soldiers and marines on Okinawa. The death of Roosevelt was announced on 13 April, but the news had little or no impact – it was in another world.

On 4 May, the remnants of 32nd Army mounted an attack that involved an amphibious landing behind American lines. The highly effective Japanese artillery moved out of cover to provide support and fired 13,000 shells in the

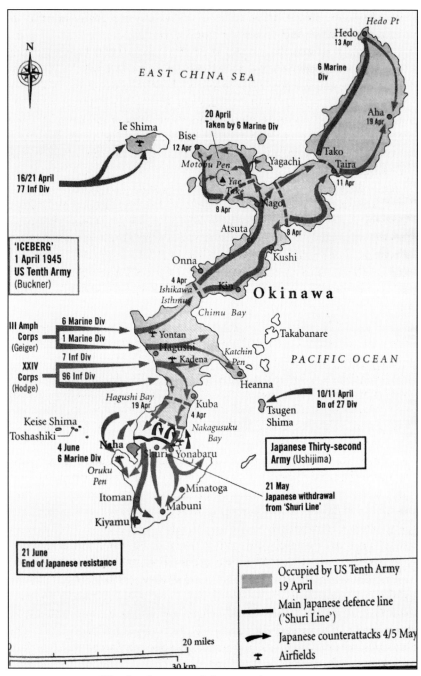

The development of the campaign. (*Hastings*)

process. However, now exposed to counter-battery fire, many valuable guns were lost along with their crews. The operation failed.

Shuri Castle was abandoned, and the remaining 30,000 Japanese soldiers withdrew in good order to the final position. It took until 27 May before Naha was taken, and Ushijima was unseated. Nevertheless, it was not the end, and the fight continued on Oruku Peninsula. The Japanese force was severely depleted and to add to its burden it had thousands of civilians in its care. Soldiers unprepared to commit suicide deserted and hid in caves. Many of those who had survived thus far committed suicide, as did tens of thousands of Okinawan civilians.

General Buckner was in an observation post on 18 June, watching an artillery barrage, when he was hit by a piece of shrapnel or coral and killed; he was 'unmourned'.[4] He was replaced the following week by General Stilwell of China fame. Japanese resistance ended on 21 June, although, as on so many other islands, some soldiers escaped to live in the countryside. Ushijima and his senior officers all committed suicide, but Colonel Yahara was denied the privilege when he was told that it was his duty to stay alive and tell the story of the battle of Okinawa. This he duly did.

The battle for Okinawa was conducted at sea as well as on land, and the USN lost more lives off Okinawa than in any other engagement in the Pacific War. At sea, the campaign was fought from 19 March to 30 July, during which time kamikaze sank or damaged over 200 Allied ships, taking 4,900 lives in the process. It was the USN Task Force 58 patrolling to the east of the island from 23 March until 27 April that was the main kamikaze aim. Its thirteen carriers provided the air cover and destroyed hundreds of incoming aircraft before they could do any damage.

The formation and deployment of a Royal Navy Pacific Fleet was an aspiration of Churchill but one that did not accord with the American wish to win the war in the Pacific single-handed. Churchill offered a fleet to the Americans in early 1944. Admiral King rejected the offer out of hand and it was only when Churchill pressed the point with Roosevelt that the President overruled his chief of naval staff. With ill grace, the offer was accepted.

The British Pacific Fleet (BPF) was accepted on the proviso that it would be logistically self-sufficient and, that being the case, it had to deploy having assembled a large supply train. The Royal Navy was equipped, trained and well-suited to the relatively short-range operations in the Atlantic and Mediterranean. The vast reaches of the Pacific were something very different, and logistically very taxing. Its aircraft carriers had reinforced flight decks and these withstood kamikaze strikes, but the carriers suffered 203 losses and downed only fifty-seven Japanese. The BPF was designated Task Force 57 and allocated a position 175 miles (280km) from Okinawa at the Sakishima Islands, there to protect the southern flank. These islands hosted kamikaze airfields, which were attacked with aircraft from the four large and six escort carriers.[5]

The RN ships were not air-conditioned and the heat was intense and debilitating on the lower decks. This led to low morale, and altogether, 'It was a sorry story, indeed one of the most inglorious episodes of the Royal Navy's wartime history.'[6]

US soldiers pass a dead enemy soldier, Okinawa.

American attitudes towards Britain became increasingly negative during the last months of the war. In the most senior circles, one view was:

> If we allow the British to limit their active participation to recapture areas that are to their selfish interests alone and not participate in smashing the war machine of Japan ... we will create in the United States a hatred for Great Britain ... that will defeat everything that men have died for in this war.[7]

The Japanese did not mount significant air attacks on the US fleet until 6 April. Then, 400 aircraft were launched from Kyushu. Thereafter it is calculated that 1,900 attacks were made. The pressure on senior USN commanders was such that Nimitz replaced them to rest. Spruance was replaced by Halsey and the fleet's designation changed from 5th to 3rd. The intensity of the sea battle cost Japan 1,100 aircraft.[8]

A Japanese major naval asset was the battleship *Yamato*. She was one of the most powerful ships in naval history but was generally underused as, during 1944, the USN gained naval ascendancy. She saw action, in October 1944, off the Philippines but did not make a significant contribution. In April 1945, she was sent on a one-way task to Okinawa. The captain's orders required him to beach the ship and use her guns in defence of the island. Yamato did not get as far as Okinawa as she was intercepted en route on 7 April. She was hit by eight bombs and eleven torpedoes from 5th Fleet's carrier aircraft, capsized and sank. Estimates are that 3,055 of her crew went down with her. Only 277 survived. The sinking of *Yamato* was, in effect, the death knell of the Imperial Japanese Navy.

*   *   *

The human cost of the Okinawa campaign was huge, as monuments to the dead testify. By 2010, the accounting was completed and covered the period from 26 March until the final surrender on 2 September. There are several monuments on the island and, in total, 240,931 are now commemorated. Of this number, 149,193 were Okinawan residents, 77,166 Japanese soldiers, 14,009 Americans, 365 South Koreans, 82 British, 82 North Korean and 34 Taiwanese.[9]

A feature of this campaign was that it was the first time that Japanese troops had surrendered in large numbers. Initially, 7,401 held up their hands, as did 3,400 Okinawan conscripts, but later, when reality struck home, a further 5,545 emerged from the countryside and threw in the towel.[10]

The Japanese had treated Okinawans appallingly – just as they had other Asian people who fell under their aegis. The island was a Japanese colony; the people were not Japanese, but nevertheless they lived under Japanese rule,

Japanese Battleship *Yamato*. Built in 1937, 72,000 tons, 9 × 18″ Type 94 guns – the largest ever mounted on a ship.

and had done so since 1879. They had every right to expect to be protected by Japanese soldiers, but there was no 'hearts and minds' policy here. Rape, torture and murder were all commonplace. By late 1945, the civilian dead amounted to about 50 per cent of the original population; many of these people committed suicide. The balance were murdered by Japanese soldiers, who held Okinawans in extreme contempt.

Notes

1. Costello, J., *The Pacific War 1941–45* [1981] (New York, Harper Collins, 2009), p. 555.
2. Heinl, R.D., *Soldiers of the Sea: US Marine Corps 1775–1962* (Annapolis, United States Naval Institute, 1962), p. 494.
3. Burcham, Capt Levi, 'USNA RG127 USMC Operations in WWII Okinawa', quoted by Hastings, Sir M., *Nemesis: The Battle for Japan 1944–45* (2007) (London, Collins, 2016), p. 409.
4. Hastings, p. 436.
5. Appleman, R., Burns, J., Gugeler, R. & Stevens, J., *Okinawa: The Last Battle* (US Army Centre of Military History, 1948), p. 97.
6. Hastings, p. 436.
7. United States Ambassador in London, John G. Winant, 1 September 1944.
8. Appleman, p. 102.
9. 'Number of names inscribed', Okinawa Prefecture, retrieved 18 January 2021.
10. Appleman, p. 489.

Chapter Twenty-Eight

1945

Harry Truman was awed by the magnitude of his new responsibilities, not least those resulting from the rapid development of the atomic bomb. He turned out to be a much-admired and effective president, who was the ideal foil to Stalin. Churchill lost the general election and so Clement Atlee and Ernest Bevin took their place at the top table.

By mid-summer 1945, what was left of the Japanese Burma Area Army was cut off in the Pegu Yoma hills between the rivers Irrawaddy and Sittang. It planned to break out, but a diversionary attack, by the depleted 33rd Army, in the 'Sittang Bend' failed. Unknown to the Japanese, the British had taken the breakout plan from a dead Japanese officer and were aware of the routes to be taken and the proposed location of river crossings. When the breakout started on 17 July, the Japanese ran into well-sited ambushes and artillery concentrations, which wreaked heavy losses. In addition, hundreds were drowned crossing the Sittang. In all, about 10,000 Japanese were killed.

Australians were mopping up pockets of resistance in New Guinea and dying in the process. There were several reports of cannibalism. Sometimes this was a symbolic act to demonstrate national superiority over the individual to be eaten. In the majority, it was the product of out and out hunger.

In China, Chiang Kai-shek and his acolytes continued to corruptly mis-manage American aid, to their personal advantage, whilst engaging in sporadic actions against the Japanese. Mao Zedong's forces concentrated on winning recruits to their cause as Mao prepared for the civil war he knew would soon follow.

After the conquest of Okinawa, the blockade of Japan's main islands was tightened and General Curtis Le May increased his aerial bombardment with his B-29 Fleet, now supplemented by carrier aircraft of the USN 3rd Fleet.

Mountbatten was fine-tuning his Operation ZIPPER, an amphibious assault on the coast of Malaya by British and Indian formations, despite a marked deficiency in the logistics required. The Americans had the logistic means but had no intention of assisting in any attempt by Britain to regain any of its former colonies.

The invasion of Japan's southern island of Kyushu had been named Operation OLYMPIC; the target date was November 1945. This would be the largest cross-beach landing in history and one never likely to be exceeded. Twenty-eight aircraft carriers and fourteen divisions were to be employed. Inevitably, any landing would be preceded by prolonged mass air attacks and sustained bombardment.

MacArthur had conducted himself badly during the Okinawa campaign by issuing bombastic criticism of the American leadership. He was seemingly unaware of his own deficiencies, so apparent in the Philippines in 1942 and, more recently, in June, during his 'return' campaign. He lobbied for and expected to be appointed the commander-in-chief for the invasion of Japan. Marshal and Nimitz were, arguably, better candidates. However, MacArthur's PR team had ensured that their man could not be rejected. He was widely perceived to embody all the virtues of a warrior and American manhood. On that spurious basis he was selected to command the land forces for OLYMPIC. Nimitz would command at sea. The Okinawa campaign had caused a rapid re-evaluation of the likely casualties during OLYMPIC and '1 million' was now the consensus. Invasion was a very unattractive option and total blockade was actively considered as an alternative.

The surrender of Germany was seen by strategists as releasing Allied assets for service in the Far East. However, the proposed redeployment was the cause of considerable angst among those who thought that they had 'done their bit' in Europe and who were now earmarked to play a part on Operation CORONET, the invasion of Honshu, following OLYMPIC.

The British, French and Dutch governments were, not unreasonably, bending their corporate minds to the reoccupation of their occupied colonies. The British Embassy in Washington observed:

> we must naturally be prepared for criticism from some quarters whatever we do. If we prosecute Eastern War with might and main, we shall be told by some people we are really fighting for our colonial possessions the better to exploit them and that American blood is being shed to no better purpose than to help ourselves and the Dutch and French to perpetuate our degenerative colonial empires; while if we are judged not to have gone all out, that is because we are letting America fight her own war with little aid after they had pulled our chestnuts out of the European fire.[1]

This was well judged, and a Foreign Office minute said:

> The Americans are virtually conducting political warfare against us in the Far East and are seeking to not only belittle the efforts which we have hitherto made in that theatre of war, but also to keep us in a humiliating and subsidiary role in the future.[2]

The mythical 'special relationship' had not yet been identified but in 1945 it was anything but. Harry Hopkins, Roosevelt's closest advisor, said, 'To hear some people talk … you'd think the British were our potential enemies.'[3]

American hostility was not reserved for Britain. The French were also in the firing line over Indo-China. The politics of Vietnam were vastly complex, and, in a demonstration of political naivety, the USA had embraced Ho Chi Minh at the expense of its ally, France. Suffice it to say that, eventually the USA was obliged to put its weight behind French colonialism and rejected the other option, which was Vietnamese communism. It did not end well.

The Royal Navy enjoyed modest success on 15–16 May when a destroyer flotilla engaged and sank the heavy cruiser *Haguro*, about 100 miles (161km) south-west of Phuket, Thailand. In July, miniature submarines, XE-craft, attacked the Japanese heavy cruiser *Takao* moored in the Johore Strait. The charge attached to the ship's hull blew a hole in her and she was disabled. This feat of great bravery and tenacity won two Victoria Crosses but did not in any way hasten the defeat of Japan – although it did wonders for the morale of the Royal Navy.

In July, the United States Navy, having destroyed its enemy, was free to send its aircraft to roam at will across Japan. Halsey made it his business to target the sea link between Honshu and Hokkaido islands. This vital domestic link was served by twelve rail ferries, which transported coal to Honshu and kept Japanese industry working. Eight of the ferries were sunk, two were beached and the other two badly damaged. This was a grievous blow because the Japanese had no means to replace the ferries other than the Kanmon Undersea Rail Tunnel. This ran between Honshu and Kyushu, had been completed in 1942, and allowed the movement of some traffic.

Halsey's ships, among them HMS *King George V*, were able to bombard shore installations despite sporadic kamikaze attacks. Inshore shipping was paralysed and that had a serious commercial effect. Japanese morale was lowered when American pilots flew so low that their faces could be seen. Life in Japan was grim and getting grimmer. The black market became almost institutionalised, medical supplies were as scarce as food.

Le May's B-29s were daily attacking Japanese cities in formations of up to 1,000 aircraft. He attacked sixty-seven cities with incendiary munitions to devastating effect. On the night of 9/10 March, he turned his attention to Tokyo and mounted Operation MEETINGHOUSE. This was, by some way, the most destructive air raid of the war: 1,665 tons of bombs killed an estimated 100,000 civilians, destroyed 250,000 buildings, and 16 square miles (41km^2) of the city. 'Aircrew at the end of the bombing stream reported that the stench of burned human flesh permeated the aircraft over the target.'[4] It is estimated that between March and the Japanese surrender in August,

Le May's aircraft killed about 500,000 and left 5 million homeless. Despite this appalling carnage, the Japanese soldiered on.

The development and testing of an atomic device, shrouded under cover as 'The Manhattan Project', was led by the arrogant, egotistical, bullying, unpleasant but brilliant Major General Leslie Groves. The project was close to fruition and was probably the most significant scientific advance in human history. It had cost $2 million and was completed with British assistance, which was only 'perfunctorily acknowledged'.[5]

The dropping of two nuclear weapons on Japan has already generated thousands of books and readers of military history will be aware of the central rationale, which was to save American lives and, incidentally, Japanese lives too – albeit at a frightful cost. It is not intended to rehash the events of 6–9 August 1945 here. Better to consider the machinations of Joseph Stalin. His intelligence service had breached the Manhattan Project and he was not only aware of the American success but had sufficient information to start developing a Russian atomic bomb.

Stalin had agreed, in November 1943 at Tehran, that Russia would declare war on Japan as soon as Germany surrendered. This was confirmed at Potsdam in July 1945. On that basis, the Russians did not wish to renew the 'Neutrality Pact' with Japan, currently in place, and, on 5 April 1945, they informed the Japanese accordingly.[6] This unsettled the Japanese, but the Soviets assured them that the treaty would still be in force for another twelve months and that they had nothing to worry about.[7] Of course they lied, but dishonesty was then, and is now, a feature of many international relationships.

Soviet Foreign Minister Vyacheslav Molotov sent for the Japanese ambassador on 8 August and told him that, from 9 August, a state of war would exist between their two countries. At 0001 hrs on 9 August, the Russians opened hostilities. They attacked on three fronts in the east, west and north of Manchuria with the vast army amassed for the purpose: 1,577,225 men with 26,137 guns, 5,556 tanks and 5,368 aircraft.[8]

The atomic bombs were dropped on Hiroshima and Nagasaki. The effect was utterly devastating and brought home to the Japanese and Hirohito in particular the hopelessness of their position. The Red host swept through Manchuria, seizing as war booty anything of conceivable value to the Russian state and inflicting heavy losses of its Japanese adversary on the way. On 10 August, Truman proposed splitting the Korean peninsula, a Japanese colony, at the 38th parallel with the Russians. The Russians could have occupied the whole country but, to general surprise, they agreed. Russian amphibious landings were made as part of the wider operation and by 18 August they secured South Sakhalin and part of the Chishima Islands.

On 15 August 1945, the Emperor made his momentous radio broadcast and his empire collapsed in ruins. The militaristic ambitions of its leaders had come to naught and at great cost in lives, treasure and national prestige. Japan was now a pariah state that attracted international contempt. Ever the showman, MacArthur stage-managed the formal surrender proceedings on board the battleship USS *Missouri* on 2 September.

The USA had won this war but at the cost of 116,606 dead and missing. The Japanese lost an estimated 1,744,000 and, of these, about 60 per cent died of starvation. Estimates of Japanese civilian deaths range from a precise but very low 393,400[9] to about 900,000. About 30,000 British servicemen and women died in the Far East, many of them in great privation, as prisoners.

Notes

1. Nicholas, H.G. (ed.), *Washington Despatches* (Weidenfeld & Nicolson, 1981), p. 559.
2. BNA FO371/f1955 Sterndale Bennett.
3. Sherwood, R.E., *Roosevelt and Hopkins* (New York, Harper, 1948), p. 921.
4. Buckley, J., *Air Power in the Age of Total War* [1998] (London, Taylor & Francis, 2001), p. 193.
5. Hastings, Sir M., *Nemesis: The Battle for Japan 1944–45* (2007) (London, Collins, 2016), p. 489.
6. Soviet Denunciation of the Pact with Japan, 5 April 1945 (Yale University, Avalon Project).
7. Slavinski, B.N., *The Japanese-Soviet Neutrality Pact: A Diplomatic History 1941–45* (London, Routledge, 2004), pp. 148–9.
8. Glantz, D.M. & House, J., *When Titans Clashed: How the Red Army Stopped Hitler* (Lawrence, Kansas University Press, 1995), p. 378.
9. The Pacific War, Online Encyclopedia.

Epilogue

The Second World War was at an end and the vanquished nations were ruined, domestically, militarily and financially. Their cities were razed, and their people confused, angry and leaderless. The short-lived Japanese Empire had fallen. The servicemen of all nations, or at least the survivors, had gone home. Everywhere there was a recalibrating of social norms and a counting of the costs.

The horror imposed on the world by Japan and its cohort Germany had been of a scale never experienced before in human history, and politicians and historians fell to analysing the perpetrators of so much misery and wondering how these monstrous regimes compared. The answer would not right grievous wrongs, nor resurrect millions of dead, but it might militate against anything similar ever happening again. The two nations acted independently, and the world should be grateful that they did not combine and cooperate more closely in their killing of innocents.

The guns were unmanned and silent. By September 1945, Japan was flooded by armed Americans whose initial task was to protect returning Japanese servicemen from the wrath of the disappointed, angry civilian population. It was a surreal situation matched by that in Vietnam where, in accordance with the Allied agreement of July 1945, Major General Douglas Gracey and his 20 Indian Division arrived to take control of the country from the Japanese occupiers. The tumult in the country was of such magnitude that the British were obliged to impose martial law and employ armed Japanese to maintain order until the French could return to reoccupy its colony in force.

Asia was in chaos and there was an urgent need to re-establish civilian administration throughout the region. The likelihood of post-war chaos had been anticipated, as had the need to examine and convict, where appropriate, those found guilty of war crimes.

By late 1945, General MacArthur was firmly installed as the Governor of Japan and, although he wallowed in his status, it was in this role that he displayed an unexpected degree of fine judgement, bordering on wisdom that shaped the future of Japan. Hirohito as the sovereign had, without any question, a case to answer. It was argued by many at the time that he was criminally responsible for his country's behaviour. Every one of several million deaths were caused 'in his service' and the view was that he could (some say 'should') reasonably be expected to take his share of the guilt.

Hirohito's life was in the hands of the USA and, specifically, those of Mac-Arthur. MacArthur was a mediocre general, and a view was that 'he was unsuited by temperament, character and judgement for the positions of high command which he occupied throughout the war.'[1] Hitherto, MacArthur had appeared to be politically naïve, and in conducting his campaign in the Pacific, his overriding personal ambition had been evident. Now MacArthur conducted himself with uncharacteristic dignity and foresight. He chose to portray Hirohito as a mere tool in the hands of the militarists and perceived that, if Japan was to recover from its wounds and its financial ruin, Hirohito would provide the vital unifying symbol that was needed. The Emperor renounced his divine status, was photographed beside MacArthur, who decided that Hirohito should not face any criminal investigation and that the throne would be absolved of all blame. It was a cynical, pragmatic and masterly judgement, MacArthur's finest hour. As history has now revealed, that pragmatism was an important contribution to the world order.

After any war, it is always 'Victors' Justice' that prevails, and the Second World War was no exception. The only defendants at the trials that followed the surrender of Japan were Japanese or Koreans serving in Japan's ranks. Allied soldiers had killed countless prisoners and wounded – the perpetrators would have pleaded that they had no other option, but that defence was not put to the judicial test.

The mechanics for the punishment of war criminals was put in place on 20 October 1943, when there had been the initial meeting of the representatives of seventeen Allied nations (the USSR was not present) which agreed to set up a War Crimes Commission. That body delegated to regional panels autonomy consistent with the central coordinating function of the Commission. The function of the Commission was to formulate recommendations for the guidance of governments, and, through several recommendations, the Commission influenced the development of international law in areas such as jurisdiction, extradition, belligerent occupation, personal responsibility for acts of state, the criminality of aggressive war and the protection of human rights of civil populations against violations by their own governments.

On 19 January 1946, the International Military Tribunal for the Far East was convened by a special proclamation from General MacArthur. It was patently impossible to bring to trial the hundreds of thousands of Japanese servicemen who had butchered and murdered their way across Southeast Asia nor those who had been complicit, by their inaction, to prevent atrocities. The pragmatic decision was to prosecute the leadership, both military and civilian.

Immediately after the war many high-ranking Japanese committed suicide to avoid the hangman. Tōjō Hideki decided to shoot himself and, in order not to mark his face, aimed a pistol at his heart – he missed and lived to be hanged.

Initially, twenty-eight of the most senior men were arraigned on 3 May 1946. The trial opened, in Tokyo, on 3 June, but was not concluded until 24 January 1947. Two of the accused, Matsuoka and Nagano, died during the proceedings and Ōkawa was declared unfit to plead.

There were many practical difficulties and not least of these was the need to translate every exchange. A Language Arbitration Board was established to settle matters of disputed interpretation. Seven of those original twenty-eight were duly hanged and sixteen of the others were given extended jail terms. Only one served as much as ten years and most were paroled after seven – a derisory punishment for dreadful crimes.

Two of the men executed by the USA were Generals Yamashita and Homma. They were convicted on the basis that they did not quell the barbarism of their subordinates in the Philippines. Today there is a consensus that their convictions for the events specified are unsafe, and that the trial was unfair and smacked of a kangaroo court. It has been suggested that 'the sentences represented MacArthur's personal vengeance on Japanese commanders who had humiliated him in the field.' However, Yamashita's orders for the killing of Chinese in Malaya and Singapore, for which the Americans chose not to charge him, were more than enough to justify his hanging.

The Australians tried over 800 Japanese, of whom a little less than one third were acquitted and, by February 1948, 931 Japanese had been tried by British Military Courts. China had suffered under the Japanese for fourteen years and it held thirteen tribunals that resulted in 504 convictions and 149 executions.

An overwhelming number of the grotesque crimes committed by the Japanese went unpunished as the perpetrators could not be positively identified. The criminals returned to civilian life, died peacefully in their beds, and are honoured today by a nation that will not accept its responsibility for the misdeeds of its fathers and grandfathers. The treatment of the 'comfort women' is still an issue nearly eighty years on.

It was evident that, for the Japanese, gratuitous torture of the most extreme kind was spontaneous, unfocussed and routine, and freedom of action was delegated to every Japanese soldier and sailor. Torture was an integral part of the killing process, and an overwhelming majority of front-line Japanese soldiers (except for a miniscule, statistically insignificant minority) was either an active participant in the killing of civilians and prisoners of war or complicit in that killing. The motivation of Japanese forces, in this respect, is difficult to comprehend. There was no end product, no military objective. One is drawn to enquire, was the Japanese Army between 1931 and 1945 composed of homicidal psychopaths? On the evidence, the answer would seem to be, yes. If not, what?

Torture has been a feature in all human conflict, and it is almost always as a method of extracting information. It has been happening for years in Guantanamo Bay, where it is euphemistically called 'enhanced interrogation', and the USA is the practitioner. Deplorable as current American conduct is, it pales in comparison with the most assiduous torturers in modern times, who were, arguably, the Japanese. They were not content with murdering their victims but had the need to torture them first. The victims were overwhelmingly non-combatants, and they were ill-treated less for information but more as a punishment, and frequently just as entertainment.

Torture was so central to Japanese operations that, on 6 August 1943, the Hayashi Division in Burma issued a manual on the subject. This was entitled *Notes for the Interrogation of Prisoners of War*.

In practice, torture was applied on anyone who fell into Japanese hands and there was no limit to the very extreme measures that they employed. Lord Liverpool gives the most harrowing account of the wholesale Japanese torture of prisoners. However, his well-researched and detailed book is not for those with a weak stomach.

The civilian inhabitants of even the most remote colonial territory were subject to barbarous treatment. In most cases, they had no information, were politically unaware and offered no threat. Their non-combatant status was no defence against men who tortured, raped, and killed on a whim. The educated Burmese people came to realise that the promises offered by GEACS were just pie in the sky.

A comparison of Japan with Germany is like comparing an apple and a pear. Both fruit, but from different trees in the same orchard. Both nations were indoctrinated to believe in their racial superiority. This made the acquisition of foreign territory entirely reasonable, and justified the killing of its inhabitants, who were deemed to be 'sub-human'. In both cases the only product was the deaths that each regime caused.

Looking for the differences between them would be like splitting hairs: ransacking and bombing of entire cities, mass shootings, massacres of women and children, mistreatment of POWs, looting, and other behaviour were crimes both engaged on a massive scale. The bestiality of Japanese army conduct was matched by the Wehrmacht. Nanjing, Bataan, Manila, Singapore has their equals in countless places in Europe.[2]

Estimates of war dead vary widely – they are all vast and there is no product in seeking to find definite figures. It is sufficient that tens of millions were the victims of two bestial regimes, which differed in their political structure.

In Japan there was no single party and, apart from the figurehead Hirohito, there was no unchallenged leader. The German State was set upon executing a national policy of genocide. Japan was a totalitarian state, but that was not based on national choice. It was imposed by the ruling military junta. In Germany, the converse applies as, on four separate occasions, the population voted for the NSDAP (Nazi Party) and propelled Hitler into power – democratically.

The wider Japanese public, of whom 50 per cent were disenfranchised, were unaware of the behaviour of its servicemen (Japanese women voted for the first time on 15 December 1945). News of any military reverse had been kept secret and civilian Japanese could reasonably claim an element of innocence that did not apply to Germans.

The guilt of Japanese armed forces did not apply to the civilian Japanese population that was isolated on the home islands and effectively cut off from what the Japanese military behemoth did to Asia on their behalf and in the service of the Emperor. The Japanese embrace of victimhood was certainly more valid than that of Germans in the post-war era.

Both countries committed wholesale murder. Now, eighty years on, some Western nations categorise homicide in an ascending order of magnitude ranging from involuntary manslaughter to capital murder.

To this day, Japanese schools do not expose children to the activities of their great-grandfathers. The country honours war criminals and contests any claim made by the very few, elderly, surviving comfort women. Germany repented and made reparation. The Japanese have chosen instead to ignore their bloodstained history. Mariko Oi commented on the teaching of history at her school. She said:

> When we did finally get there, it turned out only nineteen of the book's 357 pages dealt with events between 1931 and 1945.
>
> There was one page on what is known as the Mukden incident, when Japanese soldiers blew up a railway in Manchuria in China in 1931. There was one page on other events leading up to the Sino-Japanese war in 1937 – including one line, in a footnote, about the massacre that took place when Japanese forces invaded Nanjing – the Nanjing Massacre, or Rape of Nanjing.
>
> There was another sentence on the Koreans and the Chinese who were brought to Japan as miners during the war, and one line, again in a footnote, on 'comfort women' – a prostitution corps created by the Imperial

Army of Japan. There was also just one sentence on the atomic bombings of Hiroshima and Nagasaki.[3]

In the Pacific, the USA mounted the war crime trials and manipulated them to its own ends. Victors' justice was seen to be anything but just. For example, not one of the 300 people employed by Surgeon General Ishii Shirō in his thoroughly evil Unit 731 in Manchukuo was indicted by the USA. This despite their responsibility for carrying out unspeakably wicked experiments on captives. The USA decided that the product of Ishii's work, in which he developed pathogens that caused some of the world's most devastating diseases – among them anthrax, plague, gas gangrene, smallpox and botulism – would be useful to the American military. That Ishii used Chinese prisoners and Allied POWs as guinea pigs, forcing them to breathe, eat, and receive injections of deadly pathogens, was of lesser importance. Ishii provided the results of his 'research' to the Americans in return for immunity from prosecution.[4] Ishii died a painful death, aged 67, in 1959. The Russians found and arrested twelve members of Unit 731 and imprisoned them all.

About 5,700 lower-ranked Japanese were charged with war crimes in separate trials mounted by Australia, China, France, the Netherlands, the Philippines, the United Kingdom and the USA. These people were indicted for a wide range of offences including rape, sexual slavery, torture, ill-treatment of labourers, execution without trial, and inhumane medical experiments. The trials were decentralised to some fifty locations in Asia and the Pacific. Most trials were completed by 1949, but Australia held some as late as 1951.[5] Of the 5,700 indicted for Class B war crimes, 984 were sentenced to death; 475 received life sentences; 2,944 were given more limited prison terms; 1,018 were acquitted; and 279 were never brought to trial or not sentenced. The number of death sentences by country is: the Netherlands (236), United Kingdom (223), Australia (153), China (149), United States (140), France (26), and Philippines (just 1).[6] There is a discrepancy in the arithmetic as only 928 are accounted for here. Some of the condemned men must either have been reprieved or died before their sentence could be carried out.

Empires, by their very nature, are usually widespread, and of long standing. They leave behind some tangible evidence of their existence. Roman remains are cherished in the UK despite that empire functioning on slavery and brutality. The French left an architectural legacy in, what was, Indochina. The British Empire, perhaps the largest, and now much maligned by the 'woke' generation, left in its wake the rule of law, democracy, and a system of civil administration. Its former colonies embraced many British values as well as whisky, football and cricket! The Commonwealth is a positive testament to British colonial rule.

The Japanese Empire was probably the briefest. During its existence it produced only unspeakable misery and death on a vast scale. The only product of its territorial expansion was to hasten Britain's withdrawal from empire, and in this, it inadvertently shared a political success with the USA. Nothing remotely positive was produced by the Japanese and the crushing demise of its empire by the USA is to be applauded. Let there be no doubt, America won this war.

Notes

1. Spector, R.H., *Eagle Against the Sun* (New York, Simon & Schuster, 2020), p. xiv–xv.
2. Snyder, T., *Bloodlands: Europe between Hitler and Stalin* (New York, Basic Books, 2010).
3. Oi, Marika, BBC News, Tokyo, March 2013.
4. Gold, H., *Unit 73: Testimony* (Tuttle, 2003), p. 109.
5. Wilson, S., Cribb, R., Trefalt, B. & Aszkielowicz, D., *Japanese War Criminals* (Columbia University Press, 2017).
6. Dower, J., *War Without Mercy: Power in the Pacific War* (Pantheon, 1987), p. 22.

If there were to be a single image that encapsulates the Japanese Empire it would not be of Hirohito, who adorns the cover of this book, but given that 'a picture is worth a thousand words', the author believes that the photograph shown overleaf, of one of his soldiers acting 'in his service', says it all.

Serving their emperor.

Bibliography

'War with Japan', Vol. VI (RN Staff History, MoD, 1995).

Alanbrooke, FM Lord, *War Diaries 1939–1945*, Danchev, A. & Todman, D. (eds) (London, Weidenfeld & Nicolson, 2001).

Alexander, I., *Surviving Bataan and Beyond* (Stackpole Books, 2005).

Allen, L., *Burma: The Longest War 1941–45* (London, Phoenix Press, 2000).

Allen, L., *Burma: The Longest War 1941–45* (London, Orion Publishing 1986).

Allen, L., *Singapore 1941–1942* [1977] (Abingdon, Frank Cass, 2005).

Allen, R.E., *The First Battalion of the 28th Marines on Iwo Jima* (North Carolina, McFarland & Co., 2004).

Appleman, R.E., Burns, J.M., Gugeler, R.A., Stevens, J. & Love, E.G., *Okinawa: The Last Battle* (US Army Centre of Military History, 1948).

Baker, B.D., 'What if Japan Had Won The Battle of Midway?' (*The Diplomat*, 2016).

Baldwin, H.W., *Battles Lost and Won: Great Campaigns of World War II* (New York, Harper & Row, 1966).

Balley, D.E., *WWII Wrecks of the Truk Lagoon* (North Valley Diver Publications, 2001).

Barker, B., *Agincourt* [2005] (London, Abacus, 2007).

Bartlit, N., 'Japanese Mass Suicides' (Washington, Atomic Heritage Foundation, July 2016).

Bartsch, W.H., *December 8, 1941* (Texas A&M University Press, 2003).

'Battle of Leyte Gulf', World War II, Britannica.com, 2020.

Bayly, C. & Harper, T., *Forgotten Armies: Britain's Asian Empire & War with Japan* (London, Penguin, 2005).

Bean, C.E.W., *Australian Official History of the Great War* (Australian War Memorial 1920–42).

Beckman, K.B., *Personality and Strategy: How the personalities of Gen. MacArthur and Adm. King shaped Allied Strategy in the Pacific* (Fort Leavenworth, US Army CGSC, 2002).

Beevor, A., *The Second World War* (London, Weidenfeld & Nicolson, 2012).

Behr, E., *The Last Emperor* (Bantam Books, New York, 1987).

Beres, L.R., 'On Assassination as Anticipatory Self-Defense: The Case of Israel' (*Hofstra Law Review*, 1991).

Bix H.P., *Hirohito and the Making of Modern Japan* (New York, Harper Collins, 2000).

BNA FO371/f1955 Sterndale Bennett.

Bob Tadashi Wakabayashi, 'The Nanking 100-man killing contest debate. War guilt amid Fabricated Illusions 1971–75' (*The Journal of Japanese Studies*, Vol. 26, No. 2, Summer 2000).

Boyd, A., *The Royal Navy in Eastern Waters* (Barnsley, Seaforth Publishing, 2017).

Brayley, M., *The British Army 1939–45 (3): The Far East* (Oxford, Osprey Publishing, 2002).

Bruton, P. *The matter of a massacre: Alexandra Hospital Singapore 14th/15th February 1942* (Singapore Infopedia, 1989).

Bryant, A., *Triumph in the West 1943–46* (London, Collins, 1959).

Buckley, J., *Air Power in the Age of Total War* [1998] (London, Taylor & Francis, 2001).

Bullard, S. (trans.), *Japanese Army Operations in the South Pacific Area: New Britain and Papua Campaigns* (Australian War Memorial, 2007).

Burkman, T.W., *Japan and the League of Nations* (University of Hawaii, 2008).

Burrell, R.S., 'Breaking the Cycle of Iwo Jima Mythology: A Strategic Study of Operation Detachment' (*Journal of Military History*, 2004).

Burton, J., *Fortnight of Infamy: The Collapse of Allied Airpower West of Pearl Harbor* (Annapolis, Maryland: Naval Institute Press, 2006).

Carver, M., *The War Lords: Military Commanders of the Twentieth Century* (Boston, Little, Brown and Co., 1976).

Chang, I., *The Rape of Nanking* (New York, Basic Books, 1997).

Chapman, G., *A Passionate Prodigality* (London, Ivor Nicholson & Watson, 1933).

Churchill, Sir W.S., 'The Japanese Envy', *The Second World War: The Grand Alliance*, Vol. II (London, Cassell & Co., 1950).

Clodfelter, M., *Warfare and Armed Conflicts: A Statistical Reference*, Vol. 2 (McFarland & Co., 1992).

Coast, J. & Noszlopy, L., Nash, J. (ed.), *Railroad of Death: The Original, Classic Account of the River Kwai Railway* (Newcastle, Myrmidon, 2014).

Collingham, L., *The Taste of War: World War II and the Battle for Food* (London, Penguin, 2011).

Coox, A.D., 'Pacific War', Vol. 6, *The Cambridge History of Japan*, 1988.

Coox, A.D., *Nomonhan: Japan against Russia, 1939*, 2 vols. (Stanford University Press, 1985).

Corfield, J. & Corfield, R., *The Fall of Singapore* (Singapore, Talisman Books, 2012).

Correll, J.T., 'Disaster in the Philippines', *Air Force Magazine*, 2019.

Costello, J., *The Pacific War 1941–45* [1981] (New York, Harper Collins, 2009).

Day, D., *Curtin: A Life* (New South Wales, Harper Collins, 1999).

de Pizan, C., *The writings of Christine de Pizan*, selected and ed. by Charity Willard (New York, Persea Books, 1994).

Dower, J., *Lessons from Iwo Jima* (American Historical Association, 2007).

Drea, E., 'Reading Each Other's Mail: Japanese Communication Intelligence, 1920–41', *Journal of Military History*, 1991.

Drea, E.J., *Nomonhan: Japanese-Soviet Tactical Combat, 1939* (US Army Command & GSC Fort Leavenworth, 1981).

Dull, P.S., *A Battle History of the Japanese Navy 1941–45* (Annapolis, Naval Institute Press, 1978).

Dunant, H., *Un Souvenir de Solférino* (Genève: Imprimerie Jules-Guillaume Fick, 1862).

Dyer, G.C., *The Amphibians came to Conquer: The Story of Admiral Richmond Turner* (Washington DC, Department of the Navy, 1972).

Edwards, J., *John Curtin's War: Volume II: Triumph and Decline* (Melbourne, Viking, 2018).

Fay, P.W., *The Forgotten Army: India's Armed Struggle for Independence 1942–1945* (University of Michigan Press, 1993).

Fenton, D., *How many Died?* (Australian War Memorial, 2004).

Frank, R., *Guadalcanal: The Definitive Account of the Landmark Battle* (New York, Random House, 1990).

Funk, A., & Wagnalls, B., 'To instruct in doctrines; esp., to teach partisan or sectarian dogmas', I.A. Snook (ed.), *Concepts of Indoctrination* (London, Routledge & Kegan Paul, 1972).

Garver, J.W., *Chinese-Soviet Relations 1937–45* (New York, Oxford University Press, 1988).

Gillison, D., *Australia in the War of 1939–1945* (Canberra, Australian War Memorial, 1962).

Gillison, D., *Coral Sea and Midway*, RAAF 1939–42, Chapter 26 (Canberra, Australian War Memorial, 1962).

Glantz D.M. & House, J.M., *When Titans Clashed: How the Red Army Stopped Hitler* (Lawrence, Kansas University Press, 1995).

Glantz, D.M., *The Soviet Strategic Offensive in Manchuria, 1945: 'August Storm'* (Abingdon, Routledge, 2004).

Gold, H., *Unit 731: Testimony* (Tuttle, 2003).

Greenberger, R., *The Bataan Death March: World War II Prisoners in the Pacific* (Minneapolis, Compass Point Books, 2009).

Grey, J., *A Military History of Australia* (Cambridge, Cambridge University Press, 1999).

Grossman, D., *On Killing* [1995] (New York, Back Bay Books, 2009).

Grunden, W.E., 'No Retaliation in Kind: Japanese Chemical Warfare Policy in World War II', conference paper, *One Hundred Years of Chemical Warfare: Deployment Consequences*, 2017.

Hamilton, N., *Monty: The Making of a General* (Sevenoaks, Sceptre, 1981).

Hammel, E., *Guadalcanal: Decision at Sea: The Naval Battle of Guadalcanal, November 13–15, 1942* (New York, Crown, 1988).

Hansard, 8 December 1941.

Harries, M. & Harries, S., *Soldiers of the Sun: The Rise and Fall of the Japanese Army* (London, Heinemann, 1991).

Harrison, S., 'Skull Trophies of the Pacific War; Transgressive objects of remembrance', *Journal of the Royal Anthropological Institute*, 12: 4, 2006.

Hastings, Sir M., *Nemesis: The Battle for Japan 1944–45* [2007] (London, Collins, 2016).

Hayes, R., *Subhas Chandra Bose in Nazi Germany: Intelligence and Propaganda 1941–43* (Oxford, Oxford University Press, 2011).

Heinl, R.,D., *Soldiers of the Sea: US Marine Corps, 1775–1962* (Annapolis, Naval Institute Press, 1962).

Hicks, G., *The Comfort Women: Japan's Brutal Regime of Enforced Prostitution in the Second World War* (New York, W.W. Norton & Co., 1995).

Hinsley, F.H. & Stripp, A. (eds), *Codebreakers: The Inside Story of Bletchley Park* (Oxford, Oxford University Press, 1992).

Hudson, E.R.B., 'A Close View of the Disaster at the Sittang Bridge', *Michigan War Studies Review*, 2018.

Ike, N. (trans. & ed.), *Japan's Decision for War in 1941* (Stanford University Press, 1967).

Immerwahr, D., 'The Greater United States: Territory and Empire in US History, *Diplomatic History*, Vol. 40, Iss. 3, 2016).

Inouye Jukichi, *Introduction to Chushingura*, 4th ed. (Maruzen Co. Ltd., 1910).

Ishijima Noriyuki, *A History of China's Anti-Japanese War* (Tokyo, Aoki Shoten, 1984).

IWM Archive, Thompson.

James, D.C., *The Years of MacArthur*, Vol. 2 (Boston, MA, Houghton Mifflin, 1970).

Jansen, M., *The Making of Modern Japan* (Harvard University Press, 2002).

Japan Times, 10 December 2011.

Japanese Monograph, IV 17807.71–2 (Washington, DC, Office of the Chief of Military History, Department of the Army).

Java Sea Campaign (Naval History and Heritage Command, US Office of Naval Intelligence, 1943).

Johnston B.F., with Mosaburo Hosoda & Yoshio Kusumi, *Japanese Food Management in World War II* (Stanford University Press, 1953).

Jones, F.G., *Japan's New Order in East Asia: Its Rise and Fall 1937-45*. Vol II (New York, Oxford University Press, 1954).

Jorgenson N.-J., *Culture and Power in Germany and Japan* (Folkstone, Global Oriental, 2006).

Jowett, P., *Japan's Asian Allies 1941–45* (London, Osprey Publishing, 2020).

Katsuichi, Honda, *The Road to Nanjing* (M.E. Sharp, Pacific Basin Institute, 1987).

Keegan, J., *The Second World War* (New York, Penguin 2005).

Keegan, J., *The Face of Battle* [1976] (London, Jonathan Cape, 1995).

Keogh, E., *Southwest Pacific 1941–45* (Melbourne, Grayflower Publications, 1965).

Kissinger, H., *The White House Years* (New York, Simon & Schuster, 2011).

Kita Hiroaki [2003], *Niniroku Jiken Zenkenshō* (Asahi Shinbunsha, 2003).

Lai, B., *Shanghai and Nanjing 1937: Massacre on the Yangtze* (Oxford, Osprey Publishing, 2017).

Larry, D., *The Chinese People at War: Human suffering and Social Transformation, 1937–1945* (Cambridge University Press, 2010).

Lary, D., 'Drowned Earth: The Strategic Breaching of the Yellow River Dikes, 1938' (*War in History*, 2001 8 (2)).

Leckie, R., *Helmet for My Pillow* (New York, Bantam Books, 1957).

Lee Kuan Yew, *The Singapore Story* (Singapore, *Straits Time Press*, 1998).

Leutze, J., *A Different Kind of Victory: A Biography of Admiral Thomas C. Hart* (Annapolis, MD, Naval Institute Press, 1981).

Levene, M. & Roberts, P. (eds), *The Massacre in History* (Oxford, Berghahn Books, 1999).

Lewis, Dr T. & Ingman, P., *Carrier Attack, Darwin 1942: the Complete Guide to Australia's own Pearl Harbor* (South Australia, Avonmore Books, 2013).

Lodge, A.B., 'Bennett, Henry Gordon (1887–1962)' *Australian Dictionary of Biography*, Vol. 13 (Melbourne University Press, 1993).

London Gazette, The, 3 March 1951, 13 March 1951.

Louis, W.R., *British Strategy in the Far East 1919–39* (Oxford, Clarendon Press, 1971).

Loxton, B. & Coulthard-Clark, C., *The Shame of Savo: Anatomy of a Naval Disaster* (St Leonards, NSW, Allen & Unwin, 1997).

Lyall Grant, Maj Gen I., *Burma: The Turning Point* (Barnsley, Pen & Sword, 2003).

Lyman, R., *Slim, Master of War* [2004] (London, Constable & Robinson, 2005).

MacArthur, Gen D., *Japanese Operations in the Southwest Pacific Area* (Reports, Vol. 2).

MacKinnon, S.R., *Wuhan 1938* (Berkeley University Press, 2008).

Major Francis Holland, *The Oxford Companion to New Zealand Military History*, McGibbon (ed.).

Manchester, W.R., *America Caesar: Douglas MacArthur 1880–1964* (Boston, Little, Brown & Co., 1978).

Marauder.org

Masters, J., *The Road Past Mandalay*. [1961] (London, Cassell, 2002).

McAulay, L., *To the Bitter End: The Japanese Defeat at Buna and Gona, 1942–43* (Sydney, Random House, 1992).

McCaffrey, S.C., *Understanding International Law* [2004] (Carolina Academic Press, 2015).

Mead, W.R., *God and Gold: Britain, America and the Making of the Modern World* (University of Michigan, A.A. Knopf, 2007).

Miami Daily News Record (Associated Press, 22 April 1938).

Milwaukee Journal, The, 1 November 1945.

Mitchell, T.J. & Smith, G.M, *Official History of the War, Casualties and Medical statistics Imperial War Museum* (HMSO, reprinted London, 1997).

Morison, S.E., *The Struggle for Guadalcanal*, Vol. V (Boston, Little, Brown, 1948).

Morison, S.E., *New Guinea and the Marianas, March–August 1944, History of US Naval Operations in World War II* (Urbana, University of Illinois Press).

Mortensen, B.L, *Rabaul and Cape Gloucester*, Hyper-War Foundation, *Army Air Forces in World War II*: Vol. IV, 1953).

Moser, D., *China, Burma, India* (Alexandria, Va., *Time Life*, 1978).

Murfett, M.H., Miksic, J., Farrell, B. & Chiang Ming Shun, *Between Two Oceans* (2nd ed.): *A Military History of Singapore from 1275 to 1971* (Singapore, Marshall Cavendish International Asia Ltd., 2011).

Nash, N.S., *Strafer: Desert General* (Barnsley, Pen & Sword, 2013).

Nash, N.S., *The Logistics of the Vietnam Wars* (Barnsley, Pen & Sword, 2020).

New York Times, 20 July 1939, 11 February 2006.

Newell, C.R., 'Burma, 1942' (Washington, US Army Centre of Military History, 1995).

Newsweek, 2 April 1945.

Nicholas, H.G. (ed.), *Washington Despatches* (Washington, Weidenfeld & Nicolson, 1981).

Norris, J., *Fix Bayonets* (Barnsley, Pen & Sword, 2015).

O'Neal, M., 'Breaking of Japanese Naval Codes' (Encyclopedia.com).

Ohnuki-Tierney, E., *Kamikaze Diaries: Reflections of Japanese Student Soldiers* (Illinois, USA, University of Chicago Press, 2007).

Oi, Mariko, BBC News, Tokyo, March 2013.

Okihiro, G.Y., *The Columbia Guide to Asian American History* (Columbia University Press, 2005).

Olsen, L., *Citizens of London* (London, Random House, 2010).

Otterstedt, Lieut Col C., *The Kwantung Army and the Nomonhan Incident: Its Impact on National Security* (Pennsylvania, US Army War College, 2000).

Pacific War, The, Online Encyclopedia.

Paine, S.C.M., *The Wars for Asia, 1911–1949* (New York, Cambridge University Press, 2012).

Parillo, M., *Why Air Forces Fail: The Anatomy of Defeat*, Higham, R. & Harris, S.J. (eds) (University Press of Kentucky, 2006).

Parshall, J. & Tully, A., *Shattered Sword: The Untold Story of the Battle of Midway* (Virginia, Potomac Books, 2005).

Partridge, J., *Alexandra Hospital: From British Military to Civilian Institution* (Singapore, Alexandra Hospital, 1998).

Perez, L.G., *League of Nations, Mandates. Japan at War* (ABC-CLIO, Ed, 2013).

Perry, J.K., 'Powerless and Frustrated: Britain's relationship with China during the opening years of the Second Sino-Japanese War, 1937–39', *Diplomacy and Statecraft* (2011).

Perry, M., *The Most Dangerous Man in America: The Making of Douglas MacArthur* (New York, Basic Books, 2014).

Petillo, C.M., 'MacArthur, Quezon, and Executive Order Number One', *Pacific Historical Review*, February 1979.

Potter, E.B., *Nimitz* (Annapolis, Naval Institute Press, 1976).

Pownall, Gen, H., *Diaries*, Vol 2., Bond, B. (ed.) (London, Leo Cooper, 1972–74)

Reardon, T., *Winston Churchill and Mackenzie King: So Similar, So Different* (Toronto, Dundurn Press, 2012).

Rems, A., 'Two Birds with One Hailstone', *Naval History Magazine*, Vol. 28, 2014.

Research Report No. 122, AWM55 12/94, *Antagonism between Officers and Men in the Japanese Armed Forces*.

Reynaert, F., 'Dans les bordels de l'armée française' (L'Obs.com, 2014).

Richardson, W.R., Lieut Gen USA, in a foreword to Drea's paper (1981), 'Nomonhan: Japanese – Soviet Tactical Combat 1939'.

Richmond, K., *Japanese Forces in New Guinea* (Australian War Memorial, 2003).

Rooney, D., *Wingate and the Chindits* [1994] (London, Cassell, 2000).

Rottman, G.L. & Gerrard, H., *Saipan & Tinian 1944: Piercing the Japanese Empire* (Oxford, Osprey Publishing, 2004).

Rottman, G.L., *Guam 1941 & 1944 Loss and Reconquest* (Botley, Osprey Publishing, 2004).

Russell, Lord, of Liverpool, *The Knights of Bushido* (London, Cassell, 1958).

Saggers, Maj A.E., *To Hellfire, Purgatory and Back* (Perth, WA, Optima Press, 2000).

Sakai, S., *Samurai* (Four Square, E.P. Dutton & Co., 1974).

Sangmie Choi Schellstede, *Comfort Women Speak: Testimony by Sex Slaves of the Japanese Military* (New York, Holmes & Meier, 2000).

Sato, Kyozo, 'Japan's Position before the outbreak of the European War in September 1939', *Modern Asian Studies*, Vol.14.

Scott, J.M., *Rampage: MacArthur, Yamashita, and the Battle of Manila* (London, W.W. Norton, 2018).

Sherwood R.E., *Roosevelt and Hopkins* (New York, Harper, 1948).

Shores, C., *Duel for the Sky: Ten Crucial Battles of World War II* (London, Grub Street, 1985).

Skates J.R., *The Invasion of Japan: Alternative to the Bomb* (University of South Carolina Press, 2000).

Slavinski, B.N., *The Japanese-Soviet Neutrality Pact: A Diplomatic History 1941–45* (London, Routledge, 2004).

Slim, Gen W., *Defeat into Victory* (London, Cassell, 1956).

Smith, R.R., *The Approach to the Philippines (United States Army in World War II)* (Washington, US Army Centre of Military History, 1996).

Snyder, T., *Bloodlands: Europe between Hitler and Stalin* (New York, Basic Books, 2010).

Spector, R.H., *Eagle Against the Sun* (New York, Simon & Schuster, 2020).

Stuart, R., 'Air raid, Colombo 5 April 1942: The fully expected surprise attack', *Royal Canadian Air Force Journal*, 2014.

Symonds, C.L., *World War Two at Sea: A Global History* (Oxford University Press, 2018).

Takafusa Nakamura, *History of Shōwa Japan* (University of Tokyo Press, 1998).

Tanaka, Y., *Hidden Horrors*: *Japanese War Crimes in WWII* (Oxford, Westview Press, 1996).

Tanaka, Yuki, *Japan's Comfort Women* (Oxfordshire, Routledge, 2001).

Taylor, G.E., *The Struggle for North China 1940* (New York, Institute of Pacific Relations, 1940).

Thompson, J., *Forgotten Voices of Burma* (London, Ebury Press, 2010).

Time Magazine, 13 January 1975.

Toland, J., *The Rising Sun: The Decline and Fall of the Japanese Empire 1936–45* [1970] (New York, Modern Library, 2003).

Toll, I.W., *The Conquering Tide* (USA, W.W. Norton & Co, 2015).

Totten, S. & Bartrop, P.R., *Dictionary of Genocide* (Connecticut, USA, Greenwood, 2007).

Tsuji, M., *Japan's Greatest Victory, Britain's Worst Defeat* (Singapore, da Capo Press, 1997, Howe, H.V. (ed.), Lake, M.E. (tr.)).

Tuchman, B.W., *Stilwell and The American Experience in China 1911–1945* (New York, Random House, 1970).

US Army Military History Institute, Hostetter MS, p. 89, Newman Papers.

US NGA COMINCH signal log, 18 May 1942.

USAMHI Rodman papers, Box 5.

USNA RG127 *USMC* Burcham, Capt Levi, *Operations in WWII Okinawa*.

Van Emden, R., *Meeting the Enemy* [2013] (London, Bloomsbury Publishing, 2014).

Veterans.sa.gov.au, *The Bougainville Offensive*, 2019.

Watt, D.C., *How War Came* (New York, Pantheon Books, 1989).

Weglyn, M.N., *Years of Infamy* (Seattle, University of Washington, 1996).

Weingartner, J.J., 'Trophies of War: US Troops and the mutilation of Japanese war dead', *Pacific Historical Review*, 61.1. 1992.

West, R., *War and Peace in Vietnam* (London, Sinclair Stevenson, 1995).

Wetzler, P., *Hirohito and War* (University of Hawaii Press, 1998).

Williams, Dr P., *The Kokoda Campaign 1942: Myth and Reality* (Melbourne, Victoria, Cambridge University Press, 2012).

Willmott, H.P., *June, 1944* (Poole, UK, Blandford Press, 1984).

Willoughby, C.A., *Japanese Operations in the Southwest Pacific Area Vol. II* (Reports of General MacArthur, US Government Printing Office, 1966).

Wilson, S., Cribb, R., Trefalt, B. & Aszkielowicz, D., *Japanese War Criminals: The Politics of Justice after the Second World War* (New York, Columbia University Press, 2017).

Wright, D., *Tarawa 1943: The Turning of the Tide* (Oxford, Osprey, 2004).

Wright, D., [1999] *The Battle for Iwo Jima 1945* (Stroud, Sutton Publishing, 2007).

Wukovits, J.F., *Devotion to Duty* (Naval Institute Press, 2008).

Wukovits, J., *Eisenhower: A Biography* (London, St Martin's Press, 2015).

www.historynet.com

Yang, Tianshi, *Chiang Kai-shek and the Battles of Shanghai and Nanjing* (Shanghai People's Publishing House, 1979).

Yoshiaki, Yoshimi, *Comfort Women: Sexual Slavery in the Japanese Military during WWII* (New York, Columbia University Press, 2002).

Yoshimi, Y. & Matsuno, S., *Dokugasusen Kankei Shiryô II, Kaisetsu* (Tokyo, 1997).

Young, D.J., 'Phantom Japanese raid on Los Angeles', *Way Back Machine, World War II Magazine*, 2003.

Yuma, T., *The Tokyo War Crimes Trial: The Pursuit of Justice in the Wake of World War II* (Harvard University Press, 2008, Asia).

Index

British /Commonwealth formations
11 Army Group, 228
6th Australian Division, 230
7th Australian Division, 157
8th Australian Division, 79, 88
11 Brigade, 213
14 Brigade, 213
16 Brigade, 213, 215
63 Brigade, 126
77 Brigade, 213, 215, 221
111 Brigade, 213, 215
Burma Corps, 128
1st Burma Division, 120, 126, 128
IV Corps, 212, 215, 226
XXXIII Corps, 215, 226
2nd Division, 221, 226, 253
3rd Division, 114
9th Division, 79
17th Division, 120, 122, 124, 126, 215
11th East Africa Division, 79, 227
14th Indian Army, 211
III Indian Corps, 79
5th Indian Division, 227
28th Indian Division, 215
14th Infantry Division, 181, 257
3 West African Brigade, 213

Chinese formations
37 Division, 22

Japanese formations
6th Air Fleet, 260
2nd Army, 230
5th Army, 129, 210, 215, 221, 226–7
33rd Army, 303
5th Division, 79
7th Division, 45
17th Division, 155, 212
18th Division, 79, 221
20th Division, 160, 221

29th Division, 251, 253
31st Division, 215
33rd Division, 126, 212, 215, 226
55th Division, 121
214th Regiment, 126

US formations
11th Airborne Division, 281
V (US) Amphibious Corps, 235, 238, 250,
  253, 288
6th Army, 260, 262
10th Army, 293–4
3rd Fleet, 272–3, 303
5th Fleet, 197, 230
7th Fleet, 263, 268
24th Infantry Division, 280
27th Infantry Division, 240
32 Infantry Division, 159
77th Infantry Division, 252, 260, 266, 294
81st Infantry Division, 257
19th Infantry Regiment, 280
28th Infantry Regiment, 46
105th Infantry Regiment, 241
1st Marine Division, 164, 174, 257
2nd Marine Division, 253
3rd Marine Division, 252, 291
4th Marine Division, 253
5th Marine Division, 291
503rd Regimental Combat Team, 303

ABDA, 86, 99, 97, 103, 105–106
Aggressive/aggression, 20, 39, 50, 54, 62,
  162, 174, 190, 309
Agincourt, 144–6
Air power, 32, 41, 56, 70, 128, 136, 236,
  238, 270, 272, 307
Aitape, 230–1, 233–5, 237
Aizawa Saburo, Lieutenant Colonel, 16–17
Aleutian Islands, 139, 185, 190, 242, 295

Alexander, General Sir Harold, 121, 126–8, 164

Ambition, 7, 16, 44, 50, 80, 156, 187, 195, 233, 241, 261, 307, 309

Anglo-American relations/Special relationship, 20, 44, 305

Anglophobia/anglophobic, 42, 44, 127, 136, 213

Arizona, USS, 73

Armour, armoured, 35, 40–1, 126, 144, 215, 236, 240, 249–50, 253, 257, 289, 294

Asaka Yasuhiko, Prince, 26–7

Asami Kazuo, 24

Assassin/assassinations, 9, 12, 16–17, 53, 62, 184–5, 242

Asymmetric war, 22

Atlee, Prime Minister Clement, 303

Atomic bomb, 188, 303, 306, 314

Atrocity, 28–9, 37

Attrition, 37, 176, 178, 190, 210, 224, 275, 290–1, 297

Attu, 185–6, 190, 279

Aung San, 122

Australia, Australians, 1, 79, 84, 85–90, 97–8, 110, 118, 131–2, 152, 155–60, 162, 164, 169–71, 176, 180, 191–2, 209, 230–34, 247, 260, 277

B-17 aircraft, 94, 97–8

B-29 aircraft, 235, 255, 286, 303, 305

Ba Maw, Dr, 194–5

Balikpapan, Battle of, 103

Bamboo, 125, 241, 253

Banzai charge, 186, 255, 257, 279

Barbarism/barbarity, 3, 29, 45, 51, 150, 245, 311–12

BARBAROSSA, Operation, 56–7

Bataan, 92, 97–9, 109–10, 112, 134, 263, 281, 312

Bayonet, 27–8, 102, 112, 159, 173, 218

Bee, HMS, 32

Behaviour, 24, 27, 29, 31–2, 45, 103, 119, 122, 148, 207, 227, 232, 246–7, 283–4, 309, 312–13

Beijing, 22–3, 34, 37, 47–8

Bengal, 120, 180–1

Bernardino Strait, 270, 272–4

Betio, 197–201

Bevin, Foreign Secretary Ernest, 303

Biak Island, 234–5

Bicycle, 81, 83, 98

Bismarck Sea, Battle of the, 160, 191

Black market, 206, 395

Blamey, General Thomas, 233–4

Bode, Captain Howard, 169, 171–2

Booby trap, 227

Borneo, 75, 97, 103, 134, 147

Bose, Subhas Chandra, 181, 195, 201, 219

Bougainville, 132, 167, 184, 191–2, 197, 234

Breakneck Ridge, 263, 267

Brereton, Major General Lewis, 93–4

Broadway, 213–14, 216–18

Brooke, General Sir Alan, 84–5, 114, 187–8, 197, 233

Brooke-Popham, Air Chief Marshal Sir Robert, 69, 80

Buckner, Lieutenant General Simon, 293–5, 297, 299

Buna, 155, 158–61, 191, 199

Burma, 20, 58, 75, 89, 118, 120–2, 124–30, 134

Burma Railway, 152

Burma Road, 42, 46, 48, 57, 129

Cairo, 188

Calories, 250

Calvert, Major Michael, 126, 182, 213, 218, 221–2

Camp O'Donnell, 112

Canada, Canadian, 108–109, 188

Cannibalism, 207, 303

CARTWHEEL, Operation, 190–1, 204

Casualty evacuation, 212, 264

Casus belli, 10, 22, 52, 64, 80

Causeway, 85–7, 164

Caution, 5, 61, 72, 137, 168, 175

Cave, cavernous, 156, 234, 241, 252, 257–8, 290, 292, 295, 299

Ceylon (Sri Lanka), 106, 130–1

Chennault, Major General Claire, 188, 211

Chiang Kai-shek, Generalissimo, 16, 19–20, 22–3, 26, 35, 37, 42, 45, 50, 52–3, 56–7, 120, 127, 129, 188–9, 196, 209–11, 303

Chindits, 181–3, 211–13, 215–19, 221, 224–5

Chindwin, river, 120, 130, 181–2, 210–11, 216, 227–8
Chinese Expeditionary Force (CEF), 127, 129, 221
Chongqing, 43, 46, 53
Chou En-lai, 19
Chowringhee, 213–14
Churchill, Sir W.S., 44, 52, 60, 70, 74, 77, 84, 86, 89–90, 103, 121, 131, 136, 179, 181, 184–5, 187–9, 196, 299, 303
Clark Air Base, 71, 77, 94, 281
Clark Kerr, Sir Archibald, 53–4
Co-prosperity Sphere (GEACS), 56, 194, 196
Coal, 10, 14, 107, 305
Colonial, anti-colonial, 20, 42, 52, 56, 61, 78, 121, 164, 187, 194, 295, 304–305, 312, 314
Combined Chiefs of Staff, 131, 187, 228
Comfort women, 114–19
Commission, Earl of Lytton, 14–15
Commission, War Crimes, 310
Commonwealth, The, 3, 44, 196, 284, 314
Communist, 6, 16, 19, 20, 26, 63, 232
Conscripts, 301
Conspirators, 10, 12, 16
Contempt, 14, 23, 67, 127, 152, 211, 302, 307
Convoy, 85, 94–5, 103, 105–106, 159, 161, 184, 265, 268
Coral Sea, 132–4, 136, 140
CORONET, Operation, 304
Corregidor, 98–9, 101, 110–12, 163, 263, 284
Coup, 12, 17–18
Courage, courageous, 3, 6, 46, 78, 86, 108, 110, 124, 156, 182, 199, 201, 203, 225–7, 232–3, 236–7, 250, 260, 263, 275, 279, 292
Craigie, Ambassador Sir Robert Leslie, 54, 63
Cross-beach, 204, 248, 252, 304
Crutchley, Rear Admiral Sir Victor, 164, 169
Culture/cultural, 3, 6, 17, 28, 31, 47, 101, 112, 116, 120, 143, 151–2, 186, 213, 240, 258, 276

Curtin, Prime Minister of Australia, John, 231–3

Darwin, 105
Deadline, 62–3
Deity, 3, 6
Diet, the (Japanese Government), 56
Diplomatic/Diplomacy, 42, 45, 52, 54, 57, 59, 62, 64, 66, 70, 75, 77, 79, 127, 197
Diplomatic code, 54, 57
Dobbie, Lieutenant General Sir William, 85
Dogra Regiment, 80
Doihara Kenji, General, 18–19
Doolittle Raid, 128–9, 139
Doorman, Admiral W.F.M., 105
Dunant, Henry, 146–7
Dysentery, 109

Economic/economy, 6–10, 13–14, 17, 24, 37, 48, 50, 54, 56, 58, 63, 194, 233, 246
Ego, 95, 110, 131, 197, 199, 236, 306
Eichelberger, Lieutenant General Robert, 159
Empire, British, 75, 121, 314
Empire, Dutch, 48, 61, 75, 95, 97, 103, 118, 128, 159
Empire, French, 3, 56, 58, 114, 121–2, 134, 179, 189, 304–305, 308, 313
Empire, Japanese, 76, 117, 130, 134, 136, 140, 147, 240, 308, 314
Eniwetok Atoll, 205, 207

Famine, 179–81
Far East Fleet, RN, 81, 130
Filipino Army, 95, 284
Flame; throwers, tanks, operators, 253–4, 290, 292
Fletcher, Admiral Frank, 132, 140, 168
FORAGER, Operation, 235
Formosa (Taiwan), 7–9, 58, 70, 93, 108, 118, 178, 189, 259–60, 278
Fortification, 190, 201, 294
Fuel, 58, 63, 72, 131, 168, 184, 204, 213, 237–8, 242, 244, 250, 253, 255, 264, 278

GALVANIC, Operation, 197
Garrison, 78, 108, 114, 137, 159–60, 201, 203–204, 216, 219–22, 230, 284, 286, 295

Geiger, Major General Roy, 251–2, 293
Geneva Convention, 143, 147, 150, 186, 246
Germ warfare, 51
German-Soviet Non-aggression Pact, 42, 50, 57, 75
Ghormley, Vice Admiral Robert, 163–4, 168, 174
Gifford, General Sir George, 228
Gilbert Islands, 197–8, 201, 259
Gliders, 213–14
Gold teeth, 244, 246
Gona, 155, 159–60, 176, 180, 191
Gratuitous, 101, 311
Grew, Joseph (US Ambassador to Japan), 52, 61–3
Guadalcanal, 132, 157–9, 162–4, 166–9, 171–5, 179, 184, 190, 198–9, 206, 279
Guam, 13, 58, 69, 75, 77–9, 81, 103, 105–106, 108, 143, 235–7, 250–2
Guerrilla war, 22, 81, 196, 211, 268
Guilt, 310, 313

HAILSTONE, Operation, 204
Halsey, Vice Admiral William, 174, 190–2, 260, 263, 266, 268, 270, 272–3, 279, 301, 305
Harriman, Averell (Lend-Lease co-ordinator), 74
Hart, Admiral Thomas, 81, 86, 97–9, 103
Hawaii, 58–9, 61, 67, 69–70, 79, 93, 106, 132, 136, 139–40, 162, 259
Helfrich, Vice Admiral C.E.L., 103, 105
Henderson Field, 167, 172–4, 184
Henry V, King, 144, 146, 160
Heroism, 35, 140
Higgins boats, 199
Hirohito, Emperor, 3–6, 20, 23–4, 62–3, 77, 174, 190, 242, 260, 282, 292, 306, 309–10, 313–14
Hiroshima, 209, 306, 314
Hitler, Adolf, 45, 56, 195, 242, 282, 313
Hollandia, 230
Homma Masaharu, Lieutenant General, 95, 97, 99, 109–10, 311
Hong Kong, 20, 42, 69, 75, 77, 108–109, 134, 143
Honshu, 14, 294, 304–305
Hora Tomio, 25

Horses, 109, 150
Hospital, hospital ship, 102, 125, 222, 226, 255
Hudson, Lieutenant E.R.B., 122, 124–5
Hugh-Jones, Brigadier Noel, 124–5
Hull Note, The, 60
Hull, Cordell (US Secretary of State), 60, 63–7, 70, 231
Humanity, 30, 32, 117, 143
Humiliation, 27, 54, 69, 89, 121
Hutton, Lieutenant General Thomas, 120–1, 126

Imperial Japanese Army (IJA), 17–18, 31, 33, 40, 58, 70, 106, 114, 129, 131, 143, 159–60, 174, 179, 184, 190, 194–6, 206, 221
Imperial Japanese Navy (IJN), 12, 59, 61–2, 70–1, 76, 95, 105–106, 129–34, 137–40, 174, 184, 190–1, 204–205, 235, 238, 259–60, 263, 276, 274, 301
Imphal, Imphal plain, 130, 181–2, 210–13, 216, 218–19, 221, 223–9
Incendiary bombs, 45, 291, 305
Incompetent, 185, 262
Independence, 14, 42, 89, 121–2, 128–9, 192, 194–7, 266
Indian National Army (INA), 195–6, 212, 216, 219, 227
Indochina, 56, 58, 60, 62, 75, 86, 118, 121, 179, 314
Indoctrination, indoctrinated, 6, 29
Industrial, 62, 75, 77, 203, 232, 236, 275
Infamy, Day of, 65
Inoue Junnosuke, Finance Minister, 16
Inoue Sadae, Major General, 257
Inoue Shigeyoshi, Admiral, 133
Intelligence, 57, 67, 69, 83, 87, 129, 134, 139–40, 155, 162, 164, 166, 173, 184, 191, 210, 234, 254, 263, 306, 273, 286
Inukai Tsuyoshi, Prime Minister, 13–14, 16
Iron Bottom Sound, 171, 174
Irrawaddy, river, 120, 126–7, 129, 303
Ishii Shirō, Surgeon General, 51, 314
Ishiwara Kanji, Lieutenant Colonel, 9–10, 19
Itagaki Seishirō, Lieutenant General, 9–10
Iwabuchi Sanji, Rear Admiral, 282, 284
Iwo Jima, 259, 286–92

Japanese ancestry, 74
Java, Java Sea, Battle of the, 86, 103, 105, 106, 130, 132
Jiro Suzuki, 24
Johore, Johor Bharu, 1, 81–2, 85–7, 89, 99, 305
Junta, 16, 312

Kamikaze, 140, 273, 275–81, 294, 299–300, 305
Kantai Kessen (Decisive Battle Doctrine), 61
Karayuki-san, 115–16
Kawabe Masakazu, Lieutenant General, 182, 210, 226
Kawamoto Suemori, Lieutenant, 10
Kenney, General George, 157, 160, 191–2
Khalkhin Gol, 39–41
Kimmel, Admiral Husband, 67, 70, 95
King, Admiral Ernest, 127, 136–7, 140, 162–3, 187, 235, 248–9, 273, 299
Kiska, 185–6, 295
Kissinger, Henry, 44
Kohima, 130, 182, 210–12, 215, 218–22, 224, 226
Kokoda Trail, 155–6, 158, 233
KON, Operation, 235
Konoye, Fumimaro Prince & Prime Minister, 32, 242
Kra Isthmus, 70, 120, 152
Krueger, Lieutenant General Walter, 262, 266, 280
Kuribayashi, Lieutenant General Tadamichi, 288–80, 292
Kurile Islands, 185, 190
Kurita, Vice Admiral Takeo, 237, 270, 272–3
Kwajalein, 139, 201, 203, 205, 207
Kwantung Army, 7, 9–12, 14, 18, 22, 24, 39, 41, 48, 211
Kyushu, 278, 293–4, 301, 303, 305

Ladybird, HMS, 92
Le May, General Curtis, 303
League of Nations, 6, 13–15
Ledo Road, 210, 213
Lend-Lease, 57, 74, 129
Lentaigne, Brigadier Walter, 218
Lexington, USS, 71, 133–4

Leyte, Leyte Gulf, 260–8, 270, 272–4, 276–7, 280, 290, 293, 295
Li Zongren, General, 34–5
Liaodong/Liaotung, 7, 9–10
Liberator, 194
Lingayen Gulf, 280
Logistic, 14, 22–3, 35, 37, 42, 48, 50, 56–8, 76–8, 81, 87–8, 99, 106, 109, 112, 128, 131, 133, 136, 139, 143, 146, 150, 155, 158, 160, 169, 176, 178–9, 185, 188, 190, 196, 199, 203, 209, 211–12, 219, 221, 226, 228, 230–1, 238, 248, 250, 252, 265–7, 272, 282, 284, 303
Long Range Penetration (LRP), 181, 196, 212–13, 216, 218–19, 224, 226
LONGCLOTH, Operation, 181–2
Los Angeles, Battle of, 74
Luzon, 70–1, 95, 97, 99, 163, 260, 268, 270, 277, 280–1, 283
Lytton, Earl of, 14–15

MacArthur, General Douglas, 64, 70–1, 81, 92–5, 97–9, 101, 110, 127, 131, 155, 159, 162–3, 190–1, 204, 231–2, 234, 244, 254, 258–63, 267–8, 274, 281, 304, 307–309
Macclesfield Heath, Lieutenant General Sir Lewis, 89
MAGIC, Operation, 57–8
Malaria, 33, 109, 158, 225, 234
Malaya, 20, 42, 58, 67, 69, 71, 75, 77–9, 81–3, 85–90, 103, 118, 128, 134, 143, 152, 179, 194–6, 227, 260, 303, 310
Malnutrition, 109, 112, 150, 160, 176, 208, 227
Manchukuo, 14, 16–18, 23, 51, 55, 57, 118, 313
Mandalay, 293
Manhattan Project, The, 306
Manila, 70–1, 92, 94, 97–9, 209, 265, 275, 280–5, 311
Mao Zedong/Mao Tse-Tung, 15–16, 19, 26, 45, 303
Marco Polo Bridge, 19, 22–3, 37, 53, 211
Mariana Islands, 78, 108, 235, 250
Marshall, General George, 110, 162–3, 187, 196, 244, 248
Marshall Islands, 203–204
Maryland, USS, 73, 271

Matsuoka Yosuke, Foreign Minister, 50,
  55–7, 310
MEETINGHOUSE, Operation, 305
Merchant shipping, 76, 130, 172, 178–9,
  190, 203, 205–206, 242
Merrill, Brigadier General Frank, Merrill's
  Marauders, 196, 209, 212–13, 221, 223–5
Midway Island, 71, 79, 99, 132, 136–40,
  142, 155, 190
Mikawa Gunichi, Vice Admiral, 168–70, 172
Military necessity, 146, 160
Milne Bay, 169
Mindanao, 95, 97, 235, 254, 260
Mitscher, Vice Admiral Marc, 191, 235–7,
  268, 273
Mogaung, 221–2
Monsoon, 211, 222, 227–8, 262, 264
Mopping-up, 230–1, 233, 237
Morale, 35, 45, 87, 99, 108, 114, 158–60,
  174, 182, 184, 190, 198, 203, 206, 226,
  297, 300, 305
Morotai, 244, 254–7
Mount Suribachi, 286, 289–90
Mountbatten, Admiral Lord Louis, 194,
  196–7, 215, 224, 228, 303
Mukden, 7, 10, 12–16, 22, 24, 52, 312
Mules, 109, 213–15
Murder, 16, 31–2, 52, 78, 102, 109, 117,
  150, 194, 260, 302, 312
Mutaguchi Renya, Lieutenant General, 101,
  210–15, 219, 221, 226
Mutilation, 27, 258
Myitkyina, 221–5

Nagano Osami, Admiral, 62–3, 175, 310
Nagasaki, 209, 306, 313
Nagata Tetsuzan, General, 16–17
Nagumo Chūichi, Vice Admiral, 67, 71–2,
  130, 139, 241
Nanking, 24, 26–9, 31–3, 35, 37, 54
Netherlands, 75, 86, 254–5, 313
Neutral, 137, 147
New Guinea, 118, 132, 155, 159–60, 162,
  169, 178, 191, 206–209, 230–1, 233–5,
  242, 260, 279, 303
Nimitz, Admiral Chester, 131–2, 134, 137,
  139–40, 162, 163–4, 166, 174, 191,

200–201, 203, 235, 259, 261, 273–4,
  281–2, 286, 301, 304
Nishimura Shōji, Vice Admiral, 271, 273,
  304
Nomonhan Incident, 39–40, 46, 48–9, 56
Non-aggression Pact, 42, 50, 57, 75
Non-combatant, 97, 151, 311

Obata Hideyoshi, Lieutenant General,
  251–2
Oil, 84, 87, 103, 105, 120, 126, 128, 131,
  138, 162, 179, 197, 204, 206, 249, 278
Okinawa, 14, 259–60, 277–8, 293–7,
  299–304, 314
Oldendorf, Rear Admiral Jesse, 258, 262,
  271
OLYMPIC, Operation, 303–304
Ōnishi Takijirō, Vice Admiral, 270, 275
Ormoc Bay, 265–7
Orote Peninsula, 252
Osmeña, Vice President Sergio, 98
OVERLORD, Operation, 188–9
Owen Stanley Mountains, 155–6
Ozawa Jisaburō, Admiral, 236–8, 270

Palau, 13, 204, 237, 258
Panay, USS, 32–3, 51
Papua, 155, 157, 159–60, 178
Parit Sulong Massacre, 86
Pearl Harbor, 16, 52, 62, 65, 67, 69–71,
  73–5, 77, 79, 83, 85, 87, 89, 91, 93–5,
  113, 130–2, 134, 192, 235, 260
Peking, 22
Peleliu, 255–8
Percival, Lieutenant General Arthur, 70, 79,
  85–90, 110
Perpetrators, 10, 283, 308–10
Phibun, Prime Minister Songkhram
  (Thailand), 75
Philippines, 8, 13, 20, 58, 64, 69–71, 75, 77,
  79, 81, 92–9, 101, 103, 105–106, 109–13,
  143, 163, 192, 195, 209, 230, 235, 243,
  254–5, 258–63, 268, 270, 278, 281, 284,
  286, 301, 304, 310, 313
Philippine Sea, Battle of the, 75, 236–8,
  270–1, 279
Phillips, Admiral Sir Tom, 81, 83
Piccadilly (airstrip), 213–14, 217

Poison gas, 24, 51
Port Arthur, 7
Port Moresby, 132–3, 137, 155, 158
Pre-emptive, 61–2, 65, 67, 75, 184
Prince of Wales, HMS, 60, 71, 81–2, 84
Prisoners of war (POWs), 142, 148, 150, 282, 310–11
Propaganda, 61, 66, 74, 99, 110, 182, 188, 194, 201, 210, 212, 244–5, 278
PROVIDENCE, Operation, 155
Psychopaths, 284

Quebec, 188, 196, 212
Quezon, President Manuel, 98–9, 101

Rabaul, 146, 155–6, 159–61, 163, 168, 179, 191–3
Racial superiority, 311
Rangoon (now Yangon), 120–2, 124–9, 152, 180, 182, 196, 210, 228
Rape, 114, 117, 241, 283, 302, 312–13
Ration, 162, 249–50
Redoubt, 110, 218, 291, 296
Refugees, 33, 37
Report, The Lytton, 37
Repulse, HMS, 71, 81–4, 174
Resignation, 63, 242
Resupply, 76, 126, 128–9, 158, 205–206, 211–12, 219, 228, 267, 286
Rice, 10, 116, 131, 158, 173, 178–81, 206–207, 227, 261
Roosevelt, President Franklin D. (FDR), 42, 44, 51–2, 57–8, 60–4, 66–7, 70, 74, 77–8, 92, 99, 110, 121–2, 127, 163, 184, 187–9, 231, 246, 259, 282, 293, 297, 299
Royal Navy (RN), 21, 278
Royal Navy Pacific Fleet (BPF), 299
Rubber, 61, 162

Sacsac, 207
Saipan, 13, 71, 117, 235–6, 238, 240–2, 248, 250, 252–3, 257, 286, 292, 295
Saito Yoshitsugu, General, 13, 238, 240–1
Sakai Takashi, Lieutenant General, 108–109
Sakishima Islands, 300
Salt, 178–9, 206
Salween, river, 120–1, 129
Saratoga, USS, 71, 134, 192

Satō Kōtoku, Lieutenant General, 215, 219, 221, 226
Savo Island, Battle of, 170–4, 176
Schmidt, Major General Harry, 253, 288
Scoones, General Sir Geoffrey, 211, 228
Scrub typhus, 235
Sembawang Officers' Mess, 1, 102
Shanghai, 23–4, 33–5, 37, 64, 70, 77
Shima Kiyohide, Vice Admiral, 271
Shimura Kikujiro, Private, 22–3
SHOESTRING, Operation, 166
Shuri, 294–5, 299
SIGINT, 57, 134, 184, 134
Simpson, Brigadier Ivan, 87
Singapore, 1, 20, 42, 55, 69–71, 81, 83, 85–91, 101–103, 117, 134, 143, 152, 194–6, 198, 210, 227, 232, 260, 270, 310–11
Sino-Japanese War, 16, 22, 24–5, 27, 29, 31, 33, 35, 37, 42, 151, 176, 312
Sittang, river, 120, 122, 125–6, 129, 303
Skull: stewing, polishing, 244–7
Slim, Lieutenant General Sir William, 212–13, 215, 219, 221, 226–8
Smith, General Holland, 235, 240, 290, 293
Smyth, Major General Ralph, 240
South Pacific Area (COMSOPA), 163, 174
Special relationship, 44, 305
Spontaneous, 7, 150, 310
Spruance, Rear Admiral Raymond, 139–40, 204, 235–6, 238, 240, 268, 288, 294, 301
Stark, Admiral Harold, 67, 98, 232
Starvation, 37, 150–1, 160, 178, 192, 205–206, 219, 226, 234, 268, 280, 284, 307
Stilwell, Lieutenant General Joseph, 209–10, 213, 219, 221–4, 299
Stimson, US Secretary for War Henry, 64, 99
Stopford, Lieutenant General Montague, 215, 226
Strategic/strategy, 3, 10, 27, 37, 39, 50, 55, 71, 87, 99, 110, 132, 136, 140, 162–4, 178, 191, 209, 231, 233, 254, 259, 283, 285
Suicide, 18, 117–18, 176, 186, 222, 224, 241, 252–3, 258, 276, 278, 292–9, 294, 297, 299, 302, 310

Surabaya, 105–106

Surprise, 7, 17, 50, 62, 67, 77, 124, 130, 132, 137, 173, 190, 230, 260, 289, 306

Surrender, 186, 188–9, 192, 243, 253, 261, 275, 284, 286, 301, 304–305, 307, 309

Survivors, 32, 97, 106, 118, 126, 160, 205, 218, 226, 279–80, 283–4, 308

Sutherland, Brigadier General R.K., 94, 101

Suzuki Sōsaku, Lieutenant General, 263, 266

Sword, 26, 28, 30, 186, 290

Taierzhuang, 35

Takagi Takeo, Vice Admiral, 132, 242

Tarawa Atoll, 192, 197–201, 203, 234, 252, 292

Task Force 52, USN, 292

Task Force 57, British Pacific Fleet, 199

Tatekawa Yoshitsugu, General, 10

Tehran, 189, 306

Tenaru, Battle of, 174–5

Tennessee, USS, 73, 208, 271

Tennis court, 219–21

Terauchi Hisaichi, Field Marshal, 226, 260, 265

Thailand, 58, 69–71, 73, 75–7, 79–81, 85, 87, 118, 120–1, 152, 195, 221, 305

THURSDAY, Operation, 212–13, 218

Tientsin, 44, 52–4

Tinian, 235, 252–5, 257

Tōjō Hideki, General & Prime Minister, 241–3, 288

Tokyo, Tokyo Express, 10–12, 14, 16, 24, 26, 32, 39, 41, 50, 54–5, 61, 69, 71, 76, 95, 106, 109, 128, 136, 166, 175, 187, 196, 240–1, 255–6, 260, 286, 291, 293, 305, 310

Topography, 263, 295

Torture, 27, 52, 54, 78, 207, 283, 302, 310–11, 313

Toshiaki Mukai, 2/Lieutenant, 24–6

Trade embargo, 60

Training, 31, 46, 48, 73, 90, 92, 143, 212, 215, 236, 253, 260, 276

Translation, 64, 275

Trophies, 244–5, 247

Truk, 13, 192–3, 203–205, 261

Tsuji Masanobu, Colonel, 80

Tsuyoshi, Noda, 2/Lieutenant, 24–5

Tulagi, 132, 163–6, 168

Tunnel, 98, 290, 305

Turner, Admiral Richmond K., 164, 168–9, 172–3, 197, 235–6, 241, 294, 297

Two-Ocean Navy, USA, 54

ULTRA, 57

US Navy Seabees, 166, 173

Ushijima Mitsuru, Lieutenant General, 293, 295, 297, 299

van der Ploeg, Ellen, 118

Vandegrift, Major General, 164, 175

Vanity, 98, 232

VENGEANCE, Operation, 184, 276, 305

Victoria Cross (VC), 108, 110, 122, 135, 169

Victory Disease, 242

Vietnam, 1, 44, 56, 81, 121, 149, 179, 189, 250, 305, 308

Vouza, Sir Jacob, 173–4

Vulnerable, 23, 45, 108–109, 128, 148, 252–3, 289

Wainwright, Major General Jonathan, 97, 110–11

Wake Island, 13, 58, 64–72, 75, 77, 79, 106–109, 143

Wang Ching-wei, 54, 63, 195

War crime, 27, 30, 102, 117, 144, 201, 313

Waste, 110, 250

WATCHTOWER, Operation, 164

Water, 7, 80, 87, 89, 102, 112, 136–8, 139, 182, 188, 198–9, 206–207, 218, 234, 248–9, 252, 267, 281, 289

Wavell, General Sir Archibald, 86–7

Wealth, 77, 179, 194, 203, 248

West Point, US Military Academy, 93

West Virginia, USS, 72–3, 271

Wewak, 191, 230, 234

White City, 215, 217–18, 222

Wingate, Acting Major General Orde, 181–3, 196, 211–13, 218

Wisdom, 56, 308

Withdrawal, 63, 126–7, 158, 168, 172, 183, 212, 226, 240, 257, 272, 314

Wuhan, 23, 34, 37

Xuzhou Campaign, 33–4, 37

Yamamoto Isoroku, Admiral, 61, 67, 73–4, 138–9, 184–5, 190
Yamasaki Yasuyo, Colonel, 185–6
Yamashita Tomoyuki, General, 54, 79, 87–8, 101, 143, 260, 263, 265, 268, 280–2, 284, 310

Yangtze, river, 24, 32–3, 37
Yellow, river, 37
Yorktown, USS, 132–4, 140, 204

Zero, 236
Zhang Zuolin/Chang Tso-lin, 8–10
Zhukov, General Georgi K., 40–1
Zinc, 14